Dodie Frad

S0-AKP-106   8

ABDICATION

Abdication

BY

BRIAN INGLIS

THE MACMILLAN COMPANY

NEW YORK

Copyright © 1966 by Brian Inglis. All rights reserved. No part of this book may be reproduced or utilized in any form or by any means, electronic or mechanical, including photocopying, recording or by any information storage and retrieval system, without permission in writing from the Publisher. Library of Congress Catalog Card Number: 66-20212. The Macmillan Company, New York. Printed in the United States of America.

FIRST PRINTING

To

MY GRANADA COLLEAGUES

CONTENTS

V AFTERMATH

PREFACE

Two public faces dominate my memories of childhood: Kaiser Wilhelm, and Edward, Prince of Wales—ogre and hero. Edward was then on the world tours which were to make him internationally the best-known personality of his time. Aunts and schoolteachers never ceased to marvel at "Britain's best ambassador," with his engaging looks, his inexhaustible energy—and his inherent goodness. The most often quoted example has been recorded in a variety of forms, but the version that I recall concerned an incident during a visit he had made to a hospital just behind the front during the Great War. The Prince was shown a man who had been so terribly wounded that he was deaf, dumb and blind. Deeply moved, the Prince took the only way open to him to express his feeling: he stooped to kiss the man's mutilated cheek.

Throughout the 1920s such stories continued to attach themselves to the Prince of Wales. Often they concerned his ability to make friends with all sorts and conditions of men and, very important in royalty, to remember names—even to remember the conversation he had had years before in, say, a dugout near Bapaume, so that the conversation could now be resumed in Banff or Wagga Wagga. But new themes began to emerge: his independence, his dislike of formality, his inclination to evade stuffy protocol. Stories proliferated of how the Prince had cut dances promised to the wives of local notabilities in order to fox-trot—or sit out—with some local beauty. And the partners he chose often did not feature in the social register, much to the indignation of the girls who did—and their mothers. This only made us like the Prince the more. Clearly, he was of his time—the twenties being a great sweeper-away of antiquated notions and customs.

When he came back to England, the Prince consolidated his hold on our imaginations. He was always in the news—attending ceremonials, laying foundation stones, making after-dinner speeches. He had the knack of throwing out appropriate remarks casually, without pomposity—often, it seemed, without preparation. And for all his new immersion in his royal chores, he continued to be a pace-setter, scattering outmoded convention. He appeared in formal dress without spats, which until then had been considered *de rigueur,* and he abandoned a top hat for the more informal bowler. He was even seen, rumour had it, wearing a soft collar in public.

By the 1930s, although the Prince no longer held the world lime-light—his position as the best-known personality of the era had been usurped by Al Capone—he was an institution. To most of us he was still dashing and young. We hardly realized that he was approach-ing middle age, which was not surprising, as he showed no sign of it. I saw him in person for the first time when he came down to a commemoration ceremony at my school, to be shown around, to lay a foundation stone, and to make a speech. He performed impec-cably, to our way of thinking, but he mildly scandalized some of the parents who were present. In an introductory speech the head-master, a genial, portly clergyman with a flow of orotund clichés to match his figure, extolled him not merely because he was a prince, but because he was *such* a prince. At this point Edward, who pre-sumably had heard every conceivable permutation on this theme, ostentatiously picked up a newspaper and began to read it.

Or was it a newspaper? Perhaps memory has played a trick—more probably it was the speech-day programme. No matter, an-other bubble of pomposity had been punctured. The next day, one of the science masters admiringly reported that the Prince, on his tour of the school—seeing things he must have seen scores of times—had been observed to pause, chuckling, in front of a research project in one of the science laboratories. Mystified, the master had checked to see what could have caused the Prince's mirth. It was a notice saying, simply, "The Acid Test."

A couple of years later, the Prince had become King. In less than eleven months he had abdicated and, as Duke of Windsor, had begun his long exile.

In the autumn of 1961 I was invited by Granada Television to take on, as writer and commentator, their "All Our Yesterdays" programme, a review of the events of twenty-five years ago, week by week. It happened that I joined the programme in November—the month when, a quarter of a century before, the abdication crisis was coming to a head. The abdication had never been tackled on television or radio in Britain. The best way of handling the subject, we decided, was to devote two programmes to it: one dealing with Edward VIII's career up to that point, the other with the abdication itself—the events immediately leading up to his renunciation of his throne.

Preparing the first script brought back memories of the Prince buried since childhood, a reminder of how strong an influence he had been. Yet when I tried to remember what impact the abdication itself had had on me, I could recollect nothing—no feeling, one way or the other. This was the more puzzling as at the time of the crisis I was up at Magdalen College, Oxford—Edward's old college. There if anywhere, surely, feelings should have been strong. They weren't. My old tutor, I was to find, also had no recollection of the occasion, although he held strong views on the monarchy and with a group of other young dons had stayed away from the cele-bratory dinner at the time of King George V's jubilee, the year before.

Some of my contemporaries, I found, had been left similarly un-moved, and this, too, was surprising, as Magdalen students relished controversy. There was a frenetic campaign at this time, spearheaded by the college medical students, to ensure that all milk sold from the buttery was in bottles, instead of being ladled out of a can (which traditionalists preferred—they thought it tasted better). There was an angrily conducted poll on whether the college tie should, or should not, have a stripe. Yet the impending departure of Magdalen's most famous alumnus had, apparently, no repercussions. Of course the Christmas vacation was imminent when the crisis broke. But would we have demonstrated in Edward's favour had the vacation not intervened? It seems unlikely.

Why? Looking back twenty-five years later over the old news-reels of Edward—as a boy playing soldiers, as a young officer in Flanders, on his Empire tours, doing his royal duties at home—and recalling his popularity, it is difficult to understand how he could have gone with so little fuss. There was, admittedly, vigorous con-troversy in the press in the final stages, when the story of the King's love for the twice-divorced Mrs. Simpson was finally dis-closed to the British public, but that was—literally—a nine days' wonder, as some headline writers described it at the time. At the end of it, the country settled back to its Christmas shopping as if nothing had happened. And in a sense nothing *had* happened. Arguments had raged in pub and club over whether the Duke of

Windsor, as he had now become, had been the victim of his own folly, or of a conspiracy engineered by the Prime Minister, the editor of the *Times,* and the Archbishop of Canterbury. But though they were sometimes heated, and though they often aroused anger at the Archbishop, they were rarely productive of anything more than mild sympathy for the Duke.

In the celebrated though uncharacteristic purple passage from his *French Revolution,* Edward Burke expressed his astonishment that ten thousand swords had not leapt from their scabbards to avenge even a look that threatened Queen Marie Antoinette with insult. A century and a half later a British king who, as Prince of Wales, was more the people's favourite than Marie Antoinette had ever managed to be was eased off his throne with no effective champion—only noises-off in Fleet Street (he was to have his Burke, in Sir Compton Mackenzie, but that came later). "Funny, when you come to think of it," Professor Richard Hoggart remarked in a letter describing to me the feelings on the abdication in the working-class district where he grew up, "that practically nobody felt it worth while to *do* anything about it." Again, why? That is the question that I have tried to answer.

THE ADVERSARIES

OCTOBER 20, 1936

I was at the door to receive the Prime Minister when, punctually at ten o'clock, he crunched up the drive in a tiny black car which did not seem half big enough for him.

Friendly, calm and discursive, he might have been a neighbour who had called to discuss a dispute over a boundary fence. He complimented me upon the beauty of the grounds, the arrangement of the garden, the silvery radiance of the birch trees, and the delicacy of the autumn tints. We repaired to the octagonal drawing room and sat down in front of the fire, he in an armchair and I on a sofa. Yet he could not have been as calm and composed inside as he looked, for he became restless and finally asked, almost apologetically, if he might have a whiskey-and-soda.

That Stanley Baldwin, epitome of the calm Englishman, should have asked for a whiskey at ten in the morning greatly tickled King Edward VIII. He was to recall the request in this passage from *A King's Story* and again in his commentary for the film made of it nearly thirty years later. Englishmen, the implication was, simply did not drink at that time of the morning, unless they were alcoholics—or having a "hair of the dog," to counteract a hangover, but then they would do it in private.

But Baldwin at the best of times was far from being as calm and composed as he appeared on the surface, and he had good reason to be nervous. For some weeks, the King's name had been closely and sometimes scabrously linked in the foreign press, particularly in the United States, with a Mrs. Ernest Simpson. It was not unusual for foreign journals to speculate on the nature of a king's affairs, or his matrimonial intentions—Edward's name had also recently been linked with a variety of other possibles, notably a Greek princess whom he was rumored to be intending to visit on the cruise he had taken down the Adriatic that summer. Mrs. Simpson was different. The stories about her were more persistent and better documented. So long as she was married to Ernest Simpson, they could be discounted, but now it had been announced

(3)

that Mrs. Simpson was going to divorce her husband and that her petition was due to be heard in a week's time. The time had come, Baldwin had realised, when he must act.

Baldwin was later to give an account in the House of Commons of this meeting with the King, and in *A King's Story,* Edward—though claiming that the Prime Minister had actually been less sympathetic than he was to make himself out to be in the Commons—was to admit that the substance of the conversation had been much as Baldwin described it. As soon as Baldwin had settled down to drink his whiskey—and to smoke his pipe, a rite in which Edward was able to join him, to promote their mutual relaxation—he explained that he had two great anxieties. One was the possible effects on the Dominions of a continuance of the kind of press comment that had been appearing—particularly the effect on Canada, next door to the United States. The other was its effect on the institution of monarchy. A respect had gradually been built up for the monarchy over the preceding three generations, Baldwin pointed out, but to judge by what was being published abroad, it might take a far shorter time to lose.

The advice Baldwin tendered was that the King should use his influence to stop the Simpson divorce proceedings. According to Edward's version, Baldwin did not come right out and ask him in so many words to intervene to stop them, but gradually it became clear that this was what he was hoping for. He did not, however, demand an immediate answer. He was satisfied, he claimed, that the ice had been broken. Edward, less satisfied, thought of replying that so far as he could see the only ice that had been broken had melted in the Prime Minister's whiskey. Still, they parted without bitterness. In fact, as Baldwin took his leave, Edward remembered that he "complimented me again on the beauty of my garden, and volunteered an excellent suggestion for replanting the herbaceous border in the coming spring."

Up to this time the King had been content to let events take their course. Obviously he could not afford to do so any longer. He had insisted that he had no right to interfere with any individual's private affairs and that it would be wrong for him to try to influence Mrs. Simpson "just because she happened to be a friend of the King's." But he knew that he did not want to influence her against continuing the divorce proceedings. He wanted her to continue them so that she would become free to marry him. The divorce petition, assuming that it was granted, was the necessary preliminary. It would give Mrs. Simpson a decree *nisi*, a decree "unless"—unless somebody intervened on legal grounds. But the decree could not be made absolute until six months later, and it was obviously those six months that Baldwin was worried about. If a decree *nisi* was granted, he had intimated, it would leave the matter in suspense for a period during which everyone would be talking about it. When the British press joined in, as sooner or later it must, a most difficult situation would arise for both the King and the Prime Minister. The public might take sides, and factions might arise where none had existed before.

Baldwin did not hold a pistol to the King's head. He threatened no reprisals if Mrs. Simpson went through with her divorce case. There was no outright declaration of war. But the King had been given clear warning of Baldwin's suspicion that the divorce was going through so that a marriage could be arranged. And in fact it had already been arranged. Five months before, according to the Duchess of Windsor's account in *The Heart Has Its Reasons,* Edward had proposed to her—albeit obliquely. Telling her that he was inviting Baldwin to dinner, he had added, "It's got to be done. Sooner or later my Prime Minister must meet my future wife." Though it was the first time he had put the idea into words, she was expecting it. "They," she replied, "would never allow it." But he had brushed aside her objections, and it had come to be regarded as settled. Now, Baldwin's visit was a warning that "they" were going to do their best to prevent it. Events could no longer be left to take their course, for Baldwin would inevitably regard the decision to press on with the divorce as a declaration of intent—as, in effect, a gage thrown down, a challenge. And he would be right.

The issue on which the contest would be fought was, admittedly, not yet clarified. The Prime Minister had not told the King that his government objected to his marrying Mrs. Simpson, and the King had not told the Prime Minister that he was determined to marry her. There was, therefore, time for both sides to inspect the ground, to review their forces, and, above all, to decide how best to muster and lead those forces when the clash came.

KING'S STORY

On the face of it, King Edward was in a strong position. He had come to the throne in January 1936 to the accompaniment of the usual barrage of compliments, unusual in that for once they were genuine. His great-grandmother, Victoria, had ascended the throne at a time when its reputation and popularity were low, and she had been greeted with relief rather than affection. King Edward's grandfather, Edward VII, had been popular enough, but some raffish episodes when he was Prince had given rise to doubts whether he would make a satisfactory king. He gave satisfaction, but this only raised doubts about his son, George V. It seemed improbable that George, a relatively colourless personality, could do as well. That George actually did even better, and by the time of his death had brought the monarchy to its highest-ever point of popularity and esteem, might have raised similar doubts about his heir; but it did not, at least as far as the general public was concerned. George had appeared to be the father of his people—honourable, wise, just. But he was a Victorian by temperament and in his standards, and for all their admiration of him, the British were quite prepared for a more modern-minded successor, a king more in tune with the democratic trends of the time. Edward's accession was welcomed with spontaneous delight by people of all political persuasions (except for a handful of Communists and republicans) and of all social classes. And although he did not immediately make as much of an impact as King as some of his more fervent admirers had expected, he did not, in the first few months of his reign, tarnish the image he had won as the Prince of Wales. At the time of the encounter with Baldwin, his popularity was to all appearances as great as ever.

To those who had dealings with him, though, it had become apparent that the qualities that had helped to make his reputation as Prince of Wales were not necessarily going to help him as King. Edward himself had not changed, but his circumstances had, and his personality was much less suited for the tasks he was now required to perform. As Prince of Wales he had been a star performer, and he had adapted himself to the role's requirement, identifying himself with it so well that there had hardly seemed any distinction between prince and man. But to be King required a casting change, and his background and upbringing had conspired to unfit him for the new part.

This was not realized at the time. Even if it had been, it would have won him little more sympathy. Admittedly the analytical theories of Freud and Jung, with their restatement of the old idea that the child is father to the man, were permeating through society at this time. They were even reaching people who were never likely to read a line Freud or Jung had written (and who would have been horrified if they had) but were absorbing some of the jargon and the ideas and accepting that repressions and complexes might arise out of childhood trauma. But people who would have been prepared to be tolerant about a "difficult" friend or relative—would have attributed his failings to an unhappy or (a term just beginning to come into favour) a maladjusted childhood—were rarely inclined to give that benefit to a king. The British were then much more sentimental about the monarchy than they have since become. The now widespread attitude that as an institution it is archaic but that it should be preserved because it works better in practice than a presidency was far less often encountered. Kings might no longer be conceded any claim to divine right, but they still had an aura to which many of their subjects were susceptible—and the more loyal the subject, the less tolerant he or she might be of imperfections. The fact that Edward's family background had had some unfortunate consequences would hardly have been accepted in extenuation, even if it had been known.

Childhood

As a child, Edward had suffered from the lack of understanding of his parents, especially of his father, Prince George.

The grandson of Queen Victoria, the second son of Edward VII, George had been allowed to make a career for himself in the navy, in the full expectation of serving out his time and the full hope of ending up as an admiral of the fleet through his own merit rather than through his family connections. And although the death of his elder brother meant the end of his naval career, he had continued to apply the same quarter-deck principles to his new tasks as heir to the throne and, later, as King. The transfer proved astonishingly successful so far as his public life was concerned. In the home, it was to prove less satisfactory.

At first this was not apparent. George appeared singularly fortunate in his marriage. It had been arranged for him by his grandmother, Queen Victoria, who considered that falling in love should play no part in royal matrimonial arrangements—a view which George, with his strongly developed sense of duty, accepted. Princess Mary of Teck had originally been betrothed to the elder brother, the Duke of Clarence, heir to the throne. The German duchy from which she came was of little account, but it was considered expedient to marry young Eddie off quickly to somebody suitable rather than allow him to get involved with somebody thoroughly unsuitable, as he had shown himself inclined to do. The opinions of the betrothed pair were hardly considered, but they behaved, as convention demanded, as if it had been a love match. Perhaps it might have been, but six weeks later the Duke was dead. He had caught influenza, which had developed into pneumonia.

The tragedy made it seem all the more important to Queen Victoria that Prince George, himself recovering from an attack of typhoid, should marry somebody suitable and begin producing a family. And who could be more suitable than the girl who would have been Queen if Eddie had lived? Not unnaturally, Princess Mary did not relish the prospect. Although she had nothing against George, the contrivance was a little too blatant. But Queen Victoria was persistent, and time played its traditional healing role. Little more than a year later, Prince George and Princess Mary became engaged. Heads were shaken, but the best face possible was put on the marriage. The editorial writer in the *Morning Post* commented (prophetically, as it turned out), "The marriage of one who is ultimately heir to the throne is not an event which can be regarded as purely of a private character." The *Times* went so far as to claim, "There is even ground for hoping that a union rooted in painful memories may prove happy beyond the common lot." The forecast was correct. It proved extremely happy. But the benefits of the arranged match were to be felt more by George and Mary than by their children.

Prince Edward was born on June 23, 1894, and named after his deceased uncle—against the wishes of Victoria, who pointed out that Eddie had not been the Duke of Clarence's *real* name. He had been christened Albert. To pacify her, the Prince was christened Edward Albert Christian George Andrew Patrick David—and thereafter called David by his family. (The second son could not escape: He was born, to his parents' embarrassment, on the anniversary of the Prince Consort's death. But as Prince George's father pointed out, he had always been called "Bertie" in the family. So "Bertie" it became.)

George never managed to establish with his children the same easy relationship he had had with his father, soon to ascend the throne as Edward VII. Edward had been one of those men, common enough, who are inconsiderate, often caddish, to adults, but wonderful with children. Frightened of him at first, George's relations with his father became close and affectionate. But George, though far more considerate than his father to other people, could not get along with his children, as the records left by both father and son agree. "A sweet little boy," George wrote in his diary, recording the arrival of his son and heir. "Somehow I imagine," that son was to recall over half a century later, "this was the last time my father was ever inspired to apply to me that precise appellation."

Entrusted to the care of nurses and nannies, governesses and tutors, David grew up meeting his family usually only in what, for a child, are formal circumstances—when he was brought down to the drawing room for tea, when he was summoned to his father's study to be complimented for some achievement or, far more often, reprimanded for some misdeed. Even Harold Nicolson, whose sympathies as King George's biographer were won by his subject, felt bound, "if only to assure the reader that no single shadow has been shirked," to allude to the fact that the King "failed to establish with his children, at least until they married, those relations of equable and equal companionship that are the solace of old age." And this is hardly surprising, in view of George's observation to Lord Derby: "My father was frightened of his mother; I was frightened of my father; and I am damned well going to see to it that my children are frightened of me."

George was obsessed with ideas of naval discipline, and he resented the new license that was being accorded to youth, by contrast with the relatively spartan regime of his childhood. As a result he never really understood his eldest son or learned how to get on with him. He was to express his feelings in a letter he wrote to congratulate his second son, Bertie—by this time Duke of York—on his marriage to Lady Elizabeth Bowes-Lyon in 1923: "You have always been so sensible and easy to work with and you have always been ready to listen to any advice and agree with my opinions about people and things that I feel we have always got on very well together. Very different to dear David."

Dear David's relations with his mother, a naturally gay and ebullient personality, might have been closer. But she was determined to adapt herself to her husband, and this thrust her into what her biographer, James Pope-Hennessy, stigmatized as "this ingrowing and unnatural form of living"—court life. She did it most effectively, becoming in due course a queen to the manner born, but in the process she mislaid her natural self, with unfortunate effects on her relations with her children. Like her husband, "she had no automatic or spontaneous understanding of a child's mind or ways." Later, the fact that her husband came to the throne influenced her still more strongly: "I have always to remember," she was heard to say about her children, "that their father is also their King." The result was that although the family atmosphere was sometimes quite cosy, it never became uninhibited.

George and Mary were incapable of realizing that young children, even if members of a royal family, are not naturally obedient, neat and well-behaved. They worried because David was a "fidget," yet so remote were they from what was going on in their own household that for years they were unaware that his nurse was in the habit of pinching and twisting his arm to make him cry before bringing him into the drawing room—so that he would promptly be dismissed from it for his bad behavior, thereby restoring the nurse's ascendancy. Her technique was discovered only when she had a nervous breakdown after, it was disclosed, three years without a holiday. It cannot be denied, Pope-Hennessy reluctantly concluded, "that between them, King George and Queen Mary managed to be rather unsuccessful and somewhat unsympathetic parents."

Education

Edward's education was misguided. A tradition had begun to establish itself that the best training for a boy in the royal family was to prepare him for a career in the navy, and at the age of thirteen Edward was removed from his tutor and sent to the Royal Naval College at Osborne. But, unlike his father and numerous uncles and cousins, he was not intended for a naval career. He was put through Osborne, and later Dartmouth, because of his father's belief that the tough nautical training they gave helped to form character—the same argument that was coming to be used in favour of the English public-school system. Edward was adaptable, and the existence was not uncongenial to him, but it was not designed to bring out the sides of his personality that most needed developing. Whatever value the training might have had for him if he had intended to become a naval officer, for an heir to the throne it was staggeringly irrelevant.

Edward passed through Osborne and Dartmouth without greatly distinguishing himself—though with less difficulty than his brother Bertie, for whom it was quite an achievement to avoid last place in the term rankings. A three-month spell followed as a midshipman on a battleship. Then, just when Edward was beginning to enjoy his naval career, it was abruptly terminated by his father's orders. Instead, he was to go to Magdalen College, Oxford.

This was not George's idea—he had never thought highly of academic institutions. But he had at last allowed himself to be persuaded that his son needed intellectual attainments which the navy had so far conspicuously failed to provide. The decision, however, turned out to be even more ill-advised than putting the Prince through Osborne and Dartmouth. They at least had meant something to him. Oxford was to mean little. Edward was not academically oriented enough to benefit from what the university had to offer.

"Ever since I can remember," he was to recall, "I have always preferred outdoor exercise to reading. And, ever since I can remember, it has been from people rather than from textbooks that I have got my education." Only when he was allowed to choose his own subject on which to write his weekly essay for the pompous president of Magdalen, Dr. Warren, was an occasional spark of interest aroused, because he could deal with historical characters who were real people, such as Captain Scott of the Antarctic. But Oxford at that time was an unpromising source for such material. Warren claimed that though the Prince was not "bookish" (a term of mild contempt in the English upper classes), "he was learning more and more every day of men, gauging character, watching its play, getting to know what Englishmen are like, both individually and still more in the mass." But if that was what Edward required, Oxford was the last place for him to find it. After two years, he managed to persuade his father to let him leave.

War

The new idea was that Edward should travel for a while, before joining the army. But the year was 1914. When war broke out in August and he told his father he was in no mood to wait, no obstacle was put in his way—at first. He was given a commission in the Grenadier Guards, for which his naval career, followed by experience in the Oxford University officers' training corps, made him better qualified than many who were gazetted at the time. He was only five feet seven inches tall, compared to the minimum of six feet ordinarily required—a pygmy, he described himself, among giants. But this was a source of pride to him rather than embarrassment, and he looked forward to going with his battalion to the front. But when the time came, the Prince found himself left behind: "A terrible blow to my pride, the worst in my life."

This is unlikely to have been an exaggeration. Edward was becoming preoccupied, almost to the point of obsession, with the need to prove himself the equal of his fellow guardsmen. They might think that he was taking advantage of being Prince of Wales—a title he had been given in 1911—to avoid the real war. He wanted to prove to them that from his point of view, being the Prince was a *dis*advantage, keeping him, as it did, from sharing their life, and that his sheltered existence was not of his own designing. Given the opportunity, he was determined to sacrifice ease, comfort, rank and title to be with them wherever duty might take him.

It took him to France, but not to the front. He found himself attached to the staff of Sir John French, commander in chief of the British Expeditionary Force. He did not lack courage. He would have liked to have done his stint in the trenches—or, rather, being sensitive, he could hardly have liked it, but he felt that to be at the front for a time was necessary to acquire self-respect. However, the Secretary of State for War—the formidable Lord Kitchener—was adamant. If he were sure the Prince would be killed, he said, he did not know if he would be right to hold him back, "but I cannot take the chance, which always exists until we have a settled line, of the enemy taking you prisoner." Even when a settled line was achieved, though, the ban remained. The Prince, embarrassed, decided not to wear the Russian and French decorations that he had been awarded. He explained why to his father, who had written to rebuke him:

I think you know how distasteful it is to me to wear those two war decorations, never having done any fighting and having always been kept well out of danger! I feel so ashamed to wear medals which I only have because of my position, when there are so many thousands of gallant officers who lead a terrible existence, in the trenches, and who have fought battles of the fiercest kind (many severely wounded or sick as a result), who have not been decorated. No doubt I look at this thing from a wrong and foolish point of view, but this is the view I take . . .

A week later—this was in September 1915—the Prince came under shellfire for the first time, seeing the evidence of an attack that had just taken place in the form of unburied corpses on what had been no man's land. When he returned to his car it was to find that his driver had been killed by shrapnel. The episode only led to requests from Buckingham Palace for greater care in keeping out of risk's way, and although it made a deep impression on him, it underlined his feeling that he was not really a full combatant.

His brother Bertie was more fortunate. He had become a junior officer on HMS *Collingwood*. Although he suffered from recurring bouts of some illness that the doctors could not diagnose, he was at sea with the fleet for the battle of Jutland and emerged from the sick bay to play his appointed part in this, the last of the great purely naval battles. (Those of the Second World War had air power to complicate them.) The experience did not enable him to throw off his outward symptoms of uncertainty—shyness, coupled with a speech impediment—but it helped to build a measure of inward self-confidence that was later to surprise all but those who knew him best, and even some of them.

What Edward could do to reassure himself, he did. Whenever opportunity presented itself he went up to the front line, where his presence became considerably more familiar than that of many of his senior officers. Quoting the remark of a regimental officer that "a bad shelling will always produce the Prince of Wales," Philip Guedalla suggested that the cause lay in the bias of Edward's mind, "which led him to dislike intensely those humiliating precautions which were the due badge of his rank, and to crave instead the still-higher privilege of sharing the common lot." This was true, but there was more to it. The Prince felt continually compelled to test himself. Not out of any craving for popularity or esteem—on the contrary, the notion that they could be bought so easily would have embarrassed him. It was not the world but himself that he wanted to reassure.

Travel

Reassurance followed after the end of the war. Before it had broken out Edward had badgered his father to let him travel, and George V was sympathetic, recalling his own experience when he had been despatched early in his father's reign to open the first Australian Commonwealth Parliament. George's tour had lasted eight months, extending to South Africa and Canada, and he had been impressed, having had no idea of the reserves of loyalty to the mother country that lay waiting to be tapped. But taking him away from the benevolent but sometimes formidable presence of his father and the nervous watchfulness of his mother, Queen Alexandra, it had helped to give him independence and to broaden his horizons and sympathies. Australia, and still more New Zealand, had already advanced some way toward the welfare state, along the political road that Britain was just beginning to travel. The advance had been undertaken without civil commotion and carried through successfully by men of limited education and no social graces. Meeting them had prepared George for the possibility of a Labour government in Britain, should one materialize, as seemed likely, and he was grateful for the experience. It was natural that he should decide to let his heir go on similar tours as soon as he was old enough, in the hope that he would obtain similar benefit.

But the conditions were not the same. Edward, though in some ways more receptive than his father, was less mature. He lacked the solid grounding of a career (George had, after all, held independent commands in the navy before leaving it), and he lacked the stabilising influence of a wife (George had brought Mary with him). Nor did Edward see the tours simply as a royal duty. He wanted to enjoy them as any other young man, suddenly presented with such an opportunity, would want to do.

Wherever he went, in or out of the Empire, the Prince of Wales was rapturously greeted, and unquestionably he was good value for his reception. He was something more than a young man who happened to be a Prince, going through the stock motions. To begin with, he looked younger than his twenty-five years, and there was something delightfully appealing in his eager face. For he was enjoying himself, at least where convention was relaxed enough to allow him to, as it often was. He won Canadian esteem by insisting upon being allowed to ride a bucking bronco at a rodeo, and he impressed the potentially critical newspapermen in the United States by his ability to answer questions without hedging or affectation.

By his own account, Edward's curiosity about the United States had been aroused by his contacts with American troops during the war, and though the intention had been that his first official tour in 1919 should be confined to Canada, he managed to get permission to extend it to take in Washington and New York. In the capital he met the dying President, Woodrow Wilson, at the White House, and the Assistant Secretary of the Navy, Franklin D. Roosevelt, at Annapolis. He had his first taste of an American-style motorcycle cavalcade and of Prohibition. But it was New York that really appealed to him. He was welcomed at the Battery by Grover Whalen and given a ticker-tape parade—an enlivening and also occasionally alarming experience, as from time to time objects more solid than ticker tape would land with a thud beside them. His escort explained that they were only parts of telephone books—"Some of those people are too damn impatient."

The visit left a deep impression on Edward. From his conversations he gained an insight into the mind of Americans—something very few Englishmen had at the time. But what lingered on "was not so much the grand things that happened to me—and grand is the only word for the welcome that was given me—rather it was a haunting little song that I heard at the Ziegfeld Follies: *A Pretty Girl Is Like a Melody.*"

On his return, his father was delighted with a verse he brought back from a Canadian border town:

> Four and twenty Yankees, feeling very dry
> Went across the border to get a drink of rye
> When the rye was opened, the Yanks began to sing
> God bless America, but God save the King!

But the King was less enthusiastic about *A Pretty Girl Is Like a Melody.* "What's that damn tune that you are whistling all the time?" he asked. It was just something, the Prince replied, that he had picked up in America. But he had also picked up a lasting admiration for Americans, their easy social ways, their wisecracks, and their vitality.

His later tours took him to the Antipodes, via the Panama Canal and Honolulu, in 1920; to India, via Suez and Aden, in the winter of 1921 and then on in the new year to Ceylon, Singapore and Tokyo; to Canada again in 1923 and 1924, with a further visit to the United States; and in 1925 to South Africa and Rhodesia, before crossing the South Atlantic to Montevideo and Buenos Aires. When he returned in October 1925 he had travelled the equivalent of six circumnavigations of the world without showing any signs of strain—except once, and that was later to provide the most engaging sequence of the film of his life story. It showed him shaking hand after hand, hand after hand. . . . George V, according to his biographer, had had to shake the hands of 24,585 people on his tour, but perhaps his more reserved manner had led to a more formal, less enthusiastic grip. For Edward, the salutation began to become a martyrdom. Eventually he had to put his right hand in a sling. The film went on to show him shaking hands with his left. Yet, even then, the face was still lit with interest. A little wry, perhaps—a little as if he might be thinking, "When is it going to end?"—but not forced, and with no trace of the boredom that was sometimes to be observed on it later.

Edward, in fact, had kept throughout his interest in what he saw and heard. Because he was so obviously interested, his hosts were delighted with him wherever he went—even if he did occasionally forget a dance with the wife or daughter of a local dignitary in order to enjoy it with some more attractive partner who had caught his eye. Never before had a prince established himself so firmly in the hearts of people, all over the world.

At court

Up to this point the Prince's career seemed to be a heartening illustration of how a man in his position could break the royal mould and establish his own pattern of princedom. But now his past caught up with him. The visit to Africa and South America in the winter of 1925 was his last official tour. It was thought to be time for him to settle down. But when he came back, the Prince was disconcerted to find that there was no real place for him at home—none, that is, that gave him scope to exercise his talents. He spent quite an agreeable holiday cub hunting—pursuing young foxes, in order to train young foxhounds—and he attended the funeral of his grandmother, Queen Alexandra. But as for settling down . . . settling down to what?

There were plently of royal duties to be performed. The Prince was greatly in demand for public ceremonies of every kind, all over the country. But proficient as he had become at laying foundation stones, declaring new institutions open, presenting prizes, and replying to toasts, he could not help feeling that there should be more important tasks for the heir to the throne. Here he came up against his father, and by this time King George had become inflexible.

The long absences from his family, during which he had established his independence, might have been expected both to liberate Edward from his father's dominance and to give his father a healthy respect for him. They did neither. All they did was to make communication more difficult. They had taught Edward to pride himself on being up-to-date, and he returned to England to find the court cocooned in the past, hidebound by convention in a way that made his grandfather's court seem in retrospect positively modern.

Edward VII's company had been reasonably cosmopolitan, including Continental families, Jews—even Americans. Members of other royal families occasionally came to stay at the court of George V, but for the most part it was confined to the home-bred aristocracy, and a narrow segment of it at that. To George, a court *was* a court: it should consist of the highborn—the royal family flanked by the upper echelons of the aristocracy. Commoners were rarely invited, except in their official capacity as politicians, doctors or churchmen. The kind of people whom Edward encountered at court, whether he liked them or not, rarely shared his interests, still less his tastes. Most of them were older, and though his father and mother would have been delighted to bring in young princesses from the courts of Europe or respectable home blue blood, the scent of matchmaking put Edward off.

In any case, he found the formality stifling. Once the younger members of a house party at Windsor Castle stayed up after their parents had gone to bed, rolled back the rugs, and had the military band play wheezy fox trots. But the experiment failed: "The ancient walls seemed to exude disapproval. We never tried it again." Court life became something alien to Edward. He avoided it when he could.

In particular, he disliked the way that the court was cut off from the rest of society by its own top-heaviness. How could his mother, for example, stay with anybody but the very rich, when she could not move away from home without a retinue? According to Lady Diana Cooper's autobiography, those who had the Queen to stay found that she required two dressers, a footman, a page, a chauffeur, a lady-in-waiting, a lady-in-waiting's maid, and a detective. Every evening, too, a chair had to be prepared outside her room, on which the footman and the page (who turned out to be about fifty) could take turns to sit all night.

The object of all this retinue, James Pope-Hennessy candidly surmised, "was to protect the Royalty in the centre of the hive from any form of avoidable anxiety and from crude contact with the outside world, so as to preserve Him or Her healthy, serene, and intact for the performance of Royal duties with the maximum of efficiency and the minimum of worry." But crude contact with the outside world was precisely what Edward had been experiencing. He had enjoyed it, and he wished to continue it. He therefore took up social work of a kind that no prince had ever engaged in before, for ex-servicemen, for youth clubs, for the unemployed. The monarchy, he decided, should be brought nearer to the people—would have to be, in fact, if it were to survive as an institution. In the 1920s George V had hardly begun to touch the affections of the British. He was respected, but not loved, and Edward understandably felt that in the long run what would be required was a king whose relationship to his people was of the kind which he, as Prince, had achieved around the Empire. He set about preparing himself for that role.

According to one of his biographers, Hector Bolitho, the origins of the Prince's social-welfare consciousness could be traced to an episode in 1923. He was being shown a soup kitchen in an English provincial town and saw, among other signs of extreme poverty, a man who had no shirt under his coat. Afterward the Prince walked up and down, pressing his hands together and saying, 'What can I do? What can be done?' " When he came back from the last of his official tours he began to try to get to know the people of Britain in the same way as he had got to know them in the Dominions. In the process he began to acquire the same kind of aura that he had won during the war. A New York *Tribune* journalist who accompanied him on one of his tours of the north described how he used to choose houses at random to call on. At one, the miner who came out recognized him and said his wife was sick. She was in fact in childbirth. "If you wouldn't mind holding her hand," the miner said, "she'd never forget it." And the Prince did. Similar stories continued to be published and spread by word of mouth. No doubt many of them were elaborations of more prosaic incidents, and some may have been inventions, but the picture they presented was not false.

Again, though, he found himself thwarted. George V had often been perturbed at some of the stories about his son's casual ways on his world tours, but they were so successful that it was hard to be disapproving. For the Prince to do the same kind of thing at home was different. It might cause trouble.

But what, then, *could* the Prince do? He would have liked to take a hand in affairs of state, but this his father would not allow. Edward found himself, as he was later to describe it, in a position that "at times seemed to leave me dangling futilely in space between the ceremonial make-believe, symbolizing the power of high and mighty princes, and the discouraging realities of a world that insisted upon relegating even a conscientious prince to a figure-head role." Even association with ministers of state, of the kind that might have kept him in touch with what was happening, was frowned on by his father, though "at the same time, in a manner never defined, I was expected to remain conversant with all that was going on in the world and to give the impression of being knowledgeable and well-informed."

The Prince's difficulty was real, but it is hard to avoid the suspicion that if he had been deeply interested in politics, home or foreign, he would have found ways to get around his father. The fact was that his tastes did not lie in this direction. Even if he did not have access to state documents, he could, if he had really been interested, have studied the background—history, current affairs, and so on—as his father had done. There is no evidence that Edward did, and plenty of evidence, some of it provided by himself, that he did not. He still did not enjoy reading. It was as much as his aides could do to get him to sit down and go through the digests they prepared to brief him for visits to new places or for speeches.

This did not detract from his ability to impress and to charm audiences. Any lack of knowledge of what a factory was doing was more than made up for by the interest he showed in its work when he was being taken around. His questions were often the livelier for being unrehearsed, and his mind was quick enough to pick up the gist of what he was being told faster than the telling. But the capacity to notice, ask about, and understand some new mechanical device or invention and to make an apposite comment on it from his own experience was self-limiting. It did not broaden his outlook. Neither did it help him to understand the problems of, say, the financing of industry or of labour relations—let alone of the wider economic, social and political issues with which, as King, he would have to concern himself.

Nor, when the Prince was free from his duties, did he seek out the company, informally, of those from whom he might have learned —industrialists, trade-union leaders, scientists. He would certainly not have had the least difficulty in attracting such men around him. Both as heir to the throne and as an interesting young man in his own right he would have found it easy to win their confidence and their confidences. He encountered such men from time to time in the course of his duties, but he did not draw them into the inner circle of his friends.

One reason was that in his free time his craving was to release his energies, which remained inexhaustible. The desire to test himself, to prove himself, was as strong as ever. He now found riding the most satisfactory method. It had not come naturally to him. While he was at Oxford his father, seeing him looking ill-at-ease on a horse, insisted on his taking lessons—horsemanship being considered an essential accomplishment for princes. Had he suffered from an unsympathetic teacher, he would probably have remained bored with it all his life. But he began to enjoy it, and as soon as he graduated to the stage where he could hunt, the excitement carried him on.

In the 1920s he took up steeplechasing, and this, more than any of his other activities, helped to provide him with the rigorous self-testing he craved. He had not been a natural-born rider, and he never even became a good one. But nobody doubted that he had guts. He rode with splendid determination. Occasionally he even won races. He also had spectacular falls, and the falls attracted public attention more than the victories. Eventually he suffered a concussion following a fall in an army point-to-point and had to stay in bed for nearly a month. Both the Prime Minister and his father begged him to give up steeplechasing, and eventually, after his father's near-fatal illness in 1928, he complied with their wishes. It was a double blow, depriving him as it did of a sport that he enjoyed and of one of the two tests (hunting being the other) that "satisfied the latent desire in me to excel, to pit myself against others on equal terms, to show that, at least in matters where physical boldness and endurance counted, I could hold my own."

With steeplechasing barred, the Prince tried to find some other way to prove he could hold his own. He took up flying. At this time, and for some years to come, learning to fly was not considered a pastime. It was more like auto racing, for example, than like driving. Though the risks may have been exaggerated, it also required courage. For some reason his father, who had imposed the ban on steeplechasing and who disliked the idea of flying, did not object. Edward was allowed to buy a training airplane in which, in due course, he went solo. Then, once again, he showed that it was the need to test himself rather than the desire to learn a new craft that had interested him. Although he travelled frequently by air, the act of flying the airplane, once he had learned how to do it, held little further interest for him. He was reduced to golf.

"Those vile bodies"

The other release for his energies was parties. The twenties were the great age of parties in Britain. As Evelyn Waugh was to describe them,

. . . Masked parties, Savage parties, Victorian parties, Greek parties, Wild West parties, Russian parties, Circus parties, parties where one had to dress as somebody else, almost naked parties in St. John's Wood, parties in flats and studios and houses and ships and hotels and night clubs, in windmills and swimming baths, tea parties at school where one ate muffins and meringues and tinned crab, parties at Oxford where one drank brown sherry and smoked Turkish cigarettes, dull dances in London and comic dances in Scotland and disgusting dances in Paris—all that succession and repetition of massed humanity . . . Those vile bodies . . .

The bodies might be vile, but the Prince appears never to have tired of the parties, in spite of the fact that he had many formal evening engagements to fulfill as well. On free evenings, or after the formal engagement was over on evenings that were not free, "Fruity and I would go out and have a good time"—Fruity being Edward Dudley Metcalfe, an officer in the Indian cavalry who had attended the Prince on his Indian tour and subsequently joined his permanent staff as an equerry.

Their evenings out were unlikely to be sedate. In the early 1920s, as Edward was often nostalgically to recall, the party round was almost continuous: "One might receive invitations for as many as four parties the same evening . . . if the first failed to please, one could always move on to another." If all failed to please, or when the last was over, there were the fashionable night clubs: the Café de Paris, Ciro's, the Kit-Kat, or his particular favourite, the Embassy. And night clubs were not then, as they later tended to become, places of soft lights and sweet music, with intertwined couples imperceptibly shuffling round a tiny floor. They were bright, noisy and gay, and the dancing was energetic, doubtless the more so because that was the way the Prince liked it—"For a brief period I counted the music of the Charleston and the Black Bottom among the foremost American exports to Britain."

This was the era of the bright young things—Britain's contribution to the jazz age. (Some photographs suggest a fleeting resemblance between the Prince and Scott Fitzgerald.) But the participants were often no longer young—they were the Prince's own generation moving into their thirties. Their brightness, too, was frenetic rather than gay. Evelyn Waugh was to capture it in his *Vile Bodies*. The craving was for something different. Simple fancy dress was not enough. Eccentricity was sought after—as on the evening described in a letter by Lady Diana Cooper:

There was a fancy ball at Ava Ribblesdale's last night, and all the women looked 50% worse than usual—S. as Little Lord Fauntleroy quite awful, P. as a street arab just dirty! . . . The rest of us were porters. We thought we were pretty funny all darting into the room shouting "*Porteur, porteur!*" Gerald Berners . . . had announced his intention of going as Nurse Cavell but was dissuaded. Winston [Churchill] as Nero was good. F.E. [Smith —Lord Birkenhead] went as a cardinal. . . .

King George, when he heard about these parties, found them acutely distasteful. He would have preferred his son to put such frivolity behind him and to enter into the settled routine of court life. But this was precisely what Edward could not face, and it is easy to sympathise with him. Not only was the company uncongenial to him, the protocol was stifling.

George had an obsessive devotion to traditions, forms and ceremonial. One of his less endearing characteristics was his constant worry about procedure, and in particular sartorial precision. When the first Labour government came into office in 1923, he was for a time far less exercised about how, with their inexperience, they were going to govern the country than about what they were going to wear when they came to court. Edward, on the other hand, was busy leading a rebellion against stuffy formal dress and in particular against what he described as "the tyranny of starch"—spats, hard collars, hard cuffs, and especially the boiled shirt for evening dress, which he denounced as the "horrible garment" that had "given us so much untold misery."

His father was shocked, and the publication of a picture of the Prince of Wales wearing a bowler instead of a top hat at some official function led to his being reproved by the Keeper of the Privy Purse, Sir Frederick Ponsonby. The Prince, Ponsonby warned, was taking a risk in making himself too accessible: "The Monarchy must always retain an element of mystery . . . must remain on a pedestal." Times, Edward protested, were changing. Replying that he had served Edward's father, grandfather and great-grandmother, Ponsonby reiterated that Edward was mistaken.

From Edward's point of view, the resounding success of his world tours, in which there was informality whenever he could extract it, proved his point. He was moving with the times. His father and Ponsonby and their like were not. He could even justify his reluctance to wear a top hat—except at weddings and formal court occasions—on the ground that cartoonists had adopted it as the symbol of predatory capitalism, an argument which, he was later to claim, exhibited "a certain sagacity in what are now called public relations." He might also have pointed out that formal dress has always been subject to changes of fashion, and for a court to try to resist the changes after they have become established is to invite ridicule. King George, however, was unable to grasp the distinction between being unconventional (and therefore reprehensible) and being in step with the times, so his son's appearance was a continual source of worry to him.

Nor were Edward's clothes the King's worst worry. Almost all Edward's tastes were anathema to his father, who "disapproved of Soviet Russia, painted fingernails, women who smoked in public, cocktails, frivolous hats, American jazz and the growing habit of going away for week-ends." They could agree on outlawing Soviet Russia, but Edward could see nothing glaringly reprehensible about accepting the rest. The result was that father and son drifted farther apart. No doubt Edward's still strikingly youthful appearance contributed to the misunderstanding. Pictures taken of him during the war, in uniform, had shown the face of a boy who might have been barely into his teens, and when in 1925 he returned from his last official tour he could still have passed for a teenager, though by this time he was over thirty. And when he insisted on behaving like a teenager (from the King's point of view), it was taken as evidence that he was not yet ready for responsibility.

Yet this was only a royal rationalisation. The King was similarly unable to allow his second son, Prince Albert, any real responsibility, in spite of the fact that he was more docile and had done what his parents most wished his elder brother would do, by finding a suitable wife.

After the war Prince Albert had left the navy for the new air force, and while his elder brother was enjoying the world limelight, he had quietly done all that was expected of him. He had learned to fly, he had gone to Cambridge for a year, and he had been made Duke of York. But even when he did something useful, and did it well, as when he acted as King George's representative at the coronation of King Ferdinand of Rumania in 1922, George was unable to give him credit. In George's eyes, his sons remained children.

Then, in 1923, the Duke of York became engaged to Lady Elizabeth Bowes-Lyon, daughter of the Earl of Strathmore. Although strictly speaking she was a commoner, her charm and suitability in all other respects enabled the King and Queen to accept her as an admirable match. The public would have been better pleased if it had been the Prince of Wales who had won her hand, but the wedding was spectacular—the first time a British prince had been married in Westminster Abbey since the fourteenth century. It was celebrated with due pomp and pageantry. The marriage, his biographer thought, was the first great climacteric of Albert's life. It made him a public figure, albeit on a more modest scale than his brother.

By taking him away from the parental nest, marriage also seemed to hold out the prospect of convincing his parents he was grown up. "By your quiet useful work," his father wrote to him after the wedding, "you have endeared yourself to the people." The Duke looked forward to extending his activities. He worked assiduously on industrial relations, and he followed in his brother's footsteps with a protracted Empire tour. But when he returned, anxious to utilize his knowledge in affairs of state—particularly those that concerned the Dominions—he found his father as reluctant as before to allow him any responsibility. According to Sir John Wheeler-Bennett—echoing Edward's own recollection—the King continued holding the view that it was no part of the duties of his elder sons to have access to such confidential information, "ignoring the fact that they were expected, in some indefinable manner, to appear conversant with world affairs and to give the impression of being informed and knowledgeable." All that the brothers were allowed to see was a limited selection of Foreign Office and Dominion Office cables—"and this only with the greatest misgivings and after considerable resistance."

This barrier was never broken down, because the sons never managed to overcome their awe of their father sufficiently to impress him with the fact that they were grown up. Only within the family circle did things become a little easier for the younger brothers when they married. After the King's death the Duchess of York was to recall that "unlike his own children, I was never afraid of him," and the fact that she was not afraid of him eased his relationship with the Duke. But no suitable wife emerged to smooth his relations with his eldest son.

With Queen Mary, too, though Edward continued to feel a filial tie, he found communication increasingly difficult. After a meeting with him she commented, "We talked a lot but of nothing very intimate," and this was to be the theme of their relationship. The longer the reign lasted, the less easy Queen Mary found it to achieve the necessary spontaneity to make contact with her son. She had become one of the most regal queens in the country's history, but only at the cost of loss of her own identity. "It is possible that today nobody knows what Queen Mary of England is really like—not even Queen Mary," Janet Flanner (Genêt of the *New Yorker*) wrote of her in *An American in Paris* in 1940. "For over thirty years she has given twelve to eighteen hours of her days, and the total of her energy and conscience, to not being herself."

In different circumstances, Edward might have formed an alliance with his brothers. Together, they could have been quite a formidable combination, especially as they had a useful lever, the withholding of their royal services, with which to exert their influence. But there were temperamental incompatibilities, and after his return from his tours, the only brother with whom Edward enjoyed a close friendship was the youngest, Prince George, Duke of Kent. Prince George was the best-looking of the four and in personality the most immediately attractive. His tastes ran to gay bohemian parties and beautiful women, and Edward, visiting Spain and Canada with him in 1927, found him congenial company. But he was nine years younger and still in the navy. The stolid Harry, Duke of Gloucester, was in the army, and Edward does not appear to have pined for his company. And the Duke of York had after his marriage quickly settled down to a staid, almost bourgeois family existence that for Edward held few attractions.

Looking at the Prince of Wales' position in 1928, it could have been argued that the only possible way out of his difficulties would be for him to become King, and he very nearly did. That winter his father fell dangerously ill. Had he died, the course of Edward's reign would have been very different, and not simply because he had yet to meet Mrs. Simpson. He was still adaptable enough, at that time, to have found being King the same exhilarating challenge that he had found being heir to the throne. He would certainly have thrown himself into his duties with verve. But the King recovered, and his recovery meant that Edward was back where he had been before. He was still much in demand for all manner of ceremonial occasions, but he had no work of the kind he could really get his teeth into, and he was still to be found at night clubs in company of which his parents disapproved.

His parents thought, or at least hoped, that if only Edward could find a suitable girl and marry her, he would soon find a settled fireside life as agreeable as Bertie did. But though Edward had no trouble in finding girls, the trouble was that they were rarely suitable, and when they were, their attraction did not last. It was as if the Prince's journeyings had conditioned him, condemning him to be everlastingly susceptible to the liner-style romance that traditionally ends when the liner docks. In any case, marriageable debutantes, of whom he could have taken his pick, did not appeal to him. He preferred the company of actresses, who were amusing and made fewer demands on him.

The first woman with whom he fell in love, by her account—they saw a lot of each other for some years—was Thelma, Lady Furness. She was one of the Morgan twins, whose faces and figures had made their fortunes in the twenties. Her sister, Gloria, had married a Vanderbilt. Thelma herself married at sixteen and divorced in her early twenties, then married Viscount Furness, a shipping magnate. This marriage did not work out either. When the Prince met her at a county agricultural show, she was living apart from her husband. The Prince invited her to dinner, to further dinners, to a safari in Africa. And they fell in love.

The Prince's circle had always been considered gay, and gay it remained. The artist Sir Francis Rose was later to recall how, in the late 1920s, he used to see the Prince, "who was trying hard not to lose at baccarat," walking jauntily toward the Tire-à-Pigeon, "like a small edition of George IV, with the exquisite Daisy Fellowes on one arm and Lady Furness on the other; not hanging or hugging like the present-day miss, but pressing bejewelled fingers in a far more delicate way." But now—or so it seemed to observers—the Prince's set began to move over the invisible border that distinguishes gay from "fast," a convenient term in common use at the time—convenient because it was descriptive without being libellous. There is no reason to believe that Lady Furness, her sister Mrs. Thaw, her brother-in-law Benjamin Thaw (a U.S. diplomat), or his other close acquaintances of this period were any more "fast" than Edward's previous company. But they were more sophisticated, and, what was to be important later, they were American—alien.

The Prince and his acquaintances were also growing older. What had been condoned as innocent high spirits in the early twenties was more likely to be regarded later as irresponsible nuisance-making, especially when it took the form, as it often did, of the scavenge hunt. This developed out of an adult version of the child's treasure hunt. At first it had been innocuous. The contestants would be provided with a list of clues, often couched in doggerel, each saying where the next clue was to be found, and the pair (or carload) that completed the sequence first was the winner. The scavenge, or scavenger hunt offered greater possibilities for excitement. Each car team was given a list of objects to be brought back. At first the items to be obtained were straightforward: a bay leaf, a cuckoo clock, a pinecone. But the more daring, the more shocking, the items listed, the more likely a hostess' party was to be remembered. So her guests would be asked to get a policeman's helmet, a chamberpot from the Ritz or from some local mansion, an item of underwear from the wardrobe of the major. And the convention had been established that such objects must be acquired without the owner's knowledge or consent.

In her *The Light of Common Day*, Lady Diana Cooper recalled some of the scavenge hunts. "Quick thought, luck and unscrupulous driving might bring you first to the coveted prize. Duff disapproved and disbelieved in the wild ecstasy until one night when the meet was at Gower Street and the Prince of Wales was to be a hunter. Duff must have felt it loyal to join in, for he went with me in our little open car, caught the fever, and shouted, 'Faster, faster! It doesn't matter about the bobby. What's the matter with the car? Step on it!'" They won, and they also won a scavenge hunt in which a special award for the most unique object went to the man who had "a coutil-busked corset belonging to Mrs. Lewis of the Cavendish Hotel, signed, cross-signed and undersigned with the names, quips and quizzes of her noble and notable clients."

The Prince revelled in this kind of fun. The twenties might have been made for him: He could have passed for the prototype of the extrovert, who, to quote the psychologist Professor H. J. Eysenck's definition,

is sociable, likes parties, has many friends, needs to have people to talk to, and does not like reading or studying by himself; he craves excitement, takes chances, acts on the spur of the moment and is generally an impulsive individual. He is fond of practical jokes, always has a ready answer and generally likes change; he is carefree, easy going and likes to "laugh and be merry." He prefers to keep moving and doing things, tends to be aggressive and loses his temper quickly; his feelings are not kept under tight control and he is not always a reliable person.

But by the thirties some of the gloss was beginning to wear off Edward's existence. Young though he continued to look, he could not entirely disguise from himself that he was no longer really a member of the younger generation. As he was to write in the introduction to *A King's Story*, "I was eight years old before I switched on an electric light, had my first ride in a horseless carriage, or listened with mystification to a phonograph. I was a fifteen-year-old cadet before I saw an aeroplane in flight and almost thirty before I heard a spoken message broadcast by radio." He could hardly be considered a product of the Edwardian (let alone the Victorian) era, because he was so obviously a man of the twenties, as they so suited his particular brand of ebullience. But the twenties were deceptive. They gave the opportunity, the cover, for men to behave like college boys (and women like college girls) without feeling embarrassed. The bright young things enjoyed what was in effect a prolonged dispensation from adulthood. Having enjoyed it, they did not like to let it go, and some of them had become bright middle-aged things without being aware of it.

The difficulty was how to grow up. Edward had few inner resources, and in any case, the gay life continued to attract him. Late nights at the Embassy Club or Quaglino's appealed to him when he had reached an age at which most men prefer, except on special celebratory occasions, to go home to a nightcap and bed. Some of his circle found the life exhausting. Thaw used to come into the American embassy the mornings after, read his correspondence and dictate replies, and then make up for the night's lost sleep on a handy couch. Others were able to maintain a febrile gaiety for the party round only by increasing consumption of alcohol—the theme of Terence Rattigan's second play, which came on in the West End shortly before the war. Unlike its successful predecessor, *French Without Tears,* it received quite respectful attention from the critics, but it was a box-office failure. Perhaps the sight of the bright young things clinging to their brightness but unable to cling to their youth was too painful for the London theatregoer.

Fort Belvedere

As if he sensed that the end of an era had been reached, Edward made a decision in the spring of 1930 that was to have a profound effect on his life. One of the "grace and favour" houses, as they had come to be called—residences at the disposal of the King, which he can present to members of his family or to loyal servants on their retirement—was vacant: Fort Belvedere, near Windsor. It was undeniably ugly, looking as if it had been put together by some eccentric who liked to feel he was living in a fortified private house—"a castellated conglomeration" was Edward's own description. But it had grounds of its own, which could be made attractive. Edward had occasionally rented houses, and he had formed a liking for gardening. Now he determined to indulge it. And very soon, "the Fort" became his home. York House, his official residence, became merely the place where he stayed when he was in London.

For the first time, Edward was able to indulge himself in that most absorbing of pursuits, the restoration of an old, shambling property into a reflection of the owner's taste. Ideas that were a quarter of a century before their time in England—a bathroom to each bedroom, central heating, built-in cupboards—were incorporated in the Fort itself. And the Prince himself made changes outside: "The sheer pleasures of creation took possession of me; the landscape gardener displaced the foxhunter and, to some extent, the golfer." The Prince found a new contentment in working about the Fort with his own hands, cutting down trees and shrubs, replanting, making a swimming pool and a rock garden. "Soon, I came to love it as I loved no other material thing—perhaps because it was so much my own creation. More and more, it became for me a peaceful, almost an enchanted anchorage, where I found refuge from the cares and turmoil of my life."

A man in the grip of a love affair of this kind is apt to become a little restive when he is kept away from his mistress for no essential purpose. Royal chores which the Prince had once accepted as a matter of course now sometimes became irksome. Duty beckoned, yes, but need it beckon quite so often? There were, after all, other members of the royal family available, now that his brothers were finding themselves wives. If they all did just a little more, they would hardly notice the increase of duties spread among them, and Edward would be free to return more often to his passion—especially as the Duke of Kent was now out of the navy and ready to take his share of the royal burden.

This did not mean that Edward went into any kind of monastic retreat. After his father's illness he was at last permitted to take over a few responsibilities, notably the entertaining of distinguished visitors from abroad. But it meant that he began to think for the first time in terms of two separate lives. One was lived from his London residence; it was formal and convention-bound. The other was lived at the Fort, informal, unconventional and altogether delightful. The only snag was that after the first passion had begun to fall off, there were so few people he really enjoyed being informal and unconventional *with,* other than Thelma and her rather light-weight friends. But it was at this point that Thelma was responsible for his introduction to the woman who was to provide the fuller companionship he had so long needed: Mrs. Ernest Simpson, born Wallis Warfield.

Wallis Simpson

Wallis Warfield came of established American stock. Her cousin Upton Sinclair put it higher than that, insisting that she was a descendant of the legendary Indian princess Pocahontas. For a time after the death of Wallis' father, her mother was in financial difficulties and was compelled to take boarders. Mayfair gossips were later to sneer that Wallis was "only a landlady's daughter." But she did not lack well-off relatives, and they were ready to help. She was sent to fashionable schools—one of them, according to her biographer Geoffrey Bocca, so snobbish that they did not even compete at games with other girls, preferring to play among themselves. And in due course, Wallis was presented with the rest of the Baltimore debutantes at the Bachelors' Cotillion Club, the social event of the season.

Later in her coming-out season Wallis married Win Spencer, a pilot in the U.S. naval air service. Although the marriage was a failure, its final disintegration introduced her to China, where she spent what she was to describe as a lotus year after leaving her husband— enjoying the life in Peking and losing what remained of her provincialism. By the time she returned to the United States she had acquired, by her own account, "a taste for cosmopolitan minds." She found one in Ernest Simpson, a New Yorker by birth, a Harvard graduate, but such an Anglophile that after service in the Coldstream Guards at the end of the war he had decided to become a naturalised British citizen. A quiet-spoken, cultivated shipping broker, Simpson had a wife, but his marriage was breaking up. Wallis found him congenial company, and in 1928 they were married in a London registry office. London became her home.

Some time between her marriages, Wallis had lunch with a friend who told her of a wonderful experience she had had at a critical time of her life, when a woman astrologer had cast her horoscope. Wallis, who thought of herself as a realist, replied that she did not believe in that rot, but she went to visit the astrologer. In middle life, she was told, she was going to exercise "considerable power of some kind," but not in her own right: "You will lead a woman's life, marrying, divorcing, marrying again, with several serious emotional crises. The power that is to come to you will be related to a man."

Recollecting the episode in *The Heart Has Its Reasons*, the Duchess claimed that she had not been aware of being influenced by the prophecy, but "perhaps subconscious decisions are not always based on conscious reasons." It is not necessary to believe in precognition to realize how powerful an influence a fortune-teller can be. If the prediction points in some interesting direction, it may lead people to make decisions or take courses of action that they might not otherwise have considered. It is not unreasonable to suppose that Wallis was influenced to pursue the future that the clairvoyant had promised, or at least to accept it as a natural development when it happened. When she met her fate she was at least prepared for it, and this may have lent her the confidence that was to make all the difference in getting to know the man from whom her power was to flow.

By her own account, Wallis was not impressed with the awe in which the average Briton of that period held titles. She regarded them as irrational in a country that claimed to be democratic. But her curiosity was aroused by the court *Circular*, which records the engagements and appearances of the royal family. "The stately language, suggestive of another epoch, delighted me: 'His Majesty graciously replied—' 'His Majesty was pleased—' " She was amused that the formal comings and goings of a single family should be followed with such rapt attention—even by her husband, who tended to speak about what the King or the Queen was doing in hushed tones. But even if Wallis had been more cynical about the royal family it would have been hard, in the society where she found herself, to remain disinterested, owing to its members' appetite for gossip, particularly about the Prince of Wales. Long before she had met him, it was established in her mind, "from the gossip shuttling across the bridge tables, that he was a gay blade."

The fact that Wallis was intrigued by the royal family—not dazzled by it—was to prove important. Edward would immediately have detected and spurned the ordinary social climber. Nor was Wallis tempted to shed her Americanism. The American woman of her generation "judged it important to be a little different, or in any case interesting, and was prepared to pit her ideas spiritedly against those of the male." When on her arrival in England she found that English women were still accepting the status of an inferior sex—"If they had strong opinions they kept them safely buttoned up"—she refused to allow herself to be over-awed, continuing to speak her mind as freely as before. Sometimes this startled people, sometimes it annoyed them. Anti-Americanism was quite common in the circles in which she found herself, and though women were allowed a certain latitude, they were not thanked if they tried to give their views on the topics of the day. That was for men. But Wallis refused "to cancel out my own personality and substitute an artificial one, made to an English pattern. . . . I clung the more fiercely to my own American ways and opinions—possibly to the point of exaggeration."

In London, Wallis became friendly with Benjamin Thaw and his wife Consuelo. Through them she met Consuelo's sister, Thelma Furness, and in November 1930 the Simpsons were invited to a house party with Thelma at Melton Mowbray, the Prince of Wales being among the guests. Wallis had a heavy cold. The weather, which was miserable, may have been responsible—or, as she surmised, the excitement. But in Edward's recollection, she did not allow it to disturb her composure. When, finding that she was American, he remarked that she must miss central heating, she declined to make the conventional reply. His gambit, she said, had disappointed her: "Every American woman who comes to your country is always asked that same question. I had hoped for something more original from the Prince of Wales."

In *The Heart Has Its Reasons,* the Duchess was to give a different version of their first meeting. She had been warned by her friends not to be controversial, and in any case her cold—and her nervousness—left her in no mood to be. Presumably the Duke's recollection was of some later conversation. No matter—the point was that when Wallis established herself in his mind, it was as a woman of independence and spirit, different from the ordinary run of new acquaintances in that she stood up to him firmly, but not rudely. When she came to be presented at Buckingham Palace, he was also struck by her grace and dignity. Thereafter their friendship ripened. Wallis was attractive and good company—and she attracted good company around her. But the quality Edward most admired in her was her forthrightness, her ability to speak her mind.

The penalty of being a prince, however informal, had been that his companions were always compelled to walk a social tightrope. If they were tactful he might despise them as obsequious, if they were brash he might resent them as presumptuous. And as Edward's attitudes and feelings were not consistent, his companions required considerable intuitive powers to keep the balance. Wallis' intuitive powers were well-developed. She knew how to gauge his moods and when she could be outspoken. Her detractors claimed that it was calculation rather than intuition, but they were mistaken. Where she disagreed with Edward, she said so—not cockily or derisively, but in the same way as she would disagree with some other guest. This side of her, Edward recalled, enchanted him. "A man in my position seldom encountered that trait in other people. Never having believed that my offhand judgments were infallible, I always welcomed a chance to argue them—perhaps because I had so few opportunities of doing so." But of course he had had ample opportunity. What he had lacked was the stimulus, and this Wallis gave him.

There was another difference between her and Thelma Furness, or any of his other companions in the past. They lacked Wallis' intellectual equipment. She read the newspapers, she "kept up with"— Edward's description—the latest trends in literature and the theatre, she was in her depth wherever the swirl of conversation might take her. And—the decisive thing about her, so far as he was concerned— she was capable of becoming genuinely interested in what he was doing and what he planned to do. Assuming that his protestations of a desire to get away from it all were genuine, most week-end guests were careful to avoid introducing "shop," and when the Prince brought up the subject of his work himself, he was to recall, his accounts of what he had had to do produced only sympathy: "Oh, Sir! how boring for you. Aren't you terribly tired?" He had no objection to sympathy, but it was not what he needed. His real requirement was the kind of positive interest and comment that would lend his chores a new interest. Social services, to the server, may be a bore or a labour of love, according to mood. Wallis' interest helped to remove, or to allay, the boredom.

Edward had never lost interest in his work. All that he had lacked was the stimulus. As soon as he knew Wallis well enough to confide in her, he began to discuss it with her, to explain what he hoped to do, to outline the creative role he thought the monarchy could play. He also "dropped a hint of the frustrations he was experiencing," and in so doing gave Wallis insight into his character. His keenness for the job, she decided, and his ambition to succeed in it, were "not dissimilar to the attitude of many American businessmen" she had known.

It was a perceptive impression. At the time she came to know him, Edward was in the position of heir apparent to a business firm whose owner had been running it successfully on traditional lines. There was little Edward could do so long as his father was alive, be-

cause their ways were diametrically opposed. It was not a case of
one being right and the other wrong. Either way, traditional or modern, might have worked. Traditional, in fact, *did* work—as the growing public esteem for the monarchy showed. But Edward had little
interest in the monarchy in that form. He was only waiting until his
succession to change it. In the meantime, his tendency had been to
shut it out of his mind whenever he could, particularly at Fort
Belvedere.

This was one of the first things that Wallis noticed when she was
first invited to stay there, with her husband, in January 1932. She had
been watching the Prince's progress through the depressed areas in
newspaper reports, but the subject was never mentioned, and she got
the impression that there was a tacit understanding among the company that official concerns would be put aside. It was not, in fact, an
unspoken agreement. The Fort, Edward explained later that evening, was a place to which he came for rest and change. The effect,
however, was to compartmentalize his life and to make him think of
his circle of intimates, Wallis among them, as apart from his public
life. "I call it my Get-Away-From-People house," he told Wallis, but
it was also his get-away-from-all-thoughts-of-work house. Now, with
Wallis, he at last found that he could talk about his work and enjoy
talking about it.

Ironically, Wallis might have facilitated the conversion of Edward into an effective king, though of a very different character from
his father. To those outside the circle it seemed that she was distract-
ing him from his current duties, but in fact she was the first to
unleash the interest and enthusiasm pent up inside him as a result
of his father's different concept of the monarchy and his own past
lack of friends in whom to confide. The Prince, she found—as soon
as they knew each other well enough to be at ease alone in each
other's company—"seemed to have a new enthusiasm with every
visit." Some were trivial—a new idea for the Fort grounds, even a
new jazz record—but others reflected a potential enthusiasm that
could have been nourished, given the opportunity: plans for housing
developments, or for expanding British trade. It did not matter at
this period that she could be little more than a sympathetic listener.
That was precisely what he needed. And Wallis was also growing
more attractive, not only to Edward. The society photographer Cecil
Beaton, who had met her for the first time in 1930, recalled that she
was then "somewhat brawny and raw-boned" and that her voice had

a high nasal twang. Five years later, when he met her again, she looked "immaculate, soignée, fresh as a young girl; her skin was as bright and smooth as the inside of a shell, her hair so sleek she might have been Chinese."

While Wallis was gradually establishing herself in the Prince's affections, Thelma Furness remained to outward appearances the chief object of his attention. But then, in 1933, the Prince presented Wallis with an orchid plant on her birthday, telling her that if she followed his instructions it would bloom again within a year. Sure enough, one afternoon a year later the plant flowered as he had predicted. Afterward she was to feel this was symbolic. It was during this time that Thelma, on a visit to America, had attracted the ardent and much publicized attentions of Aly Khan, then making his reputation as the great lover. When she returned, it was to find that Wallis had replaced her in the Prince's affections—leading Elsa Maxwell to assert years later in her column that but for Aly, Edward might still be on his throne. And it was that summer of 1934 that Wallis and David—as by this time she could call him, instead of "sir" —realized that they were no longer just good friends. They were taken for a cruise on a yacht owned by Lord Moyne, of the Guinness family, a rising member of the Conservative Party whose career was later to be cut short during the war by an assassin in Egypt. In the course of it, they realized that they had "crossed the line that marked the indefinable boundary between friendship and love."

Ernest was not on the cruise. Business had taken him to America. Still, it was his continued existence as Mr. Simpson that made the love affair possible. As some expatriates do, he had become more English than the English. He even looked English, a typical former Guards officer, not unlike a plumper Duff Cooper in appearance. His life was tailored to a conventional pattern, like his clothes. An episode the Duchess was to recall in her autobiography is revealing about him. In 1930 they were on a motor tour on the Continent, staying at a hotel in The Hague, when there was a fire alarm. Wallis and her Aunt Bessie fled downstairs in their nightgowns, but for a while there was no sign of Ernest. "Then, just as I was growing desperate, an immaculate figure appeared at the head of the stairway—Ernest, complete with bowler hat, Guards tie, handkerchief neatly folded in his breast pocket, his suitcase in his right hand, and in his left the inevitable umbrella." No Guards officer likes to appear in public improperly dressed.

For Ernest, the royal family could do no wrong. Whatever he might think of his wife's growing fondness for the Prince, and the Prince's for her, he was not prepared to intervene. And with her Aunt Bessie as an unobtrusive chaperon, the "indefinable boundary" was not difficult to cross. As well as being an agreeable companion and an admirable hostess, Edward now found Wallis was capable of sharing his romantic moments.

Their similar taste in music helped. They had both grown up into an era, as Wallis was fondly to recall, when jazz was new and exciting. Edward had been unable to get the tune of *A Pretty Girl Is Like a Melody* out of his head when he came back from America. To the Duchess, it shared with *Avalon* a place in her recollections as one of the twenties' most haunting tunes. Their delight in listening, and dancing, to the evocative music of the period continued. When early in 1935 they went to Budapest, they were taken by a young Hungarian diplomat to a small café where half a dozen violinists played *Chi Chi Chi*, a song which, their escort told them, told of the sound of the rain falling softly on the rooftops. Wallis "had the feeling of being torn apart, of being caught up in the inescapable sadness of human suffering." From the look in David's eyes, she knew that *Chi Chi Chi* was having the same effect on him.

Anybody as much in love as Edward was with Wallis at this time could hardly be expected to make the wider political and social contacts that he would need, in due course, to ensure that Wallis was well-known and well-liked in influential circles. He wanted her, understandably, for himself, and as soon as the week's royal chores were completed, he would hasten back to the Fort, there to enjoy her company with their few chosen friends. The only other places where he was likely to be found with her in company were the salons of the day. Hostesses had formerly despaired of persuading the Prince to come to them—or, if he did come, to evince any interest in the proceedings. But Wallis was delighted to accept invitations from, among others, Lady Cunard, a California girl who, like Thelma Morgan, had married a shipping magnate. She had exchanged her own name, Maude, for Emerald, on the ground that she liked Emerald better; and she had worked her way up to near the top of the London hostesses' league.

Other hostesses, envying Lady Cunard her prize, had also begun to cultivate Mrs. Simpson. Wallis was under no illusions about the reasons for the invitations that poured in on her: her prospective hostesses hoped that she would bring the Prince along, too. Sometimes she did, because she liked moving in such society. Edward did not like it, nor did it provide him with the kind of social intercourse he really needed. People who secured introductions to him were usually would-be social lions or lionesses, and at their parties, individuals whose company he would have relished were too often inhibited—or even sorry for him, that he should be so visibly bored. But casual observers did not realize this. They assumed that the Prince had been caught up in "that raffish group"—a contemporary critic's view, which Compton Mackenzie quoted—"which now lords it over London society, that mongrel pack of mainly immigrant aliens, naturalized or otherwise, the Invaders, the most heartless and dissolute of the pleasure-loving ultra-rich, the hardest and most hated people in England." A kindlier critic, Lord Winterton, though admitting it was "disloyal, impertinent and ungenerous" to criticize an heir-apparent for his choice of a circle of friends, suggested later that the choice of Victoria, George V, George VI and Queen Elizabeth II was "greatly to be preferred." The English aristocracy would have agreed with him.

And Wallis was blamed, although her social gifts excited the admiration of most people she met, even those who had been prepared to find fault. "Wallis is admirably correct and chic," Diana Cooper reported, with surprise, after their first meeting at the Fort. Lady Diana arrived with her husband, after midnight, to find Edward dressed in "plus twenties with vivid azure socks." The following day, Anthony Eden and Esmond Harmsworth came to tea at 6:30, as everything was later at the Fort; Lady Cunard arrived at 8:30 for cocktails (which she did not drink, in spite of the fact that the Prince insisted on preparing them himself). For dinner the Prince changed into a Donald tartan dress kilt, "with an immense white leather purse in front," and after dinner, having first fetched his bonnet, played the bagpipes. This was surely a new atmosphere, Lady Diana felt, for courts. New it was, but hardly raffish.

King George V

All this time, Edward had said nothing to his family about his affections or his intentions. In his autobiography he claimed that he had meant to have the matter out with his father. But after the silver jubilee of George V's accession in the early summer of 1935, which would hardly have been a propitious moment, the holiday season interposed itself. The Prince was with Wallis on the Continent, and the King went to enjoy the deer stalking on his highland estate, Balmoral. Afterward, "a remarkable concatenation of events left me no opportunity to talk things over"—the concatenation consisting of his brother Harry's marriage, a general election, the death of King George's favourite sister, Victoria, and the international crisis precipitated by Mussolini's invasion of Abyssinia. At Christmas the family gathered as usual at the King's favourite country residence, Sandringham, but the King looked so old and ill that it would have been heartless to confront him. Less than a month later, he was dead. Whether the Prince could have nerved himself for the confrontation even if opportunity had offered must remain doubtful. Nor, presumably, would it have made much difference, except possibly to reinforce Edward's fear that he would have to put from his mind any ideas of keeping Mrs. Simpson and at the same time keeping the throne.

By this time King George had become an institution the like of which had not been known in the history of the monarchy and would not be known again. The process of converting him from a respected, trusted and liked king to a loved one had begun with his illness in the winter of 1928 and his protracted convalescence. But the transformation was finally accomplished by the jubilee of his reign, in 1935, which revealed a hitherto unsuspected depth of feeling for him among all classes.

George was particularly moved by his reception in the East End of London. This district was still, at that time, one that respectable bourgeois citizens would have thought twice of driving, let alone walking, through. Policemen, school children used then to be told, always went in pairs if they had to go to the East End. The King—his nurse, Sister Catherine Black, noted—was tired after his East End tour, "but radiantly happy: 'I'd no idea they felt like that about me. I'm beginning to think they must really like me for myself.'" And, in a way, they did.

According to Ernest Jones, Freud's pupil and biographer, constitutional monarchy arose to satisfy emotional starvation—as if people had decided to preserve kings "to satisfy the beneficent elements of the mythology in man's ineradicable unconscious that will enable us to deal with the more troublesome elements." No king has ever better satisfied the beneficent elements. In the twenty-five years of his reign, his biographer Sir Harold Nicolson claimed, "his subjects had come to recognize that King George represented and enhanced those domestic virtues that they regarded as specifically British virtues. In him they saw, reflected and magnified, what they cherished as their own individual ideals—faith, duty, honesty, courage, common sense, tolerance, decency and truth."

For most of his reign, George had been a remote and reserved figure, cut off from his people by rigid court protocol. The jubilee revealed that this barrier had been broken down. His reception was anything but formal, such slogans as "Lousy but Loyal" decorating his route through the slums. Puzzling over "the spontaneous hilarity of the celebrations, and the note of direct personal affection by which they were inspired," Nicolson surmised that one reason was the King's annual Christmas message on the radio. Radio at that time was just becoming a mass medium, and the King, who had previously inspired loyalty through awe rather than affection, was heard speaking as a benevolent, sentimental father of the family. He had, as Nicolson recalled, "a wonderful voice—strong, emphatic, vibrant, with undertones of sentiment, devoid of all condescension, artifice or pose." He was capable of saying, as he did after his jubilee celebrations, "I can only say to you, my very very dear people, that the Queen and I thank you from the depths of our hearts for all the loyalty—and may I say so?—the love with which this day and always you have surrounded us." And he was able to make it sound as if he meant it—and as if it were off-the-cuff, which it can hardly have been.

The image George presented was not of a traditional king, but of a simple man who happened to be a king. The historian A.J.P. Taylor was to bring out this contradiction, noting that George became the epitome of a monarch without the personality to explain it: "Meeting him you would have thought there wasn't much to him. And you would have been right. There wasn't. He never made an interesting remark, never hit on a fresh or new idea. In appearance, in his opinions, in his beliefs, he was unfailingly ordinary." And that, Taylor thought, was his strength: Wherever he went he carried "the majesty of the ordinary man."

But there is another possible interpretation of the people's enthusiasm for King George. It can be argued, and has been, that it represented the grand climacteric of what the Continental peoples regard as English cant—that he was revered not so much because he reflected all that was best in the English character but because he enabled the English to continue to believe that he did, that he reflected their essential dignity, courage, virtue and downright common sense when in fact at this time they were very far, as a people, from maintaining these virtues. The English were undergoing a character-change, forced on them by circumstances and by changing economic, political, social and moral ideas. Their old beliefs and assumptions were being eroded. They did not care to admit this, and the existence of the monarchy helped them to delude themselves into thinking that they were not really changing. But they were. The actions and inactions of their governments were beginning to lend justification to the growing assumption on the Continent that the British had become decadent. Admittedly, when the test came in 1939, and still more after Dunkirk, they were able to reveal that those qualities had not been lost but merely mislaid, and George VI was sufficiently in his father's image to give some help to Churchill in bringing them out again. But at the time of the jubilee they could hardly lay claim to the qualities that they liked to think their King mirrored.

Still, the strength of the monarchy that Edward VIII inherited, a few months later, lay in the conviction that the King was the father of his people, good, wise, God-fearing, and with a strict sense of duty. Edward would have to live up to it—or set about creating a new role that he could play to the public's satisfaction.

"Hatless from the air"

This prospect was by no means hopeless. As Prince of Wales, Edward already had acquired a public image, and a highly flattering one. He might not be thought of as good, in the puritanical sense, but he radiated good-fellowship. He loved his fellow men, and was not that the essential Commandment? He might not be wise, but he was certainly shrewd, quick-witted. As for being God-fearing, a people who had long since ceased to be a nation of Christian churchgoers (if they ever were) ought not to object if their King's attendance at divine service was a little irregular. And as yet there had been nothing to indicate, at least as far as the general public was concerned, that he was any less dedicated than his father.

Hardly a weekday had passed, it seemed, without his bobbing up at some function or other, and if he liked his week-ends off, good luck to him.

He had one great asset, too: he was of his time. Older citizens might have their doubts, as expressed in John Betjeman's verses on the death of George V, inspired by a newspaper report on Edward VIII's arrival in the capital:

> Old men who never cheated, never doubted,
> Communicated monthly, sit and stare
> At the new suburb stretched beyond the runway
> Where a young man lands hatless from the air.

But for many of the younger generation, the change was welcome. Politically and economically, Britain was stagnating. The new King might help to stir things up.

Not everybody felt that this would be to the country's advantage. Even before Edward came to the throne, references to him by the Archbishop of Canterbury, Cosmo Gordon Lang, in an after-dinner speech had struck Hector Bolitho as being "heavy with foreboding" —though the Prince himself thought them fulsome. And on his accession, an editorial in the *Times* remarked that "in the life of responsibility, day in and day out, which will henceforth be his, he will lack the help and counsel of a consort." Geoffrey Dawson, the editor of the *Times,* knew about Mrs. Simpson. Gossip about her had not yet soured into scandal, but it was common enough in Fleet Street, in London clubs and at Mayfair cocktail parties.

Still, the general disposition was to give the new King an enthusiastic send-off and hope that, like Shakespeare's Prince Hal, he would send his Falstaffs and Doll Tearsheets packing and emerge as an illustrious monarch. Certainly he started off with one great advantage. "Few, very few of his subjects," the *Times* editorial noted, "can rival the knowledge which his travels have brought him of every part of the Empire." In those days the term "Empire" was still more likely to bring a thrill of pride than a twitch of guilt, and in 1931 the Statute of Westminster had closely identified the monarchy with the Dominions (Australia, New Zealand, South Africa, Canada, and the Irish Free State) by making it the formal constitutional link—all executive links were severed. It therefore seemed particularly important to have a king who knew the Dominions and was known by them. In this respect Edward was ideal. His qualities, too—the *Times* continued—"could hardly fail to command the popular confidence and honest liking with which, in full store, he begins his reign." It went on to list them: physical courage, utter freedom from all trace of affectation and pretentiousness, zest for new experience—"Such is the personality which has put so remarkable a spell upon the imagination of the many communities within what is henceforth his realm."

And at first—at least so far as the public was concerned—the course of the reign appeared smooth enough. For a while, court mourning circumscribed Edward's activities. The fact that he shortened its duration was generally regarded as sensible—formal mourning was becoming unfashionable. Outwardly, at least, he performed his royal functions to the manner born, and foreign visitors who had audiences with him found him very much on top of his job—the Aga Khan, for one, who saw him in the spring, reported that he had undergone from the King "one of the most searching, serious and well-informed cross-examinations that I have ever experienced." Duff Cooper, the Minister for War, was to recall that one morning soon after the accession, the King granted an audience to Field Marshal Sir Cyril Deverell, chief of the Imperial General Staff, "a Yorkshireman of few words, not prone to enthusiasm, but on this occasion his tongue was loosened and his eyes were dancing." Deverell had been deeply impressed by the King's obvious love of the army and his interest in it—"The interview was really inspiring."

The King's first broadcast to the nation, too, on St. David's Day, suggested that he would be well able to carry on the radio tradition his father had begun. Although his speaking voice was less attractive and less effective—except when he was talking off the cuff—he hit the right note: "I am better known to you as the Prince of Wales, as a man who, during the war and since, has had the opportunity of getting to know the people of nearly every country of the world under all conditions and circumstances. And although I now speak to you as the King, I am still that same man who has that experience and whose constant effort it will be to promote the well-being of his fellow-men."

In the summer, Edward even enjoyed the benefit of the bonus to a national figure's popularity which comes from an unsuccessful assassination attempt—or, in this case, what looked like one. He had been presenting new colours to some Guards regiments, and while he was riding back at the head of the battalions, a man pushed his way through the watching crowd and hurled toward the King something "bright and metallic," which was naturally assumed to be a bomb. It turned out to be a loaded revolver thrown by—or perhaps knocked out of the hand of—a paranoiac journalist, who later claimed he had only wanted to make a disturbance to draw attention to some grievance. The King's demeanour, though, and the way he quipped with the general beside him immediately afterward, made an excellent impression.

The only outwardly disturbing signs of the times, in fact, were certain omens. The British do not believe in astrology or in the occult, but millions of them follow their horoscopes in newspapers and journals with an avidity that is hardly accounted for by the usual explanation—that it is for amusement. Nor are the British superstitious, by their own reckoning, yet few of them care to dispense with the prescribed rituals to avert bad luck when, say, salt is spilled or the new moon is seen through glass. The British do not place credence in fortune tellers—but they listen to them. According to Frank Owen, co-author with R. J. Thompson of the first account to appear of the abdication crisis, the Hon. Ralph Shirley had predicted as early as 1903 that Edward would either not come to the throne or would soon leave it if he did, to be succeeded by the Duke of York; and a Scottish gypsy had told the young Lady Elizabeth Bowes-Lyon that she would someday be Queen. In 1931, too, the then famous "Cheiro" had written in his *World Predictions* that planetary influences suggested the Prince of Wales would give up everything, even the chance of being crowned, "rather than lose the object of his affections."

The British affect not to believe in omens—but they notice them. They noticed when the Maltese cross on top of the royal crown—on which there is a sapphire, flanked by eight medium-sized and ninety-two smaller diamonds—fell off when the crown was being borne through the streets of London on King George V's coffin. The draped gun carriage on which the coffin was placed had rubber-tyred wheels. The obvious explanation, that the cross had been jolted off, was consequently a little unsatisfactory. Edward himself thought it strange: "Though not superstitious, I wondered whether it was a bad omen." Lord Boothby, at that time a Conservative back-bencher, recalls that he was with Walter Elliott, the Minister of Agriculture, in the crowd close to where the cross fell, and they overheard Edward's reaction: "Christ! What's going to happen next?" "That," Elliott remarked, "will be the motto of the new reign."

For the new reign, new postage stamps had to be issued, and the King expressed his preference for simplicity instead of the traditional twirly-whirly scrolls. But he also asked that, as he considered his left profile to be better than his right, the left should be the one shown. This created a difficulty. Tradition, again, demanded that the direction in which the King's head was facing on coins and stamps should be reversed at the beginning of each new reign. It was Edward's turn to look to the right. Edward, however, was obdurate: He would *not* look to the right, and that was that. The postal authorities had to obey. But they failed to change the background, and this meant that the King appeared to be looking into the shade. This was noticed when the stamps appeared—as the *Times* recalled after the abdication, when it surveyed the portents of the reign:

> As harbingers preceding still the fates
> And prologue to the omen coming on.

"Even strong minds can yield to this weakness," the *Times* asserted, a little self-consciously, and it recalled, without derision, "the superstitious anxiety of those who shook apprehensive heads at the new stamps, because the head of King Edward VIII was turned away from the light, and looked forward into the gloom—apt symbol of a reign that began with everything in its favour and moved onward into calamity."

The Prime Minister may not have been impressed by these omens, but he would have had to admit that they were relevant. For it quickly became apparent to him that Prince Hal was not going to play Henry V. The old associates were not discarded. When a new king is proclaimed, the proclamations are read out by the heralds from four different vantage-points in London, one being St. James's Palace, and when the time came, Edward joined them there, explaining that he saw no reason why he should not watch himself being proclaimed king. Nor was there, but the fact that the newsreel cameras, trained on the apartment windows, showed him in animated conversation with Mrs. Simpson was a clear intimation that he did not intend to allow the change of his circumstances to affect their relationship—as he also made clear to her at the time.

Although he could not see her so often during the week, the week-ends at the Fort continued as before.

According to Wallis, protocol at the Fort stiffened. The red dis-patch boxes containing state documents for the King to read and sign flowed in, people arrived for audiences, his every movement was recorded in the court *Circular*. But the change, though natur-ally Wallis felt it, was not great enough to be observable to the casual eye. Lady Diana Cooper, arriving with her husband to stay for a week-end, found nothing changed except the stationery. Even the servants were "a bit hobbledehoy, because H. M. wants to be free of comptrollers and equerries, so no one trains them."

What finally banished any lingering hope that the King might change his ways was a dinner party held in York House early in the summer, with the Prime Minister as the guest of honour. Apart from Baldwin and his wife, the guests included the Mountbattens, Lord Wigram, who had for many years served King George V at court, the Duff Coopers, Admiral Chatfield, the Lindberghs, just back from Germany, Lady Cunard, and Mr. and Mrs. Simpson. Ernest's presence deceived no one. Baldwin, according to his biog-rapher G.M. Young, was intrigued to meet Wallis, though he was surprised to see her placed at one end of the table. His wife's com-ments were less charitable—"For her, and for women like her throughout the Empire, Mrs. Simpson had stolen the fairy prince."

A second dinner at York House, on July 9, caused more meaning-ful eyebrow-raising in London society. The guest list was com-parably distinguished: the Duke and Duchess of York, Samuel Hoare, who was the new First Lord of the Admiralty, David Margesson, who was the government chief whip, Major Alec Hardinge, appointed Edward's new private secretary, the Winston Churchills, the Marquess of Willingdon, who was viceroy of India, and so on. Only two guests who were at the earlier dinner were present: Lady Diana Cooper and Mrs. Simpson. No Ernest Simpson this time. It could have been, of course, that he was away, or in-disposed, but that was hardly likely. The King, it was felt in society, could hardly have made his intentions toward her clearer if he had formally announced them with the guest list, published in the court *Circular* and in the next morning's *Times*.

Hoare noted at the time that Wallis was "very attractive and intelligent, very American and with little or no knowledge of English life"—which Wallis thought an acute observation. It was, and it pointed to troubles ahead. Wallis' intuition had served her admirably with Edward himself and in the cosmopolitan circles in which they moved. It was going to be much less effective in helping him to make the right decisions in affairs of state, and already he was beginning to make mistakes. The episode that most clearly showed the direction the reign was taking had nothing directly to do with Wallis, and in itself it was trivial, but it aroused some discontent, and the Duke's description of it in *A King's Story* is detailed enough to suggest that he realized his action required some explanation.

Full court mourning for George V lasted for six months after his death, and by that time there was a long queue of "women of position" and debutantes waiting to be presented at court—about six hundred. The Lord Chamberlain, Cromer, suggested that the sensible way to expedite the introductions would be to combine them with a couple of the usual palace garden parties, on July 21 and 22, and this was arranged.

The weather forecast had warned of showers, and hardly had the ceremony begun when "a menacing cloud loomed over the immense pile of the palace." Edward watched it with increasing apprehension, but protocol demanded that each deb should have her ten seconds in which to make her curtsy, a process which was not speeded up even when the rain began to fall. Their dresses and hats, Edward pointed out to Cromer, would be ruined—"We can't let this go on." Cromer agreed, and Edward, "with a gesture intended to convey my regret over the inadvertent shower," retired to the palace.

So far from being praised for his consideration, though, Edward found himself unpopular. Some of the mothers whose daughters had not received his formal bow of recognition felt that the presentation had not really been effected, whatever protocol might say, and that the social position of their daughters was in consequence left in doubt. This, he insisted, was foolish, and it is true that the *Times* the next morning carried the announcement that "those ladies summoned to the afternoon's reception who, owing to the interruption of the ceremony by the weather, were unable to pass the King's presence, would be considered as having been officially presented at Court." But the real dissatisfaction lay deeper. It happened that photographers and newsreel cameramen were present to record the scene. The pictures which appeared in the papers the next morning, and the films, show with awful clarity the look of frozen boredom on the King's face; the films also show the perfunctory, almost irritable nod that he gave to each deb. This is in striking contrast with the lively expression almost constantly observed on his face in earlier newsreels—or, for that matter, in films taken of him later on the *Nahlin* cruise. And to point the contrast, the films show his brothers, sitting behind him, finding the proceedings entertaining—or at least productive of entertaining comment.

The King, admittedly, may not have been so much bored as abstracted. Some men present the appearance of boredom when their thoughts are elsewhere, and Edward was one of them. As Bolitho observed, his face was melancholy in repose. But the alacrity with which he closed the proceedings when the rain began to fall appeared to confirm that he was anxious to escape. It was, after all, no more than a shower. The presentations could have been resumed. Or, with his known love of improvization, could he not have found a way to complete them under cover?

Edward's own attitude was reasonable enough: "It has always seemed to me that women are prone to attach an excessive importance to these affairs." Had he made his view clear from the start and anticipated the decision made by the royal family some years later to discontinue the ceremony, his decision would have commanded general respect. But for some reason—possibly because Wallis had herself attached sufficient importance to it to be presented at court—he was prepared to be indulgent. Having decided to hold the presentations, though, the King had no alternative but to do his best to get some pleasure out of the proceedings, or at least to pretend to. To show his boredom simply created resentment.

And by this time Edward *was* bored. Not with being a king— far from it. Wallis, whose relationship with him had begun again to resemble what it had been when he first began to "drop in" for evenings with her, was impressed by his enthusiasm for his work. His mission, as he saw it, was to modernize the monarchy while preserving its traditions, and had he been allowed to carry out his project, he would have been absorbed by the task. But he was not able to carry it out—not, at least, in the ways he wanted to—and this made him irritable. He had assumed that being King would give him the responsibility he had always craved, but what it chiefly did was to give him more routine work. Some of it was of a kind that he had done for years and grown tired of. Some was of a kind he found he did not enjoy—the interminable desk work and the scrutiny of tedious state papers. Besides, work took him from Wallis. If he could have her beside him, things would be different. But this was not easy, except on holiday. . . .

The cruise of the *Nahlin*

There was nothing inherently shocking about Edward's desire to spend part of his summer holiday on the Mediterranean rather than at Balmoral. His grandfather, Edward VII, had enjoyed his Continental forays, and nobody had thought it unpatriotic of him. Had Edward's first choice—he planned to rent Maxine Elliott's villa near Cannes—been acceptable, the party might have attracted relatively little attention. But France was in a state of political crisis, which the emergence of Blum's popular-front government had not settled, and the ambassador advised against the project. Instead, the King arranged to charter a luxury yacht, the *Nahlin*. It belonged to Lady Yule, the wife of an English baronet whose business interests in India had made him reputedly one of the richest men in the world. The baronet had died and his widow lived a quiet life on her estate in England, the *Nahlin* representing her only conspicuous self-indulgence. It was, in effect, a floating villa, and Edward—hoping, according to Wallis, "to recapture the carefree atmosphere of our previous summers"—decided to undertake a cruise down the Dalmatian Coast southward to Greece.

He could hardly have chosen a route better calculated to concentrate attention on himself and his party. On the French Riviera they would have been one of scores of groups of the rich and famous, intermingling. On the *Nahlin* they were self-contained. Every time they came ashore they were watched—usually besieged. And among the besiegers were cameramen, reporters, and gossip columnists from newspapers and magazines the world over.

The publicity the cruise attracted and the attention it centred on Mrs. Simpson were later to prove decisive. But even if her presence had by some ruse been kept secret, Edward would still have managed to scandalize people. He liked whenever possible to strip to the waist. At that time it was not usual for men to leave off their shirts, except on the beach, but on the way through the Corinth Canal, in some places so narrow that it seemed the hordes of spectators had only to reach out to touch the King, he stood on the bridge dressed only in shorts.

This seemed undignified to some of the party, particularly to his equerry, the genial Major John Aird. Aird enlisted Lady Diana Cooper's assistance in a project to persuade Wallis to ask the King to keep his shirt on. It had not been the most enjoyable of holidays for Lady Diana. The early stages of the cruise had been spoiled for her by an intrusive sore throat. She joined in his entreaties, but Wallis refused to cooperate, making the feline comment that Diana ought to be the one to do it, as she had more experience of dealing with kings. Experience, perhaps, but, as she was soon to admit, less skill. When the *Nahlin* party went to dinner with the King of Greece, Diana sat dispirited on one side of him, while Wallis, on his other side, was "doing splendidly, the wisecracks following in quick succession, the King clearly very admiring and amused."

But Edward's unconventional attitude to dress was of less importance than his indifference to the fact that he was all the time being watched and photographed. In general, the British press obeyed the long-established convention that a monarch on holiday is left to enjoy it without what he does being reported or pictures being shown of him (unless convention has hallowed the occasion, as when the royal family goes to Crathie Church near Balmoral for a Sunday-morning service). But there were a few breaches of the convention, and they hinted that Fleet Street was well aware of what was going on, as some of the pictures that were published showed Edward with Wallis. Wallis was aware of the risk, but did nothing about it. When she saw the *Nahlin* for the first time from the quayside at Sibenik on the Dalmatian Coast, she was yet again reminded of her good fortune: "To come upon her so, in a picture-book setting of mountains and sunlit sea, made me appreciate as never before the pleasure and power that attended those in the company of a king." And as never again. To Wallis' surprise, she noticed from the start that she was almost as much the object of attention as Edward was. Eyes turned from him to her and back again, in what she took to be unspoken understanding. This, she felt, should have been a warning to the King.

Why not also to her? In her autobiography, she was to insist that she had already made clear to him that the idea of marriage was impossible. "They" (it was unnecessary to specify) would never let him. But common sense, even without the help of her intuition, could have told her that this *Nahlin* cruise, by making their relationship international common gossip, would make "them" determined to end

it if they could. It was desirable, then, that Edward should behave
with extreme discretion. But discretion—as he actually boasted, during the *Nahlin* cruise—was a quality he had never particularly
admired.

Balmoral

Edward had decided that he would spend the last fortnight of
his holiday at Balmoral in Scotland. Balmoral had originally been a
small country estate: Queen Victoria and the Prince Consort had
rented it for a highland holiday and, liking the place, they had
bought it and built a pseudo-baronial castle in the then fashionable
style. On Albert's death, Victoria had spent as much of her time as
she could there—as many as five months out of the twelve. She
tended to tyrannize over the establishment. Her son Edward VII did
not much care for it, and even George V went more out of duty than
for his own pleasure, as he vastly preferred Sandringham. But Edward VIII decided he would carry on his father's autumnal habit
and stay at Balmoral. It was a gesture, he thought, that would please
his mother, and when he told her about it over dinner on the night
he got back from London, it did. She hoped it presaged a return to
his father's routine. It was not, however, just for Queen Mary's comfort that he went there. He really liked the place. He had not cared
for the old, stuffy Balmoral routine, but he loved the highlands:
"The deer stalking would be at its best, there would be plenty of
grouse on the moors; and the exhilarating air and hard exercise
would put me in condition for the heavy list of appointments awaiting me."

Ironically, in the early months of his reign Edward had been
closer to his mother than he had ever been while his father was
alive. They saw each other frequently, and when he was away she
would write to him much as she had written to George V in his
absences. This was the time, if he was ever going to do it, to confide
in her. But Edward could not bring himself to do so. And the
pleasure Queen Mary had at the news was immediately banished
when she saw the list of guests. It revealed what Edward was to
recall as a "slight" departure from custom. The usual Cabinet ministers, archbishops, and admirals were not invited. Instead, Wallis
Simpson came, with two friends from Peking days, Herman and
Katherine Rogers. Their arrival was recorded in the court *Circular*
and duly published by the *Times*.

If their arrival had been arranged to give the maximum of offence locally, it could not have been better timed. Months before, the city of Aberdeen had asked the King to open some new hospital buildings, and he had declined, because he was still in deep mourning for his father. This was hardly the most convincing of excuses, as Edward had shown himself eager to modify the traditional mourning schedule. A month after his accession, *Time* magazine had reported that he had already decreed no mourning for Ascot Week. In any case, he delegated the duty to his brother the Duke of York, who presumably was in deep mourning too. And the very day that the Duke was performing the ceremony, Aberdonians saw the King arriving to meet Wallis off the train, putting her in the front seat with him, with the Rogerses in the back.

The result was the rumour that the King had ducked an official engagement in order to meet her. In *A King's Story*, the Duke made no mention of the episode. The Duchess, however, referred to it, calling it "one of those unfortunate coincidences"—something of an understatement, for by this time Wallis ought to have realized that it was unwise for her to go to Balmoral at all. She had stopped off a few days in Paris, while Edward went on back to London, and awaiting her she found letters from America, including newspaper cuttings about the *Nahlin* cruise, with pictures and gossip. The revelation disturbed her, yet she was content merely to confide her worries to Edward, who said that newspaper gossip had been directed at him before and "didn't mean a thing." It did not occur to him or Wallis that there was a fundamental difference between the kind of speculation dressed up as inside knowledge that was the standby of gossip columnists and the correct, if belated, realization that Edward and Wallis were in love. The fact that some of the accounts contained inaccuracies was irrelevant. What mattered was that the secret was out and had become a topic of conversation all over the world—except in Britain, where gossip was still confined to London society.

With the story spreading through the American papers and growing more speculative every week, it would have been difficult to delay a show-down between the King and his Prime Minister after they had both returned from their holidays. But the crisis was precipitated by the news that Mrs. Simpson's divorce case was coming up for a hearing.

In her autobiography, the Duchess claimed that during one

of her husband's absences she discovered, through a letter to him which had been inadvertently misaddressed, that there was Another Woman in Ernest Simpson's life. Up to this point he had continued, when he was in London, to act as a kind of chaperon, and perhaps if his attention had not been thus distracted he might have continued to play the part, at least long enough to enable Edward to settle more firmly on his throne after the coronation. Had the break come sooner, on the other hand, Wallis could have obtained the divorce in less difficult circumstances, while Edward was still Prince, and they would have been given more time to plan their future. But as things were to work out, the timing of the divorce proceedings was disastrous. To those who disapproved of her relationship with Edward—and to those who did not, but who wanted it to remain on the old under-the-counter basis—the news could mean only one thing: that she was determined to take advantage of the new freedom of choice that being King would give Edward by giving him the opportunity to use it by marrying her.

In society, Mrs. Simpson had not been taken very seriously. The news of her divorce proceedings meant that she was now regarded as a designing woman. And from this moment the antagonism to Edward—previously held in check by loyalty to the monarchy, by old admiration for him, and by the hope that when he came to the throne he would become more responsible—was unleashed.

Again, Wallis' intuition failed her. She was cut off at this time from most of her normal contacts—except for an occasional visit from Edward—owing to the need to take up residence in Felixstowe in order to lend some justification to her lawyer's decision that she should seek her divorce there rather than in a London court. Felixstowe lies on the eastern coast, a few miles northeast of London. In summer it blossoms with small yachts, tennis tournaments and cocktail parties, but in autumn it can be bleak. To Wallis, hanging around with nothing to do in a small house rented for the month, it was: "The only sounds were the melancholy boom of the sea breaking on the deserted beach and the rustling of the wind around the shuttered cottages." Still, the locals did not recognize her. Probably few of them were aware of her existence. The gossip, though general in London society as well as abroad, remained oddly slow to spread through the provinces. So Wallis, though bored, was not disturbed. She could face the divorce proceedings with equanimity.

Edward, too, was confident. After the Balmoral holiday ended he had a full schedule until December, some of it work of a kind that he enjoyed and had been anxious to resume, because it brought him into contact with the people—a visit to the fleet and a tour of the depressed areas of South Wales. He had only one fear, that the British press might decide to do what the American newspapers had been doing and begin speculating on his relationship with Wallis, using her divorce case as a peg. On October 16 he sent for Lord Beaverbrook—the most influential of the proprietors of the popular newspapers, and an old friend of his, though not a very close one— to ask if he thought Mrs. Simpson could be protected from this kind of publicity in the British press. Beaverbrook said he would see what could be done. He reported back that a gentlemen's agreement had been reached by which the popular papers in London and the provinces would report the divorce case, if at all, without sensationalizing it. (The quality papers, it could be assumed, would refrain from sensationalism anyway.) So that danger had been removed.

Then, just as Edward thought all was going smoothly, the blow fell. Arriving at Sandringham for a week-end of shooting, he found a message from his private secretary asking him to telephone Windsor Castle. The news awaiting him was that the Prime Minister wished to see him without delay—and not at Sandringham, a stipulation that left little doubt in the King's mind what subject they would discuss. The Prime Minister's manifest nervousness when he arrived at Fort Belvedere on the morning of October 20, leading up to his request for whiskey so early in the day, confirmed that this was to be a confrontation on the issue of Mrs. Simpson—not yet a declaration of war, perhaps, or even an ultimatum, but clear evidence that conflict was imminent.

STANLEY BALDWIN

By comparison with Edward's relatively uncomplicated extrovert personality, Stanley Baldwin's remains inscrutable, full of baffling contradictions. Was Baldwin—as Wickham Steed, a one-time editor of the *Times*, asked—the subtlest of competent statesmen or the luckiest of incompetent politicians? According to his biographer, the historian G.M. Young, what puzzled people was "whether a man so obviously good could really be so clever, or a man so amazingly lucky could really be so simple, as he appeared." Young had been an acquaintance and seemed the obvious choice to write his official biography, yet it shows many an indication of disenchantment. According to Young's All Souls colleague A.L. Rowse, Young came so to dislike the man that he had some difficulty in finishing the book. Although this dislike did not make for a dispassionate biography, it is nevertheless revealing about Baldwin.

Different though he was from Edward, they shared one common experience, a childhood under a stern Victorian father. In some studies of Baldwin, such as Francis Williams' *A Pattern of Rulers,* the apparently devious character of the man has been attributed to his upbringing. Stanley as a boy was much in awe of his father, and he remained so most of his life, finding the same difficulty of communication that Edward was to find with George V. One consequence, Williams suggested, of this strange inhibited childhood was nervous strains which "left their mark in the twitching of the facial muscles very similar to the tic from which his father suffered, and a habit of involuntarily snapping his fingers which conveyed to the observant a revealing comment on the public image he managed to impose on his followers"—that public image being a placid, pipe-smoking countryman, always in command of his emotions.

Certainly so long as Baldwin's father was alive and for some years after his death, the son's abilities were effectively disguised by diffidence. Although he had shown considerable academic promise, his school career was undistinguished, and he left Cambridge with only a Third-Class degree. "I hope," his father told him, "that you won't have a Third in Life." He very nearly did. He went into his father's prosperous business, which he detested but which enabled him to live in the style of a country gentleman, interested in local charities and cricket, a dabbler in farming. He became a justice of the peace. And the pattern of his life would have remained unchanged until he retired, and eventually died, had his father not decided that he should add a little more lustre to the family name by entering Parliament.

A hereditary principle used then to operate (it is still not quite extinct to this day) whereby the sons of fathers who have made assiduous and dutiful Conservative MPs were rewarded with constituencies—in the hope that they would follow the parental example, contribute handsomely to the party funds, look after their constituencies, follow the instructions of the party whips and, in due course, with any reasonable luck, qualify for a knighthood or perhaps a baronetcy. There was no difficulty in finding a Conservative seat for a Baldwin locally. But Stanley's career nearly collapsed before it had properly started: for once the seat turned out not to be safe—it was lost when the Liberals swept into power in the 1906 election. His father's death, however, left the constituency of Bewdley vacant, so safe that when he was nominated for it at the resulting by-election, he was not even opposed. But there was nothing to suggest that Baldwin, now in his forties, would emerge from the decent back-bench obscurity to which he promptly committed himself. And when, nine years later, he was offered a government post as Financial Secretary to the Treasury, it was assumed, correctly, that he had obtained the appointment because he had won a reputation for being safe. He had also avoided making influential enemies—important, at that time, as political jealousies were destroying many a more promising career.

Lloyd George's coalition government—in which Baldwin found himself, as the country emerged from the Great War—was one of the most star-studded in history. Lloyd George himself was still a comparatively young man, and with all the prestige of having won the war, as Prime Minister. Under him served Arthur Balfour, who was the former Conservative Prime Minister, Austen Chamberlain, who had narrowly failed to succeed Balfour in the party leadership before the war, Lord Curzon, who was a former viceroy of India, Lord Birkenhead, and Winston Churchill. There was also Bonar

Law, who had become leader of the Conservative Party on Balfour's resignation—he retired from the leadership and the Cabinet owing to ill-health in 1920, but remained a political force to be reckoned with. All these men were Baldwin's contemporaries, give or take a few years, and nobody thought of Baldwin as a possible future leader of the party. It came as a surprise when in 1921 he was promoted to be President of the Board of Trade. Even his own former leader, Bonar Law, had no great confidence in Baldwin's ability to make a good head of a government department, and, writing to congratulate him on his promotion, Law suggested one of the reasons why: "You have what I am told was one of my defects, too much modesty; so my advice to you is to get rid of that defect as soon as possible." Baldwin took the advice. As a minister, he made no great impression. But that summer he went for the first time to Aix-les-Bains for his holiday, spending long hours walking the hills, turning over in his mind his party's future and in the process deciding his own.

Baldwin had two insights denied to his more famous colleagues. He realized that the Lloyd George coalition was cracking up, and he understood why. For all his gifts as a wartime leader, Lloyd George had become too self-satisfied, and his government too corrupt. In particular, the sale of titles had become a national scandal. To redeem itself, Baldwin decided, the Conservative Party must cut itself away from the coalition, even if this meant leaving behind some of its most eminent figures.

The leading Conservatives in the government, he found, were not prepared for the break with Lloyd George. So he concentrated his powers of persuasion on Bonar Law, whom he had earlier served as parliamentary private secretary. In spite of his cautious estimate of Baldwin's abilities, Law trusted his judgment and allowed himself to be persuaded to lead the party back to respectability. At a meeting of Conservative MPs at the Carlton Club in October 1922, Austen Chamberlain sought to persuade them to go to the country at the coming general election as part of the coalition, but Baldwin, making a spech that crystallized the objections to the party's continued support for Lloyd George, emerged for the first time as a political force. The dissidents won, and the Conservative Party formed a government with Bonar Law as Prime Minister and Baldwin as Chancellor of the Exchequer.

Had Law lived, the Conservative coalitionists—Austen Chamberlain, Churchill, Birkenhead and others—could have been brought back into the party under his leadership, as Curzon was. The succession would then have gone to one of them, presumably Chamberlain. But six months after he had become Prime Minister, Law died of cancer, leaving only two possible contenders for his post. The obvious choice was Curzon, with his long ministerial experience. But if ever a man had been strung up for life on a lampoon, it was Curzon. Years before, while he was still an Oxford undergraduate, someone had written of him:

> My name is George Nathaniel Curzon,
> I am a most superior person,
> My cheek is smooth, my hair is sleek,
> I dine at Blenheim once a week.

The reputation of being a supercilious snob clung to him—never, he complained in 1920, had more harm been done to an individual "than that accursed doggerel has done to me." His superciliousness, though, was not the real cause of his downfall. He had crept back into the party from the coalition only at the last moment, and this had served as a reminder of his propensity, when prompted by political expediency, to desert friends and principles. In A.J.P. Taylor's phrase, "He was one of nature's rats." And by chance there was a good excuse to reject him. It was suggested to the King that in view of the rise of Labour in the House of Commons and the fact that the party was scarcely represented in the House of Lords, the Prime Minister ought to be in the Commons. The King agreed. So "little Baldwin," as Lloyd George had called him—"not even a public figure," as Curzon complained, but "a man of no experience, of the utmost insignificance"—found himself Prime Minister, at the age of fifty-six.

Prime Minister

As Prime Minister he made an inauspicious start. His first contribution to his party's fortunes was to involve it in another general election, in spite of the fact that it had a good majority in a parliament that had still some years to run, and he took it to the country on the issue of protection. The electorate showed it was not yet prepared to abandon free trade. The Conservatives remained the largest party, but they were outnumbered in the Commons by Labour and Liberals combined, and Ramsay MacDonald was called upon to form the first Labour government, with Liberal support.

For the Conservatives, the election set-back was bad enough, but to have let in the "Reds" was disgraceful. Had Labour been able to stay in power, the two wings of the Conservative Party might have had time to come together, giving Baldwin the opportunity to step down—or be pulled down, if he proved obstinate—in favour of Austen Chamberlain. But MacDonald's government was dependent on erratic Liberal backing. It made mistakes from inexperience, and after a few months it fell. The general election of 1924 brought the Conservatives back with a comfortable majority. Baldwin was re-prieved.

It now began to become clear that he had the invaluable ability to learn from his errors. He even learned to turn them to advantage. After the rebuff of 1923 he became extremely adept at what Churchill described as "the successful avowal of mistakes." If a storm broke, Baldwin later explained, "when I knew I was in the right I would let it break on me, and I would either survive it or break. If I felt after examination that there was in that storm something which showed me that, however unconsciously, I had done something that was not wise or right, I would bow to it"—an assurance, as Philip Guedalla tartly observed, which ensured that whatever happened, "Mr. Baldwin would be on the winning side."

But he was not moved simply by political expediency. His civil service secretary, Tom Jones (who knew him as well as anybody), insisted that Baldwin really had the humility that admits mistakes: "He felt things deeply and his conscience was more active than his intellect." The discovery that the public, far from resenting his admissions of past incompetence, liked and trusted him the more for them was an unexpected political bonus. The realization that he was "capable of leaving an unforgettable impression by his staggering candour" naturally encouraged him to use it, and he began to do so with gratifying effect. The frankness was not spurious, but it had one unforeseen consequence. If Baldwin could be confident of extricating himself from difficult situations caused by his own or his government's errors, and if he could actually gain electoral kudos thereby, he had less cause to worry about whether his government's policies were sound. He could let things drift until the ship of state was almost on the rocks—and then, steering her to safety, be hailed as the pilot who weathered the storm.

Up to this time, Baldwin had been a leader without a policy. Now, something emerged that was recognisable as Baldwinism—even if it was not so much a policy as a political attitude of mind. The objective was One Nation, on Disraeli's pattern: a rejection of the inevitability of class warfare—the Socialist thesis—in favour of . . . what? It was never very clear, in Baldwin's mind or anybody else's, but it amounted to a mildly paternalist society, rather on the the lines of the Baldwin family business, in which the employer regarded himself as the head of the family, stern to offenders, but just and kindly—the employer being willing in hard times to share his last crust with his men. There was little egalitarianism about it. There was not even much sympathy for worker-management co-operatives of any organized kind. The basic idea was to take the social system as it stood and, through round-table discussions, make it work with less friction.

Baldwinism's first test came with the general strike of 1926. The Prime Minister's handling of the negotiations which led up to it could be criticised, and he was partly responsible for their eventual breakdown, but, ironically, he emerged from it with his reputation enhanced. "He blundered," Tom Jones thought, "in agreeing to war," but then he regained control, "declared peace and insisted upon peace." He acquired so enormous a popularity in the country, the left-wing weekly *New Statesman* had to admit, "that he could afford to let all his colleagues resign if they wanted to"—a result achieved "mainly by one effective broadcast in which he seemed to embrace the mass of his countrymen with affection and understanding, to which the response was immediate." Some members of his own party were less enthusiastic. They thought Baldwin had shown himself a fumbler, a putter-off of decisions. But he learned another lesson from the general strike. If he could get public opinion behind him, he need not worry overmuch about political rivals. He might be no nearer an effective One Nation policy than before, but what he now had was the capacity, which he relentlessly exploited in crises, to convince the public that they could rely on him—with the unspoken implication that other politicians were less trustworthy.

For party political purposes, though, Baldwinism had one obvious disadvantage. It was uninspiring. Attitudes of mind do not make good election slogans or good campaign platform programmes, and the best that Baldwin could do in this line—"Safety First"—was

not good enough to win the 1929 general election. It had no relevance to the main political problem of the day—unemployment. The
defeat was no worse a setback than the Conservatives could have
expected, after five years of office with nothing spectacular to show
for it. But the fact that Labour was now for the first time the largest
party in the Commons alarmed the Tory right wing, and the
industrialists whose funds supported the party. Soon, mutterings of
"BMG"—originally applied to Balfour, now meaning "Baldwin must
go"—began to be heard.

But who could succeed him? Churchill was back in the party—
he had been Baldwin's Chancellor of the Exchequer—but few Conservatives trusted him. Besides, he was manœuvering for another
coalition with the Lloyd George Liberals, a prospect from which
his colleagues shrank. Austen Chamberlain, in spite of the reputation he had won as Foreign Minister in the Baldwin government,
had eased out of the running—he had lost too many times for his
party to have confidence in his powers of leadership. His half-
brother, Neville, was the most likely successor, but Neville was not
disposed to risk defeat in a premature coup to take on the leadership.
And no other serious contender was available.

Nevertheless, discontent grew, and a dissident Conservative
right-wing group began to threaten danger. In February 1931 the
chief agent of the Conservative Party formally advised that it would
be in the party's interest that its leader should "reconsider his position." Baldwin did: he actually offered to resign. Then he thought
better of it. The fighter in him took over, and he decided to stake his
future on the result of a pending by-election in the St. George's division of Westminster, where Duff Cooper was to stand as his champion against the dissidents. Duff Cooper won the seat convincingly
enough to reassure doubters, and then the economic crisis distracted
attention from the party's internal squabbles.

The Great Depression, which had hit the United States a little
earlier, now had Britain in its grip. Unemployment was heavier than
it had ever been, and there was a run on the pound. To restore confidence, the government's financial advisers in the City insisted, there
must be retrenchment: cuts in welfare services, in pensions, in the
"dole," as unemployment relief was called. Labour ministers found
this difficult to swallow, and the Cabinet was divided. And to solve
their difficulties the idea was put forward that a national government

should be formed from the three political parties, Labour, Conservative and Liberal, so that any harsh measures that had to be taken would not be blamed on a single party.

It was typical of Baldwin that he had nothing to do with the negotiations that eventually led up to the formation of the national government to rescue the country from its difficulties. He stayed on holiday at Aix, leaving Neville Chamberlain to wrestle with the complexities of national and international finance. When he returned, reluctantly, Baldwin was annoyed at the prospect. Having destroyed one coalition, he said, he had no wish to form another. But as soon as he realized a national government was inevitable whether he wanted it or not, he took charge, with his now practiced aplomb, and his colleagues had no choice. The leader of the Conservative Party in the national government had to be a man who would have the confidence of his Labour and Liberal colleagues in the Cabinet. And as Neville Chamberlain's contemptuous attitude to Labour MPs had not endeared him to his former political opponents, Baldwin it had to be. When the general election of 1931 gave the National Government an immense majority, heavily weighted with Conservatives, Baldwin became its most influential member, even though the former leader of the Labour Party, Ramsay MacDonald, remained nominally Prime Minister.

Soon, though, Baldwin was again in trouble with his party as the result of a by-election at Fulham in 1933, where a seat that had been won by the "National" candidate with a massive majority was lost to a Labour candidate—and a pacifist. It was not certain that the result was a vote against rearmament—some observers believed that it reflected working class resentment at some of the stringent measures which the National Government had imposed to counter the economic crisis. But the general impression was that pacifism had become an issue, and this was clearly going to benefit Labour—led by a pacifist, George Lansbury. The party had been almost annihilated at the general election of 1931: now, only two years later, it seemed to have miraculously recovered. Although the Government could still command a huge majority in the Commons, its authority was shaken.

So was Baldwin. Like many of his generation, he had been deeply affected by the First World War, and the prospect of another horrified him. Some advisers warned him that militarism in Japan, in Italy and now in Germany was increasing the risk of war, and that Britain must rearm or risk abject humiliation. But here was the electorate apparently demonstrating its desire for *dis*armament. In desperation, Baldwin resorted to the old device of saying that there were difficulties in telling what he knew: "If I were to stand here and to say what the difficulties are, and who are the people who raise those difficulties, it would be impossible ever to advance one inch with regard to disarmament. One's lips are sealed." Baldwin's friends were dismayed by his prevarication, and his opponents were delighted—the cartoonist Low, beginning to make a name for himself, used to portray him with his lips sealed by sticking plaster.

Once again, some of Baldwin's colleagues began to wonder if he was losing his grip. He was in any case unpopular with the imperialist wing of his party for accepting a pledge made earlier by the Labour Government to help India on the road toward self-government. Churchill, among others, felt that the cause of empire was being betrayed. The India Defence League had been set up to provide a resistance movement with the Conservative Party, and although it did no more than give the India Bill a rough passage, damage was done to party unity and morale. Even more alarming than Fulham, too, was the "Peace Ballot" of 1935, the most extensive public-opinion poll—other than general elections—ever carried out in Britain. Over eleven million people voted, coming out overwhelmingly in favour of disarmament. The Conservative Party, long identified with the policy of a strong Britain, could take little comfort from this result; and it made things particularly difficult for ministers, who were being warned by their foreign experts and their service chiefs that British power on land and sea and in the air, already dangerously weakened, would soon be menaced by a re-armed Germany if Hitler had his way.

By 1935, then, Baldwin's position was—in his colleague Sir John Simon's words—"difficult, if not precarious." But once again, he revealed his political acumen. The peace ballot had left him one opening. The voters had indicated overwhelming support for the League of Nations. If he could exploit that, all might not yet be lost.

Baldwin chose his time with care. That summer the demonstration of affection for George V at his jubilee could be interpreted as evidence of the success of Baldwinism, to the extent that it showed the Nation was indeed One. Soon after, on Ramsay MacDonald's retirement, Baldwin became Prime Minister, which put him in a position to go to the country whenever he chose. Then, in October,

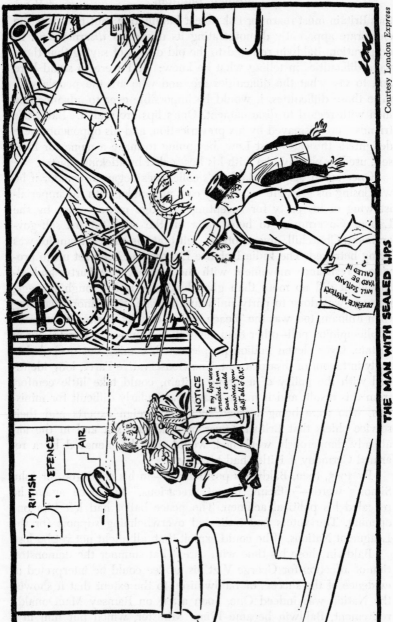

Courtesy London Express

the Italians invaded Abyssinia. There was an upsurge of hostility to Mussolini and sympathy for the unfortunate Emperor of Abyssinia. But in order for Britain to fulfil her League obligations to the Emperor, she must rearm. Baldwin seized the opportunity to hold a general election, making a series of campaign speeches—including a very effective one for the newsreels—about the need for a modest measure of rearmament to enable Britain to fulfil her League commitments, with his personal pledge ("and I think you can trust me") that it would not be allowed to develop into an arms race. The plan worked. In November the Conservatives were returned with a majority which, though reduced, was still handsome.

When Baldwin succeeded MacDonald as Prime Minister, Walter Lippman opened his New York *Times* article with the comment, "No other man in the United Kingdom could begin to command the confidence which Stanley Baldwin inspires at home and abroad." Some British eyebrows had been raised at the notion, but the election had abundantly vindicated it. Up to this time the suspicion had remained that Baldwin had simply been lucky. Now, the verdict of Harold Laski, the archetype of the Socialist intellectual of the thirties, had to be accepted: Baldwin had the Englishman's genius "for appearing an amateur in a game in which, in fact, he is a superb professional." He had reached the peak of his prestige. In a few months, he told friends, he would retire. But in the meantime he could enjoy his power, prestige and popularity to the full.

Hoare / Laval

Hardly was the election over before Baldwin suffered the biggest humiliation of his political career. His lack of interest in foreign affairs may have been exaggerated—there was even a rumour that he slept through Cabinet discussions on them—but he tended to leave them to his Foreign Secretary. He would admit this occasionally. Young, reminding him of a talk he had had with the French Prime Minister Poincaré, asked if he had ever talked to any other of the leading men of Europe. Baldwin's reply was no—he didn't like them: "Ribbentrop once lunched, and recited *Mein Kampf*," that was all. Baldwin obviously did not intend the remark to be taken seriously, but he certainly gave much less attention to foreign than to domestic affairs. In all his years of visits to Aix, he had only once bestirred himself to visit the nearby Geneva headquarters of the

League of Nations. It had suited his convenience to praise the League for campaign purposes, and probably he thought that the traditional dispensation for the breaking of campaign pledges after an election has been won would apply to this one, too. Whatever the reason, his professions of faith in the League, as Young recalled, "went so far beyond what he really felt that they might almost be called insincere."

To Baldwin, reconciliation with Mussolini was now desirable, and there were plenty of people ready to advise him that it was also necessary—to meet the greater threat of Hitler and of Japan. The Foreign Secretary, Samuel Hoare, happened to be about to go to Switzerland on medical advice. It was agreed that he should stop off in Paris to see the French Prime Minister, Pierre Laval, and discuss the prospects. And at their meeting, the soon to be notorious Hoare-Laval "pact" was agreed upon. Under its terms Mussolini was to keep what he had conquered. Abyssinia was to be compensated by giving her an outlet to the sea through British Somaliland.

The reaction in Britain was immediate. For people who cared about the League, the Hoare-Laval pact simply confirmed that an aggressor, if ruthless enough, could dictate the terms under which he would consent to stop fighting in order to enjoy the spoils he had won. Even those who had little faith in the League were affronted by what appeared to them to be the humiliation that Britain, as a member state, would suffer at the hands of Mussolini. The most influential of British newspapers, the *Times,* took a strong anti-Italian line, culminating in an editorial entitled "A Corridor for Camels"—a derisive reference to the fact that the compensatory access to the sea did not even have, and was not going to be permitted to have, a railway. Anxious though everybody should be to bring the belligerents together, it said, Britain could not "endorse an unjust peace."

The *Times* alone would not have been able to swing public opinion, but it was already clear that the *Times* was not alone. Some influential Conservatives—including Austen Chamberlain, by now the party's elder statesman—were against the pact, and responsible public opinion as a whole was disgusted by it. After some hesitation, Hoare was instructed to reject his own plan. He preferred to resign, and although the government survived, its treatment of him added to its unpopularity.

Again, Baldwin was shaken. According to Young he "wore the

air of a man crushed by some appalling disaster," and he confided
to Tom Jones that the affair had "knocked him endways." The
Foreign Office, Baldwin complained, had declared the agreement to
be the best day's work a Foreign Secretary had done for years—the
Foreign Office at the time being under the domination of Sir Robert
Vansittart, whose mistrust of Hitler had made him regard Mussolini
with a benevolent eye. It had not occured to Baldwin that the British
public—usually no more interested in foreign policy than he was—
would be capable of getting so worked up about Abyssinia. "My
worst enemy," he was accustomed to claim, "could never say that I
do not understand the people of England," and the conviction that
he could sense their moods had become essential to him because,
lacking any particular political philosophy, he depended on it as a
built-in compass to tell him what way the electorate was moving.
Now his compass had let him down.

Baldwin could still sense what people wanted, but he could no
longer judge what they needed—which they sometimes realized they
needed. His policy was based on satisfying their wants. Now they had
exposed its shallowness, nearly unseating him in the process. Among
those who observed his discomfiture from the gallery of the Commons was the Prince of Wales, who came to hear his friend Hoare's
resignation speech, and he came away from the debate with no high
opinion of Baldwin's judgment.

A month later, the Prince had become King Edward VIII. The
funeral of his father and the accession ceremonies distracted attention from politics for a while, but as the winter drew on there were
further humiliations for the government. Early in March Hitler sent
troops into the Rhineland, demilitarized under the Treaty of Versailles. The British and French governments could not agree on
what action to take and ended by taking no action. The League of
Nations had imposed sanctions on Italy, but not the essential sanction, an embargo on oil, so the Italians were able to continue their
advance into Abyssinia until resistance there collapsed and Haile
Selassie had to leave his country. Discontent with Baldwin began to
spread not only on the party's right wing, but in the centre, from
where he had drawn his staunchest support.

The normally dispassionate *Annual Register* said that Baldwin
had done nothing to retrieve himself from the discredit that his
conduct over the Hoare-Laval pact had brought upon him and
claimed that "opinion was freely expressed that his days as leader

of the Conservative Party were numbered." David Maxwell-Fyfe—
later to be British prosecutor at the Nuremberg trials of the Nazi
leaders, but in 1936 a back-bencher new to Westminster—felt sufficiently alarmed to get together with other young Tories to form a
pressure group, with the intention of fighting the party's parliamentary battles more vigorously than their leader could do. Tom Jones'
diary and correspondence at this time were full of references to
Baldwin's unpopularity. At a week-end at Cliveden, the home of the
Waldorf Astors, Jones found himself cornered by a group of women
all bent on attacking his friend because—as one of the group, the
MP for Frome, put it—Baldwin's "capacity for hiding his incapacity"
could no longer be tolerated. Had there been an obvious alternative
leader, Baldwin would certainly have fallen, but Neville Chamberlain, in line for the succession, was still disinclined to gamble for the
leadership immediately, knowing that it was Baldwin's intention to
retire after the coronation, in 1937. And there was no other obvious
alternative.

Then, during the summer, civil war broke out in Spain. Although
a non-intervention agreement between Britain, France, Italy and
Germany was arranged, to prevent the war from spreading, reports
soon made it clear that Mussolini, in particular, was ignoring it and
sending units of the Italian army to fight for Franco in Spain. His
submarines were also active in the Mediterranean, a threat to British
shipping. The outlook was depressing. Lobby correspondents had
noticed in June that Baldwin looked—as one of them put it—"the
picture of forlorn misery." They were now told that his medical advisers, fearing overstrain, had told him to rest. He did not even feel
up to going to Aix. Instead, he went to Wales, and later to Norfolk,
to stay with friends. His colleagues were begged not to worry him
with affairs of state, and Neville Chamberlain was glad to take over
in his absence.

Withdrawal and return

Baldwin was away for over two months, in the course of which
the King's relationship with Mrs. Simpson became front-page news
in America. Was Baldwin really so ill that he could not be confronted with the evidence? Or was he simply unwilling to make any
move? And if so, why? On the answers to these questions must depend the verdict whether Baldwin handled the abdication impec-

cably—as his supporters, and many people who were ordinarily his opponents, came to believe—or whether he helped to precipitate it by his failure to act soon enough to settle the King's matter without a constitutional crisis.

Baldwin's prolonged rest cure was the subject of hostile comment at the time in his own party. Robert Boothby made a speech in September in his constituency in which he complained that the international storm signals were up: "Under such conditions, there is one place for the captain, and that is the bridge. Stalin has recently given forcible evidence to the world that he has not left Moscow. Mussolini has not ceased to preside over his own cabinet; and we have not read in the newspapers that Hitler was too tired to attend the Nuremberg Congress." Boothby's implication was that Baldwin was not so much ill as lazy and indifferent, a view that was widely shared. Certainly there was nothing seriously the matter with him. He had simply lost his nerve, Tom Jones thought, so that "every burden became a nightmare." This could be accounted for by his worry over the international situation and by the crumbling of his political authority, but it seems likely that he had also come to realize that he was going to be forced into a conflict with the King and that he was anxious to postpone it as long as he could.

The conflict was not, at least at this stage, over Mrs. Simpson. Baldwin may have had his suspicions, but so long as she was with her husband—as she was at the York House dinner which Baldwin and his wife attended—the danger was not immediate. What more concerned him was the King's reluctance to carry out his royal duties according to the book—the book being, in effect, the set of precedents established by his father.

Even before Edward came to the throne, the story had got around among Labour circles that Baldwin had made a cryptic comment about the succession: "The Yorks will do it very well." At the accession council he told Clement Attlee, the Labour Party leader, that he had grave doubts whether the new King "would stay the course." And as the weeks went by, his foreboding was justified. Relations between the King and his government grew progressively more strained.

Members of the Opposition became aware of the ministers' worries, and so did the press. American newspapers and magazines began to make references to the King's habit of intervening, in ways that would have shocked his father, to tell his ministers what they ought to think or do. Earl Reeves, for example, who had been chief London correspondent of the International News Service, claimed in the magazine *Liberty* that the King was interfering in foreign affairs: he had insisted that discussion between the French and British of the re-militarization of the Rhineland must be held in London rather than in Geneva, where there was a risk that the Russians might sway the assembly into demanding action against Germany.

Improbable though the story sounded (and it is not confirmed by Lord Avon), there was later to be independent evidence of the King's attitude to the Rhineland coup. A young German journalist, Fritz Hesse, had come over to London the year before as director of the German news agency and press attaché to the German embassy. At first he was regarded with suspicion by the ambassador, von Hoesch, who thought that Hesse had been sent by the Nazis to spy on him—Hoesch being an old-style career diplomatist. But eventually his suspicions were lulled, and he began to take Hesse into his confidence.

When the Rhineland was re-occupied, Hoesch feared that the Francophile belligerents in England—Churchill, Duff Cooper and others—might rouse public opinion in favour of restoring the alliance and helping the French to eject the German forces. According to Hesse's account in his *Hitler and the English,* Hoesch took advantage of the fact that he "had been on terms of intimate friendship" with Edward for many years to make a direct secret appeal to the King, promising, among other things, that Hitler was ready to replace the old Locarno Treaty by a new one and that if the Rhineland question was solved Germany would return to the League of Nations. Hesse was doubtful of the promise to return to the League, knowing Hitler's views—nor was it likely to appeal much to the King. However, Hoesch went one night to see the King in secret to put forward his case, and the King promised to send for Baldwin.

Hesse was with the ambassador when the telephone rang.

Von Hoesch whispered to me: "The King!" and handed the second receiver to me, so that I could listen to the conversation.

"Hullo," a voice called, "is that Leo? David speaking. Do you know who's speaking?"

"Of course I do," replied von Hoesch.

"I sent for the Prime Minister and gave him a piece of my mind. I

told the old so-and-so that I would abdicate if he made war. There was
a frightful scene. But you needn't worry. There won't be a war."

The ambassador was delighted with himself: "I've done it, I've
outwitted them all, there won't be a war!" And his action, Hesse
thought, "did indeed seem to produce a change in the situation."

It is difficult to accept the account as it stands, because there was
no need for the King to threaten abdication. Baldwin had no more
idea of declaring war than he had. The "change in the situation," if
it took place, was probably coincidental. Yet Hesse is unlikely to
have invented the conversation. What seems more probable is that
the King said roughly what Hesse attributed to him, but that he was
being flippant. Flippant or serious, an intervention of that kind
would not have been welcome to Baldwin, who was having enough
trouble with his party at the time without having the King chivvying
him too. And Hesse's conclusion may be accurate: the conflict between the Prime Minister and the King over Mrs. Simpson "may already have been playing its part in the background of world events."

There were two main grounds of complaint about the King. As
Claud Cockburn's newsletter *The Week* was to recall at the height
of the abdication crisis, rumour had asserted that he was neglectful
of his duties and that he interfered in state affairs. To Cockburn—a
former *Times* correspondent who had joined the Communist Party
and then found his real *métier* in the editing of his news-letter—the
two complaints appeared mutually contradictory. But were they?
The King might well have interfered in those state affairs that interested him and neglected those that did not. With his disinclination
for reading, the arid columns of state papers and memoranda could
have been expected to prove indigestible, but this would not have
prevented him from expressing himself forcibly on Hitler or on
unemployment. In any case, even if the rumours were grossly exaggerated, what mattered was that they existed and spread. Little
though Labour MPs cared for the Conservative government, they
would feel bound to support it on this issue, for if they did not, they
could expect trouble themselves if they returned to office.

At least one of Edward's entourage at this time has continued to
believe that Baldwin realized even before the summer holidays that
the King would have to be brought under control or compelled to
leave his throne. A row blew up between them when Edward was

told that he should not go to the villa in the south of France, because
he did not consider the explanation adequate—that the government
was worried by France's political situation and the Spanish civil war.
Still, his second choice, the *Nahlin* cruise, promised to give the privacy that he desired for the party. Then he was informed that if he
proposed to go on a cruise in the Mediterranean, his yacht must be
accompanied by two destroyers and he must take with him a secretary of state. The King had no objection to the company of the
secretary of state in question—Duff Cooper, who was an old friend
—but to be ordered to take a government representative on board
and to have the destroyers in attendance infuriated him. Apparently
he did not attempt to disguise his irritation.

But why, if Baldwin realized a showdown was inevitable, did he
delay so long before confronting the King? The answer lies in his
character. Outwardly, he was the essence of English imperturbabil-
ity: a solid, John-Bull-like figure, homely, placid, phlegmatic, a pipe
usually stuck comfortably in a corner of his mouth. His speaking
voice conveyed the same impression: relaxed, free from the usual
politician's mannerisms, and eminently reassuring. But this portrayal
of himself "as a countryman, plain and simple almost to imbecility,"
Tom Jones explained, was an act, laid on as a reaction against the
rule of the brains of the Lloyd George era. Baldwin was anything
but placid. "Within him," an American newspaperman had observed
at the time of the general strike, "storms a chaos; he has himself
under admirable control, but everything he does is the issue of tense
inner conflict." The tension manifested itself in his chronic facial tic
and in the habit, which Edward had observed when they had
crossed Canada together on one of the royal tours, of "snapping and
cracking his fingers with a quick flip of the hand past the right ear."
But at times the stress grew too great for such casual release, and
then Baldwin would suffer from nervous prostration.

One attack had followed the general strike, and the illness in the
summer of 1936 was another. The idea of coming into direct conflict
with the King, after all, was far more disturbing to Baldwin than it
would be to a present-day politician. People were then much more
susceptible to the awe that hedged a king, particularly a George V,
and whatever they might think of Edward as a man, much of
George's royal aura remained. The prospect of a constitutional crisis
over the boundaries of the royal prerogative was disconcerting.

It is possible, too, that Baldwin had begun to realise that the King proposed to marry Mrs. Simpson. Early in July, after a rest at the Prime Minister's official country residence, Chequers, Baldwin surprised everybody by being at his most ebullient in the Commons, as if he had quite recovered. But a week later, the second of the York House dinner parties was held, and Ernest Simpson's name did not appear in the list of guests. Years before—according to his son— Baldwin, though not normally psychic, had had a premonition. He had to meet the Prince of Wales at Folkestone on his return from Africa to be at his father's bedside, and he was overcome by a sudden "feeling of certainty that one day he most certainly would have something to say to him, and that it would be about a woman." Perhaps he now realized that the day was not far off.

Baldwin was used to political crises, but this meant a trespass on his religious and moral beliefs, all the more distressing to him because—according to Tom Jones, again—he was one-half contemplative and non-political, "more a preacher than a statesman." He had a profound belief in God and in his own destiny as the chosen servant of God.

When he came down from Oxford, Baldwin had wanted to become a clergyman, a wish his father refused to grant. Later, when he became Prime Minister, he thought he could see the hand of God in it: "I recognised that my peculiar life had been a preparation for the very work that lay before me . . . I knew that I had been chosen as God's instrument." This was not cant. It was still conventional to claim God's special interest in such matters, and Baldwin, for all his political suppleness, was a genuinely religious man. "Every morning," his wife once said, "we kneel together before God and commend our day to Him, praying that some good work may be done in it by us. It is not for ourselves that we are working, but for the country and for God's sake. How else could we live?"

Baldwin, therefore, would feel little sympathy with a king who had the reputation of being irreligious, still less for the idea of his marrying the twice-divorced Mrs. Simpson. Nor were their personal relations such that Edward could hope to bring him around. The recollections of their previous encounters described in *A King's Story* may be unreliable, written as they were with the acerbity of hindsight. It seems probable that Edward quite liked Baldwin, who certainly did what he could to help him when he came to the throne. But no rapport had been established between them, and the prospect of a confrontation on the subject of Mrs. Simpson could only be embarrassing. "When I was a little boy in Worcestershire reading history books," he had told Tom Jones, "I never thought I should have to interfere between a king and his mistress." It was not a subject one talked about in public, except perhaps in the club or over a glass of port when the ladies had left the table. The King's generation might have learned to discuss such matters freely, but not Baldwin's.

In any case, both by temperament and by political training Baldwin was a man who put off making decisions, in the conviction that, at least so far as he was concerned, this was the most effective way of handling a crisis. Whenever he or his governments had initiated policies, the results had been unfortunate. Occasionally, as in the Hoare-Laval affair, they had been nearly disastrous. The experience had taught him that if he saw a group go down for a swim on a beach where the currents were known to be dangerous, there was no point in advising them to go elsewhere. His job was to wait—and be ready to call the life-boat.

The most likely explanation, then, is that Baldwin had known what was likely to happen, but had decided to wait, recognizing that past experience had shown that masterly inactivity until the right moment came was the best way of handling such situations. And it is just possible that he had another reason for his prolonged summer retreat. He had become a believer in periodic withdrawal from the scene of action, as at Aix, before the events that led to the Conservatives leaving the Lloyd George coalition—not so much to work out a plan of action as to let intuition regain mastery after being overlaid by political expediency. Perhaps he had read that section of Arnold Toynbee's monumental *Study of History,* in the volume which had been published in 1934, dealing with the theme of "withdrawal and return" and its recurrence in the lives of great men—the need to commune with God, or nature, expressed in Moses' ascent of Mount Sinai, Jesus' forty days and nights in the desert, and countless similar episodes. The "withdrawal and return" theory had aroused considerable interest. Baldwin, even if he had not read the book, would certainly have heard about it, and he could hardly have failed to be impressed by its relevance to his own career. Here was notable justification for his method! As Harold Nicolson noted, he had never been addicted to intellectual analysis—"He regarded logical processes as un-English; he preferred to rely upon instinct, and would

sniff and snarl at problems like an elderly spaniel." Now, Toynbee
had demonstrated not merely that he had been wise to indulge himself in this way—to opt from time to time for withdrawal, to allow
instinct to resume its domination over him—but also that he had
been in excellent historical company in so doing.

It is highly improbable, then, that Baldwin was unaware of the
spate of scandal in the American press up to the time he returned to
work on October 12. He spent several hours studying the correspondence that had come in during his absence, some of it concerning Mrs. Simpson, but the following day, when he went to the
palace, the subject was not brought up. He might have hesitated
even longer, but he had been invited to spend the week-end of
October 17 and 18 at Cumberland Lodge, another of the royal "grace
and favour" establishments on the Windsor estate. His host was Lord
FitzAlan, an old friend and admirer of King George V. According
to Sencourt, FitzAlan had arranged the house party—"the most important he had ever had"—because of anxiety for the future of the
crown. As well as the Prime Minister, he had invited the Duke of
Norfolk, who was to be in charge of the coronation ceremony, Lord
Salisbury, who had been a leader of the government peers in the
House of Lords, and Lord Kemsley, one of the Berry brothers, now
both ennobled, who had built up the most influential newspaper
chain in England, including the *Daily Telegraph,* the *Sunday Times*
and the *Financial Times.*

The King's secretary, Hardinge, was called in, and after conferring with him, Baldwin agreed that there could be no further
delay. Hardinge telephoned Sandringham, where the King had gone
for the shooting, only to be informed that the King was not available.
He had probably, Baldwin surmised, "been at Lowestoft with the
lady." (He presumably meant Felixstowe, where the lady was
establishing her "residence" for the purpose of the divorce.) Baldwin
was prepared to go to Sandringham, but Hardinge felt that his appearance there might attract undesirable publicity, and when the
King eventually came through, it was arranged that he should return
to Fort Belvedere on Monday night and that Baldwin should see
him there the following morning.

Now that the time for confrontation had come, Baldwin was prepared. But this would not have helped to make him less nervous. He
could not know what the King's reaction was going to be—whether

he would regard his Prime Minister's intervention as justifiable or as intolerable *lèse-majesté*. And even if by good fortune the King was prepared to be understanding about Mrs. Simpson, the vexed problem of his attitude to his duties would remain. Tranquillizers had not been invented, and Baldwin might have been shocked at the idea of taking them, but whiskey was sanctioned for their purpose, even if ten o'clock in the morning was unusually early.

Nervous he might be, but the King could not hope to reap more than a temporary advantage from that. Baldwin, he realised, was going to be a powerful adversary. Not that "adversary" was, as yet, the correct term—certainly Baldwin would have repudiated it with genuine indignation. His function as Prime Minister, as he saw it, was to give the King all the help and advice he could. So long as he did not know what to advise or how to help, he had kept silent. Now he had been forced to tell the King what was in his mind. But it was still up to the King to make the next move. There was no constitutional issue, yet.

Obviously, though, there was going to be if the King announced his intention to marry Mrs. Simpson. At that point, Baldwin would be compelled to make his own views clear, and they could not be expected to be favourable. The chances of Edward's persuading him to change his mind and to accept Mrs. Simpson as the King's wife-to-be were negligible. He must be treated, then, as an adversary, for such he was now bound to become.

Yet formidable though Baldwin would be, his career had been too checkered to suggest that he was politically invulnerable. He had made so many mistakes, the Hoare-Laval affair being the latest —and potentially the most damaging, because it had so tarnished Baldwin's man-of-the-people image. If it were to become a struggle between the King and the Prime Minister, Edward ought not to lack allies, provided that he could rally them to his side in time. The Fleet Street "gentlemen's agreement" not to sensationalize the divorce case would give time. The question now was: Where could the allies be found?

IN SEARCH OF ALLIES

KING'S FRIENDS

By the nature of his position, an heir to the throne meets many of the influential men of his time. If, like Edward, he is outgoing, observant and keenly interested in what is happening around him, it would be reasonable to expect that he will collect an unusually varied range of acquaintances and a circle of friends drawn from men and women in positions of power and responsibility, whose worth he knows at first hand and whose advice he can trust. Edward, looking around him, did not find himself so well-endowed. There was hardly anybody in his immediate circle who could be expected to be of much help to him in this situation. In the wider range of his acquaintanceship, though there were a few influential men who would be delighted to find themselves his advisers, the advice they had to give was unlikely to be either consistent or sound.

One reason was hinted at more than once in *A King's Story* and by Edward's biographers. At the time he grew up, he had not been given the chance to settle down and *make* friends. He had only been in the navy for a few months when his father ordered him home and told him he must go to Oxford, and he left Oxford after only two years, without ever becoming absorbed in the life there. During the war he was constantly being shifted from unit to unit, job to job, country to country, and, in the meantime, many of those who had begun to be or might have become his close associates were killed: his equerry soon after war broke out, two equerries of his father's, and his cousin Prince Maurice of Battenberg. The war had hardly begun before he was writing in his diary, "I shan't have a friend left soon." Hardly an exaggeration—this was the theme of countless journals and letters of the war years. And after the war—when he would have liked to stay on in the army, in a regiment—his father again intervened to compel him to take up his duties as Prince of Wales. Thereafter for the next few years he was almost continuously on the move, on his world tours.

When he returned to London, as Bolitho noted, he was almost a stranger. His few Magdalen friends had been scattered, and his army acquaintances had settled into new grooves. His chief interests were of a kind that dispersed rather than concentrated his activities. His work for ex-servicemen, particularly the disabled, brought him to endless hospitals, clinics, sales of work, exhibitions, and so on, just as his public appearances introduced him to a diversity of audiences. But they did not bring him the continuity of acquaintanceship that provides the material from which friendships arise.

Most people have some opportunity of living in enclosed communities—college, a regiment, a job, a suburb, a back street—for long enough to gain friends, or at least to enjoy the companionship that passes for friendship when not too harshly tested. And such friendships, though they may not survive separation, often linger in memory, so that a man has the comfort of imagining that he has old friends even if he rarely meets them and finds little to say apart from reminiscence when he does. But Edward was always being transplanted before he had put down roots.

The Fort had provided Edward with his first real opportunity to collect a circle of close friends around him. But not many of those who came there on week-ends were likely to be of much help to him. Of his brothers, only the Duke of Kent had been a regular visitor, and when in 1934 he married the beautiful Princess Marina of Greece, he came less frequently. The only other member of his family who was often at the Fort was his cousin Lord Louis Mountbatten, great-grandson of Queen Victoria and son of Prince Louis of Battenberg, who had been First Sea Lord when the First World War broke out but was compelled to retire because of his German background. Mountbatten had gone into the navy, but—as Wallis, who knew the species well from her first marriage as well as from encountering it in London, was interested to find—he had refused to conform to it. Like Edward, he was interested in the whole range of problems of his time and class, from unemployment to polo strategy. "He bombarded the Prince with pamphlets, books and clippings all carefully annotated or underlined and all urgently commended to the Prince's attention." But he was a serving naval officer and was kept busy by his work.

The Prince, too, had made few close friends—apart from Duff Cooper—among people who were, or might become, politically significant. Anthony Eden, the youthful and popular Foreign Secretary, was invited once or twice to the Fort, but he was too immersed in his work to provide the kind of light-hearted company that Edward enjoyed. For similar reasons, influential men from industry or the professions whom the Prince met and admired on his royal round rarely moved into the inner circle of his acquaintances. Temperamentally, he was better able to make contact with people than to keep it. His interest in new ideas attracted people to him, but before they had become part of his life and he of theirs, some fresh idea would remove him to new company. His circle of close friends therefore had remained small, and it consisted mainly of congenial companions who could be relied upon to join in the fun when he was released from his duties—to go dancing at a night club or to relax at the Fort.

The people whom the Prince had found the most time for, who "spoke the same language," were of a type not uncommon in the years between the wars, though less often encountered today. They were not conventional—that would have bored him—but their unconventionality was predictable. There was Colonel Rivers Worgan, who, Edward thought, "might have galloped straight out of the pages of Kipling." He was always immaculately turned out and, "if a trifle pompous, was an eight-goal polo player and a very brave soldier." There was the dashing Irishman Captain Edward Dudley ("Fruity") Metcalfe, "gay, handsome . . . another bold and accomplished horseman," whose sympathy and understanding on the Indian tour so impressed the Prince that he took him on as equerry. Fruity, who was eventually to be best man at his wedding, shared in Edward's eyes the trait that had endeared Wallis to him. "Of all my friends," Edward was to write in *A Family Album*, "it was he alone, with his informal and expansive Irish nature, who behaved towards me, not as though I were a prince, but as though I were an ordinary human being like himself." He recalled as typical of his friend's easy familiarity—which some people found shocking—an incident on the hunting field when Fruity, finding his matchbox damp, "light-heartedly struck a match on the sole of my boot—an impulsive and characteristic gesture which amused and delighted me."

Edward's closest associate was the "gallant and charming Grenadier Guardsman, Brigadier-General G.F. Trotter." Usually known simply as "G," he had lost an arm in the Boer War but had not allowed that to dampen his zest for life and for good living. He became the Prince's constant companion "in the things pertaining to the lighter side of my princely role . . . I suppose I learned from 'G' Trotter that life should be lived to the full."

There had been a few exceptions. Edward Grigg, later Lord Altrincham, was likewise a former Grenadier Guardsman with a good war record, but he was also a scholar, a journalist and an expert on imperial affairs. Yet most of the Prince's close friends were what would have been dismissed by the intellectuals of the time as "hearties"—hard-riding, hard-drinking and, to anybody who did not share their interests, distinctly hard-going. To the Prince, who could admire intellectual capacity but did not feel any desire to live with it, their tireless undemanding bonhomie was comforting. But in a crisis such as this, the amount of help they could give would obviously be limited. Nor could much be expected of most of the friends he and Wallis had later attracted around them, many of them Americans. They were more sophisticated and more intelligent, but they were not versed in constitutional niceties.

COURTIERS

The first place that a king would normally expect to find allies would be in his court. Edward made no serious effort to enlist them there, and rightly. His courtiers appear to have made a conscientious effort in the early part of his reign to adapt to him: according to the Aga Khan, everyone at court insisted that Edward "had it in him to be the greatest king in the history of our country." But it may be that they knew this was the Aga Khan's opinion and were tactful enough not to attempt to disabuse him. The chasm that lay between them and the new King was too great to be spanned, and the first action of his reign made it clear that he was not greatly concerned to attempt the feat. His father had kept the Sandringham clocks half an hour fast. As soon as he died, Edward had them put back to Greenwich mean time.

The reason the Sandringham clocks had been put forward was that Edward VII had found it a good way to make the most of the few hours of winter light, for shooting—a do-it-yourself form of daylight-saving to which he had been introduced by a county neighbor, who liked to ensure that guests were at their appointed places in time to make the maximum use of what little daylight there was. To Edward VIII, who had little patience with such devices and who realised the confusion they could cause, there seemed no point in perpetuating the practice. Nor was there, but the abruptness with which the tradition was broken suggested that he was indulging an old promise to himself to make it clear from the start that things were going to be done *his* way. The Archbishop of Canterbury recorded the putting back of the clocks in his diary: "I wonder," he speculated, "what other customs will be put back also!"

Very soon, rumour began to spread of disaffection in the court. It was alleged—Alan Hodge and Robert Graves recalled, in their history of the thirties, *The Long Week-End*—"that he was impatient of dull functions, and had even, on occasion, by ordering the drastic curtailment of a musical programme, hurt the feelings of the loyal performers. And how insensate it had been to remove from Windsor

Great Park the herd of royal goats that had pastured there for generations, and confine the poor creatures to a paddock at the Zoo!" For his part, Edward was irritated by the way even his most modest innovations were met by the court functionaries—as he complained to Wallis, over their evening cocktails at her flat—with unimaginative opposition.

The courtiers naturally did not put the reasons for their opposition into words, except, presumably, in private. But their attitude was understandable. They had been deeply involved with the monarchy as it had existed in the reign of George V. The resounding success of his technique of kingship appeared to them convincing proof that it was the right approach, and they believed that Edward, when he had thrown off his juvenile habits, would realize its value. They felt it was important, therefore, not to give him his head in the early days, in the hope that as soon as he had become accustomed to the tight reign of custom and protocol, he would cease to chafe under it and in time come to respect it.

Edward simply had not the temperament to get around their opposition by guile. As during his father's lifetime he had taken himself away from the court, he had no idea how to handle his father's courtiers—little idea, in fact, how to handle even his own. A court is a massive vested interest. When it is threatened, the entire establishment is liable to react defensively with an instinctive appreciation that its members' livelihood—their whole way of life—is in danger. In such circumstances, Edward either had to declare war on his courtiers, which he was naturally disinclined to do, or to generate among them a new "King's party" that would have sufficient confidence in him to accept his lead. But this would have required time, patience and subtlety. Edward had no subtlety and little patience. Nor was he prepared to spend much time away from Wallis.

Often what he was doing was "right" so far as he was concerned —part of his plan to knock the stuffiness out of the monarchy. But in trying to do this he sometimes managed to alienate even those who might have been brought around to his side. In the course of the *Nahlin* cruise, for example, the King accepted an invitation to dine with the Earl of Dudley in a small garden café in Athens. His equerry, Aird, had to think of the repercussions if somebody chose to make an anti-monarchist demonstration—which in the disturbed state of Greek politics at the time seemed only too likely, as the

Greek king had but recently returned to the throne. Aird begged Wallis to intervene. Edward dismissed his objections "in the airiest manner," and what she remembered as a "really embarrassing situation" ended with the rest of the party going to the café while Aird dined alone on the *Nahlin*. As it happened, Aird's alarm proved to have been unnecessary, but it may not have been unfounded, and the reference to Edward's "airiest manner" is revealing. By this time, tact was ceasing to rate high in the list of Edward's qualities.

It was much the same with his attitude to what he wore. By later standards he was usually only being sensible, but sometimes the parading of unconventionality was embarrassing to his companions. Edward, after all, could ill-afford at this point to give any additional impression that he was going to bring the monarchy into disrepute. As he needed allies around him if his plans were to be given time to mature, he could not afford to alienate his courtiers unnecessarily. This did not mean that he must give way to them. It meant simply that he must go out of his way to convince them that what he did was for sensible reasons, so that even if they were not persuaded by the arguments they would at least remain certain of his motives. But Edward failed to realize the importance of—to put it at its most pragmatic—humouring his court.

Over Sandringham, Edward showed a measure of shrewdness. Sandringham House in the county of Norfolk had been bought by the Prince Consort for his eldest son. Architecturally, like most of the royal residences, it was undistinguished, but the shooting on the estate was excellent, and it exerted a powerful attraction on some members of the royal family. According to Neville Williams' *Royal Residences of Great Britain*, George V used to refer to "Dear old Sandringham, the place I love better than anywhere else in the world," but the remark "could have been made equally well by his father or his second son."

Not, though, by his first son. Whatever happy memories Edward had had of the place from his childhood had been banished during his father's reign. It was at Sandringham, he felt, that his father, in his war with the twentieth century, had won his most convincing victory. In any case the Fort was now too well-established in Edward's affections to brook such a rival. But the upkeep of Sandringham was extremely expensive, and he had no desire to squander his income unnecessarily. How, then, to reduce this drain on his resources without giving offence? He hit upon the idea of asking his brother the Duke of York to make a survey, with the aim of finding ways to cut down running costs. It was a shrewd move because the Duke, much as he loved Sandringham, relished a task that taxed his abilities as a landowner. He approached it realistically, and the resulting report, according to Sir John Wheeler-Bennett, was "a remarkable example of clarity and common sense, which would have done credit to his great-grandfather, the Prince Consort." On the basis of the report, reforms were put in hand, and those who suffered from the squeeze could hardly blame the King, as it was his brother who had recommended them.

But they did blame the King. They knew, or guessed, that the squeeze would not have been applied without his prompting. And when it came to applying similar retrenchment policies to Balmoral, Edward was too impatient to adopt a similar technique. Perhaps he felt that the Sandringham proposals were insufficiently ruthless. More probably he was content to leave Sandringham to his brother's inquiry because he did not care for it. But Balmoral was another matter. He enjoyed spending part of the autumn there, and he was determined to make the changes he desired immediately, so that the place would be run to his satisfaction, not to the memory of his father's. He made changes in the staff and in the management of the estate without consulting the Duke of York, though the Duke was staying nearby, at Birkhall. "David only told me what he had done after it was over," the Duke complained in a letter to his mother, "which I must say made me rather sad. He arranged it all with the official people up there. I never saw him alone for an instant."

The changes might make the Duke, who loved Balmoral, feel sad. They made other people feel alarmed. Most of Edward's efforts to impose reforms and economies on the royal households were sensible enough. He reduced the number of staff canteens, he travelled with a greatly reduced retinue, he preferred to sleep in a simple bed rather than a four-poster. Many of the changes, too, were designed to save trouble for those who served him. But those who served him did not necessarily see it that way. They felt their livelihood threatened. When he dispensed with the old custom of the servants lining the Balmoral drive to greet him on arrival, it did not make them feel—as he thought it would—that he was being considerate, because he failed to put it across that this *was* the reason. The assumption was that he wished less formality, which might mean that he would soon be able to dispense with the services of some old retainers.

The new informality, too, did not always mean less work. It could mean innovations, such as Wallis' "contribution to the traditional grandeur of Balmoral"—the introduction of the three-decker toasted sandwich as a late-supper item, after the movies. This proved very popular with the guests, but, as she admitted, it "hardly endeared the new reign to the household staff." Late suppers were a minor irritant, but this was a time when the King could not afford to make any more enemies. Court gossip travels fast.

The fact, too, that Edward so obviously did not care for Buckingham Palace did not pass unnoticed. He had allowed his mother to stay on there after George V's death, but during the summer she moved to Marlborough House, and he no longer had the excuse to stay away. He took up formal residence in the palace after his return from Balmoral, but without enthusiasm. "Buck House," as it had come facetiously to be known, was another of George IV's contributions to posterity, and perhaps the least appealing. For a bachelor not much interested in court ceremonial, it was like living in a museum. The "dank, dusty smell" that he associated with the building still pervaded it. He jibbed at occupying his father's old rooms, moving instead into the suite normally kept for visiting royalty. In *A King's Story* he claimed that he had a presentiment at the time that he "might not be there very long," and he continued to feel that he did not belong there. If buildings can create moods, Buckingham Palace could be claimed as an ally by the forces that were now combining to thrust him from his throne.

If the changes that Edward made had been simply the product of a reforming or innovating mind, his courtiers might have put up with them, reflecting that George V had done things his way and that the new King was entitled to his own ideas. But this was not the impression that some of them received. They read into what was happening not so much an alteration as a disintegration. Under George V, the court's movements, its ceremonial, its protocol, even its relaxations were fixed and largely immutable. The further that court life was removed from what was going on outside, the more important it seemed to the King to preserve it. And the astonishing culmination of George V's reign, the jubilee, seemed to be proof that he had been right. It followed that what Edward was doing was wrong.

Even if Edward had gone about it more tactfully, it is improbable that he could have persuaded his courtiers of the need for drastic changes. They were too set in their ways. The official retiring age for court dignitaries was sixty, but King George had liked to keep his old friends around him, and he had ignored it—some were over seventy. The result was that when Edward came to the throne the court was still run almost entirely by men of George's generation, tastes, and habits of mind. In ordinary circumstances, a new king could be expected to want to keep on tried and trusted court functionaries at least until he has settled in. But Edward realized that his father's courtiers were incapable of changing their ways. It would be useless, and painful, to try to make them. And on July 16, the magazine *News Review* revealed that the King, "determined to have a modern Court around him," was replacing the old guard by men "whose ages average 20 years less than those of retiring officials."

The most important of the courtiers was the King's private secretary. Lord Wigram was sixty-three and totally identified with George V. He had first encountered George as his ADC on the Indian tour of 1905, joining his staff five years later as deputy to the then private secretary, Lord Stamfordham, whom he succeeded on his death in 1931. The fact that Wigram had been content with the subordinate position for a quarter of a century suggested he was a man of loyalty and devotion, but not of any originality of mind. He and his colleagues had helped to mould court life into the pattern enjoyed by George V, and they had not noticed how fossilized it had become. Obviously he would not have fitted into the new style demanded by Edward. In any case, the death of King George had been a heavy blow to him. So Edward cast around for a successor.

He needed two successors. After the death of the Keeper of the Privy Purse the previous year, Wigram had taken over his functions, too, though ordinarily both were full-time jobs. The Keeper of the Privy Purse was the royal manager and accountant, and for this post Edward selected Major Ulick Alexander, another product of Eton and the Guards, but with the requisite qualifications from a subsequent business career. It proved an admirable choice. Alexander was to retain Edward's confidence in the closing stages of the crisis.

The other choice was to prove less happy. A king's private secretary, as Edward was to recall, "is a personage of higher order than the current usage of the term might imply." Apart from being the King's chief adviser and general assistant, it had come to be accepted that the private secretary had a civil-service function. He was the normal channel of communication between the King and the government. It followed that the man chosen should have the confidence of both. The King's wish was to have Sir Godfrey Thomas, who had been his private secretary when he was Prince of Wales, for over fifteen years: "He had been with me on all my official overseas tours; he had shared my princely vicissitudes and had in no small measure contributed to the technique with which I had conducted my duties as Prince of Wales." But Thomas felt he did not have the necessary experience of the court, and instead he recommended Major Alexander Hardinge, the son of a former viceroy of India, who had been one of George V's assistant private secretaries since 1920.

Hardinge had the background and the qualifications, but—as with Wigram—he had been long in the old court, and this might have been a warning that he would not fit easily into the new. "The appointment," Edward was to admit in *A King's Story*, "was a fateful one, as events soon to unfold will show." Hardinge had arranged the confrontation with Baldwin, and this also might have given the King due notice where Hardinge's sympathies lay. Of all the people around him, the King most needed a private secretary in whom he could confide and in whom he could trust. Hardinge was a simple, honorable man, dedicated to do his duty as he saw it. But he saw that duty as to the monarchy, not to the monarch, and this impelled him onto Baldwin's side.

The changes in the court reduced the average age and held out promise that it could become less stuffy, but they did not bring in people upon whom Edward could rely to stand by him. When it dawned on them that Mrs. Simpson was not his mistress, which they could have accepted, but the woman whom he was proposing to marry—and in due course, perhaps, make his Queen—some of them were deeply shocked. No doubt they had heard some of the current scandal about the King's circle, and perhaps they discounted it. But as soon as they began to suspect the King's intentions, they began to think that the scandal must have been right—that Mrs. Simpson must be a designing woman who had got the King in her clutches. As few of them really knew her, they had no means of realising that this was unfair. Nor, even if they had met her, and liked her, did they necessarily sympathize. Even if not deliberately, they felt, she was nevertheless making a fool of the King, who really ought to see that a twice-divorced woman, with two husbands still living, was simply not a suitable person to be his companion in public, let alone his wife.

CABINET MINISTERS

Another potential source of allies was the Cabinet. In theory at least, with Baldwin's political position so shaky, some of his colleagues who were anxious to get rid of him might be disposed to back the King, if by doing so they could help themselves to power. If any such idea presented itself to him, though, he must soon have put it out of his mind. Less promising material for enrolment as a group of King's friends, on this issue, could hardly have existed.

Ramsay MacDonald

The senior member of Baldwin's cabinet was his predecessor as Prime Minister, Ramsay MacDonald, but by this time he was taken seriously by nobody. "That sheep in sheep's clothing," the *Daily Express* columnist "Beachcomber" had dubbed him—echoing a Max Beerbohm quip—while he was still Prime Minister. With his departure from office his mind, which had long shown signs of wandering in his parliamentary speeches, began to soften. "He floats around like a wraith," Baldwin told Tom Jones in May 1936. "He held on as Prime Minister till the Jubilee, and will hold on now as Lord President till the Coronation. I have heard of carrying on with a sack of flour fastened to your back; Ramsay is an eiderdown round my head."

Even if MacDonald had surprised everybody by recovering full possession of his faculties, he would not have been tempted to take Edward's side. He had been deeply grateful to King George V for his efforts to help the Labour government when it first took office, and he had adored the whole court paraphernalia of uniform and protocol. King George had also been largely instrumental in bringing about the national government of 1931 and keeping MacDonald at its head. The remark MacDonald made to his Chancellor of the Exchequer, Philip Snowden, after it had been arranged—"Tomorrow every Duchess in London will be wanting to kiss me"—indicated not weary cynicism, but relish at the prospect. Nuisance he might be, but Baldwin could count on him in any contest with King George's scapegrace son.

Neville Chamberlain

Baldwin's second-in-command was Neville Chamberlain. In certain ways, Chamberlain was by this time almost as influential, at least in the Cabinet, as Baldwin himself. The reins of administration had been left largely in his hands. It would not have been easy, had the two men fallen out, for Baldwin to resume control. Chamberlain's attitude, therefore, would be important.

Neville was the son of Joseph Chamberlain—one of the most influential politicians of his time, even if the highest honours eluded him—and the half-brother of Austen Chamberlain, who had come even nearer to the premiership than his father, though in the end it had eluded him, too. Beside them, Neville had seemed insignificant. He did not even attempt, as a young man, to enter Parliament. Instead, his father sent him out to further the family's business interests, as a sisal-grower in the Bahamas.

It proved an unfortunate venture. Neville knew nothing about sisal, nothing about the Bahamas, and nothing about the market. But he threw himself into the work with energy, and his letters continued to exude bland confidence, even in the face of accumulating evidence that the scheme was not prospering. Gradually, the realization was forced on him that the project was an utter failure and that much capital had been squandered uselessly because of his want of judgment. He had undertaken a task for which he was unfitted, and he had refused to recognize that unfitness until it was too late.

He returned to Birmingham and local politics, over which his family still exerted masterful control. Impressed more by his name than by his reputation, Lloyd George appointed him Director-General of National Service in 1916. In this post, too, he was a failure, and he soon resigned. Nothing could have seemed less likely, at this time, than that he should be on the verge of a successful political career. But two years later, at the age of forty-nine, he became a Member of Parliament. When the party split, he broke with his half-brother to follow Bonar Law, who rewarded him with office, and in the Baldwin administration of 1923, he became

Chancellor of the Exchequer. Again, it was a tribute to his name rather than to his talents, but politically he had arrived.

Neville made a reputation in his own right in the second Baldwin administration. The disparaging verdict attributed sometimes to Churchill, sometimes to Birkenhead, that Chamberlain "would have made a good lord mayor of Birmingham—in a lean year," was unjust. He made an efficient Minister of Health. It now became clear that the earlier failures were not due to any lack of ability, but to the fact that it had been misplaced. Anything that could work, he could make work smoothly. It was simply that both the earlier projects had been basically unworkable.

Finding him so able an administrator, Baldwin began to delegate more and more to him, so that by 1930 he was beginning to be considered for the succession. He was even tempted to claim it when Baldwin appeared to be on the point of resignation. But when Baldwin recovered his authority, Chamberlain was content to serve in the national government—as Chancellor of the Exchequer, again —and await his next opportunity. Gradually he established an ascendancy over the Cabinet second only to Baldwin's—in day-to-day matters, greater.

In some ways, Chamberlain's early career had had a curious resemblance to Baldwin's. Both had been businessmen of no particular ability who had entered politics late in life with no substantial expectations, and both had succeeded suddenly and surprisingly. The resemblance ended here. Baldwin's life had kept him close to what he might have described, and probably often did, as the heart of England. He was prepared to take his time from its pulse beat. Chamberlain's experience had shown him that his talents lay in administration, with efficiency as his guide. Baldwin, it could be said, liked to give the people what he thought they wanted, Chamberlain what he thought they should receive.

Chamberlain was an admirable man for his ministerial colleagues to bring their difficulties to. He would go into the matter, Sir John Simon recalled, "as though it was his personal problem, test it at every point, listen in a business-like fashion to what one had to say, and then state his conclusion with the finality of a general manager conducting a company's affairs." But outside company affairs, Chamberlain lacked vision. More important, he lacked humility. Before he returned from the Bahamas he had blamed himself for the failure of the venture, but this was something that he found increasingly difficult to do as he grew older. His senior ministerial colleagues, Baldwin and MacDonald, were to his way of thinking inefficient bumblers. He had little confidence in most of his junior colleagues and less in the leaders of the Opposition. By the middle thirties he had become consumed with political vanity: he could not recognize when he was wrong.

Chamberlain's part in the Hoare-Laval affair is revealing. When the news of the Hoare-Laval pact was leaked, Chamberlain's first instinct was to accept it, and it was he, more than Baldwin, who held the Cabinet together behind Hoare. When Duff Cooper came to explain to Chamberlain on behalf of some of the younger members of the government that they felt Hoare should be asked to resign, Chamberlain replied with some hauteur—according to his biographer, Iain Macleod—"that to demand a colleague's resignation in his absence would be unprecedented and improper and that, since the whole Cabinet had accepted responsibility for the Hoare-Laval pact, the House would condemn it now for making a scapegoat of the Foreign Secretary."

This attitude, Macleod claimed, showed that "his loyalty to his friend burned brightly as the shadows fell." It burned brightly only so long as there seemed a chance of the government's surviving without his friend being ditched. But at this point Lord Halifax, to whose opinions his Cabinet colleagues attached weight, intervened. Might not the moral force of the government suffer if Hoare stayed on? Chamberlain suggested a compromise: Hoare should offer his resignation, and they could refuse to accept it. His colleagues were unenthusiastic. They urged Chamberlain to make Hoare lie the government out of its perilous situation by disowning his own plan and saying it had all been a mistake. This Chamberlain did. His loyalty to his friend was by this time burning very low indeed. Hoare tendered his resignation, the government accepted it, and Chamberlain carried on as if nothing untoward had happened.

At each stage of the negotiations, Chamberlain's bland self-assurance manifested itself in the assumption that his stand at that particular moment was the only possible one, politically and morally. It would never have occurred to him afterward to make a comparison between his own arguments—to contrast his initial assertion that the sacrifice of Hoare would be impossible and absurd with his later decision that the sacrifice must be made in order to keep the government in office. No doubt Chamberlain could have produced retrospective excuses for his shifts, just as Hoare later did in his own case. But Chamberlain did not realise that there was any need to justify himself.

Again like Baldwin, different though they were, Chamberlain was not deliberately equivocal. He simply lacked insight, as Anthony Eden soon found. As Minister in charge of League of Nations affairs, Eden had been shocked by the Hoare-Laval pact and relieved when it was repudiated, especially when, as a reward for his resistance to the temptation to embarrass the government by resigning, he succeeded Hoare as Foreign Secretary. And he was gratified to find that Chamberlain appeared to have been converted from his earlier cynicism: His support of Eden's arguments for maintaining sanctions was "consistent and firm."

By the early summer of 1936, however, it was clear that the policy of limited sanctions—no embargo on oil, no closure of the Suez Canal—had failed. To Eden, this made it all the more important to preserve the League's united front. Sanctions must sooner or later be abandoned, but the aim should be to see that they were abandoned collectively, to prevent the damage that would obviously be done to the League if countries began to renege individually. This was the policy that Eden was preparing to carry out when Neville Chamberlain made a speech to a Conservative political club, on June 10, in which he described continued sanctions as "the very midsummer of madness." "Is it not apparent," he went on, "that the policy of sanctions involves, I do not say war, but a risk of war? . . . Is it not also apparent from what has happened that, in the presence of such a risk, nations cannot be relied upon to proceed to the last extremity until their vital interests are threatened?"

Coming from Chamberlain—who had freely ridiculed the Peace Pledgers because they supported collective security only so long as it did not lead up to the ultimate risk, war—this was a specious argument. Even if it had been justified, the timing, as Eden complained, was explosive. It turned Italy's defeat of the League into a humiliation. Chamberlain did not have the excuse that more had been read into his words than he intended. He knew what he was doing. According to his diary, he did it deliberately, "because I felt that the party and the country needed a lead, and an indication that the Government was not wavering and drifting without a policy.

. . . I did not consult Anthony Eden, because he would have been bound to beg me not to say what I proposed."

By 1936, therefore, Chamberlain's political image was already established, and it was not attractive. "His public personality," Francis Williams recalled, "and indeed, except in his most intimate relationships, his private one also, was frigid and condescending. Contemptuous of emotion, which he thought of as sentimentality, and of the half-educated fools with whom he felt himself surrounded, he gave the impression of being painstaking, methodical, but unhumourous and implacable in his dislikes, arrogant and narrow-minded. . . . It was his misfortune that even when he most wished to be amiable, his face seemed to wear a sneer." Sneer is too strong a word—on the newsreels, at least, his expression was more often one of self-satisfaction rather than of contempt for others. But the impression given was disagreeable.

In his *Inside Europe*, first published in 1936, John Gunther expressed the then common view of Chamberlain, that he was a reactionary, a distruster of idealism, who commanded "the complete confidence of the plutocracy in the City." He had won the City's confidence as an administrator, and having won it, Chamberlain assumed that his ability as an administrator qualified him for the highest office. Sir John Simon, singling out "steady persistence—some would say obstinacy" as the strong element in his character, explained that Chamberlain "had so often found the right solution, in municipal affairs or at the Treasury, by the hard labour of his own brains, that he was inwardly confident that world problems would in the end yield to his treatment."

A man who was so convinced of his destiny, his rightness, and his rectitude, who admired efficiency above all other political virtues, and who looked forward to succeeding Baldwin as soon as and as smoothly as could be arranged was unlikely to be sympathetic toward the King. In any case, Chamberlain was a Unitarian, and less tolerant than most of that faith—Gunther thought him as "orthodox as a Bishop." The prospect of the King consorting with, let alone marrying, a twice-divorced woman was repugnant to him. At the beginning of the new reign, Chamberlain expressed anxiety in his diary: "I do hope," he wrote, "he pulls up his socks and behaves himself now he has such heavy responsibilities, for unless he does he will soon pull down the throne."

Even more irritating to Chamberlain than the King's private life was his failure to conform to the pattern of duty established by his father. Being so deeply concerned that the machinery of state should run smoothly, Chamberlain craved reliability and assiduous attention to detail above all other monarchical virtues, and more than any other member of the Cabinet he resented the slack way the King performed some of his chores and the impression he gave that he might break away from strict constitutional precedent. In particular, he was worried at the way Edward looked at industry —as if it were, or should be, a kind of social service. This was a notion to which Chamberlain could have been sympathetic only if it were made abundantly clear that the service was to be provided by the capitalists in their capacity as employers of labour, not supplied or interfered with by the government. Fear that the King would adopt a different attitude made Chamberlain likely to be a much more dedicated opponent than Baldwin if trouble between the King and his ministers arose.

But it was also very desirable for Chamberlain's peace of mind that if a constitutional or political crisis arose, it should not be of a kind that might conceivably let in his potential rivals outside the Cabinet. His brother Austen might now be discounted, but Churchill, Lloyd George, Amery and other critics of the government had been attracting dissidents. While Baldwin was away during the summer of 1936, Chamberlain was careful to consolidate his position so that when, early in October, he took the premier's place at the annual Conservative Party conference he was able to boast in his diary that its main result appeared to be "a general acceptance of my position as heir apparent." He was naturally anxious that nothing should happen that might jeopardise the transition to the premiership, which could be expected after the coronation, but the lesson of his father and his brother, both of whom had been denied the highest office, was there to remind him of the uncertainty of the political game.

Still more important, he knew Baldwin's guile. When in 1931 the party organizers had expressed their dissatisfaction with Baldwin's leadership, it had been Chamberlain who carried their message to Baldwin. When he heard of Baldwin's decision to resign, Chamberlain, confident of obtaining the succession, himself resigned the chairmanship of the party organization—only to find he had been outmanoeuvered: Baldwin had decided to stay. In in-fighting of this kind, Chamberlain was no match for his leader. His wisest political course, therefore, would be to back Baldwin—to give him what support he needed, and if possible to push him into decisive action, but to remain as his ally. In such circumstances, the King could expect no sympathy or help from Neville Chamberlain.

Sir John Simon

Of the other members of the Cabinet, the most important by both seniority and experience in office was Sir John Simon. He had the further claim to consideration that he was the leader of the National Liberals, the branch of the Liberal Party that had gone over to the national government and stayed over when their former colleagues, under Sir Herbert Samuel, left. The "Simonites" were already fast becoming indistinguishable from Tories. It was in the Conservative Party's interest to keep them that way and not to do anything that might lead them to regret their decision to break away again. So Simon's susceptibilities had to be watched.

A lawyer by profession, Simon had entered parliament as a Liberal in 1904—lucky in his timing, as at the general election two years later the Conservatives suffered their catastrophic defeat. He showed himself a good parliamentarian, and in 1910 he was made Solicitor General, a post that carried an automatic knighthood. It was a distinction that, he later claimed, he would have preferred to dispense with, because he felt it was attached to the office rather than to the merit of its holder. The post of Solicitor General, too, did not greatly attract him, for fear that it might lead to his being "typed" as a law officer. He had never disguised the fact that the legal profession was for him simply a stepping-stone to a political career, but he found that his profession was a positive handicap. When David Maxwell-Fyfe was elected to the Commons for the first time in 1935, Simon told him, "Remember this is the only legislative assembly in the world where lawyers as such are unpopular," and Maxwell-Fyfe found that he was right.

For a while, though, Simon could not break away. In 1913, he succeeded the Attorney General when he was promoted to be Lord Chief Justice. But in the first wartime coalition government, when Simon was actually offered the Lord Chancellorship—the highest legal office in the government, with an automatic peerage attached—he turned it down, because it would be "a removal, at too early an age, from the centre of parliamentary life to a bourne from which no politician returns." Instead, he was appointed Home Secretary. He was only forty-two. If ever there was a Prime Minister in the making, it was surely Simon.

By the following year, however, he was out of office, and he was to stay out for nearly fifteen years. He had resigned rather than support the bill introducing conscription. With uncharacteristic humility, he was later not merely to admit he had been wrong, but also to point out why he had been wrong. His argument had been that conscription would not bring in enough men to compensate for the disadvantages—a view that the Minister of National Service in the later stages of the war was to accept: "On balance, the imposition of military conscription added little if anything to the effective sum of our war effort." But what Simon had failed to grasp was the psychological effect, "alike on our allies and on the men in the field, who were hard pressed, and their anxious relatives at home." The allies, who had imposed conscription earlier, felt that the lack of it in Britain showed the British were not really trying—a theory gratefully seized upon by German propagandists, with their re-iterated theme that "England will fight till the last Frenchman." As for the men at the front—and, still more, their relatives at home— they were easily roused by stories of the slackers evading their duty and holding down cushy jobs for the duration. It was to fulfil this psychological need that the legislation had to be introduced. He had been wrong, Simon admitted, to oppose it, "and such mis-takes have to be paid for at a heavy price. In my case, it meant not merely the abandonment of office, but a long setback in my political career." By 1918 he was out of the Commons as well—as a follower of the former Liberal leader, Asquith, he did not benefit from the Lloyd George "coupon" awarded to those who supported his coalition. And though he soon regained a seat, it was only to rejoin the now small Liberal parliamentary party in opposition.

Simon might have expected to gain prestige by his demonstration of his integrity in resigning, but not everybody believed that his explanation of his motives was the correct one. In the view of Asquith's successor, Herbert Samuel, Simon had also been influenced by his belief that conscription would be extremely unpopular, with unfortunate consequences for the minister who would be most closely identified with the stern measures that would be required to enforce it—himself. Simon had the unfortunate capacity to make members of all parties, but particularly his own, mistrustful of him, and his political movements in the next few years confirmed their suspicions. With the Socialists coming up on the Liberal left, he moved steadily rightward, eventually leading a breakaway movement within the party to join the Conservatives in opposition to the second Labour government. When the national government was formed in 1931 the Simonites—as they were called to distinguish them from the Samuelites—joined it, extracting the prize of the Foreign Secretaryship for their leader. He had previously, by his own description, been a "full-blooded old-fashioned Free Trader." Now he became a protectionist, a change of policy that enabled him to remain in the national government when the Samuelites left. That Simon had convinced himself of the need for protection—that he was not simply lured by the love of office—even his former colleagues reluctantly conceded, but it did not make them more fond of him that he had been able to change his mind so profitably.

No politician of his day aroused more dislike. Naturally the Samuelites resented him, as a turncoat and a time-server, and Lloyd George, who once described him as "lending one of his countenances to a measure," was also credited with the comment, "Simon has sat so long on the fence that the iron has entered his soul." Lloyd George could be savage, as well as playful. Many a better man, he said, than Simon had crossed the floor of the House, but none had left such a slimy trail of hypocrisy behind him. And he was far from being alone in this attitude. "Simon we knew as Sir John Snake," Kingsley Martin has recalled. When editor of the *New Statesman*, Martin once felt he had to delete from a profile of Simon a passage beginning, "Many of those who have shivered when he took their arm . . ." John Gunther's sketch of him in *Inside Europe* was little more than a collection of sour anecdotes about him, most of them the stock apocryphal stories that attach themselves to unpopular politicians. ("Simon, finding an acquaintance of long standing to be useful, came up to him, put his arm around his shoulders—and called him by the wrong Christian name.")

The explanation, Gunther thought, was that Simon, being an exceptionally shy man, lonely and anxious to be popular, was too afraid to offend people. To judge from Simon's autobiography, this is probably close to the truth. "If people have sometimes thought me frigid and unresponsive," he wrote, "there was an explanation from earlier fate"—his first wife had died giving birth to their only

son. He was not ambitious in the most ruthless sense of the term—
he did not sacrifice principles or colleagues to his overriding political
needs. But he was just too determinedly a career politician for
comfort, and too humourless to realize that what he meant as
bonhomie was regarded by those who suffered it as calculation.

It was this lack of any sense of humour that prevented him from
seeing that he had no chance of attaining his ultimate goal of the
premiership. In 1936 he could hardly claim, even to himself, that
he had been a striking success at the Foreign Office, before Samuel
Hoare had succeeded him. But he had worked his passage back into
the mainstream of politics, and once again the premiership seemed
a theoretical possibility. He was in his sixties, and although this was
no bar in itself, he knew he had to wait not merely for the retirement of Baldwin, which could hardly be long delayed, but also
of Chamberlain. But if chance or accident removed Chamberlain
from the succession—Simon must have felt—his prospects looked
quite good. Hoare had probably disqualified himself by the disastrous deal with Laval, and Eden was too young. That he should
be compelled to wait a little while longer would in any case have
caused Simon no concern. The fact that he was a National Liberal
rather than a Conservative was still against him, but presumably
time would blur that distinction—as indeed it was rapidly doing.

Simon, therefore, had every reason to keep his nose clean. And
apart from political calculation, neither by upbringing nor by
temperament could he be expected to have any sympathy with the
King in his predicament. He came of Welsh stock. His father was a
Congregationalist minister, and his grandfather was the deacon of
the local chapel, so he grew up in an atmosphere of nonconformist
piety. (Although Jewish in name and appearance he had no Jewish
blood, a fact that he felt constrained to publicize when he became
Foreign Minister, in case people should suspect his policies might be
affected by his racial sympathies.) It would have been a futile
waste of time for Edward even to try to win him over.

In reality, there was not the slightest chance of Simon's becoming
premier. The Conservatives preferred to have him on their side
of the House, for he could still be a formidable debater, and he
lent an air of experienced distinction to the front bench. He might
have been mistaken—the observant "Watchman" (Vyvian Adams,
a Conservative MP) noted in his *Right Honourable Gentleman*, a
study of the politicians of the thirties—for a bishop, or a banker,

even if he never quite looked the part of a statesman. But the Conservatives would never have tolerated him as leader. As Lloyd George had prophesied, they would hail with delight his criticism of his old friends: "They will applaud him. They will use him to the utmost—all his powers and all his gifts," but "when he ceases to be useful to them, they will fling him aside." Simon, though, could not bring himself to admit this, and while he remained hopeful, he would remain a Baldwin man.

Lord Halifax

Potentially the most influential member of the Cabinet, at least on an issue of this kind, was Edward Wood, Lord Halifax. There was nothing in his character or career to suggest that his influence would be exerted on behalf of the King. His family had been Yorkshire landowners for generations. His father was president of the English Church Union and a pillar of the Anglo-Catholic movement, to which the son was faithful: "His dedication to Anglo-Catholicism," his latest biographer, the second Lord Birkenhead, has claimed, "was far the most important side of his life."

At Oxford, his family background and skill in the hunting field marked him out for the highest office in Loders, a select club whose members frequently met to get drunk and then to hunt on foot, as a pack, whatever quarry presented himself—an aesthete was very welcome, particularly if his room could be sacked. But such sport was not for young Edward Wood. According to an earlier biographer, Alan Campbell Johnson, "Loders under Wood's regime was no longer merely convivial, but developed into a society of moral improvement. Its dinners every other Sunday had about them the aura of a Young Men's Christian Association." And one of his earliest friends was the future Archbishop of Canterbury, Cosmo Gordon Lang, who used to go on holidays with him and his family in Italy.

Eton, Oxford, a Fellow of All Souls . . . Halifax had the qualifications, and the manner: "a privileged, solemn, intellectual young man," in Francis Williams' description, "towering above his contemporaries from the lanky height of six foot five inches." He also had a lisp. His manner, though, as well as his height, gave the impression that he was above politics, and this had led in 1925 to his being sent to India as viceroy. In this capacity, although he did not achieve anything spectacular, he was a success. Little though he cared for Indian nationalism, he respected Gandhi's moral qualities, and Gandhi admired him, which helped to ease a situation that might otherwise have become explosive.

The difficulty was to know what to do with him after his return. A man of high principle who seems to be above politics can be a liability when quick and perhaps unscrupulous party political moves have to be made. But he showed himself pleasingly flexible. If Edward Halifax did not feel it was necessary to resign over the Hoare-Laval pact, other ministers need not feel guilty about their own conduct: "Halifax carried most weight," Chamberlain noted in his diary, "when he said that unless Sam went, the whole moral force of the Government would be gone." Halifax became a kind of barometer which ministers tapped when they wanted to make sure that a policy or an action would not prove embarrassing. Baldwin, particularly, who described him as "a man whose ideals and views in political life approximate most closely to my own," often drew comfort from consulting him.

What has remained uncertain is the extent to which Halifax was actually influential during the abdication crisis. But his biographers have been in no doubt that he played an important part. "His friendship with Stanley Baldwin," according to Birkenhead, "was of much comfort to the latter as he groped his way through the shoals and quicksands of the Abdication crisis." Campbell Johnson had earlier been even more emphatic: "It is fair to suggest that history may well adjudge that upon Halifax rested the ultimate responsibility, not merely in his constitutional capacity as the Leader of the House of Lords and Lord Privy Seal, but as the all-powerful middle man between Church and State, between Lambeth Palace and Downing Street, the trusted friend who gave shape and substance to Baldwin's advice to the King."

The very fact, though, that Halifax was Baldwin's trusted friend makes it harder to estimate his influence on events at this time. When a politician, particularly a Baldwin, is engaged in intricate constitutional manœuvers he is not always aware that he is being influenced. The comments of a political colleague, a wife, a friend, or a taxi-driver may be important—not in altering a decision, but in confirming that it is the correct one in the circumstances. To have influenced Baldwin, it was not necessary for Halifax to argue with him or even to talk to him: It was enough that Halifax should nod assent, or give it by silence. Had Halifax taken a very different line, such was his authority on matters pertaining to public morality that he would have been listened to with attention and respect. But as his views so largely coincided with Baldwin's, Baldwin may well have evolved his plan of campaign, and carried it out, without Halifax contributing anything except moral support.

Still, "Certain it is," Campbell Johnson concluded, "that Halifax and all that he represented, whether as a social, political or moral leader, was bleakly opposed to the new pretensions of the King and his Court. The resistance to King Edward's New Order significantly came first of all from Yorkshire, and it was sustained throughout by the landed gentry of the shires by High Churchmanship, and by the overwhelming mass of political 'Moderates'—all embodied in the ideals and position of the third Viscount Halifax."

Sir Thomas Inskip

Then there was a newcomer: Sir Thomas Inskip, Minister for the Co-ordination of Defence, an important-sounding title that failed to disguise the fact that its owner was one of the lowest-powered political figures of the day. Inskip had been a barrister, and not a particularly successful one, but he was likeable and well-connected —he had married an earl's daughter—and like Simon he had climbed the rungs of the law officers' ladder, becoming first Solicitor General, then Attorney General.

He was a large bumbling fellow who often looked as if he was about to fall over, and an occasional impediment in his speech helped to make him a mildly comic figure. But his modesty kept him generally popular in the House. It was assumed that in due course he would become Lord Chancellor, and that would be the respectable end of his political career—as indeed it was eventually to be, though he went on to become Lord Chief Justice. But in March 1936, the announcement that he had been given the important new Defence Department caused stupefaction to his political friends and foes alike. According to Malcolm Muggeridge, the news sent the House into uncontrollable laughter. "Cato," on the other hand—the author of *Guilty Men* ("Cato" was in fact three young journalists, Michael Foot, Peter Howard and Frank Owen)—thought that the laughter came from parliamentary officials and newspapermen when the appointment was posted up in the lobby. One aged correspondent fell off his chair in a faint, though "Cato" did not report whether this was attributable to the convulsions of laughter or the shock. And after first surmising that it must be a clerical error, an MP—Churchill, it was thought—remarked that there had been no similar appointment "since the Roman emperor Caligula made his horse a consul."

The reason the choice fell upon Inskip, according to Chamberlain, was that his appointment would create no jealousies. "He would excite no enthusiasm, but he would involve us in no fresh perplexities"—unlike Churchill, the obvious candidate for the post. John Gunther found that the stock explanation circulating was that Baldwin had gone to great pains to find someone for the job "even less brilliant than himself." Nobody was more astonished at the appointment than Inskip—a modest and delightful man, according to Robert Boothby. It simply had not occurred to him, he said, that he would be asked to undertake such a responsibility, and "nor did it ever occur to me—I can say this in all seriousness—that I would ever be able to discharge these duties even if they were offered to me." It was unfortunate that it also did not occur to him to refuse the proffered post. His modesty did not, apparently, extend so far.

Ludicrous though his appointment was, the fact that he had been thus elevated immediately led to speculation whether he might be the coming man in the Conservative Party. At the end of July, Lloyd George was actually tipping him to succeed Baldwin, on the ground that Neville Chamberlain was too old—only a couple of years younger than the premier. A poll of the Tory Party, Lloyd George estimated, would give Inskip eighty percent of the votes, and although Tom Jones thought it too high, he did not dismiss it as absurd, as he would have done a few weeks before.

Inskip, then, could not be altogether excluded from the King's calculations. But even if he turned out a force to be reckoned with, he could be relied upon to be on Baldwin's side. A devout churchman, puritanical in his leanings, he was president of the Lord's Day Observance Society, the Y.M.C.A., and the Church Pastoral Aid Society. If "Cato" is to be believed, he was known to his political antagonists as "that bum-faced evangelical."

Sir Kingsley Wood

One other member of the Cabinet may have played a more important part in the crisis than has been recognized. How important, though, is difficult to judge, because of the way in which he exercised his influence.

Evelyn Waugh's *Scoop*, first published in 1938, was to describe some of the celebrated foreign correspondents of the thirties, barely disguised by fictional names. One was "Wenlock Jakes," whose column was syndicated all over America. It was Jakes' habit to describe riots and revolutions from the safety of his hotel. On one occasion, when he had been sent to the Balkans to cover a revolution, he went by mistake to the wrong town. All was quiet there, but his story ("barricades in the streets, flaming churches, machine guns answering the rattle of his typewriter as he wrote, a dead child like a broken doll, spreadeagled in the deserted roadway below his window") was splashed in his newspaper. Under the impact of Jake's reporting, the local stock market collapsed, followed by mobilization, panic and mutiny. Revolution broke out, and Wenlock Jakes won the Nobel Prize for his harrowing descriptions of the carnage. In *Scoop* Wenlock Jakes was engaged on a treatise, whose nature Waugh indicated from time to time by quotations—for example, "the Archbishop of Canterbury who, it is well known, is behind Imperial Chemicals." And one of Jakes' assessments was that "the dominant member of the new Cabinet was colourful Kingsley Wood."

From the readers of *Scoop*, when it appeared, the idea of Kingsley Wood being either dominant or colourful would ordinarily have provoked only a snigger. To outward appearances he was an insignificant, bouncy little man with a high-pitched giggle. Somebody said of him that except for his glasses he would have been hard to distinguish from an animated verson of one of the stone cherubs so popular among Georgian architects. But precisely because he seemed no more than an amiable cypher, he had already managed to acquire more power than was realized, even by his own colleagues. Wenlock Jakes was not so ludicrously wrong as he seemed. Beneath the ebullient, boyish exterior a calculating political mind was at work.

Kingsley Wood had entered politics through the London County Council, in which he concerned himself with social-welfare problems, housing, pensions, and particularly health. He first attracted attention when he joined the movement to found the Health Ministry. Lloyd George approved, the ministry was established, and Kingsley Wood's reward for his services was a knighthood. In 1918

he entered Parliament, becoming private secretary to successive
Ministers of Health before achieving junior office in the ministry, as
its parliamentary secretary. Here he began to reveal talent in debate.
His touch, "Watchman" recalled, was "light and impudent—as comic
as a tickle, and far more damaging." More important, he won the
confidence of his minister, Neville Chamberlain, "the friend," according to Iain Macleod, to whom Chamberlain "would now increasingly turn."

In the national government, Kingsley Wood found himself in
the office of Postmaster General, not previously highly regarded but,
as it happened, becoming more important because this was the
period when the future of broadcasting became a controversial issue.
The relationship between Kingsley Wood and Sir John Reith, Director-General of the British Broadcasting Corporation, became the
subject of some amused speculation in private and occasional caustic
public comment. They worked together, "Watchman" thought, surprisingly well: "Double bass and high falsetto contrived a passable
harmony," and he thought some credit should go to Wood "for his
patient relationship with one who had the embarrassing reputation
of being a superman." The harmony was less apparent to Reith. The
comment that Wood's attitude "seemed to be determined by considerations of personal expediency," which occurs in Reith's biography, expressed a feeling that some of Wood's colleagues were
soon to share. But his ability as a minister was considered impressive
enough for him to be brought into the Cabinet, still as PMG, in
1933, and when Baldwin took over from MacDonald two years
later, Wood went back to his old Department of Health, this time as
minister.

With Baldwin leaving day-to-day administration increasingly
in Chamberlain's hands, Kingsley Wood now emerged as the government's chief "fixer"—or rather, he did *not* emerge, for he went
about his task so skilfully that his activities rarely attracted attention.
Eden, however, noticed them and recorded a number of examples in
his memoirs of the period, notably on the occasion when the possibility of holding staff talks with the French became an issue, following the German re-occupation of the Rhineland in March 1936.
Eden was grateful for the opportunity to do something that, he
thought, would restore French confidence in the Alliance. But when
he went to see the Prime Minister, before presenting the project
formally to the Commons, he found Baldwin anxious. Kingsley

Wood, Baldwin explained, had been around to warn him, "in characteristic fashion," that the staff talks "were unpopular on the Conservative back benches. 'The boys won't have it' was his verdict." Eden did not believe this. The intervention only spurred him to make a less diplomatically phrased, more vehement speech on the subject in the Commons than he would have otherwise attempted. He found the House sympathetic, the majority of Conservatives being fervent in support. Evidently Kingsley Wood had been experimenting with a gambit frequently employed by the practised fixer: he had been pretending to give a consensus of opinion while really giving his own—or, more probably, Chamberlain's.

That he would also share Chamberlain's views on the King was never in doubt. He was a political animal and knew where his future lay—with Chamberlain. (At least until Chamberlain was about to fall, in 1940: it was Wood who gave him the final push.) Colin Coote—later to be editor of the *Telegraph*—knew Wood, and liked him, but regarded him as an extremely barometrical politician" and in 1925 composed a verse about him:

> Kingsley would
> If he could
> But if he shouldn't
> Kingsley wouldn't!

Kingsley, too, was the son of a Wesleyan minister. He could not merely be numbered with certainty among the King's adversaries, he could also be expected to work energetically and effectively against the King. There is some evidence that he did.

Anthony Eden

Of the senior members of the Cabinet when Edward came to the throne, there was only one whom he could think of as a friend. Anthony Eden, the Foreign Secretary, as well as having actually spent week-ends at the Fort, was almost a contemporary—in fact he was a few years younger than the King.

If a blueprint had been made for a coming leader of the Conservative Party in the years between the wars, it would have come out looking like Anthony Eden. As many observers—including the indefatigable Gunther—noted, he had all the right qualifications:

educated at Eton and Oxford, a good war record, an attractive wife and two sons, as well as good-looking—albeit almost too conventionally. If more of his contemporaries had survived the war—two of his brothers were killed in it—he might not have made his mark politically as he was not at first ambitious in that direction. But young men of his stamp were hard to find in the 1920s, and the only early obstacle to a successful political career was his initial reluctance to embark on it. He entered Parliament in 1923, and three years later became Austen Chamberlain's parliamentary private secretary at the Foreign Office, a post he filled so satisfactorily that Baldwin recommended him for the parliamentary undersecretaryship in the national government. Eden's interest in the League of Nations during the next two years led to his becoming, in effect, a secretary of state for the League, and in 1935 *de jure* recognition was given to this status when he was brought into the Cabinet as Minister Without Portfolio in charge of League affairs.

It was not, as ministries go, a particularly responsible post. As events were soon to show, Eden was still very much at the mercy of Foreign Office decisions. Eden had been working to strengthen the League, and the Hoare-Laval pact terms, when they were disclosed, seemed to him to amount to betrayal. He was tempted to resign, but it was difficult to do so during Hoare's absence in Switzerland, because some reasonable explanation might be forthcoming—to have condemned Hoare without a hearing, too, would have seemed disloyal. In his memoirs, Lord Avon blames himself for allowing his loyalty to obscure his better judgment, but as things turned out, public opinion did not identify him with the pact or with the government's waverings after it was disclosed. When, on Hoare's resignation, Baldwin asked Eden to become Foreign Secretary, there was general satisfaction. Now, at last—it was felt—Britain would begin to honour her obligations to the League. No doubt this was why Baldwin appointed him. As Gunther noted, Eden's presence in the Cabinet was valuable to Baldwin because he was the darling of the pacifists and Peace Balloters, "so much so that his departure from the Government might easily have wrecked it." To a quite remarkable extent Eden had managed to win the confidence of his political opponents, and more important, of the public.

So when Edward came to the throne, a few weeks later, Eden was establishing himself not merely as Foreign Secretary, but as the white hope of the progressive-minded voters. If Edward had decided to cast around for a champion within the government he could not have chosen a better one—in theory at least—than his friend.

But from the start, the two men did not hit it off. There is a complication here as their divergences, though common gossip at the time (and since), are only touched upon in *A King's Story* and not mentioned at all in the Avon memoirs. But the reasons for them are clear, and the most important was their respective attitudes to the League of Nations.

Eden had worked in and for the League almost all his political life. As an institution, it was cosier than the United Nations was later to be. Foreign ministers and secretaries of state attended the regular meetings of its council, getting to know each other better, and they had more authority to take decisions. For a time in 1934 it really seemed to Eden as if the League was going to justify its founders' hopes: "Our authority and the League's stood higher than at any time in the National Government's life." Mussolini's invasion of Abyssinia had been a blow to the League's authority and the Hoare-Laval pact a blow to Britain's honour, but this damage could now be repaired, Eden felt, provided that past mistakes were recognized and admitted and that from this time on Britain fulfilled her obligations in the spirit, as well as to the letter, of the Covenant.

In *A King's Story* Edward was to reveal rather less interest in international affairs than could have been expected in view of his much-travelled existence, but his comments leave no doubt that he held strong opinions. Early in the 1930s he met King Gustav of Sweden on a visit to Scandinavia and was impressed by his analysis of the European situation. King Gustav dissected the Treaty of Versailles, "that hodge-podge of conflicting ideologies that neither reconciles the vanquished to accepting the status quo nor destroys their power to rise against it." Versailles, he concluded, "has sowed the whirlwind, and unless you can effect peaceful adjustments very quickly you will reap it. Your only other hope is to become strong, very strong." Edward passed these views on to Whitehall, where, he complained, "they were received with the complacency that passed for statesmanship in those days." In his autobiography he did not disclose which of the two courses urged by King Gustav he would have preferred at the time, but he appears to have favoured an amalgam of both. He would have liked to revise Versailles peacefully, but also, in case of accidents, to have Britain rearmed and strong. What he did not care for—he did not trouble to disguise his contempt for it—was a foreign policy based, as Britain's then theoretically was, on fidelity to the Covenant of the League of Nations.

Whereas to Eden the growing authority of the League in the early 1930s had been heartening, to Edward it was a cause for concern. He was perturbed, he recalled, over "whether our foreign policy should be based on realism or on the League of Nations"— that will-o'-the-wisp in pursuit of which his country "might foolishly neglect the strength that had been its sure recourse in the past against aggression." This was not an unusual point of view to hold, at the time. Many Conservatives shared it, though few cared to avow it so explicitly. But what Edward did not see was that the League, for all its deficiencies, could have worked if the British government had been more resolute in its backing. In any case, right or wrong, his views were not calculated to endear him to his Foreign Secretary, and it would have been out of character if Edward, holding his opinions as strongly as he did, did not express them forcibly.

Edward was not simply critical of the League as an institution. He actively disliked its intervention over Abyssinia, he objected strenuously to the adoption of sanctions against Italy, and he made no secret of where his sympathies in the conflict lay—with Mussolini. A year before, this would not have been unusual. Mussolini had had many admirers in Britain. He was the man, they believed, who had rescued the feckless Italians from the consequences of their political ineptitude, had drained the Pontine Marshes, had made the Italian trains run to time. And Edward had a personal reason to be grateful for this last achievement. When George V had fallen ill in 1928, Edward had been on safari in Tanganyika, and cables arrived urging him to return as quickly as possible. A cruiser brought him from Tanganyika to Brindisi. There he found Mussolini's private train waiting to take him across Europe, the journey being facilitated by personal orders from Il Duce to clear the tracks all the way to the Swiss frontier.

By 1936, though, there had been a change of feeling. As the reaction to the Hoare-Laval pact had first shown, sympathy for Haile Selassie, and disgust with Mussolini, was widely felt even by people who had cared little for the League. It was not just the fact that Abyssinia had been brought into the League under Italian sponsorship, nor that the invasion had been begun on trumped-up pretexts, whose spuriousness Mussolini scarcely troubled to conceal. The methods used in the campaign, such as the spraying of poison gas from the air, were of a kind that, it had been hoped, had been banished forever after 1918. The Fascist leaders, too, so far from trying to disguise them, actually boasted about them. One episode in particular caused revulsion the world over: a report by Vittorio Mussolini, the Duce's son, of a bombing raid from his pilot's-eye view—particularly the passage, "One group of horsemen gave me the impression of a budding rose unfolding as the bomb fell and blew them up. It was exceptionally good fun." If it were necessary to set a precise date upon which the British public abandoned its illusions about Italy, it was the day on which that report was first published and began to acquire its notoriety.

Sympathy for the Emperor increased when he was forced to leave his country. Cinema audiences were able to follow his movements in exile, and he made a profound impression by the sad dignity of his appearance before the League, when he was barracked by Italian newspaper correspondents. There was a general welcome for the proposal that he should be offered sanctuary in Britain, and when he was due to arrive, Eden suggested that it would be a popular gesture if the King were to receive him at Buckingham Palace.

Popular with whom? Edward sourly replied—"certainly not with the Italians!" It was important, he insisted, not to offend Mussolini any further, and Eden did not press the point. All that the King would concede was that his brother Harry, who had represented George V at Haile Selassie's coronation, should "call upon him at his hotel."

In *A King's Story,* as if to justify this rudeness, Edward went on to show he was not alone in his attitude. Stanley Baldwin, apparently, when surprised a few days later by the approach of Haile Selassie and his party on the terrace of the House of Commons, avoided them by the expedient of ducking around the tables, "hiding his face in his hands," to escape to his office—and there locking the door. But there was, Edward thought, "an important, if concealed, difference of opinion between my Ministers and me regarding Italy. They had embarked upon a futile policy of coercing Mussolini which had utterly failed in its purpose and was only forcing him into ever closer relations with Hitler." Aggression must be condemned, he agreed, but "I could see no point in indulging in half-measures that could not succeed. It was more important in my eyes at this stage to gain an ally than to score debating victories in the tottering League of Nations."

Again, in this view the King was not alone. Many influential people—including Robert Vansittart, the powerful civil servant who was at the head of the Foreign Office—held it. It was nonetheless mistaken, as events were quickly to show. Mussolini could no longer, at this stage, have been won back to the Alliance. His grandiose plans for conquest could be carried out only at the expense of of France (from whom he coveted Djibuti, Tunis, Corsica and even Savoy) and Britain (whose control of Egypt barred his path to the Middle East). Except in the Balkans—his squalid Albanian adventure was still to come—there was no way in which he could gratify his imperialist dreams except by conflict with the Allies.

Mussolini's disenchantment with the British dated, in fact, from some time before sanctions were imposed, and the form British attempts at appeasement took had only helped to enrage him— notably an offer by the British government to cede a strip of British Somaliland to Italy: "I am not," he said angrily in an interview, "a collector of deserts." The idea that he might be won back to the Alliance by appeasement was just as unreal as the idea of appeasing Hitler was later to prove.

The British public's hostility to Mussolini, though, was not based on awareness of his ambitions, which were never taken very seriously. It rested on the assumption that he had behaved despicably and on the well-founded belief that if the League of Nations could not act effectively to punish Italy for this act of aggression, the chances of its ever being able to act effectively again in any circumstances would become remote. And this was not a narrow Opposition view. It was shared by many Conservatives, including Churchill. The King, however, did not share it, and he made little attempt to disguise his contempt for those who did.

In *A King's Story*, Edward recalled that the arrangements for the *Nahlin* cruise led to a further brush with Eden, which left Eden apparently unmoved, but irritated the King. When his intention to have his holidays in a villa on the French Riviera had had to be abandoned, leading him instead to charter the *Nahlin*, he had the agreeably romantic notion that the party should board the yacht in Venice. Nothing could have suited Mussolini better than that the King of the nation that so recently had imposed sanctions on Italy should now present himself as a guest, but naturally the plan outraged the French, who were not sorry to have the chance to criticize *Albion perfide*—particularly when it was reported that Edward was going to see Mussolini during his stay.

This story was officially denied, but it was decided that the King had better not go to Italy, and the Foreign Secretary had to go around to explain why. The reason ought to have been self-evident: Edward's failure to appreciate the effect of his decision to visit Italy was the measure of his insensitivity in such matters. But he was not content to accept the Foreign Office's advice with good grace. He reacted like a petulant small boy, denied a promised treat. He was not quite sure, he recalled, which Eden feared more—"that I might be jeered by the Italians because my government had imposed sanctions, which would be bad for British prestige; or that I might be cheered by the same people as a friend of Italy, which would have offended the faithful supporters of the League of Nations."

Again, the sneer at the League: clearly the refusal to allow him to go to Venice touched on his vanity. A king on holiday, he appears to have thought, should not be subjected to such ridiculous restrictions. And the humiliation was still rankling when the time came for him to write his memoirs. He had to agree to switch embarkation to the Yugoslav port of Sibenik, and "in thus bending my plans to suit the expediencies of British foreign policy, I subjected myself to an indescribable night journey by train into Yugoslavia and a clanking and jolting such as I had never before experienced."

As if in an attempt to justify himself, Edward emphasised the fact that the *Nahlin* cruise was not all holiday. He was also to pay visits to Prince Regent Paul of Yugoslavia, King George II of Greece, Kemal Ataturk, dictator of Turkey, and King Boris of Bulgaria. But of these, only the visit to Ataturk was welcome at the Foreign Office, and in fact it was added to the royal itinerary at its request, after the original plans had been announced. The British government had no great respect for the slippery Paul and even less for George, who had only recently been brought back to the Greek throne after eleven years of exile spent in his London residence, Brown's Hotel. As he complained to Edward, George was King in name only: he had just been compelled to rubber-stamp General Metaxas' dictatorship by agreeing to dissolve the legislature and proclaim martial law. As for King Boris, he was a joke. One of his hobbies was engine-driving, and he allowed Edward to join him on the footplate and to toot the whistle of the royal train at crossings. Edward's last glimpse of him was at the frontier, arguing with his brother who should drive the train on the way back.

In any case, what Edward neglected to mention in his memoirs was that his decision not to keep the cruise simply as a holiday enraged Mussolini, who had decided that the Balkans should be kept within the Italian sphere of influence and who resented British meddling there. Had Edward read the Italian papers of the time, he might have altered his belief in Mussolini's friendship for Britain—and for himself. Their tone was contemptuous. Edward was being humoured by the Foreign Office, the general attitude was. He need not be taken seriously, but he should learn not to meddle in matters that were not his concern.

By 1936, though, what Mussolini might be doing was coming to be of less concern than what Hitler intended to do. And as things turned out, Edward's attitude to Germany was to have considerable bearing on his future, not simply because he held strong views, not even because of the tactlessness with which he was capable of expressing them, but because rumour was to fasten on his—and, still more, on Mrs. Simpson's—supposed closeness to the German government and to make it one of the strongest arguments for not supporting him when the crisis came.

When Edward came to the throne it was still quite widely felt in Britain that what the Nazis were trying to do for Germany was admirable: restore the economy, ruined by the Depression and the collapse of the German currency, and, still more important, restore German self-respect. Hitler the demagogue, it was surmised, was a necessary evil—when his party was settled in, its seedier elements would be discarded, and along with them into the discard would go Hitler himself, as soon as he had outlasted his usefulness. If he did not want to go or if his party was reluctant to lose him, the army would surely step in—the army, after all, was still the real power in Germany.

Even before Edward had come to the throne, though, there had been incontrovertible evidence of what Nazism meant: the Reichstag trial, the concentration camps, Jew-baiting, the murder of the Austrian Chancellor Dolfuss in an attempted Nazi putsch, the purge of Roehm and his followers (and many who were not his followers, but whom Hitler wanted to be rid of) in June 1934. It was this purge, Lord Boothby was to recall, that settled the issue for him and for those he was with when the news came in: "The Nazis had been shown up for what in fact they were—unscrupulous and bloodthirsty gangsters. In future they should be treated as such."

The British government, however, preferred to try appeasement, and in 1935 its first fruits emerged with the Anglo-German naval pact. Hitler had ordered the rebuilding of the German navy, in defiance of the Treaty of Versailles; but in 1935 he told the British government that he was prepared to limit German naval strength to thirty-five per cent of Britain's. His offer was made as if he were granting Britain a favour, and it was accepted as such, though in view of Britain's overseas commitments, it was almost a claim to naval parity in the North Sea. Hitler claimed that he was not breaking his pledges—that whenever his word was voluntarily given, it would be kept. The Germans, he said, would "scrupulously observe every treaty voluntarily signed by them, even if it was drawn up before they took over the government"—including the Locarno Pact of 1925, by which Germany had been brought back into respecta-- bility, as it were, after her Versailles punishment, in return for a guarantee of the French, Belgian and German frontiers, with Brit- ain and Italy as additional guarantors. On this basis the Anglo- German naval deal was concluded, and as late as January 1936, Hitler's foreign ministry was reiterating his government's gratitude and its determination to stand by the Locarno Pact, as Hitler had promised.

Hitler's attitude to the Locarno Pact, therefore, could be re- garded as a clearly defined test case. Unlike Versailles, it had not been imposed upon the German nation. It might earlier have been possible to argue that Germany, at the time she agreed to the pact, was not in a position to demand anything better. But now that Hitler had explicitly avowed his continued faith in it, he had forfeited that excuse. Yet, in March 1936, when his forces reoccupied the Rhine- land, Hitler had not merely repudiated the Versailles Treaty, he had rejected the Locarno Pact, too. It had, he said, "lost its inner meaning, and ceased in practice to exist."

It was argued at the time, and has often been asserted since, that Britain and France should have embarked on what would have been no more than a police action—quite easy to take owing to the over- whelming superiority of the French army at that time. Baldwin did not agree. In this he was supported not only by the great majority of his party, but also by the Opposition and by public opinion in general. "I suppose," Eden's Foreign Office driver commented, "that Jerry can do what he likes in his own back garden," and the phrase, subsequently attributed to Lord Lothian, reflected the common view. As A.J.P. Taylor has argued, too, the simple act of driving the Germans back out of the Rhineland would not necessarily have settled anything. But what was clearly of vital importance was the evidence that Hitler was not concerned simply to right the wrongs that had been done to Germany. "The myth is now exploded," Eden wrote in a memorandum, "that Herr Hitler only repudiates treaties imposed on Germany by force. We must be prepared for him to repudiate any treaty even if freely negotiated (a) when it becomes inconvenient (b) when Germany is sufficiently strong and the circumstances are otherwise favourable for doing so."

Eden had a personal reason for feeling this way. He now knew that Hitler was a liar, because Hitler had earlier treated him to an earnest discourse on the value of Locarno. Eden shared the view that there was nothing that could be done about the Rhineland, but at least he realized from this point that Hitler was not to be trusted. He could not understand why Hitler should be allowed to repeat the Rhineland exercise elsewhere in later years and yet still continue to find apologists. The answer, he thought, "is probably to be found in any intelligent dictator's understanding that the democracies are passionately sincere in their love of peace, and in his consequent ability to exploit this sentiment for his own ends." But for Eden himself, the Rhineland episode was decisive: "I could not forget how Hitler had spoken to me of Locarno; if he was not to be believed in this, he could not be believed in anything."

Eden was not alone in his view. The American commentator Dorothy Thompson warned that in future, in international affairs, what would be needed was not translators, old-style, who converted one language into another, but a new breed who could translate from one psychology into another, and she offered some of her own definitions. Peace, she wrote, in the dictionary of democracies is "a desirably permanent condition of amicable relations with all other nations." But in the dictionary of dictatorships, peace means "a quiet and undisturbed period in which to prepare for war." She continued,

> *Morality*, in the language of all dictatorships, means, not a devotion to an abstract standard of conduct but blind obedience to the dictates of State. And *truth* is not conformity with fact, or fidelity to an ac-

cepted standard of abstract principle, but is quite frankly whatever may serve as an instrument of national policy, there being no higher agency than the State and no higher good than that of the nation. *Unity,* in fascist terms, means uniformity; *freedom of conscience* means insubordination; *co-ordination* means coercion.

Whether Europe would ever again speak a common language, Dorothy Thompson thought—and if so, which dictionary would be used—was the real issue.

It followed, then, from Eden's point of view, that even if nothing could be done about the Rhineland, it must be made absolutely clear to Hitler that he was not going to be allowed to get away with the use of force again. Negotiations over grievances would not be precluded, but if they were undertaken, it would be in the knowledge that Hitler's word was not trustworthy. And in the meantime, nothing should be done that would encourage the Germans to believe that the British approved of what Hitler had done and was doing.

The King's views on Germany were very different. He had already become a Germanophile before the Great War—a marked contrast to his grandfather, Edward VII, who had done so much to restore Anglo-French friendship. Before he went to Oxford, Edward had been sent on a four-month trip to France. It bored him, and it proved unprofitable so far as one of its primary aims, the learning of the language, was concerned. His professor, he later recalled, could at first hardly speak a word of English, but after four months, "out of sheer necessity of communicating with me, he had gained a far greater mastery of my language than I had of his." German, by contrast, came relatively easy to him. He was related by ties of blood or marriage to most of the German royal houses, still flourishing at the time, and he enjoyed himself so thoroughly when he went to stay with some of them in 1913 that at the end of his trip he was barely conscious of any crisis in Anglo-German relations. He was actually looking forward to returning the following year. Nor did the war disillusion him with the Germans: he attributed it to the madness of their leaders. Germany itself, he thought, was a prosperous, industrious and agreeable country, which "echoed with work and song."

Edward's reaction to Hitler's rise to power was to work more energetically for Anglo-German harmony, a fact promptly noted by the German embassy, which made arrangements to exploit it. Edward and Wallis were invited to the embassy, and ways were suggested to him whereby he could help the cause further—for example, through the British Legion, of which he was still an active member.

As Edward was to recall in *A King's Story*, "A proposal had been advanced within that organisation that, as a gesture of friendship and good will, a small group of members should visit Germany in the near future and shake hands with some of those whom they had fought so bitterly in the past. This struck me as an eminently reasonable idea, and at the suggestion of the Chairman of the Legion I agreed to commend the proposal." The terms he commended it in, though—as the press reports show—went beyond what might be regarded as brief. He felt, he said, that there could be no more suitable body to stretch out the hand of friendship to the Germans "than we ex-servicemen, who fought them in the Great War, and have now forgotten all about that."

It was an astonishingly naive statement, considering how Hitler had ridden to power on the back of German memories of humiliation in the war. King George, when he read a report of the speech in the *Times* the next morning, was worried. He sent for Edward to tell him that he must not mix in politics, and especially in foreign affairs —"The views you expressed yesterday, however sensible, are, I happen to know, contrary to those of the Foreign Office." Edward pointed out that he was only endorsing a British Legion resolution. George replied that that was beside the point: "You must never speak on such controversial matters without consulting the Government."

This was a lesson that Edward would not learn. "The rebuke disturbed me. It seemed to settle nothing; our foreign policy, the more I thought about it, seemed paralysed." It did not occur to him that his qualifications for assessing British foreign policy, let alone pronouncing upon it in public, were slender, and he was unable to make the distinction, by this time second nature to his father, between statements that were unexceptionable and statements that were politically loaded. And as by this time he was not a man to keep his opinions to himself, the rumour soon got around of his pro-German attitude.

Edward was not an admirer of Hitler. There is no reason to doubt his recollection that the Führer "struck me as a somewhat ridiculous figure, with his theatrical posturings and his bombastic pretensions." But it was not necessary for the King to approve of Hitler to further the Nazi cause. What Hitler needed most, in fact, was not slavish admirers like the British Fascists, who were an embarrassment, but men of standing and independence who would take the German side and thereby indirectly help—much as the Communists liked to have their fellow travellers.

It was not enough, therefore, for Edward to claim that his activities had only been pro-German, not pro-Nazi. In his memoirs von Ribbentrop insisted that his "Bureau," which arranged goodwill tours such as those welcomed by the King and undertaken by the British Legion, "never did anything except promote good will;" but that, of course, was the design. Any attempt to use the tours to promote Nazism directly would have discredited them. In any case, Hitler genuinely wanted England's goodwill and friendship—provided that it was on his terms. He was anxious to convince people in positions of influence that he had no designs on England. And there was plenty of pro-Germanism of this kind about—as John Gunther found: Edward's views were shared by many Tories ("stupid ones think of Hitler as a sort of guarantee against future encroachments"), by the City, with its heavy investments in Germany, by Lord Lothian and his coterie, "the nucleus of the appeasers-to-be," and to some extent by the *Times,* which gave Hitler rather more than the benefit of the doubt.

For this reason the Nazis, who in this period were showing themselves uncharacteristically subtle, had begun to pay court to Mrs. Simpson. Their efforts do not appear to have gone beyond the usual invitations to embassy parties and luncheons, but simply by accepting them, Wallis became caught up in the intrigue. It was very much in the interest of the embassy to emphasize the importance of its contacts. Naturally they made much of the link with Mrs. Simpson, known to be the Prince of Wales' friend. Ribbentrop, intrigued, decided to investigate for himself. In her memoirs, the Duchess could recall only two meetings with him, both at Lady Cunard's, and her only recollection of Ribbentrop was that he held forth "in his best champagne-salesman manner" on what Hitler was doing for unmarried mothers in Germany. All that Ribbentrop wanted at that time was to get to know her. It was not the intention of the Nazis to try to use her as an agent, or even as a dupe. Their aim was simply to establish a contact that might be useful later. But they were not quite subtle enough. The connection was noted, and the Foreign Office was disturbed. Wallis found herself begged to stay an extra night at a house party—which surprised her, as she did not know her hosts very well. The reason, she eventually realized, that she was being kept was so that she could be inspected by Vansittart, deeply hostile to the Nazis. She found him "looking over me, dissecting me, no doubt, in the light of what he had been reading about me in his Foreign Office digest of the overseas press."

Edward and Wallis, then, were not so much rash as gullible. They did not realize the Nazis were seeking to exploit them. When Edward ascended the throne it became of greater importance that he should not appear to be favouring the Germans, particularly in view of the country's strained relations with France, but the press, ever on the watch for signs of his pro-Germanism, kept on reporting examples. When he held his first reception for members of the diplomatic corps in Buckingham Palace, early in February, it was noticed that he had chatted longest—half an hour—with the German ambassador. There was a perfectly innocent explanation: Edward enjoyed speaking German. But the frequency with which he went out of his way to remind people of his preferences was unfortunate. He even made a practice of inquiring, when he went to school ceremonies, whether German was taught as well as French; and this would be reported in the papers. In ordinary times, this would have been attributed to a worthy desire to banish English insularity. In the mid-thirties, it only aroused suspicion that he was too pro-German for comfort—or safety.

If it had been merely a matter of the King presenting arguable points of view, this would not have mattered. George V had never hesitated to express what was in his mind, when he happened to disagree with his ministers. But he had usually managed to state what was in his mind as if it were a possible alternative, reached after weighty consideration. Edward could not disguise his impatience with what he regarded as wilful blindness on the part of Eden, who advocated courses that, in his opinion, could benefit only Russia. The impression Edward made on Eden—to quote one of Eden's biographers, Bardens—was of "an impetuous and often opinionated man who did not understand the limits imposed on a modern monarch, and lacked his father's intimate knowledge of foreign affairs. Whereas his father knew much and interfered little, he knew little and interfered much." And it was not only the Foreign Secretary who aroused the King's irritation. When Duff Cooper made a speech in Paris during the summer, arguing that the Germans would be encouraged in their plans for aggression if the British and French did not stand together, he found the King's face "heavy with displeasure" on his return.

In April, von Hoesch, the German ambassador in London died, and that summer, the announcement of his successor set rumours seething. It was to be Joachim von Ribbentrop, and the obvious interpretation was that he would be arriving to exploit the influential contacts he had made on his earlier visits—in particular, Mrs. Simpson, and through her, the King.

For once, rumour was not far off the mark. Ribbentrop asserted in his memoirs that Hitler had offered to make him his foreign minister. Ribbentrop, though grateful, had suggested it would be better if he went to London. The reason he gave was that although the prospects for Anglo-German understanding were poor, "at the same time, from what I heard, King Edward VIII was not ill-disposed toward Germany." In ordinary circumstances, Ribbentrop admitted, a British King could exert little influence on his government's policies, "but if the King were to give his support to the idea of Anglo-German friendship, his great popularity might well help to bring about an understanding." Hitler agreed, and after the Berlin Olympics, Ribbentrop set off for London—not, perhaps, with massive expectations, but certainly in the knowledge that the King and his circle offered him the best available opportunity to pursue his objectives. The Foreign Office was no use to him because of Vansittart's resolute hostility to Nazi aspirations, and although individual members of the Cabinet might be friendly, they would be reluctant to commit themselves. The King, on the other hand, "had shown his sympathy for Germany on several occasions"—and in public, particularly in supporting the meeting of German and British leaders of ex-servicemen's organizations, which Ribbentrop himself had arranged. He had even granted audience to the German delegations, when they had arrived.

As rumours were building up about the King's desire to marry Mrs. Simpson, it was inevitable that those rumour-mongers who were hostile to the idea should seize on every scrap of evidence that could be used for purposes of denigration—in particular, Mrs. Simpson's supposed friendship with Ribbentrop. Owen and Thompson in their book on the abdication, not unsympathetic to Edward, were prepared to condone his pro-Germanism as being no more than the natural affinity for the race of his origin, but they took it for granted that he had been influenced by "Mrs. Simpson's private, personal friendship with the German ambassador, Herr von Ribbentrop, and his friends." And some members of the Labour Party, when they were faced with the decision whether to support Baldwin or seek some compromise that would keep the King on his throne, were influenced by their belief—as Hugh Dalton, then spokesman on foreign affairs in the Labour shadow cabinet, recalled in his autobiography—that the King was unduly sympathetic to the Nazis.

No hint of this appears in Eden's memoirs. But in a dispatch that autumn to Beneš, President of Czechoslovakia, Jan Masaryk—the Czech ambassador in London—reported an interview with the Foreign Secretary in which Eden had disclosed how worried the Foreign Office was with the King's increasing and disturbing intervention in foreign affairs. Eden had actually remarked that if the King went on like that, there were ways and means of compelling him to abdicate. Even if Masaryk was taking what he heard too seriously, the fact that he should have come away from the meeting with this impression, at a date before the abdication crisis had arisen, is an indication of the extent to which the King had already managed to antagonize his Foreign Secretary.

On the main issues of the day, then, the King and Eden were at loggerheads, but even if they had been in agreement, it is doubtful whether Edward could have won Eden to his side. During the summer the Foreign Secretary was immersed in the negotiations for a non-intervention pact over the Spanish civil war. When he returned to London in October, he was unaware of the impending crisis. To his surprise and irritation, he found Baldwin's mind even further removed from foreign affairs than usual—he actually begged Eden not to trouble him with them. As it was three months since any direction had come from him, Eden assumed that this was only another example of Baldwin's reluctance to face unpleasant realities —the "daily fare at the Foreign Office." But Eden's irritation disappeared when he examined the letters that were coming in from overseas, commenting on enclosed press cuttings about Mrs. Simpson. By his own account, he was never in any doubt that the course Baldwin was taking was the right one. Ironically, Eden twenty years later was to become the first prime minister to have been through the divorce courts.

"THE VALUE OF THE CROWN'

Individually, then, the members of the inner Cabinet circle were unlikely to look sympathetically on the King's desire to marry Mrs. Simpson. And collectively, they were disturbed by what appeared to them to be his potentially unconstitutional behaviour, in contrast to his father's strict adherence to the rules. Or was this just an excuse? The contrast between the two men as monarchs was not quite so great as ministers thought. Edward could, in fact, have argued that he had taken up where George V left off.

George had based his conduct as King on Bagehot's *English Constitution*. He had learned it under the instruction of the historian J.R. Tanner, summarizing for his own benefit:

The value of the Crown is in its *dignified* capacity . . . it makes Government *intelligible* to the masses . . . it makes Government *interesting* to the masses . . . it *strengthens* Government with the religious tradition connected with the Crown. . . .

And

The existence of the Crown serves to *disguise* change and therefore to deprive it of the evil consequences of revolution: (e.g. the Reform Bill of 1832).

George, in fact, saw himself with a positive role. He was something more than a catalyst. But what he must not do, he realized, was allow his personal views to dictate his actions. And at the very beginning of his reign, he had shown how far he was prepared to go against his own instincts, and those of his court advisers.

He ascended the throne in 1910 at a time of grave constitutional crisis, with a conflict raging between the House of Lords and the House of Commons over the proposed curtailment of the Lords' constitutional powers to reject legislation. Asquith's Liberal government threatened to resign unless the new King would give them his pledge, in secret, that as a last resort he would create new peers in sufficient numbers to secure a government majority. Edward VII, aware that he might be confronted with such a demand, had not been able to decide what he would do. The obvious precedent for such a step—William IV's promise to the Liberals in 1832 that he would create peers to get the Reform Bill through—was not necessarily relevant, because there was little indication in 1910, as there had been on the earlier occasion, that the government's proposals enjoyed the overwhelming support of the British people. When George came to the throne, however, he gave the required pledge, acting against his own inclination and against the strong advice of his respected private secretary, Sir Arthur Bigge, later Lord Stamfordham. He felt that the dangers of acting on his own judgment, even if it proved correct, would be too great. His duty was to facilitate the constitutional process: he had to support his government, and that he might disapprove of what the government was doing was beside the point.

To act unconstitutionally, though, a monarch does not have to defy his government. He may be in effect unconstitutional by helping his government to take courses that are politically expedient to them—courses that the King's sanction encourages them to take but that are not in the national interest. By the 1930s, King George had begun to lose his political detachment and to give free reign to accumulated prejudices—for example, as Nicolson noted, in connection with the threatened departure of the Liberals from the national government in 1931. As soon as George V had accepted the idea— implanted in his mind, ironically, by the Liberal leader, Herbert Samuel—of a national government, he had become infatuated with it. "The country had to be saved," he told Ramsay MacDonald, "and there should be a combination of all decent-minded politicians towards this end: party differences should be sunk." George did not object to the Socialist opposition—its members might not be decent-minded, but that was understandable, considering their background. That the Liberals should contemplate leaving the national government, though, seemed to him disgraceful, and Samuel, whose clear-headedness he had so admired a few weeks before, now was "quite impossible, most obstinate . . . God knows what can be done!"

What George could do, and did, was to tell MacDonald that his resignation would not be accepted if it were tendered, thus compelling the loyal MacDonald to stay in office and find a way out of the dilemma. The way out he chose was to hold a general election, with the already Tory-dominated government parading as "National" and asking for a "doctor's mandate"—a mandate to do whatever it should think fit. With both the Labour and the Liberal Parties hopelessly sundered, and with the British system of single-member constituencies, the result was inevitable. The "national" government won 558 seats, the Labour Opposition holding only 52 and losing many of their most able parliamentarians. And whatever might have been the arguments for a national government at this time, this overwhelming victory—for which the King was largely responsible—was to prove unfortunate. But George did not realize this, and his advisers encouraged him in his belief that all had been done for the best. His private secretary, Wigram, was enthusiastic. The King, he wrote in 1932, "never had such a good set of Ministers. . . . It is wonderful how we can put a strong team into the field whenever required—even our second eleven would defeat most other countries."

To imply, then—as many of his critics have done—that Edward was on the way to becoming an unconstitutional monarch, in contrast to his strictly constitutional father, is to exaggerate the difference between them. It happened that King George's attitude toward the end of his life rarely clashed with his ministers'. Had a Socialist government been in power, he might have recollected his Bagehot philosophy and behaved impeccably, but some of his actions in connection with the national government were, in a sense, more unconstitutional than anything his son was to contemplate.

The real difference between them lay in the fact that George had gone with his ministers, Edward threatened to go against them. George, too, was predictable, whereas they never knew what Edward might be up to next. Newspapers and magazines were continually hinting that Edward was waiting to play a more decisive part in politics. His father's speech in Belfast in 1921 had helped to bring about the treaty that gave the Irish Free State her independence. Now—the magazine *News Review* asserted on July 2—"acting within his rights as Constitutional Monarch, the King will give his attention to the long-standing quarrel between Northern Ireland and the Irish Free State"—by asking the Northern Irish Premier to smooth the path for a three-party meeting between Northern Ireland, the Irish Free State and Britain: "The King himself may open the discussion."

Ministers might suspect that this was simply guess-work on the writer's part, but, as they never knew what was in the King's mind, they could not be sure. Nor could they be sure that the public would disapprove if the King played a more dynamic role in politics. The government was sufficiently unpopular to suggest that a well-timed royal intervention might capture public approval—as, indeed, it was to do, on the occasion of his visit to South Wales.

And because ministers were nervous, Edward's failings seemed the more intolerable. The King, Tom Jones noted, "has done the popularity side supremely well—he has the memory for persons, a quick if shallow intelligence, and a sense of drama. But he dislikes work and escapes from it, and delays and postpones its performance." Chamberlain in particular was irritated, and it did not help when the King prodded him into discussions about new ideas for housing, only to lose interest in them when they grew out of the idea stage. These annoyances would have been patiently borne if the King in other respects had continued to give satisfaction—or even if he did not, so long as no excuse presented itself to take action against him. But now the excuse was being presented, and it was of a kind calculated to unite the most influential members of the Cabinet. The Nonconformist element in the Cabinet was strong: Chamberlain, Simon, Kingsley Wood. To them, as to Halifax, Inskip and Eden, the idea of the King wanting to marry Mrs. Simpson and stay on his throne was inconceivable. Had they really wanted him to stay on his throne—had he made himself as popular with them as he had earlier made himself popular with the public—they would have been prepared to cast around for some way out of the dilemma. It is just possible that they might have been prepared to contemplate some variation on the morganatic marriage idea. But as things stood, they did not trust Edward, they did not like him, and they did not want him as King. There could be no doubt that, should a constitutional crisis arise, they would be ranged against him.

THE ESTABLISHMENT

It was not absolutely necessary for the King to win ministers to his side in order to defy Baldwin. He had another source of potential allies, which might be even more valuable. It was not easy to define, but its existence had been demonstrated, not for the first time, by the reaction to the Hoare-Laval pact. What (or who) had compelled the government to reject the pact and to let Hoare resign? The credit was usually given to the abstraction "public opinion." As Lord Tweedsmuir—John Buchan, the novelist and historian—wrote from Canada, where he was Governor General: "I don't profess to understand exactly what happened, but what seems plain is that public opinion suddenly took a hand in directing the game, which is a most interesting phenomenon and proves that after all we are a genuine democracy." But did it? Why should public opinion, which over other matters so often failed to change the government's course, became suddenly so effective? The likeliest explanation is that it was not public opinion in the general sense of the term, embracing the entire community, that had been effective, but the opinion of what later came to be known as the Establishment.

Inner Circle

Until the 1950s it was customary to assume that power in Britain rested in the hands of the executive, with checks and balances provided by the legislature and the judiciary. From time to time, however, commentators suggested that this was an oversimplification, or even a delusion. Socialists complained that the City was the true seat of power, at least while Conservative governments ruled the country—the City itself being to some extent a puppet manipulated by faceless international financiers. There was also "big business," organized into giant cartels and rings, a law unto itself. But the possibility that there was another source of hidden power began to excite speculation: the Establishment. The term had been used in the eighteenth century to denote people of influence, but later for a while it drifted out of use, presumably because the controversy over Church Disestablishment led to some terminological confusion. In 1955, however, it was revived and quickly became common currency.

The term still does not have a generally agreed meaning. It has sometimes come very close to Professor C. Wright Mills' concept of the "power elite" in the United States—a group of people who in theory at least can be identified, holding power through their jobs. But the more common view of the Establishment is that it consists of individuals with a common social and educational background, and shared beliefs and aims, who constitute a kind of informal club —though they are not necessarily aware of it and are often amused or annoyed if they are named as Establishment figures. Some of them hold positions of importance, but this is not necessary. Influence may be exercised as effectively, and sometimes more effectively, through go-betweens—for example, through society hostesses. The essential point is that power is exercised indirectly, and often secretly. One definition of the Establishment is "that part of our government which has not been subjected to democratic control."

Although the actual term "Establishment" was not to be used for another twenty years, there was some recognition of its existence in the 1930s. Rudyard Kipling had described its processes:

> For undemocratic reasons and for motives not of State
> They arrive at their conclusions—largely inarticulate
> Being void of self-expression they confide their views to none
> But sometimes, in a smoking room, one learns why things were done.

John Gunther was one of those who speculated on the subject, after his visit to Britain when he was preparing *Inside Europe*. Gunther's work was to come in for some harsh handling by critics, both then and later—not entirely unjustified. Working journalists, as Malcolm Muggeridge later recalled (he was one, at the time, in Fleet Street), found it difficult not to feel a cerain derision for the method Gunther employed—"One recognized a good many of the anecdotes and observations as current in the twilight world where politics, journalism, diplomacy and public relations come together in the early evening hours over free cocktails." But this gives Gunther's impressions an interest of their own: they may not describe what was really happening, but they certainly reveal what people who regarded themselves as well informed *thought* was happening, and this can be illuminating in its own right.

It was suggested to Gunther that the former British ruling classes had developed some kind of underground organization to maintain their supremacy, and though he could not find any evidence of a close oligarchy, such as he encountered in France, what he heard made him believe in the existence of what he called an "inner circle" of men of power, including Baldwin, Chamberlain, Lord Salisbury, Lord Derby, the editor of the *Times*, and the governor of the Bank of England. He admitted, though, that no two people, asked to name the inner circle, would have presented the same list, and this was understandable, as the great strength of the English ruling classes was their flexibility.

From the evidence that has emerged since, it is clear Gunther was on the right track. An inner circle, or Establishment, did exist, and it did develop owing to the desire of the English ruling class to preserve its power. The process, however, had not been entirely deliberate. The Establishment had grown up, like so much else in English life, by a series of purposeful accidents.

Eton and Harrow

The base of the pyramid of which the Establishment constituted the apex was the English public school system. The system had evolved owing to what was felt to be the need to remove boys from the beguiling influence of their homes, in order to toughen them and stamp them in a mould whose emphasis was on character rather than personality, before sending them out as empire builders. But it had as a by-product the creation of a devoted loyalty not simply to the code instilled, but to the school which instilled it—quite the most remarkable example being the case of Stanley Baldwin.

At the age of sixteen young Baldwin, whose record had hitherto been sound, was discovered by his headmaster at Harrow in possession of some pornography. In the eyes of the school authorities, though not of the boys, this was considered to be a particularly heinous offence. Baldwin was nearly expelled. Only the intervention of his respected father caused the sentence to be reduced to a severe flogging. Henceforth the privileges which Stanley could have expected toward the end of his school career, such as being a prefect,

were denied to him. Naturally the rest of that career was unhappy—
as well as being academically wasted. Baldwin had good reason to
loathe Harrow, and the system. Yet he was capable, years later, of
saying, "I will, with God's help, do nothing in the course of an
arduous and difficult career which shall cause any Harrovian to say
of me that I have failed to do my best to live up to the highest
traditions of the school." And, apparently, he meant it.

A statement of Baldwin's that is more often quoted, though, suggests that his tongue was in his cheek. "When the call came to me
to form a government," he claimed, "one of my first thoughts was
that it should be a government of which Harrow should not be
ashamed. I remembered how in previous governments there had
been four or, perhaps, five Harrovians, and I determined to have six.
To make a cabinet is like making a jigsaw puzzle fit, and I managed
to make my six fit by keeping the Chancellor of the Exchequer for
myself." Yet whatever Baldwin may have been thinking, most of his
audience would have found nothing odd, certainly nothing sinister,
about an Old Harrovian Prime Minister packing the Cabinet with
as many Old Harrovians as he could muster. Old Etonian Prime
Ministers, after all, did the same. The only difference was that they
were not aware they were doing it. They chose the men that they
considered most suitable. It simply happened that the men they considered most suitable were usually Old Etonians (as late as 1964,
there were seven of them among the inner twelve of Sir Alec Home's
Cabinet).

It had been expected that the influence of the public schools
would begin to wane as the franchise extended. The expectation was
not fulfilled. Even before the First World War, A.L. Lowell in his
Government of England was claiming that the prophecies that
democracy would have a levelling effect in England had proved
fallacious: "Where political class jealousy is weak, social ambition
and social cohesion are among the strongest forces in human nature,
and in a society as centralised and powerfully constructed as that of
England they are not likely to fade quickly into the background."
They didn't. Following up Lowell's forecast half a century later,
W.L. Guttsman found that so far from the spread of democracy and
the rise of the Labour Party between the wars helping to broaden
the social base of the Conservative Party, it had had the opposite
effect. In *The British Political Elite,* Guttsman showed that whereas
one-third of Conservative MPs in 1918 had received a public-school

education, by 1945 this figure had risen to almost two-thirds, and "the proportion of those recruited from the most exclusive public schools actually doubled."

All Souls

It was primarily the most exclusive public schools that provided the recruiting base for the Establishment—though a Scots education, paradoxically much admired in England for its democratic content, was permissible. The next desirable, though not essential, qualification was a university, but it had to be either Oxford or Cambridge. The great majority of public-school and "Oxbridge" men, of course, went on to work in the professions or in the colonies, drifting out of the running for qualification as members of the Establishment. But for those who were ambitious, two university institutions were particularly helpful.

One of them was the Union, which provided a debating society at both universities where they could test each other out and where they could meet eminent and influential men of the time. The guest speakers were frequently distinguished. The officers of the Unions made good use of the opportunities afforded. In 1965 the *Sunday Times* published a list of Oxford and Cambridge Union presidents since 1918, and the success rate, especially in politics and journalism, was astonishingly high—a good deal higher than could be accounted for by their ability, as the Unions' electoral systems were not calculated to recognize talent. They were a breeding ground for ward politicians.

But still more important, at least for the thirties, as a breeding ground for the Establishment was All Souls, at Oxford—a college without undergraduates, which liked to skim the cream of each academic year. All Souls created a loyalty among its alumni even more intense than was felt for the Old School, and after they had gone forth to their jobs—in the Empire, in journalism, in the City, or in politics—the college continued to provide them with a club where they could meet, from time to time, shedding their inhibitions and renewing old ties. The list of All Souls men influential in different walks of life began to attract attention between the wars, so much so that in 1932 a journalist, Charles Brodribb, wrote the skit *Government by Mallardry*—the mallard being the college emblem—pointing out the extensive nature of their operations and describing the

Mallards as "an unofficial club for running, or helping to run, the destinies of the British Empire."

The influence of All Souls in this period was to be attested to by many of its Fellows, by none with greater thankfulness than Sir John Simon. The foundation, he conceded in his autobiography, "might seem to do too much for the favoured few," but it attached to itself, at the beginning of their lives, a lucky selection of men. "While many of them afterwards advance to divers positions where they serve in Church or State, or in the higher studies, all remain a band of brothers . . . a society of men of all ages, who never lose a sense of equality as between themselves, and preserve a common devotion to the place itself." Simon thoroughly approved. "What amazing good fortune," he recalled, "for me to be made, at the age of twenty-four, a member of this select company, and to be a member of it still! Looking back, I feel that, apart from domestic happiness, nothing in my life has meant as much to me as the companionship, now extending over more than half a century, of the fraternity of All Souls."

The fraternity was later to be surveyed with a more detached eye by one of its junior Fellows in the thirties, A.L. Rowse—unusual in that he was a Socialist and anti-Establishment-minded. "What a galaxy they constituted!" he recalled, in his *All Souls and Appeasement*. Viceroys and foreign secretaries—Curzon, Chelmsford, Halifax. Eminent lawyers and Cabinet ministers—Simon, Amery, Somervell (Inskip's successor as Attorney General). Bankers and empire builders—Lord Brand, Lionel Curtis (founder of the Royal Institute of International Affairs). There were also Cosmo Gordon Lang, Archbishop of Canterbury, the headmasters of Eton and Winchester, and Geoffrey Dawson, editor of the *Times*.

The Fellows of All Souls, Rowse was careful to emphasize, did not have a united political outlook. And although he disliked their views, he liked them. "Though I was a young fanatic of the Left, in constant opposition to them in politics, I never received anything but kindness and forbearance from them. For my part I regarded them not merely with admiration, though unflinching disagreement, but with affection; for nearly all of these men I had a liking, of some of them I was really fond." Rowse even liked Sir John Simon. There seems to have been something in the atmosphere of the institution that brought out amiable qualities. Certainly they were not wicked or designing men, conspiring to subvert democratic processes. But the Fellows of All Souls were not much troubled by intimations of humility. "One thing dominated them all—the sense of public duty; there was nothing they would not do if they were convinced it was their duty." They saw nothing wrong, if duty called, in an action that others might justifiably regard as unscrupulous or unfair. The trouble was that as they were not all gifted with insight, what they thought was their duty was often in reality their self-interest.

Although the Fellows of All Souls did not form a cabal, or seek to exert their influence by stealth, they had great influence and were constantly exerting it through their political and social contacts. Baldwin was not a Fellow of All Souls, but he greatly admired the institution. As Vansittart unkindly put it in his autobiography, "Baldwin liked a Fellow of All Souls better than other fellows." The Fellow, therefore, had available to him an impressive range of contacts in every walk of life, many of which he could utilize without apparently making any effort to do so, over a drink or at dinner. It is impossible to assess the precise influence of the college or its members, but it was undoubtedly considerable.

Milner's Kindergarten

The Establishment of the 1930s, however, derived its initial dynamic from a decision taken by Lord Milner when he was given the task of reconstructing South Africa after the Boer War—a task whose successful outcome used to be regarded as imperialism's finest monument, though later events in South Africa demonstrated how far Milner had been from getting to the roots of that country's problems. "I mean to have young men," Milner wrote in 1900, describing how he wanted to set about the job: "I value brains and character more than experience." The trouble, he realized, was that first-class men with experience were not likely to be lured away from their presumably successful careers. If one qualification had to be sacrificed, he preferred to make do with first-class men without experience. "When I go," he concluded, "I mean to leave behind me young men with plenty of work in them."

He did. "Milner's Kindergarten," as it was first derisively, then enviously known, included such men as R.H. Brand (later Lord Brand), John Buchan (the novelist), Hugh Wyndham (later Lord Leconfield), Lionel Hichens (later chairman of Cammell Laird), Lionel Curtis, Patrick Duncan (later Governor General of South

Africa), Richard Feetham (later a judge), Philip Kerr (who as Lord Lothian was to be British ambassador in Washington during the war), and Geoffrey Dawson (editor of the *Times* with one short break from 1911 to 1940).

Milner not merely had the knack of selecting to work under him young men likely to succeed, he also indoctrinated them with the philosophy that helped to give them the required incentive. He was a racialist—he believed it was the destiny of the English to guide, if not to rule, mankind. And because of this, he despised democratic institutions, which might be infiltrated and used to dissipate English resolution. His young men did not necessarily go all the way with him in his doctrines, but they caught something of the messianic fervour—particularly his loathing of what Lothian described as "the slipshod compromises, the optimistic slogans, the vote-catching half-truths with which democracy seemed to compromise the majestic governing art." If a sufficient number of dedicated men were to arrive at positions of authority, Milner thought—and so did the Kindergarten—it might be possible for them to take charge and guide democracy, without the demagogues and the charlatans realizing what was happening. It was not always a conscious process, but it was the driving force in the life and work of men such as Lothian and Dawson. They believed that they stood for the true values. They felt it their task to prevent the baser instincts of the mob, fed by politicians and the popular press, from destroying the Empire.

The Milner Kindergarten retained its cohesion, long after the need for it ceased to exist in South Africa, through a kind of prolonged seminar or symposium that came to be called the Round Table. Its members held regular meetings—or "moots" as they coyly called them, from the Anglo-Saxon term. To lend purpose to the discussions, they published a quarterly, called the *Round Table*. Newcomers were added including Edward Grigg and the historian F.S. Oliver, with his invaluable range of friends in politics, and Waldorf Astor. And the group became closely knit socially: Lothian and Dawson became close friends of Waldorf and his wife, Nancy, and Brand married Nancy Astor's sister.

The Round Tablers' chief aim, as Milner's biographer A.M. Gollin put it, was "to win power and authority in national and imperial affairs." Unlike most Englishmen with that ambition, however, "the Group scorned any connection with political parties . . .

they intended to gain political influence by means of their conspicuous ability, by their social contacts and by the validity of their plans"
—plans which they formulated at their moots. They were, in fact, a
pressure group, though that was not a term they would have applied to themselves, so confident were they of their own rectitude
and the purity of their motives.

The Round Tablers found that the easiest, as well as the pleas-
antest, places to meet were house parties. They were held on week-
ends, when everybody concerned could get away from their jobs. In
the country they could be self-contained and spared unwanted
interruptions. It was the essence of the Establishment—which the
Round Tablers were now permeating—that such contacts were, or
could be, on a casual social basis. There was no need for them to
meet formally to discuss events and formulate policies. Informality
was easier and pleasanter—and left fewer tracks. The ideal meeting
place was a large country house, like Lord Salisbury's Hatfield. But
the house parties that were to become most closely identified with
the Establishment were those held at Cliveden, the home of the
Astors.

Waldorf was the great-great-grandson of John Jacob Astor, the
German immigrant who had made the family fortune in America,
and the son of William Waldorf Astor, who, after an unsuccessful
attempt at a political career in New York, had been appointed U.S.
minister in Rome. Deciding to live in England, he had bought
Cliveden from the Duke of Westminster, passing it on to his son
and heir at the time of Waldorf's marriage in 1906. Ten years later
he purchased a title, becoming Baron Astor "for political and public
services," and a year after that the grateful government made him a
viscount, presumably for further services of a similar nature.

His son Waldorf might have passed for the typical English
country gentleman. He had been educated at Eton and New College,
Oxford, he hunted, he dabbled in politics as a Conservative with
some Liberal leanings, he performed good works. But Cliveden
would have remained just another country house had he not married
Nancy Shaw, née Langhorne, a Virginia girl with a mind of her own
and a determination, as soon as opportunity permitted, to indulge
it. She entered politics herself, becoming the first woman to take
her seat in the House of Commons. She became a leading spirit in
a variety of campaigns—for women's rights and for teetotalism—and

around her, at her home, she gathered what came to be known as the Cliveden set, or, less politely, gang.

"Few visitors' books," boasted Tom Jones, an assiduous Cliveden week-ender, "can show such a variegated collection of signatures. Aristocratic families: Salisbury, Cavendish, Balfour, Lansdowne, Mildmay; almost every week one or more members of the Round Table group: Philip Kerr, R.H. Brand, Lionel Curtis, Edward Grigg, Lionel Hichens; Prime Ministers, British and Dominion; American Presidents, past or future; Ambassadors; Labour politicians . . . Geoffrey Dawson, editor of the *Times,* was a regular visitor." Baldwin was not, yet the week-end before he succeeded Ramsay MacDonald in the summer of 1935, it had been at Cliveden that he reconstructed his government, and he was Lothian's guest during his convalescence in 1936. Chamberlain's visits to Cliveden were also infrequent, but he, too, was later to spend a week-end at Cliveden in March 1937 that was to be the peg upon which Claud Cockburn hung his onslaught on the Cliveden set in *The Week*—the attack which, with the help of denials by Lord and Lady Astor that they were running a conspiracy, helped to establish Cliveden in British political folklore as the GHQ of the Establishment.

Cockburn's first attack on the Establishment—though he did not call it that—was in April 1936, when he named Lord Astor and Geoffrey Dawson as being chiefly responsible for the flabby way the Rhineland crisis had been handled, the beginning of a sustained campaign in *The Week* against them. Cliveden's influence was also noted at this time by John Gunther. No one, he argued, should think that aristocratic plotters met for week-ends of conspiracy, "but suppose that the editor of a great newspaper wants to meet a promising Labour politician. The country house, like that of the Lady Astor at Cliveden, is the perfect place." Wealthy and influential Londoners, Gunther thought, had invented the long week-end to get out of their ugly and uncomfortable capital—"Their *métier* is politics, they talk politics; and they make politics, quite spontaneously."

But was there a Cliveden set, in the sense of a group of people with a common purpose, determined to carry it through? It was often to be argued that the range of Nancy Astor's taste in company, and the consequent diversity of people who came for week-ends, precluded the attainment of any real unity or planning. Lord Winterton, for example, dismissed the charge that the Cliveden set exercised a malign effect on foreign policy as nonsensical, because the feature of Cliveden gatherings "was the catholicity of opinions expressed upon every subject under the sun, and the fact that the guests might include famous men such as Lord Balfour and Mr. Bernard Shaw with completely diverse political views."

But this is to misunderstand the nature of the forces at work within the Establishment. Had Cliveden simply been a centre for a homogeneous group of plotters it would not have acquired influence. Its importance lay not in the fact that the people who stayed there all came to think alike, but that they got to know one another on easy social terms and so could know what was going on and acquire a "feel" of how to react to it.

Then, when there was a group within the Establishment with a positive attitude—as there was to be over appeasement, in the later 1930s—they were able to act with astonishing harmony. They did not realize the connection: Chamberlain, Halifax, Dawson, Lothian and the rest were genuinely irritated at the allegations that they had conspired together to reach their appeasement policy. They thought of themselves as men of independent mind who had happened to reach the same conclusions. But in reality they were very far from being independent of one another, even when apart. The headmaster of the Kindergarten had done his work only too well. Milner's conditioning continued to work on his pupils without their being aware of it, and they indoctrinated people with whom they came in regular contact, until their thought processes grew predictable. There was no rigid uniformity—certainly not on appeasement—there were remarkable similarities of attitude, and the constant social intercourse gave them a comforting sense that their views were shared by men of sense and of standing and therefore could not be far wrong. More than that, in fact, they tended to think of their views as right and to regard the expression of dissident opinions as wrongheaded, vexatious and mischievous. Public opinion meant little to them—they tuned in only to listen to broadcasts on their own narrow social waveband.

"We all assume the responsibilities of the Prime Minister," Tom Jones wrote, "and imagine ourselves in his place." In a sense, they *were* in his place, because what they thought, the Prime Minister was very likely thinking too—or would soon begin to think. And

eventually this was to prove destructive—as Michael Astor, Waldorf's son, described in his *Tribal Feeling*.

Some of the charges against Cliveden, he thought, might have
been overdrawn, but "it is nevertheless true that there was a con-
sortium of people, engaged in public life, who normally met at
Cliveden or at 4 St. James's Square [the Astor's London residence],
whose members shared a common view about the best methods of
keeping the peace in Europe"—the view being that if Hitler's
"reasonable" demands were met he would cease to make unreasonable demands. Even without benefit of hind-sight, this was wildly
divorced from common sense, indicating how far some of those who
had been nurtured in the Kindergarten had lost touch with political
realities—a process which can be traced to their basic contempt for
democracy and to the insensitivity arising out of their confidence
that they, and they only, had the knowledge, the judgment and the
rectitude to guide their country. As Boothby, himself a maverick
member of the Establishment at the time, was to recall, its members'
horizons were too restricted: "Round they hopped, like birds in an
enormous cage, from shoot to shoot, from Cliveden to All Souls, to
the Athenaeum, to the Travellers, to Grillons dining club, to Round
Table 'moots' and back again; with the result that they were out of
touch with ordinary people, with all that was happening in Europe,
and finally with reality."

The King, therefore, had more to contend with in any clash
with the Establishment than a sociological abstraction. Members
of the Establishment were capable of exerting powerful lever-
age through the institutions of which they enjoyed communal
membership—all the more powerful because they were not necessarily aware they were exerting it. And in connection with the King,
one Establishment figure in particular would acquire an importance
greater than he usually commanded. As well as being King Emperor,
Edward was also the Head of the Church of England, "Defender of
the Faith." The power and prestige of the Anglican Church might
have waned, but it was still responsible for formally installing the
King on his throne at the coronation, due to be held in the spring
of 1937. The Archbishop of Canterbury, therefore, was in a position,
if he cared—or dared—to exercise his authority and refuse to crown
the King, and rumour was already beginning to suggest that he was
contemplating refusal.

The Archbishop of Canterbury

Shortly before the turn of the century, the Liverpool *Daily Post* undertook a census of congregations in the city's churches. Out of a population of about 650,000, about 23,000, it was found, attended the morning services, and 34,000 the evening service, in Church of England churches. Publication of the figures aroused the customary lament about the decline of faith and the risk to morals, but they were then forgotten. They will serve, though, as a reminder of what a flimsy hold the Established Church had on the population—at least in towns. Earlier surveys in other regions had pointed to the same conclusion, and later surveys were to confirm it.

Nor could it reasonably be claimed that the Church, while not attracting people to its services, nevertheless remained an influence in their daily lives. All the evidence pointed in the other direction. Although most people continued to believe in a God and to pray to him, and although their mental picture of him, however confused, bore some resemblance to the God worshipped in the Church of England, the Church was ceasing to play any significant part in the life of the community. For weddings, funerals, christenings, and the "churching of women" a clergyman's assistance was still called upon, but with hardly more thought than the caterer, or the undertaker, was called upon. He was there simply to perform a function—and be paid for it.

In the 1930s, however, the Church of England still continued to present the appearance of being a nationally based and accepted institution, and it enjoyed the connivance of authority in this hoax. In the armed forces, for example, it was difficult, and usually impossible, to put "None" as an answer to the question "Religion?" Recruits who wanted to were persuaded to put "C. of E." The British Broadcasting Corporation allowed other churches a fixed ration of broadcasting time, but the Church of England, in addition to its inflated share of the times set aside for religious programmes, also virtually controlled non-denominational religious time on the air, of which there was a great deal. And the Church as an institution still commanded the respect of the English upper middle class. In practice, churches resembled the "musical banks" which Samuel Butler had described in *Erewhon*. They were often nearly empty, but not—inquirers would be told—for want of any confidence: "The heart of the country was thoroughly devoted to these establishments, and any sign of their being in danger would bring in support from the most unexpected quarters." Those members of the Establishment who were not churchgoers ordinarily still found it wise to pretend they were.

There was a strong, though not a conscious, feeling within the Establishment that the Church of England, for much the same reason as the monarchy, needed to be sustained because without it, the fabric of the English way of life would begin to disintegrate. What the Church was doing, therefore, continued to arouse an interest disproportionate to its real influence, and in lists of the most important men in Britain, the Archbishop of Canterbury was usually included. Because so many people wanted him to be regarded as important, he *was* important—or at least could be. What the Archbishop of Canterbury said in the ordinary course of his clerical duties, in sermons or speeches, was not news. But his views on social or quasi-political issues always had a good chance of making the headlines. And on this particular issue—involving, as it might do, the coronation, and the whole future of the King's relation to the Church —the views of the Archbishop could be expected to command attention.

Cosmo Gordon Lang was the son of a Scots minister. He was brought up and educated in Glasgow before going to Oxford, where he made a name for himself as a speaker in the Union, of which he was to become president. To his Oxford contemporaries he appeared a man certain to succeed. His political inclinations were manifested when he became secretary of the Canning Club, which combined social elegance, in the persons of the Duke of Newcastle and Earl Ferrers, with opinions so reactionary that even Lang was by contrast progressive. He had barely come of age when he was asked to become the Conservative candidate for the constituency of Tredegar.

Lang's chief ambition, however, was to crown his Oxford career with a Fellowship at All Souls. His first attempt ended in failure, but in 1888 he was elected. His pleasure in the association, then and throughout his life, can be judged by a Litany he used to recite:

> *Balliol* was my mother, to whom I am bound
> by ties of filial gratitude;

All Souls is my wife, who gave me a home and
most generously received me back after a
temporary residence with
Magdalen, my very beautiful mistress, for whom
during years I forsook my wife!

According to his biographer, J.G. Lockhart, he would sometimes
add that since receiving his wife's forgiveness for this lapse, their
conjugal fidelity had been unbroken.

To Lang, All Souls was more than a club. It was a place where
he could absent himself from pomposity awhile—particularly when
he became "Lord Mallard," an office he held for over a quarter of
a century. Each All Souls Night the college held a "Gaudy," at
which he would be called upon to sing the Mallard Song. Its refrain ran:

O by the blood of King Edward
O by the blood of King Edward
It was a swapping, swapping Mallard.

By his own account, four stalwart Fellows then carried him in a chair

for nearly two hours after midnight round the quadrangles and roofs of
the College, with a dead mallard borne in front on a long pole (which I
still possess), singing the Mallard Song all the time, preceded by the
seniors . . . and followed by the juniors, all of them carrying staves and
torches; a scene unimaginable in any place in the world except Oxford,
or there in any society except All Souls.

"Unimaginable" was an understatement. The mallard ceremony
was a cross between a light-hearted black mass and a parody of the
Last Supper. Early in the century, when Lang's prospects in the
Church were beginning to look distinctly encouraging, he decided
to institute certain reforms:

I thought of it as unseemly that surplices should be worn, and we contented ourselves with black gowns. There seemed something approach-
ing irreverence in the notion of making the Junior Fellows eat of the
mallard's flesh and drink its blood, so as to be incorporated into the
spirit of All Souls. Instead of this I had a small silver Mallard made and
filled with wine, which the Juniors drank.

When the bird was ceremonially burned in the small hours, some
of the junior Fellows "could not be restrained from eating portions

of his charred flesh," but at least Lang had made his gesture. He was to continue to carry out his duties as Lord Mallard until he was appointed Archbishop of York, and even then, he so far lamented what he described as his "excessive prudery" that he continued, though leaving the Lord's duties to deputies, to sing the Mallard Song at college Gaudies until 1945, shortly before his death.

When Lang had decided to enter the Church, the road to preferment quickly opened in front of him. Magdalen—his "very beautiful mistress"—took him as Dean of Divinity, and among the undergraduates was "a ruddy-faced boy from Eton," who was to become a lifelong friend: Geoffrey Robinson, later to change his name to Dawson. When Lang moved to take charge of a parish, too, it was from his point of view admirably situated in Portsea—across the water from the Isle of Wight and Osborne, where Queen Victoria still lived. She liked to hear good sermons, but good preachers were rare. Lang proved to be an exception, and at Osborne he made the social acquaintance of the royal family.

Although at pains to acquit Lang of the charge of being a snob, his biographer Lockhart had to admit that he gave plenty of justification for the charge. When his diary or notes alluded to someone or other as one of his "dearest and closest friends," as they frequently did, "it is to be observed that the someone or other is very often Lord This, or Lady That." Lord This and Lady That might indeed be dear friends, but the suspicion arises that had they not been titled, he would not have thus referred to them. Lockhart also recalled that his curates at Portsea sometimes laughed at "the diplomatic guns which he laid with such care, and his unconcealed taste for the society of the important. They thought that he was too often absent from the parish on outside work of different kinds, and that his intention to climb to the top of the ladder was too plain even to be questioned." The combination of ambition, administrative ability, good sermons and excellent social connections proved irresistible: Lang was made a bishop.

The Church of which he had now become one of the rulers was faced with an impending crisis. For years the country had been governed by men who, whatever their own religious views, were prepared to accept that the Church as an institution was indispensable. The Church, therefore, could carry on as if it *were* indispensable without worrying overmuch about its failure to attract worshippers to morning service. But with the rise of Socialism, this supremacy might be challenged. And the first Labour government was formed from a party that included rationalists—and even Marxists, who believed that churches were the opium of the people, and who might, given the excuse, wish to close them, or at least to strip the Anglican Church of its "Established" status.

Apart from this political threat, the Church—and Christianity in general—was beginning to feel the impact of the blows that it had received from Darwin, and later from Freud and his followers. The twenties were not so much irreligious as a-religious, and amoral, in their tendency, but this churchmen found even more disconcerting than the attacks of the atheists, which had never had much effect. In Britain, too, conventional Christianity had been exposed to the subtler repudiation of E.M. Forster, whose work had built him a small but not insignificant following. Forster's rejection of Christianity was based on a belief in "the moral and aesthetic and humane sensibility of a few enlightened people who are to be found scattered about in all nations and classes," and he believed in them not—as earlier philosophers had—because he thought they would act as a kind of yeast on society, but simply because they were right for their time. In a sense, Forster acted as a self-effacing John the Baptist for the developing humanist and existentialist thought that was beginning, though gradually, to permeate Britain in this period. This was a much greater threat to the Church, as things eventually turned out, than the assaults of rival creeds or of old-style rationalism.

What the Church needed, then, at this time, was not administrators, but evangelists who would find ways to restore it to its place in the lives and the hearts of the British people rather than simply keep it going as a club for the benefit of a dwindling minority. But it happened that in the twenties the Church had become enmeshed in a controversy which preoccupied some of its most senior divines to the point of obsession and prevented them from grasping the Church's need.

For years, disputes had raged about the Prayer Book. The relevance of many of its passages to the twentieth century was hard to detect. It was time, Church leaders agreed, for a revised version. This was duly produced, but as the Church was Established, owing its existence and constitution to the state, legislation had to be passed to permit the revised Prayer Book's use. The proposal was modest: that the new, far from revolutionary version should be optionally available. It was the fruit of nearly a quarter of a century's labours and had been gratefully accepted by bishops, clergy, and laity. Yet in 1927 the House of Commons rejected it— and not, which might have been justifiable, on secular, but on doctrinal grounds.

The absurdity of having an "Established" Church was at once apparent. It would have been difficult enough to secure agreement between the two wings of the Church, High and Low—the High (according to the Low) being barely distinguishable in their beliefs and ritual from Roman Catholics, the Low (according to the High) being no better than a rabble of Nonconformists. In the Commons, the opposition to the bill was led by two Low Churchmen, or "Evangelicals," who were actually members of the government: the bigoted Sir William Joynson Hicks—widely, though not affectionately, known as "Jix"—whom Baldwin had made Home Secretary, and Sir Thomas Inskip, the Solicitor General. But they found backing from the Nonconformists, loosely federated as "the Free Churches"—Presbyterians, Methodists, Baptists, Congregationalists, Unitarians and others. Though not members of the Anglican Church, they felt that as Protestants they had a right to watch over her to see that she did not slide toward Rome. The decisive speech, in fact—or so the then Archbishop of Canterbury, Randall Davidson, thought—came from a Scots Presbyterian MP: "a simple ultra-Protestant harangue, with no real knowledge of the subject, but owing its power to its rhetorical presentment of no-Popery phrases and arguments of a sort which are to be found in *Barnaby Rudge*, when the Lord George Gordon riots set London aflame."

The rejection of the bill created a ludicrous situation, because the chief reason for going ahead with a revised version had been the realization that the old Prayer Book was no longer being adhered to. The revised version had been designed not for the sake of novelty, but to try to bring it into line with what most of the clergy were actually doing. It would have been difficult for the bishops, after showing by so big a majority that they approved of the new Prayer Book, to attempt to discipline clergy who deviated from the old one, and no attempt was made to do so. But this meant that the Church of England laid itself open to the charge of hypocrisy—a source of embarrassment to those clergy who craved spiritual integrity in all their dealings.

For a while, especially when a revised bill was also thrown out, there seemed a risk of a Church-State crisis, and in retrospect it is easy to see that it would have been better for the Church had it occurred. Randall Davidson was eighty, and the failure of what would have been the consummation of his life's work was a blow from which he could not be expected to recover. Had a militant successor been elected, there was no telling what the Church might have done. But Baldwin, ever the peacemaker, acted quickly to prevent an explosion. The need, he decided, was for a primate who could be relied upon to damp down the smouldering fires. Lang was the obvious man, and he was hardly likely to recognize his inadequacy for the post at that particular time. Nevertheless Baldwin was taking no chances. He came to Lambeth Palace in person to tell Lang that he had proposed his name as Archbishop and that King George had given his ready assent—the first time, Lang boasted, that such a communication had been delivered by word of mouth and not by letter, except once when George III had bypassed his Prime Minister, Pitt, to make a direct offer to the man of his own choice. When Lang went into the usual polite dither about needing time to consider, Baldwin brushed his hesitation aside: "I won't hear of any refusal. You are the only man, your one and only duty is to say 'Yes' at once, before I leave." Lang, though a little disconcerted that Baldwin should smoke his pipe on so important a mission, said yes, and thereby earned the right to sign himself "Cosmo Cantuar," as Primate of the Established Church.

King George V cordially approved what in theory was his choice. He had met Lang before the turn of the century and they had become close friends. In the scale of worldly values, Lockhart claimed, nothing stood higher with Lang than this friendship: "The Royal Office, of course, had and would always have his loyal respect; but for the King as a man, for his kindliness, simplicity, religious spirit and single-hearted devotion to his duty, Lang had much more than a formal feeling." Innumerable entries in Lang's private diaries and correspondence testified to this devotion. Lang thought of himself as one of the family, accepted and trusted. He was a regular visitor to Balmoral, and he liked to recall, as evidence of his closeness to the King, an occasion when they were out stalking deer together and were caught by a heavy shower. The only shelter was an overhanging rock, under which the King lay down, with Lang—claiming it was the privilege of the subject to protect the Sovereign—on top of him. George for his part had a liking and respect for Lang and trusted in his judgment, as did Queen Mary. The Archbishop's relations with the Duke and Duchess of York were also cordial.

By this time the Archbishop had acquired a gratifyingly aristo- cratic circle of friends. Aware that this led some people to think him a social climber, he resorted to an expedient that he found com- forting: he embraced the proffered title, calling his summer holi- day round of visits his "Snob's Progress." A visit to Hinchingbrooke, the home of Lord Sandwich, "had an almost invariable place on the itinerary," his biographer recalled. Afterward he would stay at Welbeck, where the "Duchess Winnie" (the Duchess of Portland, "unchanged and unchangeable") occupied a special niche in his affection. Then "he might move on to Garrowby to visit the son of his old friend Lord Halifax, or Castle Howard, or Lumley Castle, or Alnwick, or Howick" before crossing the border to Scotland, and eventually to Balmoral. He was usually a welcome guest. There was a cachet in having the Primate to stay, and his hosts had found to their relief that he could be entertaining company, as he was a gifted raconteur.

One of the people whom Lang could not impress was the Prince of Wales. Lang had admired, as it was hard not to, the gifts, charm and promise of the Prince—though, as Lockhart put it, "with some- times a note of regret that these were not always wisely directed." But their relationship had remained distant. Edward's attitude to Lang was to be expressed in A King's Story, where he refers to the Archbishop, other than in passing, only once in the years before he came to the throne—and that reference a sour one, suggesting that it was the new Archbishop's importunities (Lang had just been ap- pointed) that had led in 1929 to the holding of a day of national thanksgiving for the King's recovery before the King had in fact recovered, the King agreeing only out of reluctance to disappoint an old friend. Considering the true state of the King's health, "those of us who were close to the sickroom were inclined to regard the Archbishop's project as premature." So it turned out. The day be- fore "the elaborate religious display" was due to be presented, the King happened to be in the company of the Labour minister J.H. Thomas, whose fund of mildly dirty jokes the King greatly relished. On this occasion, one of the jokes so convulsed him that it burst an abscess below his ribs—thereby revealing why the King's recovery had been so slow: the doctors found on opening him up again that bone splinters had been left behind in the wound after the first operation. The King nevertheless insisted on going through with the service the following day: "Whether the Archbishop ever truly appreciated how much my father suffered that Sunday in the interests of national rejoicing I never knew."

The Duke of Windsor's recollection may have been tinged with resentment at the Archbishop's part in the abdication crisis—or what he assumed that part to have been. But there is no reason to believe that they had either respect or liking for each other. George V had confided his worries about Edward to the Archbishop, and the Archbishop shared them. Edward's casual attitude to religious observance, his enjoyment of night clubs, his choice of friends—almost everything about him, in fact, after his return from the Empire tours, was likely to irritate Lang.

Edward was not lacking in religious sense, but it was unconventional. When in *A King's Story* he recalled pleasure from church services, it appears to have been the setting and the music that captured him—as with the evensong at St. George's chapel, where he would sometimes go after a Sunday's work at the Fort: "Sitting in my stall as a Knight of the Garter, I listened to the singing of its fine choir, deriving an inner comfort of the spirit that I had seldom known elsewhere." But this was not the kind of churchgoing that Lang wanted from a King. He would have preferred regular attendance, to set a good example, as Edward's father had done—though his grandfather had been less assiduous. Edward, in fact, might reasonably have argued that he initially got his lax churchgoing habits from King Edward VII. When staying at Sandringham he went to the local church, but the rector had instructions that the sermon was not to last longer than ten minutes, and as Edward invariably arrived half an hour after the service had begun ("looking as if he had been detained by matters of great moment"), his grandchildren calculated that though he could claim to be a regular churchgoer, he in fact only spent half the time in church that they did. But at least Edward VII went to church—his name could be published in the court *Circular* as having attended divine service, which was more than could often be said for Edward VIII.

Equally, Lang's social climbing and pliability were certain to annoy Edward. The prospect of their coming together when Edward came to the throne was slender, and they clashed even in connection with the funeral arrangements for George V. The Archbishop had been relieved at the declaration of accession, when the King ended his speech with the hope that God would guide him, but it was soon clear that this formal expression did not presage any change of attitude. The King informed him that when the body of George V was brought from Sandringham to lie in state in Westminster Hall, no religious service would be held, as he was "anxious to spare the Queen." Lang insisted that there must be some service and told Edward that, as it happened, he knew that Queen Mary wanted it, as she had already chosen the hymn: *Praise, My Soul, the King of Heaven.*

The Archbishop's only attempt at a rapprochement came the day after the funeral, when he went to see Queen Mary at Buckingham Palace and took the opportunity to have a talk with the King afterward. According to Lockhart, he spoke to the King frankly: "I was aware that he had been somewhat set against me by knowing that his father had often discussed his affairs with me. But I assured him—which was true—that I had always tried to put the most favourable view of his conduct before his father." And the King, Lang thought, did not resent this frankness.

In this the Archbishop was wrong. Edward did resent it. "My conduct, I wondered? What was Dr. Lang driving at? No man likes to be told that his character has provided a topic of conversation between his father and a third person." It was an unpropitious note, Edward thought, on which to inaugurate the formal relations between a new sovereign and his Primate. However, "hiding my resentment, I turned the conversation in the direction of my new responsibilities as head of the Church." But this also turned out to be an unfortunate topic. When Edward named several clerics he knew and liked, Lang's "cool and almost negative response implied that my acquaintance with Church affairs was too naïve to be pursued." According to Lang, Edward spoke to him only of "one or two" clerics he had met, "but even of these his knowledge was faint. It was clear that he knows little and, I fear, cares little about the Church and its affairs."

So in spite of the fact that Edward was "very pleasant, and seemed to be cordial," Lang went away disturbed. "There is not only a new reign, but a new regime. I can only be most thankful for what has been; and for what is to be, hope for the best." The effect of the interview on the King was even more disturbing. Lang had contrived to give the impression that "the hidden burden of his discourse" was to express his disapproval of the King's friendship with Mrs. Simpson. Lang had in fact discussed it with George V at Balmoral the previous summer in a "long and intimate talk"—one of the conversations to which he had been referring when he had begged that it should not be held against him that he had discussed Edward's affairs with his father. To the King, "the air in the room was heavy with portent when the Archbishop left"—he knew, or thought he knew, that this was what Lang was getting at, and he knew that Lang would be able to count on powerful support. Previously, Edward had been able to combine duty and personal inclinations without much difficulty. But now, "the Royal Standard flying from the clock tower of St. James's Palace was a signal that my freer days as Heir Apparent were over; and that my life and actions, already dedicated beyond recall to a secret hope, had by the circumstances of my new position become the presumptive property of a vast Imperial community that might seem to obstruct that hope."

But why, now that he realized what lay ahead, did Edward not seek advice and help on how to proceed? By his own account, the reason was that he was a fatalist: "When great questions are invoked, forces are let loose that are beyond the limited powers of personal decision." Time, he hoped, would solve the problem, and he thrust himself into the work of a king, in the hope that something would turn up. The Archbishop made no further advances, and Edward made no attempt to capture him by diplomacy. Lang being the man he was, this might not have been impossible. But Edward, being the man *he* was, was incapable of the hypocrisy which would have been involved in the effort.

Lang was not on the list of those invited to Balmoral that October. It was an omission that he was unlikely to regret, because he received an invitation to stay in company that, to him, would be much more congenial. The Duke and Duchess of York asked him to their home at Birkhall, and they were kindness itself. "The children—Lillibet, Margaret Rose and Margaret Elphinstone—joined us. They sang some action songs charmingly. It was strange to think of the destiny which may be awaiting the little Elizabeth, at present second from the throne."

The Archbishop, though, was not simply worried by "the King's matter"—as he euphemistically called it in the diary he kept during the period—because of fears about the fitness of the King to be crowned. Lang happened also to have committed himself to a scheme requiring the King's active co-operation, designed to promote a revival of the Church—a revival that was urgently needed, as recent events had demonstrated.

The collapse of the campaign to legitimize the revised Prayer Book had been bad enough for the Church's reputation, but perhaps more damaging, and certainly more humiliating, were the protracted proceedings taken in 1932 against Harold Francis Davidson, rector of the parish of Stiffkey (pronounced Stewky) in Norfolk. Davidson had been there for over a quarter of a century before facing the charges of immoral living preferred against him in a Church court. From the prosecution, it transpired that he had spent the years running a one-man mission for fallen women in London—work which, he claimed, had necessitated his spending a great deal of his time with them—the whole week, usually, while his wife and children remained in the Stiffkey Rectory, taking in paying guests.

From early spring to midsummer the Church court probed Davidson's relationships with girls, the evidence ranging from stories of petting in teashops to descriptions of his excursions with them to Paris, and the lurid details were gratefully chronicled in the popular press. Davidson took the line that he was the prostitute's padre—"to me, the proudest title that a true priest of Christ can hold"—and he cited evidence from the New Testament to suggest that Jesus, were he to return to earth, might be expected to undertake the same mission. He was an amused, and often amusing, defendant, and the public, so far from being shocked, inclined to his side. Eventually in July he was found guilty, but even then the Church's humiliations were not over. The ceremony by which he was "entirely removed, deposed and degraded" naturally excited interest. So did his subsequent career. He decided to earn his living on the Front at Blackpool, where, like Diogenes, he lived in a tub, among such attractions as the Bearded Lady and the Fattest Man in the World. And from time to time, newspaper reporters and photographers would visit him there and record his impressions.

By 1936, though, references to the rector of Stiffkey were becoming rarer even in the patter of music-hall comedians, and the Archbishop of Canterbury decided that the time was ripe to launch a counterattack on the scoffers and the backsliders. The year 1937, he decreed, was to be used for a campaign designated "A Call to Religion," and it would be pegged to the coronation.

But how could it be launched when there was the possibility that the Archbishop was going to be asked to crown a king who wanted to marry a woman who had been twice divorced? "If this looming possibility was realized," Lockhart observed, "with what force or sincerity could he speak and, above all, how could he allow the appeal to hinge on a ceremony which had become a mockery"—especially as one of its themes was to be an attack on divorce? Lockhart could find no evidence that the Archbishop had made up his mind that—as rumour claimed—he would refuse to crown the King if he persisted in his determination to marry Mrs. Simpson. But obviously the situation was fraught with potential embarrassment, whatever decision the Archbishop reached. And in the circumstances he was unlikely to make any energetic efforts to keep Edward on the throne.

The editor of the *Times*

The other influential Establishment figure who was later to be accused of conspiring to push the King from his throne was Geoffrey Dawson, editor of the *Times*—according to Gunther, "certainly one of the ten most important men in England." Although he had been editor, with one brief interregnum, for over twenty years, he was still in his early sixties—"a man of middle height," Beaverbrook was to describe him, "with a good head, going a bit bald, and a rather flushed face. He walked with a firm tread. He would have looked well, and he would have done well, on the bridge of a battleship . . . he was a *somebody*." He was also, Beaverbrook believed, the key figure behind the scenes in the abdication—of much more importance to Baldwin than any of Baldwin's Cabinet colleagues, and invariably consulted before them. Reviewing *The History of the Times* for the BBC in 1952, Beaverbrook formally put forward the thesis, which he claimed the *History* itself bore out, that Dawson (1) "was the most important factor—with the sole exception of the Prime Minister, Stanley Baldwin—in compelling the King to abdicate. (2) That he did it by methods which many would condemn. (3) That he pursued his quest with a vigour that seemed more like venom."

Geoffrey Robinson—he changed his name to Dawson during the

First World War—was not born into the Establishment, but in every other respect he was its epitome. His father was a provincial banker, devoted to the Church and to his Masonic lodge. He brought his son up in the Victorian tradition, but the boy was lucky enough to go to a preparatory school nearby that at that time had a remarkable academic record, culminating in 1887 in the winning of three out of the first four scholarships to Eton—Geoffrey Dawson taking one of them. He went on to Magdalen and in 1898 was awarded a fellowship at All Souls—the year after John Simon and Leo Amery. He had originally planned a civil-service career, but his talents were spotted by Milner, who invited him to go out to join the Kindergarten. His work in South Africa led to an invitation to stay there as editor of the Johannesburg *Star*. In that capacity he became South African correspondent of the *Times*, which liked to use the editors of respected local journals as its "stringers."

The *Times* was then in serious financial difficulties, which were eventually resolved in 1908 by allowing Alfred Harmsworth, later Lord Northcliffe, to buy it. Northcliffe had helped to revolutionize journalism in England by introducing the first popular mass-circulation daily, aimed at an audience that up to that time had read "penny dreadfuls" but not newspapers. His *Daily Mail* had broken away from the traditional Fleet Street verbosity, with short news stories, short editorials and light features. The *Mail* was followed by the *Mirror*, the first tabloid newspaper, and with the addition of a string of provincial papers and magazines, Northcliffe's empire soon dominated Fleet Street. To prove that he was not limited to the popular market, he had bought the *Observer*, which was threatened with extinction, and preserved it as a quality Sunday newspaper. With this good example before them, the owners of the *Times* were persuaded that their property, which they had come to regard more as an institution than a newspaper, would be safe in Northcliffe's hands.

His early actions suggested that they had been right. As the *History of the Times* later acknowledged, Northcliffe turned "a bankrupt nineteenth-century relic into a flourishing twentieth-century property," and to help in this process he called back Geoffrey Dawson, with the idea that he should remodel it along the lines it had followed in the time of its greatest editor, Thomas Barnes.

A century before, the proprietor of the *Times* had decided to leave his paper in Barnes' hands. Up to then, the course the *Times* had taken had been undistinguished, but Barnes was a genius. Previously the *Times* had had to rely on governments to support it. Within a decade, governments were relying on the *Times* to support them and becoming nervous when it declined to do so. Barnes kept free from party ties, bartering the *Times'* support for individual measures of which he approved—such as Catholic Emancipation, in 1829—in return for privileges, compelling even the Duke of Wellington, who hated the press, to grant it "the earliest intimation of the Duke's intentions and any advantages that the Foreign Office could give—such as intelligence from foreign countries." The result was that the *Times* began to secure a succession of "scoops," which increased its circulation, its revenue, and its influence. The status of journalists was also raised in the process. In 1829 Walter Scott could tell his future biographer that "connection with any newspaper would be a disgrace and a degradation: I would sooner sell gin to poor people than poison them that way." But when, the following year, Barnes was elected to the Athenæum, it was clear that old prejudices were breaking down. Soon, Barnes was dining in the highest social circles, and one of his hosts, Lord Lyndhurst, was not being sarcastic when he described the editor of the *Times* as "the most powerful man in the country."

Under Barnes' successor, John Thadeus Delane, the *Times* rose to even greater heights. Never in history has any newspaper wielded comparable influence. There was a difference, though, between the methods of the two editors. Barnes had supported measures, not men. Delane was inclined to attach himself to governments, and where the government was in the hands of a politician as wily as Lord Palmerston, the *Times* could be manipulated to serve government policies. As soon as Palmerston had broken down early suspicions, Delane—as the *History* admitted—"gave him firm support in matters both great and small. Palmerston could think and do no wrong, almost. His taste, even in architecture, was grounded in the verities." Delane was not aware how he was being exploited, retaining to the last his belief that he was giving Palmerston the *Times'* support because of Palmerston's merits. But in fact, Palmerston was cleverly using the *Times*. He would tell Delane of a course of action that he was thinking of taking, and Delane would publish a leading article urging that the course *should* be taken. If the response was favourable, Palmerston would then take it—his government getting the benefit of having a preview of the public reaction without having committed itself, Delane getting the benefit of the scoop.

The *Times* became even more influential. Foreign journalists and diplomats now had to read it in order to know what the government might be up to. But it lost its integrity, and after Delane's death it began to go downhill. The appearance of Reuters News Agency, with its international network of communications, and later of the telephone and the radio, meant that the chances of getting major international scoops grew more remote. The removal of the stamp duty and other taxes affecting newspapers enabled rivals to enter the field with more prospect of success. And grave errors—like the publication of letters supposedly written by the Irish leader Charles Stewart Parnell, which turned out to be forgeries—damaged the *Times*'s reputation and its finances. Its circulation fell away, and had Northcliffe not come to its rescue, it would probably have had to suspend publication.

Northcliffe had studied the story of the *Times*, acquiring a great admiration for Thomas Barnes. What it needed, he believed, was another Barnes as editor, while he managed its finances. In theory, Dawson was given editorial independence. But Northcliffe proved incapable of leaving the editorial side alone. He was too interested in it, and his self-confidence was developing gradually into megalomania. During the war years there were frequent conflicts, ending in 1919 with Dawson's resignation and—as he assumed—his final severance from the *Times*.

Then, in the summer of 1922, Northcliffe died. His brother Lord Rothermere was anxious to take on the *Times*, but John Walter, a member of the family that had owned the *Times* when it was first founded, was anxious to break the now noxious Harmsworth connection. He found a backer in the Hon. John Jacob Astor—Waldorf's brother, later to become Lord Astor of Hever. On the same day that Bonar Law succeeded Lloyd George as Prime Minister, Walter and Astor acquired the *Times*. Four days later, they dispatched Robert Brand to persuade Geoffrey Dawson to return to the editorial chair. It was appropriate that this meeting should be held in All Souls, and after some heart-searching, Dawson allowed himself to be persuaded to return to Printing House Square.

Dawson was now in an exceptionally strong position. The influence of the *Times* might have declined after Delane, but the editor had remained an important figure. His predecessor, writing to congratulate him on his appointment in 1912, had said that he had commended Dawson to his "personal friends," who included Balfour, Bonar Law and Chamberlain—as well as Milner and Curzon, whom Dawson already knew—on the Conservative side, and the chief leaders of the Liberal Party. "The Archbishop of Canterbury," he went on, "whom I know well, will be very ready to help you. I have also bespoken the friendly interests of Stamfordham, the King's Private Secretary."

Dawson was well able to keep up this tradition. As a member of the Round Table, he was in constant touch with his old Milner Kindergarten colleagues, now becoming influential in their own right. He also kept his close links with Eton and with All Souls—he always attended the All Souls Day mallard gathering, except when abroad. A gregarious man, he became a member of the Athenæum and other clubs and began to go regularly to week-end house parties. On his return from South Africa he had become friendly with Waldorf and Nancy Astor. Thereafter, Cliveden, according to his biographer Sir Evelyn Wrench, provided him with "a very stimulating background and a lovely setting for meeting old friends and making new ones." Lord Stamfordham would discuss with him such matters as whether Baldwin or Curzon should succeed Bonar Law, or who should be the recipients of the Order of Merit. Nobody in Britain had a wider range of influential acquaintances—many of them friends. In such circumstances, the *Times* could be kept exceptionally well-informed of all that was going on behind the scenes.

For a time Dawson modelled himself on Thomas Barnes. In spite of a strong dislike for Socialism, he was one of those who was prepared to give the first Labour government a fair trial. He dismissed the idea of bringing Conservatives and Liberals together in a new coalition to keep Labour out as "immoral and utterly fatuous." But the Barnes phase passed. By temperament and Kindergarten training, Dawson was more akin to Delane. When the economic crisis arose in 1931, he became active in promoting the project of a national government. According to Lady Oxford, the original idea was his, and he was consulted by George V, through Wigram, about it. He strongly urged that the King should insist on Ramsay staying on, to make sure that it appeared to be a national government. He even advised the King to use flattery, if necessary, to secure Ramsay's consent. The advocacy of the *Times* was also important in helping to remove the worries of those who, like Baldwin, were suspicious of any coalition. Dawson has a strong claim to have been, with the King, the decisive force in bringing the national government into being.

But having delivered it, Dawson could not look upon it with detachment. It was his child, and he loved it. The *Times* continued to be critical of individual government decisions, and Dawson did not think of the paper—any more than Delane had done—as the servant of the government. Yet the *Times* could say, in 1932—when the Prime Minister's mind had already begun to sag, to the frequent irritation of his colleagues—that "Mr. MacDonald has so steadily gained in strength and public estimation since he took his great decision to face the country with a National Government, that if any man could be called indispensable to the State, he has won that title today." Two years later, the *Times* could call the record of the national government in economics, social reconstruction and international affairs—which was feeble—"beyond all criticism." Politically, Dawson had begun to see only what he wanted to see.

It was typical of his lack of insight that he should not for a moment have considered that he or his paper had party political affiliations. "For myself," he wrote to Claud Cockburn, when Cockburn was resigning on grounds of political incompatibility, "I have always regarded the *Times* as something of an organ of the Left." But, he went on to add, to Cockburn's delight, "never, I hope, of the extreme Left." As time went on, Dawson grew less and less able to grasp how committed he was, politically.

The commitment added greatly to the influence, if not to the reputation, of the *Times*. Under Dawson it was restored to roughly the same standing as it had had under Delane. Dawson was known to be close to Baldwin, who was grateful for his support and his advice; he would drop in for fireside tea with the Dawsons and confide his difficulties to them. In his diaries and memoranda, Dawson recorded many instances of conversations in which he was treated less as an editor than as an adviser—for example, on the formation of Baldwin's new Cabinet after the retirement of Ramsay MacDonald in 1935. In the process Dawson naturally acquired extensive inside information about what was happening behind the political scenes, and this enabled the *Times* to report, comment and predict with unrivalled authority. Naturally observers began to realize this and to use the *Times* as a barometer of the government's moves. This was not good for the *Times'* reputation for being independent of political parties, but it meant that the paper was read with attention abroad as well as at home.

There are indications that Baldwin used Dawson as Palmerston had used Delane—to fly kites, to test out public reactions. He may well have begun to feel that Dawson needed him more than he needed Dawson. But late in 1935 he had had a salutary reminder of the influence that the *Times* could exert independently of him— the only occasion on which the *Times* came out against the national government on a major issue: the "Corridor for Camels" editorial that helped to bring down Hoare, pouring ridicule on his idea of compensating Abyssinia for what she had lost through Italian aggression by giving her access, through a desert, to the sea.

The *Times,* admittedly, was taking not so much an anti-government as an anti-Hoare line. Dawson had recommended Hoare to Baldwin for the Foreign Secretaryship and was annoyed at his protégé. Though not actively pro-German, Dawson believed, rightly, that Germany was the power to watch. He also thought that she was therefore a power to be appeased, and here his judgment was soon to be proved at fault. Hoare, he had hoped, would take the same attitude. When Hoare allowed himself to be won over by Vansittart to the pro-Italian, anti-German camp. Dawson was not sorry to have the opportunity to put Hoare in his place.

But there may have been another reason. Dawson told Tom Jones that he had offered to see Baldwin earlier in the crisis, but had not pressed the point. He had grown accustomed to being able to make his views known to Baldwin, and the "Corridor for Camels" editorial may have been a none too gentle intimation that this political intimacy should be resumed. The astute Baldwin, of all people, was likely to take the hint.

From every possible aspect, Dawson could be expected to be antipathetic to the King's project. As a man of strong religious principles, he could not have viewed the prospect of Mrs. Simpson becoming Queen with anything but repugnance. He had often heard from members of the government about the difficulties of dealing with Edward over state business, and as he was a friend of Wigram's and an acquaintance of Hardinge's, he could not have failed to have heard of the worries of the court. But what was finally destructive of any sympathy he might have felt for the King was the pile of letters and cuttings that he had begun to find every morning on his desk at the *Times*. The guiding force in his life had been the Milner concept of England and the Empire as a great moral force. The strength of that force must depend—he and his friends assumed—on the one binding link that remained: the crown. Now, here was the crown being rolled in the gutter.

There could be no question that the *Times* would take Baldwin's side. Baldwin's only cause for concern, in fact, would be keeping the *Times* on the leash. For by this time a new trait could be observed in Dawson: vanity. In his memoirs of Cliveden, Michael Astor singled Dawson out for particular criticism, along with his colleague and successor Barrington Ward. Both were industrious and eminently respectable men, believing themselves to be unusually enlightened, and they acted with a sense of mission, "but I thought at the time, and I still believe, that Geoffrey Dawson was blinded by a form of self-conceit." Dawson was a man of uncompromising honesty—except with himself. If he felt sufficiently strongly on any issue, the *Times* would cease to be reasoned and judicial. It could become relentless, and even downright unfair, in its onslaught.

The Go-Betweens

Personal power—W.L. Guttsman observed in his study of the British political elite—"may occasionally come to men who are formally lowly placed, but who occupy strategic office which either gives them intimate access to powerful individuals—such as the office of Principal Private Secretary to a high-ranking minister—or one that permits them independent action through the accumulation of know-how and experience of a special kind." The more tightly knit the Establishment, the easier it is for strategically placed individuals to exploit their talents as go-betweens, and the 1930s produced quite a crop of them. The most influential in the abdication period was Tom Jones, secretary of the Pilgrim Trust—an organization founded in 1930, with the help of a New York benefactor, to make grants for the repair of ancient monuments, the preservation of historical records, and other such objects.

The Pilgrim Trust gave Jones a base from which to operate, but he owed his influential contacts to the fact that he had earlier been private secretary to four prime ministers. In his *Diary with Letters,* he was to give a revealing glimpse of the way in which influence could be exerted by a man with a mind to exert it—or simply with a mind that revelled in the feeling of being in the centre of things. Jones was not an active wire-puller, let alone a "fixer," but he was an assiduous go-between, with exceptional facilities to indulge his hobby.

Jones' function, as he had regarded it, had not been to be a private secretary in the strict sense, but primarily to be a kind of adviser to the Cabinet and liaison officer with the various state departments. There were many opportunities, before and after meetings, for brief conversations with ministers, "and one learned to make good use of these occasions, to judge imponderables and garner impressions of value to the Prime Minister, to whom, from the beginning, I had the privilege of direct access whenever I sought it. Prime Ministers, Cabinet Ministers and Secretaries, all take in one another's advice." Jones admitted that he gave much wrong advice, as hind-sight was to show, but he made no attempt to disguise his satisfaction at having been in a position where his advice could exercise considerable influence, whether it was sound or not.

But this was only one side of Jones' life. "Though a mere provincial in speech and dress," he recalled, "sporting a superannuated bowler hat but neither the rolled umbrella nor the spats of the Foreign Office clerk, my post as Assistant, and later Deputy, Secretary to the Cabinet made me a person of some casual interest to London political hostesses, and I was increasingly asked out to luncheon and dinner. I went to Lady Carnarvon's to talk of education in Albania, to Lady Esher's to talk to his Lordship, to Lady Horner's, to Lady Cholmondley's, occasionally to Violet Markham's in Gower Street, and much oftener, and for many years, to Lady Astor's at 4 St. James's Square, Cliveden, or Sandwich . . . No one could escape at least one invitation to Lady Cunard and one to Lady Ottoline Morrell. I went to both. In addition I was welcomed to the homes and clubs of Private Secretaries: Philip Kerr, Edward Grigg, Geoffrey Fry, Patrick Duff, Robert Vansittart, James Grigg and others." And Jones might have added that, in A.L. Rowse's collection, he was "constantly in and out of All Souls."

There were also, Jones found, the wives of aspiring politicians who "desired my company at luncheon so that they might remind me, and through me the Prime Minister, of the brilliant gifts and political deserts of their husbands," but he could not reciprocate their generous hospitality. He could, however, by keeping his ears open, learn much that was of value—particularly as he did not drink and was better able than many of his associates to avoid giving away confidences. So, "more and more, the luncheon hour provided an opportunity of meeting civil servants or public persons on business of national importance rather than for entertainment or gossip."

It is difficult to assess the extent of Jones' power, because it depended on his not appearing to have any, or at least not trying too obviously to exert it. But that he influenced Baldwin, for one, can hardly be disputed. Baldwin came to appreciate Jones because he had lived for so long among the Welsh workers and therefore could be deemed to have his ear to the ground. "I seem," Jones recalled, "to have helped to relieve tension in the ministerial mind, was sought for as a counsellor and prompter in the wings, and much consulted in the preparation of speeches." The advice was not necessarily sound. What mattered was that it seemed representative, giving Baldwin the comforting feeling that if Jones thought that way, so must others like him.

Occasionally, however, Jones was able to intervene actively to promote some attitude or policy he believed in, as he did in 1936. Jones was a fervent Germanophile. "I keep on and on preaching," he wrote in a letter in February 1936, "against the policy of ostracising Germany, however incalculable Hitler and his crew may be. We have an abundance of evidence of the desire of all sorts of Germans to be on friendly terms with us. There is still a substantial element of elderly men and women in Germany who have not forgotten the war and its horrors and who are in no hurry to precipitate another."

These views came to the ears of Ribbentrop, who had been trying for some time to break into London society through certain recognized routes for climbers—the salons of Lady Londonderry and Lady Cunard. When Lady Astor chaffed him about the "bad company" he kept when in England, he excused himself by saying that they had always been extremely kind to him and his friends, but they had also been useful in introducing him to, among others, Mrs. Simpson. Jones—who, though retired, still had the ear of the Prime Minister—was an even more promising contact, and in May he received a message that Ribbentrop very much wished him to spend a week-end at his home outside Berlin. Jones protested that he was "a person of no importance, and entirely without official standing," but Ribbentrop persisted. Jones, flattered, decided to accept. He met not merely Ribbentrop, but Hitler, whom he found "a complete contrast to Mussolini." Hitler made no attempt whatever to impress "or aggress" his visitor. His aim, it transpired, was to urge the importance of an alliance between Germany and England and to indicate his desire to meet Stanley Baldwin. Jones replied that Baldwin was shy and modest—had never entirely got over his astonishment at finding himself Prime Minister. When this was translated, the Führer smiled: "And I also." As soon as Jones got back, he had breakfast with Baldwin and delivered Hitler's message. Baldwin was much impressed, interjecting at one stage, "Go on. This is like an Oppenheimer story." (Presumably a reference to the thrillers of E. Phillips Oppenheim.) Jones was invited to come down to Chequers to talk it all out on the week-end, and Geoffrey Dawson also came around to hear how the German trip had gone.

Apart from any effect this may have had on Baldwin, by encouraging him to believe in Hitler's pacific intentions, the encounter between Hitler and Jones helped to persuade Ribbentrop that he was now in a position to exercise a decisive influence in London. The King, Ribbentrop knew, was on the German side, and so was Mrs. Simpson. Now here was Jones, and Baldwin—with any luck—in Jones' pocket. The prospects seemed highly encouraging. And so they might have been, had Edward been able to stay on his throne. Ironically, though, Ribbentrop's arrival was to decrease his chances of remaining King. Because one of the most persistent and damaging rumours about Mrs. Simpson concerned her closeness to the Nazis in general and to Ribbentrop in particular, his arrival at the critical moment seemed to confirm suspicions and to diminish confidence in the King.

Another active go-between, eventually destined to be far more influential than Tom Jones, was Sir Horace Wilson, officially chief industrial adviser to the government, but seconded to the Treasury "for service for the Prime Minister." In that capacity, the Duke of Windsor was to recall, Wilson wielded power behind the scenes. His words "carried great weight in the day-to-day evolution of high government policy."

Like Jones, Wilson was not Establishment-born. His father dealt in furniture, his mother was the landlady of a boarding house. He went to a local "board school," as they were then known, and managed to get only into the second division of the civil service, the administrative grade. But administration was what he was good at.

He impressed those under whom he worked and rose rapidly, eventually leaping over the heads of those in the first, the executive, grade to become Baldwin's right-hand man. And in this capacity—the head of the Civil Service Union, W.J. Brown, asserted—Wilson held a more powerful position in Britain "than almost anybody since Cardinal Wolsey."

The way Wilson exercised it made him many enemies. Some of them later began to wonder, looking back, whether he might not have been the real back-room boy of the abdication, as well as, later, of appeasement. "Cato" in *Guilty Men* argued that he had a good deal to do with the arrangements. Certainly he was active in the final negotiations. Wilson was an assiduous churchgoer and was believed to be a member of the Buchmanite Oxford Group—later to be known as Moral Rearmament.

Of the other members of the Establishment, a few have since been named as co-conspirators, but without real evidence. One of them, however, was certainly in a position to have exercised influence: the King's chief physician, Lord Dawson of Penn. Dawson was in a unique situation as medical adviser to many members of the court and to some of the most influential men of the time, including the Archbishop of Canterbury and Lloyd George, with whom he visited Hitler at Berchtesgaden in the summer of 1936. Dawson had emerged as a figure of public eminence during King George's illness, though the course that illness took, as Edward tartly noted, was not exactly a testimonial to his treatment. But Dawson had eventually clinched his reputation with the celebrated bulletin on the evening George V died: "The King's life is moving peacefully towards its close." He had easy access to men in authority, and most of them treated his views with respect.

Dawson had liked the young Prince—dynamic, he thought, where George V had been static—but now that Edward was King, he did not feel that the Mrs. Simpson affair was any concern of his, unless, of course, Edward chose to broach it. And Edward did not so choose. Long after Dawson, like everybody else in his walk of life, knew of the gossip and the speculation in the foreign papers, the King still did not confide in him. "He never talked of Mrs. S.," Dawson recalled, "except as 'my friend Mrs. Simpson'; and thus he held himself to all, including authority, until events at Balmoral and the Simpson divorce brought his impending marriage onto the stage of possible events." There is no evidence that Lord Dawson used his knowledge or authority against the King—in fact, intervention of this sort, his biographer Francis Watson claimed, would have been out of character.

The City

Of all the outposts of the Establishment, the one from which the King could most confidently expect allies was business. Not, though, the City, whose financiers did not like to have their activities interrupted by crises which might upset the stock market—as, indeed, the threat of abdication was to do. Besides, there were influential bankers like Brand who were part of the Establishment's inner circle, and though he was to show an independent mind over appeasement, on the King's matter he was wholeheartedly behind his friend, the editor of the *Times*.

The attitude of the governor of the Bank of England, Montagu Norman, could well have been important. He figured in all lists, such as Gunther's, of the ten or twelve most important men in the country, and rightly. As a financier he clung to an arid orthodoxy, and such was his influence that successive governments meekly accepted it. As an individual, he was one of the great eccentrics of the day. "Ostensibly eschewing publicity," Boothby described him, "he moved in a perpetual limelight of alibis." He liked to travel incognito as "Mr. Skinner," but his beard and his broad-brimmed black hat made him instantly recognizable wherever he went—and when he was not recognized, he would on occasion draw attention to himself by behaving like a ham actor playing the villain in a melodrama. Norman had met the King and might have proved a useful ally if his services had been enlisted, but there is no evidence that Edward sought him out, and apparently Baldwin, though he and Norman were close friends, did not feel it necessary to consult him.

As for the City in a corporate sense, one of Edward's earliest acts as King had been to give it offence. As usual, he was trying to cut down traditional and—as he thought—time-wasting ritual. At the beginning of his reign he was told that twenty leading corporations would be coming to see him, one at a time, to deliver their loyal addresses. The King insisted that they should all come together, and most of them accepted his decision without demur. But the City delegation was furious. The City regarded itself as being in a special position vis-à-vis the King, and it was damned if it was going to allow itself to be lumped together with the Society of Friends, the Jewish Board of Deputies, the Royal Academy and other such bodies. Eventually the King had to agree to receive the lord mayor and aldermen in a separate room, before the ceremony.

Recalling the occasion, Edward said he had described "this unimportant incident only to illustrate the extent to which mere formality still, even today, claims the time of the King." It would have been more to the point if he had described it to illustrate one of the causes of his eventual downfall. To many representatives of corporate bodies, a meeting with the King represented the most memorable event of their tenure of office—but only so long as they could see him in their small corporate group and have the opportunity to exchange a few words with him. A mass meeting of all the corporate bodies was hardly more of an occasion than a royal garden party, and they resented what one of them, as Edward himself recalled, described as "His Majesty's unfortunate decision." Had Edward received them individually, and exercised on them the charm that came naturally to him, he might have won them to his side. As it was, many of them went away disgruntled, and none more than the City aldermen, fobbed off with their brief encounter in an antechamber.

Edward was also on unsure ground when he assumed that businessmen would remember with gratitude his efforts on their behalf while he was Prince of Wales. Of all the titles ever applied to him, he was to claim, hereditary or complimentary, "the ones that gave me most private satisfaction were the newspaper sobriquets acknowledging these services—'Britain's First Ambassador' and 'Britain's Best Salesman'." To have been Britain's First Ambassador he had a fair claim, but there were some who thought his reputation as Britain's Best Salesman was ill-founded.

The trouble was that he allowed his enthusiasms to run away with him. On his return from his first visit to South America, for example, he sent for the head of Reuters News Agency, Sir Roderick Jones, to say that the pro-British element in Buenos Aires were anxious to see British news and views more satisfactorily put. As things were, information from and about Britain reached South

America only through French or U.S. channels, restricted, distorted, sometimes anti-British in presentation. Jones broke with Havas and moved Reuters in—the Prince having encouraged him to believe that it would get support in the form of subscriptions to the service from newspapers and British concerns, which were very powerful in the Argentine at the time. But the promises were not redeemed. "The British protagonists," Jones complained, "whatever they may have led his Royal Highness to suppose, seemed afflicted with a palsy when it became a question of giving, or causing to be given, the necessary financial backing," and after a couple of years of heavy losses, Reuters had to withdraw again. Such stories got around, and the businessmen involved did not thank the Prince for his part in them.

The Prince could also be tactless. One of his voyages, in 1931, had had a more mundane purpose than its predecessors. He went to Buenos Aires, ostensibly to open the British Empire Trade Fair but really "to try to recapture for British commerce the great South American markets into which the competition of the United States and other countries had made deep inroads." He brushed up his Spanish before leaving and spent much of his time when he arrived seeking to find out why people were no longer buying British. In the process he collected a quantity of samples to show what was actually being sold, instead of the British commodity, and on his return he did his best to explain why. The British product, he thought, often just was not good enough. He now found no great enthusiasm, even some hostility, from the very people he had been hoping to instruct in how to mend their ways. They were offended at the idea that he should think he could teach them their business.

In any case, such benefits as Edward had brought to industry had by 1936 been forgotten. Businessmen were more likely to regard him with some suspicion, as a man who had been inclined to express heterodox views—for example, about the need for more state intervention to cure unemployment. They assumed unemployment was incurable, and some of them did not hesitate, at least in private, to admit that they were glad that it was—for how else would wages be kept down? A few individuals must have retained pleasant memories of what the Prince had done for them, either indirectly by his engaging personality or directly by some visit to their firm, but on balance there was little enthusiasm for him in the business world.

Anglo-Saxon attitudes

Clearly, then, Edward could look for little sympathy from the members of the Establishment. For apart from the reactions of the individuals who composed it, he also had to face the fact that in proposing to marry Mrs. Simpson he was going to offend the Establishment's corporate susceptibilities—for a number of reasons.

Chief among them was the feeling that marriage to Mrs. Simpson would weaken the structure of the Empire. In the Establishment the imperial dream had not yet become, as it was fast becoming outside it, a music-hall joke—the Malay planter putting on a dinner jacket every night in the jungle, the Poona army officer downing his chota pegs in the club. In most upper-middle-class families, the fact that in British atlases so many areas on the map of the world were still coloured the traditional British red was a matter for pride, not for guilt. There was satisfaction, too, that the transition to self-government—in spite of the mistakes made in America, and later in Ireland —had been on balance so smoothly accomplished. There was a strong desire that the process by which the British Empire was becoming the British Commonwealth of Nations should continue to be smooth. By removing possible causes of friction, the imperial link might even be made more binding than before. And in the inner ring of the Establishment, this feeling was even more powerful, owing to the Kindergarten influence. It could be almost religious in its intensity.

Inevitably, with the disappearance of all the legislative ties that had bound the former colonies to Britain, more and more reliance had to be placed on the last remaining formal Empire link: the crown. At that time it seemed inconceivable that any country should want to stay within the Commonwealth as a republic, not accepting the crown. It was therefore considered essential that the crown's wearer should command respect in the Empire—if he did not, what link would remain? And one thing could be predicted with total certainty: a king who proposed to marry a twice-divorced American woman, no matter what his qualities might be, no matter how much he had been admired as a prince, would not command respect. The chances were, therefore, that the whole imperialist concept would collapse. It might not collapse immediately—though even that was not impossible. But certainly erosion would set in, and the institution that had brought the men of the Kindergarten together, and had illuminated their lives, would be destroyed.

There was also in the Establishment a measure of anti-Americanism, though as this was something that its members did not ordinarily admit to, even to themselves, it is difficult to assess how much effect it had. After the First World War, anti-Americanism became endemic in the English upper middle class. They resented the neutral United States acting as profiteer-in-chief during the worst of the war and then coming in and claiming to have won it, they resented Britain's state of indebtedness to the United States, and they resented the way post-war American visitors talked big (which they often did) about their skyscrapers and their cars and their Hollywood, with the implied disrespect for lil' ole England, left on the sidelines.

The anti-Americanism was not one-sided. There was still in the United States at that time plenty of anti-English feeling, notably among the Irish immigrants and their descendants. There was also some republicanism, old-style, which manifested itself occasionally on political platforms—as when Big Bill Thompson, mayor of Chicago, had threatened to bust King George on the snoot if he came to pay the city a visit. Such views, often as brashly put, would duly be reported in the English papers, giving apparent justification for anti-American attitudes.

The main focus for anti-Americanism in England at this time, though, was Hollywood. Film stars had become the pace-setters of the new morality. In the films themselves, the Hays Office could order the covering up of over-exposed bosoms, but the Hays Office had no control of the bosoms or the extra-marital relations of the stars off the set. Publicity men used to devote much of their energy to promoting the "true love" and "this time it's for keeps" line about the stars whenever they were married, which they frequently were, but this only made Hollywood morality sound all the seedier when, with painful regularity, the marriages broke up again in a few years, or perhaps a few weeks.

Most notorious of all in England were the American divorce laws. It had become obvious that the marriage tie in the United States was all but meaningless, if any husband or wife could go to Reno or some such place and get it dissolved in a matter of days.

And this gave the term "American divorcée" a special connotation: she must be fast, or loose—"no better than she should be." But what finally damned Mrs. Simpson in Establishment eyes was that not merely was she an American who had been divorced, but in order to be free to marry the King, she was now going to get a divorce for the second time.

It happens that Establishment attitudes to divorce in England at that time are unusually well-documented, because a Bill was on its way through Parliament to reform the Divorce Law. The Bill was the product of some unusual circumstances. It had been introduced by A.P. (later to become Sir Alan) Herbert, who had attracted a reputation for himself as author, wit and controversialist. His normal pulpit was *Punch*, in which articles by "APH" were a regular feature. One of his interests was divorce reform, and in 1935 he had written a devastating exposure of the effects of the law as it stood, in the form of a novel, *Holy Deadlock*. It described the experiences of a couple seeking to get a divorce, and managed to make the law look as ridiculous as it was.

The divorce law as it stood was the product of an uneasy compromise. The Established Church of England looked with disfavour on divorce, believing as it did in the sanctity of the marriage tie. But the Church could not entirely ignore the fact that it owed its very existence to a divorce. As an anonymous Irish poet had proclaimed:

> Don't talk of your alien Minister
> Nor his Church without meaning or faith!
> The foundation stones of its temple
> Are the bollocks of Henry VIII.

For centuries it had been possible to obtain a divorce by an individual Act of Parliament. But, like the Catholic Church's "annulments," this escape was available only to the rich and well-connected. With the spread of democracy, there had been growing an eventually successful pressure for legislation to enable people to obtain a divorce from an unfaithful partner as of right. But hardly had this concession been extorted when people began to realize how illogical and indeed how unjust it was to regard "unfaithfulness" as the only proper ground for divorce. What about persistent cruelty? Or the incurable insanity of one of the partners? Adultery was ceasing to be regarded as a mortal sin, and when it came to be considered as a peccadillo (or even in some distinguished circles, such as the court of King Edward VII, as an agreeable pastime), the absurdity of allowing it as a ground for the breakup of a marriage, while refusing to terminate marriages that had in fact already been broken up by far sadder circumstances, began to be recognized.

Attempts to secure a reform of the law, though, broke down because of the resistance of the churches—the Catholic Church in particular. To them, the argument about the relative unfairness of the law's accepted grounds for the divorce was irrelevant. They did not want divorce anyway. If they could, they would have restricted it still further. "As you have made your bed, so you must lie on it" was an often quoted tag. It was still sometimes argued that an unhappy marriage must be the judgment of God. Attempts to reform the law by extending the grounds for divorce, therefore, seemed doomed to failure.

There was, however, one feature of the law as it stood that irritated and embarrassed the leaders of the churches, particularly as they felt in a sense responsible for it. By their rigorous insistence upon adultery as the only proper ground for divorce they had created a new industry, designed to facilitate divorce by disguised collusion. It had to be disguised, because the courts ruled that if both parties to a marriage had been unfaithful to each other, then their sins cancelled each other out, and they must remain married. But where both parties were anxious to terminate the marriage they were often willing to make a private compact that one of them should accept the status of guilty party. Almost invariably the man played the guilty role, as it was considered the honourable thing for the man to take the blame even if in fact he had not been the original guilty party—even, in some cases, if he had not strayed at all but nevertheless felt he must give his wife her freedom. In these cases, it became necessary for him to commit adultery, or at least give the appearance of having committed adultery, in order to provide his wife's lawyers with the necessary evidence of his infidelity. If he had a mistress, his wife might be able to obtain the evidence herself, with the help of a private detective agency. But again, where there was collusion, the husband very often did not want his mistress to be named as corespondent. So it would be agreed that his infidelity should be staged with some other woman.

Holy Deadlock was a work of fiction, but A.P. Herbert's description of the process by which his antihero provided the evidence for his wife to try to divorce him was duplicated in scores of real-life cases. Divorce lawyers told their client, in confidence, where he could be fixed up. He would go to an agency, who would direct him to one of the hotels that catered for this trade, and introduce him to a girl who specialized in it. Together, after signing the register, they would go upstairs to their bedroom and there spend a decorous night (if he attempted to obtain additional services from her, he would forfeit his deposit). They could talk or doze, the man, per-haps, in an armchair. The following morning they would get into the double bed together in time to be "surprised" by the chamber-maid, bringing the tea. The receptionist and the chambermaid would then give evidence in court, and provided that the husband and wife did not make the mistake of letting it be known around that the whole thing had been prearranged between them, a decree *nisi* would be granted to the innocent party. Six months later, the divorce would be made absolute.

Little though churchmen liked the prospect of a more liberal divorce law, they had come to regard this abuse of the law as de-plorable, and in 1936 the bishops actually had before them, in their Convocation, a motion that they later passed:

That this House, recognising that full legal enactment of the Christian standard of marriage may not always be possible in a state which com-prises all sorts and kinds of people, including many who do not accept the Christian way of life, is of the opinion that some amendment to the state law relating to the grounds of divorce may be demanded by the circumstances of the day, and that the Church should be prepared to give consideration to proposals for such amendment, provided that any pro-posed amendment does not tend to make marriage a temporary alliance or to undermine the foundations of family life.

The main reason for the proposal was undoubtedly the distaste felt for the dubious practices that the old law had encouraged, for Convocation had already passed a resolution deploring "the meth-ods of collusion and perjury which are at the present time not un-commonly employed in seeking to secure decrees of divorce."

Herbert determined to take advantage of this feeling. Although he himself was happily married with a family, the absurdity—and the cruelty, in some cases—of the divorce law appalled him, and writing *Holy Deadlock* failed to work his disgust out of his system.

He had often turned over in his mind the sort of reform he would bring in if he were a Member of Parliament, but as he was not a politician and had no party affiliations, this had remained a pipe dream. Then, shortly before the 1935 general election, somebody casually suggested to him that he should present himself as a candidate for Oxford University. At that time the university had two seats in the Commons, the electors being graduates (who therefore had two votes: one for their University, the other in their home constituencies). Herbert managed to attract the necessary quota of supporters and presented himself as a candidate. To the university's astonishment, and everybody else's, he was elected.

An independent Member of Parliament ordinarily can expect to get little help, if he wishes to introduce legislation, from any of the political parties, least of all from the one that forms the government. But Herbert, having succeeded in his first venture, boldly faced the second. He put forward his proposed divorce reform as a private member's bill. Realizing that he would get nowhere if his bill came to be regarded as an attempt to weaken the sanctity of the marriage tie, his preamble to it ran:

Whereas it is expedient for the true support of marriage, the protection of children, the removal of hardship, the reduction of illicit unions and unseemly litigation, the relief of conscience among the clergy, and the restoration of due respect for the law that the Acts relating to marriage and divorce be amended . . .

And this was not merely oratorical flim-flam. As a barrister, Herbert pointed out in *The Ayes Have It*—his account of the passage of the Matrimonial Causes Act, as it came to be entitled—he wanted the laws of England to be respected, and the main part of his case was that they were *not* being respected: the law was compelling collusion, perjury, and humbug. "My contention was that once you admitted reasonable new grounds for divorce, especially desertion, the temptation to concoct bogus adultery cases would depart, and at least the worst scandals would come to an end." To show how anxious he was to preserve the institution of marriage he even included a clause to prevent divorce petitions being presented until after five years of marriage—though this was later reduced to three. By a remarkable combination of shrewdness, pertinacity and luck he managed to steer it through all the procedural shoals that normally wreck such bills even before they get a fair hearing, and from the debates, it is possible to get an illuminating glimpse of attitudes to divorce at that time.

The antagonism of the churchmen—archbishops and bishops of the Church of England in the House of Lords, and lay Catholics and Evangelicals in both Houses—to any extension of the grounds for divorce remained. A few gave Herbert their ungrudging support. The bishop of Durham said that he thought that the bill "if it were passed into law, so far from bringing the law of England into conflict with the law of Christ, would bring the law of England into deeper and truer harmony with that law." For the most part, though, church-men mistrusted the bill. But they found difficulty in opposing it because it had been too shrewdly drafted—they might have risked being criticized as hostile to its avowed aim, "the true support of marriage," if they denounced it. Even the Catholics, with a few individual exceptions, did not come out strongly against it. As for the Church of England, its dilemma was reflected in a marvellously contorted speech by the Archbishop of Canterbury, who declared himself neutral: "I do not think it would be honest, on my part, however much on other grounds I may wish to do so, to oppose the Third Reading. . . . But as a Christian of that standard, My Lords, how can I bring myself to vote actively in favour of a bill which contains some provisions which seem to me inconsistent with that standard?"

The reason the bill went through with such little difficulty, then, was not that the Church or the Establishment was becoming more tolerant of divorce. On the contrary, the rise of the divorce rate deeply disturbed them. They supported the bill, reluctantly, only because they realized that the law as it stood had fallen into con-tempt. If they could have thought of any way to make agreed divorce more difficult, they would have welcomed it, and the act did eventually give new powers and duties to judges to prevent collu-sion, as well as imposing the three year rule to stop quick divorces. For this reason, the King could not regard the progress of Herbert's bill as encouraging. It was really thoroughly discouraging, because the reason that the Church and the Establishment supported it was their dissatisfaction with a law that had left precisely the kind of loophole that, they believed, was enabling Wallis to divorce Ernest Simpson. As was soon to be disclosed in the hearing at Felixstowe,

Ernest Simpson appeared to have used *Holy Deadlock* as a procedural handbook.

And this was why it was futile for the King to argue—and later to reiterate—that it was grossly unfair to Mrs. Simpson to single her out for disapproval as a divorcée, considering that in both cases she had been the innocent party. The very term "innocent party" was enough to enrage the Establishment, simply because it had been so grossly abused. It was known that many a man who had been the guilty party in a divorce suit had gone through the hotel-bedroom procedure because it was the honourable thing for a husband to do, even if the guilt was really his wife's. Ernest Simpson, it was assumed, was also only doing the honourable thing.

Or was he? Scandal, turning against Mrs. Simpson, began to smear him, too. It was suggested that he had been bought off. Ironically, if Mrs. Simpson had obtained a Reno-style divorce it would have been less damaging—at least it would have appeared to be in character. For her to obtain a divorce by collusion—as it was assumed to be—and to obtain it by the very means, the hotel-bedroom technique, that had brought the law into contempt, so that she could pursue her designs on the King, seemed to be the final indignity.

And yet it would be a mistake to think that the Establishment was hostile to the marriage project for specific reasons. The moral, constitutional and imperial objections were to be lodged, but they were essentially rationalizations. The real objection to the idea of the King marrying Mrs. Simpson could be expressed—and frequently was—in a single word: inconceivable. Between *the* Queen—as Queen Mary was still called—and Mrs. Simpson the disparity was too great. It did not matter what Mrs. Simpson was like, or how justified her divorces had been, or how good a wife she would make Edward. These things seemed unimportant. Colin Coote, then on the staff of the *Times,* was to sum up the Establishment's attitude in his autobiography. For himself, he recalled, he found Wallis charming and intelligent, and he found it difficult to object to people on the ground of their race or morality. "But all that was irrelevant. The real puzzle was how anybody would ever have thought it possible for her to become Queen of England, and of seven British Dominions as well."

THE FOURTH ESTATE

Baldwin, then, could count on almost solid support from the court, the Cabinet, and the Establishment. But would that be enough? There was no precedent for voluntary abdication, and the enforced abdications had been for misdeeds more serious than a liaison, however unsuitable. In any case, they had taken place before the development of a constitutional monarchy. The final arbiter now was the electorate, and the electorate's opinon was un-predictable.

Again, in ordinary circumstances Baldwin would have counted on his ability to gauge the public reaction. But the circumstances of 1936 were not ordinary. The shadow of the Hoare-Laval fiasco still hung over him, and his authority had seemed to be slipping away. The German re-occupation of the Rhineland, the collapse of sanc-tions, mounting social unrest at home—particularly in the depressed areas, still unable to recover from the slump—and now the Spanish civil war, bringing almost daily humiliations at the hands of Musso-lini and Hitler: all these were sapping Baldwin's self-confidence. Certainly the public would not like to hear that their former idol the Prince of Wales had allowed himself to be infatuated with an American divorcée. But was it not possible that they would accept her, however reluctantly, to show their greater contempt for the unpopular premier, and to keep the popular King on his throne? Particularly if the King invoked the aid of friends who controlled the popular dailies, with their big circulations, and used them to put his case and the case against his ministers, with all the new Fleet Street tricks of presentation and display?

Baldwin could count on the *Times,* easily the most influential newspaper in the country. He could also, on this issue, rely on the *Morning Post,* an old established organ of diehard conservatism, now in decline. It was soon to be swallowed up by the *Daily Tele-graph,* which already had a considerably larger circulation than the other two "quality" newspapers, as they were called in the trade. But the *Telegraph,* Baldwin had reason to know, was also safe. It was part of a newspaper empire developed by two Berry brothers. Baldwin had obtained peerages for both of them. One of them, Lord Kemsley, had been at the FitzAlan house party at Windsor. Baldwin had taken the opportunity to have a private word with him on the subject and to ask what he thought. "Prime Minister," Kemsley replied portentously, "the Nonconformist conscience is not dead." According to Young, Baldwin laughingly told him, "I believe you ought to be in charge of this, not I." Kemsley probably thought he meant it. As for his brother, Camrose, Baldwin had a safe channel of communication through their mutual friend John Davidson, Chancellor of the Duchy of Lancaster.

But the combined circulation of the quality papers did not add up to the circulation of one "popular," and it was the popular newspapers that, for Baldwin, represented the unknown quantity. True, they had not been conspicuous for their ability to influence public opinion in the past, but they had never been provided with an issue of this nature before.

Up to this time, few attempts had been made in the British press to link Mrs. Simpson's name with the King's, in spite of the temptation afforded by the existence of avid speculation about them in the American press. It had begun after the court *Circular* of May 27, which had given the guest list of the dinner party at St. James's Palace. The presence of an unknown couple among all the rest of that distinguished dinner party naturally excited curiosity, which *Time* magazine promptly proceeded to gratify. In its issue of June 8 it described Mrs. Simpson as the King's favourite dancing partner, "his companion on numerous holiday excursions." But it was the next dinner, at York House, that really awoke the American press to a realization of what was happening, because Mrs. Simpson was not in the company of her husband. The inference was not lost on *Time,* which quoted the odds against the King's marriage as shortening from 11-1 to 5-1 and the following week ran pictures of Mrs. Simpson at home.

The only British journal to refer to the gossip in America was *Cavalcade,* a recently founded news magazine on the *Time* model. It had put "The Duke of Lancaster and guest" (Edward had borrowed one of his grandfather's aliases for the occasion) on the cover of its issue for August 15, with further pictures inside identifying the King and Mrs. Simpson. The pictures had been taken at Salzburg, where the *Nahlin* guests had broken their journey down to the

Adriatic. In its next issue, *Cavalcade* showed more from the cruise itself—its cover picture being destined to become the best known of all, showing the pair of them in a dinghy, Wallis with her hand on Edward's arm. And now, on October 24—three days before the divorce—*Cavalcade* devoted a brief feature to Wallis, referring to the gossip in the American press, along with a page of pictures—mostly concerned with her move from Bryanston Court to Cumberland Terrace. The *Cavalcade* material, though, was presented in a way that would have suggested to most readers that it was idle gossip. The impact it made was small.

And otherwise the press contained few clues to what was happening. The *Telegraph* was so circumspect that when it gave the list of the guests on the *Nahlin* cruise, it omitted Mrs. Simpson. The photographer of a tabloid paper, the *Sketch*, took pictures of the King and Mrs. Simpson in Salzburg, one of which was printed, but the *Sketch's* owner—the other Berry brother, Lord Camrose—gave instructions that there must be no repetition. Only the *Referee*, one of the lesser Sunday "populars," gave pictures of the *Nahlin* cruise, naming Mrs. Simpson. In general the British press followed the editorial line laid down in Lord Rothermere's *Sunday Dispatch:* that, as his Majesty was on holiday, his "natural desire for occasional respite from the public attention focused upon his movements by responsibility and tradition" should be respected. Arthur Christiansen, editor of Beaverbrook's *Daily Express*, recalled in his autobiography that when he printed the picture of Edward in the dinghy, he cut out Mrs. Simpson, and felt "no spasm of conscience over this decision." The standards of the press at that time, he thought, in relation to intrusion into people's private affairs, were considerably higher.

Convention did not protect the King only when he was on holiday. It had also begun to ordain that royalty should not be criticized or written about in such a way that critical judgment might result. This protection was of comparatively recent origin. George IV and William IV had both been savagely lampooned, and Victoria, at some stages of her reign, had excited hostile comment. But with the enthusiasm that grew for her after her jubilee in 1887, criticism had dwindled. Royalty, it came tacitly to be agreed, was not fair game because, by etiquette, it was forbidden to reply. The last recorded offence—according to Hodge and Graves in *The Long Week-End*— was in a sporting sheet that gratuitously announced one week that there was "nothing whatever between the Prince of Wales (the future Edward VII) and Lily Langtry," adding, the following week, the apparently unrelated remark: "Not even a sheet." But that had been nearly fifty years before.

The growing respect for George V had made the idea of criticizing the monarch unthinkable, and to mention Mrs. Simpson might have been construed as criticism of his successor. On balance, the editors were relieved to have the excuse that was later to be given by the *Morning Post,* that "it was no part of the function of the press to publish gossip possibly injurious to such an institution as the monarchy, and until the time when the King's friendship for Mrs. Simpson passed from the region of vague rumour to that of substantial fact, the friendship seemed to be a matter of private rather than of public life."

This attitude was not confined to Britain. In France, for example, *Figaro* published brief references to the *Nahlin* cruise, but did not mention Mrs. Simpson. Instead, it remarked on the difficulty that beset a party of this kind in trying to avoid publicity. It blamed the attendant swarm of reporters and photographers, rather than the local populace, for the crowds that appeared wherever the royal party landed. Whatever other French newspapers might do, *Figaro* was to make no mention of Mrs. Simpson until after the story had broken in the British press. An editorial on December 3 announced that it had deliberately refrained from making any allusion to the rumours about the King's matrimonial intentions circulating in London and New York, out of respect for the proprieties.

There is no reason to suspect, then, that any outside pressure, other than that of convention, had been put on British editors to make them keep silent. But this meant it was difficult to be certain that the press silence would be maintained. With the American newspapers splashing the rumours daily—"Mrs. Simpson" had by this time become "Wally" for convenience—Fleet Street's position was becoming daily more uncomfortable; and with her divorce petition due for a hearing at Ipswich on October 27, the risk that the story would break had become serious. Up to this time, the newspapers had had nothing to go on but the fact that the King and Mrs. Simpson spent a good deal of time in each other's company, but the divorce case would give an obvious peg on which they could hang stories and features about her.

They would not be able to report the details. In 1926 Parliament had passed an act to restrict the publication of reports of divorce proceedings. Ostensibly this was to "prevent injury to public morals" —the injury supposedly being done by the publication of intimate details of the sexual tastes and aberrations of the parties to the divorce. What had made the act appear necessary, though, was the fact that most divorce suits were still, at that time, between members of the well-to-do. The aristocracy, in particular, suffered a disproportionate number of broken marriages. Probably this was less because of the aristocracy's traditional license, dating from the days of the *droit du seigneur*, than because its members had more money, more leisure, more opportunity to travel and grow apart from each other than the middle and working classes. But whatever the reasons, it gave an unfortunate impression—particularly as the sexual inclinations of the erring husbands, often a product of their monastic public-school education, were remarkable, embodying ingenious variations of sadism and masochism that had proved all too compulsively readable when laid out in the popular newspapers.

The Conservative government, alarmed by the rise of Socialism, felt that cases of this nature were giving hostages to the enemy in the class war. The Home Secretary, too—"Jix"—was rabidly puritan-minded. It was decided to put a stop to reports of the evidence and proceedings in divorce cases. The newspapers were permitted only to print the court's judgment, which occasionally, where the judge felt it was his duty (or where he relished the task of composition), could be revealing and entertaining enough. But only the fact that Mrs. Simpson got her decree *nisi*—or the fact that it was denied her, if for some reason it was—could be printed, if the judge did not choose to make any observations.

There was nothing, however, to prevent the papers from using the case as an excuse to recount the life story of Mrs. Simpson, and the temptation to exploit this opportunity would be considerable. Something, the King decided, was bound to give before long, and this was why, "believing in the direct approach, I decided to try to enlist the aid and understanding of two powerful newspaper friends, Lord Beaverbrook and the Hon. Esmond Harmsworth, now Lord Rothermere."

If some demon had been working on him to enlist the advisers who were least likely to guide him successfully and most likely to deliver him over, bound and gagged, to Baldwin, he could hardly have chosen more perceptively. Beaverbrook and Rothermere were old antagonists of Baldwin's. Over the past twelve years they had been involved in many disputes, some of them extremely bitter, and Baldwin had emerged the victor with such unfailing regularity that they ought long before to have realized they were no match for him. Under Baldwin, even Beaverbrook's genius stood rebuked.

Beaverbrook and Rothermere

The young Max Aitken had come over to Britain from Canada, where he had amassed a fortune. Apart from his wealth and his business sense, he had only one potential asset when he arrived in 1910: an acquaintanceship with Bonar Law, another New Brunswicker who had settled a few years before in England and had become a Conservative MP. They became close friends. Soon, Aitken had become a Conservative MP himself. Early in his political career, according to his biographer Tom Driberg, somebody suggested he ought to study Edmund Burke, and he found a passage that he was to learn by heart, for future quotation: "The world is governed by go-betweens. Those go-betweens influence the persons with whom they carry on intercourse by stating their own sense to each of them as the sense of the other; and thus they reciprocally master both sides." The future Lord Beaverbrook made this advice his motto, and very effectively he exploited it.

The year after Aitken's arrival in England, Arthur Balfour resigned from the leadership of the Conservative Party, and the succession was contested between the two front-runners, Austen Chamberlain and Walter Long. They had agreed that if neither could win overwhelming support from their fellow MPs, they would both withdraw, to allow in a compromise candidate. With remarkable ingenuity, Aitken, by his own accounts, managed both to arrange that the contest between them should end in a deadlock and that the compromise candidate chosen instead should be Bonar Law.

In 1916 he had an even more spectacular success as a go-between, in the intrigue that got rid of the Prime Minister, Asquith, and replaced him with Lloyd George. But at this point, Aitken made what was later generally acknowledged to be his gravest miscalculation. He expected Lloyd George to give him office. Instead, he was offered a peerage, which he took. King George was "surprised and hurt" that he had not been consulted—presumably because Lloyd George realized that if he *had* been consulted, he would have protested vigorously at this abuse of the honours system. It was unfortunate for Beaverbrook that the King had not made his disapproval known in time. The days when a peer could expect to become Prime Minister were ending, and even on a lower level of ambition, it was soon clear to Beaverbrook that going to the Lords had been fatal to his political prospects.

An alternative road to political power, however, presented itself to him. The press had played, or at least seemed to have played, an important part in the replacement of Asquith by Lloyd George. In particular, Beaverbrook had found the *Daily Express* useful when he wanted to leak inside information to further his intrigues. Impressed by the possibilities, he bought a controlling interest in the paper just before Asquith resigned, and after the war, when the death of Bonar Law deprived him of his last opportunity to control the Conservative Party through its leader, he turned to newspapers to bring him the power he desired.

Up to this time Lord Northcliffe had been the dominant figure in Fleet Street, but on his death most of his empire—though not the *Times*—was acquired by his brother Harold, Lord Rothermere. At this stage, Rothermere was chiefly interested in newspapers for their profit potential, and Beaverbrook was able to do a deal with him, acquiring control of the London *Evening Standard* to add to his *Daily Express* and the *Sunday Express*, which he had founded. Beaverbrook began to build them up into a new style of newspaper, whose primary function was propaganda. There was nothing new, of course, about using journals to promote political causes, but this was the first time that the promotion had been carried out with such journalistic flair, assisted by striking presentation. The circulations of the Beaverbrook papers began to climb rapidly, and Rothermere, who saw his own papers' circulations being overhauled, was tempted into imitation. Both men assumed that the influence of their papers should be roughly proportionate to the number of readers they attracted. In this they were soon shown to be wrong.

Beaverbrook's first propaganda aim was to discredit traditional free trade and win acceptance, in the Conservative Party and in the electorate as a whole, for imperial preference—or, as it came later to be called, Empire free trade, with its concomitant of tariffs on food imported from countries not in the Empire. Baldwin was prepared to go forward in 1923 with a program of protection, but not of imperial preference. Beaverbrook, dissatisfied—and also annoyed that Baldwin, rather than he, should have been Law's heir—opposed him, and a number of newspapers, including the *Observer* and the *Morning Post,* actually attributed the Conservative defeat in the general election to the resultant disunity.

This alone would have been enough to embitter Baldwin, but after the election, he found himself blamed for the defeat in the Beaverbrook newspapers, which began to call for a new leader and a new party policy. In 1924, Winston Churchill was induced to stand at a by-election as an Independent Conservative, against the official party candidate, on the issue of imperial preference, with the backing of both the Beaverbrook and the Rothermere presses, and he failed to win the seat by only forty-three votes.

It was a declaration of war, and Baldwin struck back with an ingenuity that revealed again just how wrong his party colleagues had been in thinking him "safe" but rather dim. He allowed himself to be interviewed for the *People,* a Sunday newspaper that was engaged in a long and in the end successful climb to prosperity, mainly through the publishing of lurid stories about crime and vice, but with occasional muckraking as a public service. In it, Baldwin was quoted as saying that he did not care about the attacks of the "press barons," as they had come to be called. They were not worth bothering about: "They are both men I would not have in my house. I do not respect them. Who are they?" Rothermere? His brother Northcliffe had a spark of genius—"But this man . . . ! " As for Beaverbrook, what was riling him, Baldwin thought, was that since Bonar Law's death he was no longer able to obtain, and misuse, inside information. "When I came in," Baldwin explained, "that stopped. I knew I could get his support if I were to send for him and talk things over with him. But I prefer not. That sort of thing does not appeal to me." He went on to surmise that this silent contempt might irritate the press barons more than if he had actually spoken out against them, and—the interviewer reported—he "yawned with disgust and weariness at discussing for so long so unpleasant a subject."

If Baldwin had lashed out angrily at his tormentors, Beaverbrook would in fact have been delighted. It was the silent contempt—and the yawn—that was infuriating. But what was really diabolical, so far as Beaverbrook was concerned, was that Baldwin promptly repudiated the interview, sending a disclaimer to each of the persons named. Quite apart from the improbability that any journalist would invent an interview of that nature, it carried conviction—in Driberg's view—on the internal evidence. This was precisely how Baldwin wrote and felt. And the story also enabled the *Morning Post,* far too respectable and Tory to publish an interview of that kind itself, to quote it at length and to argue that even if it were an invention, there was so much truth in it "that it is almost as good as if he had said it." Baldwin, Driberg concluded, had "hit on a technique of character assassination that had no comeback, and was, accordingly, more simple and more cunning than anything devised since by Goebbels or Senator McCarthy."

Had the reporter been fired, or the *People* taken for heavy damages, Baldwin might have found the ruse dangerous, in the long term —journalists would never again have trusted him. But it was realized for what it was, an ingenious and effective trick. The press barons, the general feeling was, had only got what they deserved. A verse that acquired popularity at the time expressed the prevalent feeling. Of several versions, the commonest ran:

> If once again the fount of Truth
> Should flow both pure and clear
> We'll have to dam the Beaver Brook
> And drain the Rother Mere.

Beaverbrook was prepared to forgive his enemies when he had vanquished them, but he could not forgive himself for having been worsted by Baldwin. What made it all the more galling was that Beaverbrook had himself—or so he later claimed—helped Baldwin to leave political anonymity on the back benches during the war, by recommending him to Bonar Law as his parliamentary private secretary on the ground that he was "rich, reticent and neutral in character." Beaverbrook determined on revenge. The opportunity presented itself when, during the second Labour administration of 1929 to 1931, influential members of the Conservative Party began to grow discontented with Baldwin's leadership—or the lack of it. This was the time, Beaverbrook and Rothermere decided, to revive the campaign for Empire free trade and to promote it through their newspapers, which by now had massive circulations.

Beaverbrook was still under the impression that he could acquire through his newspapers the political power that had so far eluded him. But his choice of ally proved unfortunate. Northcliffe, before he died, had suffered from advanced megalomania: it was already incipient in his brother Rothermere. Although outwardly anxious to put himself under Beaverbrook's leadership, Rothermere was really engaged in his own quest for power, and showed it. Baldwin made what appeared to be a conciliatory speech, and Beaverbrook took the excuse to abandon his partner.

Up to this point, Beaverbrook had not seriously damaged his reputation within the Conservative Party. Empire free trade might not be taken very seriously by the party leaders, but it was quite popular with the rank and file, and the fact that Beaverbrook had left Rothermere when he saw the way Rothermere was going could be held to be a sign of his political maturity. But no sooner had he come to terms with Baldwin than he found that he had been deceived. Baldwin had been prepared to be nice about Empire free trade only so long as there was the threat of a party split. The moment that the threat receded, Baldwin let the matter drop. Beaverbrook, exasperated, began to think that he had been right, after all, to hold the idea of setting up a rival organization rather than a pressure group within the party. He returned to his Empire Crusade and to Rothermere, who accepted him back. Their earlier plan to run unofficial Empire candidates against the official Baldwinite Conservatives at by-elections was revived, and a London seat was actually won by an Empire Crusader.

Just as the danger seemed greatest, Baldwin was given the opportunity he had been awaiting. Rothermere arrogantly set out in writing the terms on which he would support Baldwin. Not merely must he be informed precisely what Baldwin's policy was going to be and how it was going to be carried out, he must also be "acquainted with the names of at least eight, or ten, of his most prominent colleagues in the next Ministry." Baldwin had only to read out the Rothermere ultimatum at a political meeting for the audience to be disgusted at the transparent egocentricity. "The Lord," Baldwin was fond of recalling, "had delivered him into my hands." It was the end of Rothermere politically.

Beaverbrook remained to be dealt with, and Baldwin took the opportunity to pull him down along with Rothermere. In a speech on behalf of Duff Cooper at the St. George's by-election of 1931, Baldwin left political issues in order to consider the influence of certain newspaper proprietors—Hearst in America, Beaverbrook and Rothermere in Britain:

What are their methods? Their methods are direct falsehood, misrepresentation, half-truths, the alteration of the speaker's meaning by publishing a sentence apart from the context, such as you see in these leaflets handed out outside the doors of this hall: suppression and editorial criticism of speeches which are not reported in the papers. These are methods hated alike by the public and by the whole of the rest of the press.

As an instance, Baldwin cited an attack on him that had appeared in the *Mail*, suggesting that as his father had left him a fortune that had since largely disappeared, he was hardly the right man to restore the fortunes of his country. The suggestion that his fortune had been dissipated, Baldwin said, was a lie, and he had been advised that it was libellous. But:

I shall not move in the matter, and for this reason. I should get an apology and heavy damages. The first is of no value, and the second I would not touch with a barge pole. What the proprietorship of these papers is aiming at is power, and power without responsibility—the prerogative of the harlot throughout the ages.

The phrase—provided by Baldwin's cousin, Rudyard Kipling—stuck to the two newspaper barons for the rest of their lives. Their newspapers did not suffer—millions of Britons continued to buy them, for the same reason, Driberg suggested, that millions of Americans bought the Hearst newspapers: because of their technical competence and their entertainment value. "But it is one of the more hopeful aspects of western democracy that so many of the people have so far refused to be guided politically by the newspapers which they prefer to read." Sales of the *Daily Express* might continue to rise, but Beaverbrook's journalistic reputation sank. So did that of the journalists who worked for him and his imitators, pilloried by Humbert Wolfe in *The Uncelestial City:*

> You cannot hope to bribe or twist
> Thank God! The British journalist
> But seeing what the man will do
> Unbribed, there's no occasion to.

Rothermere's reputation sank even lower. In its obituary in 1940 the *Times* was to describe him as "the best of sons, the most affectionate of parents, and the most generous of men," but politically he was infantile. In a last bid for power, he began to correspond with

Hitler, to extol Fascism and to back Oswald Mosley's blackshirts, and although the flirtation with the British Union of Fascists did not last for long, it was enough finally to discredit him. "An ignorant and megalomaniacal businessman," Francis Williams was to recall, "self-deceived, as his more able brother had been, into believing that wealth and possession of newspaper properties gave him the right to dictate what national policy should be." And though it was Rothermere's son Esmond, of milder political temper, who was to be directly involved in the events that led up to the abdication, he had not yet moved out of his father's shadow, and it was generally assumed at the time that what he did was on his father's behalf.

FACE TO FACE

FIRST CONFRONTATION—OCTOBER 20

These, then, were the friends on whom the King was forced to rely. At least he had had the sense to call on Beaverbrook first. For all his mistakes, Beaverbrook was a remarkable personality—and had a remarkable appearance, which Driberg, a columnist on his *Daily Express*, was to describe: a "powerful head, broad, rather flat-topped, bulging—almost as if its contents were pressing the bone structure outwards"; a face "dark in hue, a mottled tan, permanently sunburned"; and a mouth "just as in every cartoon of him by Low or Vicky; a satchel mouth, bisecting the face in an enormous grin." Long years of life, Driberg continued, had "not modified at all the Canadian resonance of his voice. Sometimes it is loud, grim and rasping; sometimes it sinks to a melancholy or a coaxing purr. . . . The rest of his appearance is an anticlimax. He is five feet seven inches in height, slight of build, with a suspicion of a paunch." Anticlimax it might be, but it did not detract from the dominating impression that he managed to transmit.

Gentlemen's agreement

Few things could have given Beaverbrook more pleasure than to be invited to Buckingham Palace on such an errand. Not that he was either by upbringing or by temperament a royalist. On his first visit to London, according to Driberg, he had seen a man weeping over the ticker-tape announcement of King Edward VII's death: "This was astonishing to the young Canadian then, and a comparable demonstration would be almost as incomprehensible to him today [1956]; he accepts constitutional monarchy as a convenient and expedient arrangement, but any sentimental or mystical concept of kingship is alien to him." And by his own account Beaverbrook knew the King only slightly. But he admired Edward, and in any case, he realized that it was a wonderful opportunity to exercise his talents as a go-between, to demonstrate the extent of his influence over the popular press, which he rightly believed to be strong, and, above all, to embarrass Baldwin. All through the year, the Beaver-brook papers had been campaigning to get Baldwin out, and al-though by this time their campaigns were not taken seriously, the government was so shaky that Conservatives found it hard not to lend at least some credence to what the papers were saying. "There is no doubt the Government is thoroughly discredited," Tom Jones told a Canadian friend in April, "and Rothermere and Beaverbrook, Winston and Austen are seizing their chance to promote disunity in their party." "Who will bring Baldwin down?" was one headline of the time. Now it looked as if the chance to bring him down was being offered to the man to whom it would give a most pleasurable revenge.

At first, though, it was not so much Beaverbrook's advice that the King needed as his help. There could be no question of hushing up the news of Wallis' divorce case. All he wanted was to protect Wallis from publicity arising out of it. Beaverbrook had already been con-sulted by one of his editors, Percy Cudlipp of the *Evening Standard,* about how the case should be handled, and he had told Cudlipp that he was in favour of reporting it. But then he had second thoughts—or perhaps he was working to a plan. He knew Theodore Goddard, the solicitor who was acting for Mrs. Simpson, and he rang him up to tell him what to expect. Goddard at once came around, "understandably anxious to secure privacy for his client," but Beaverbrook declined to reassure him. It was Goddard's report of this meeting, presumably, that made the King realize that he would have to recruit Beaverbrook if the press silence was to continue.

Beaverbrook was suffering from a severe toothache when the royal summons came, but when, a couple of days later, he had ex-tricated himself from his dentist, he went to the palace, heard the King's case, and said he would do what he could. Together with Walter Monckton, one of the King's legal advisers, he went to the chairman of the Newspaper Proprietors Association—who happened to be Rothermere's son Esmond Harmsworth. Harmsworth readily agreed to co-operate. He called a meeting of the NPA at Warwick House to confer with the proprietors of the other national news-papers—except those of the *Times,* the *Morning Post* and the *Daily Telegraph.* (As George VI's biographer, Sir John Wheeler-Bennett, put it, "Their discretion was not in question.") Out of this meeting emerged the "gentlemen's agreement," by which it was established that the Simpson divorce case reports, if published at all, should be used unobtrusively.

The only proprietor who was hesitant was Sir Walter Layton of the liberal *News Chronicle*, but Beaverbrook went personally to see him and won him over. Many of the provincial newspapers were in chains that could be controlled from London, but Beaverbrook also contacted the proprietors of independent Scottish and Irish newspapers. All were compliant. Beaverbrook even went so far as to contact Jean Provoust, the owner of *Paris Soir*, which—unlike *Figaro* —had been regaling its readers with the Mrs. Simpson story, extracted from the American newspapers. M. Provoust wrote back to say that he had ordered his editors to desist.

Decree *nisi*

When it was held, on October 27, the divorce case appeared to pass off smoothly enough. In London, the King carried on as if nothing was happening. Ironically, this was the morning chosen for his now worried private secretary, Alec Hardinge, among others, to be sworn in as a member of the Privy Council. The King did his best to perform his duties "with my usual punctiliousness," though part of his mind was preoccupied with what was happening at Ipswich—as well it might have been, because the gentlemen's agreement could have collapsed if, for example, there had been scenes inside or outside the court.

Mrs. Simpson's solicitors were taking no chances. They had briefed Norman Birkett, the leading advocate of the day, as counsel, and it was at his suggestion that the case should be heard at Ipswich. This was to avoid publicity, according to one of his biographers, Denis Bardens. According to the other, Montgomery Hyde, it was because the London lists were full. To her alarm, Wallis immediately sensed the hostility of the judge, Mr. Justice Hawke. He was puzzled why the case should be heard at Ipswich, until a whispered colloquy with the clerk of the court seemed to reassure him, and he then listened suspiciously to the employees of the Hotel de Paris, in Bray-on-Thames, giving evidence that Ernest Simpson had spent the night with a lady. At the end he still seemed dissatisfied. Birkett, trying to reassure him, only made him more suspicious. "I assume," Birkett suggested, "that what your Lordship has in

mind . . . " Mr. Justice Hawke testily interrupted, demanding to be
told just how Birkett could know what was in his mind. Birkett had
to use flattery—verging, according to Bardens, on the obsequious—
to explain to the judge that he need not worry about the absence of
the lady's name, as it had been mentioned in the original divorce
petition. What Birkett did not say was that her name happened to
be Miss Buttercup Kennedy, which might have aroused the judge's
suspicions still further. With manifest reluctance, he announced that
he had come to the conclusion that adultery had been committed
between Mr. Simpson and the unnamed lady in the Bray Hotel.
Mrs. Simpson was granted her decree *nisi*, and she drove back to
London with Theodore Goddard, who "exuded an air of quiet
triumph."

But although the decree *nisi* had been acquired, the proceedings
were to leave an unpleasant aroma. To begin with, the evidence on
which it had been granted too closely resembled A.P. Herbert's *Holy
Deadlock* for comfort. If ever a divorce looked as if it had been
obtained by collusion, this one did—particularly as it was held at
Ipswich. To Wallis' surprise there were only two members of the
public sitting in the court: the judge's wife and a friend, Goddard
told her. But it was unlikely that the judge's wife would have been
sitting there, alone, if the judge had not known what kind of a case
it was he was being called upon to try. And the American papers
were quick to point out that Mr. Justice Hawke had known, and
actually worked for, the King. He had been legal adviser to the
Duchy of Cornwall.

The precautions taken, too, suggested that "they" must have been
at work on the King's behalf—whoever "they" might be. Two press
photographers had their cameras smashed by the police. At the end
of the hearing, too, the police forcibly prevented reporters from
following Mrs. Simpson. Inevitably, the story got around that the suit
had been fixed for the King's benefit. As it could not be fully reported, the manifest suspicions of the judge were not made known.
It was assumed he must be in it, too. And this was to have a particularly unhappy effect on the very people whom Edward, lacking
support in the government ranks, might need to attract to his cause.
A traditional working-class grievance was that there was one law for
the rich, another for the poor—"The courts of law," a tag of the time
ran, "are open to all—like the Ritz Hotel." The belief that the courts
had been rigged to suit a King's convenience enraged some left-wing

MPs, and one of them—George Buchanan, from Glasgow—was to give expression to his resentment after the abdication, when he denounced the government for its hypocrisy in aiding and abetting the Simpson divorce, but then turning on the King. If an ordinary workman had got into a mess of this kind, Buchanan complained, MPs would have been ashamed of him and refused him benefit. But here, there had been collusion. "The whole law courts were set at defiance for this man. A divorce case was heard when every one of you knows it was a breaking of the law. What are you talking nonsense about? The law is desecrated. The law courts are thrust aside."

William Randolph Hearst

The morning after the case it was clear that the gentlemen's agreement had been kept. The *Times* gave the divorce suit thirty lines under the headlines "Undefended divorce suit at Ipswich Assizes," and no newspaper tried to make a story out of the proceedings. The first crisis had been surmounted, and the Duke of Windsor, looking back on what happened, could write, "The British press kept its word, and for that I shall always be grateful."

But now the King was facing a new threat. Up to this time, whatever people might have suspected, there had been no positive evidence that he intended to marry Mrs. Simpson when her divorce was made absolute. It was a reasonable speculation, but no more. On the day before the divorce hearing, however, an article had appeared in the New York *Journal* giving what appeared to be the first authoritative account, from an inside source, forecasting the marriage. The article appeared under huge headlines, KING WILL WED WALLY, and though it was unsigned, it was generally assumed to have been written by the *Journal's* proprietor, William Randolph Hearst. Hearst had been on a visit to England and, it was believed, had visited Fort Belvedere. It stated positively, without equivocal mays and mights, that eight months after her divorce was through, Mrs. Simpson would marry Edward, and that after the coronation he would take her as his consort.

Considering their reputation, the Hearst papers had been relatively circumspect about the Mrs. Simpson story up to this point, perhaps because Hearst, with Marion Davies in his life, could hardly allow his newspapers to mock Edward. This gave the article more of an impact than it might otherwise have had. The writer went on to give a clue how Edward proposed to justify his choice—on the ground that it would be a mistake to marry into any of the European royal houses "and so involve himself and his Empire in the complications and disasters of these royal houses"—not to mention "all the physical as well as political disabilities likely to result from that outgrown custom," and he pointed to how happy and fortunate the Duke of York had been in his marriage to "a lady of the people, a commoner, so-called." Edward, the writer continued, believed that "the most important thing for the peace and welfare of the world is an intimate understanding and relationship between England and America, and that his marriage with this very gifted lady may help to bring about that beneficial co-operation between English-speaking nations." This might have been designed to win American sympathy, but it could also be read as a warning to Englishmen who might be tempted to oppose the match: they should realize this would be construed as anti-Americanism.

It was immediately assumed that Hearst was saying what the King wanted to be heard. But was he? The question of how Hearst got the story aroused considerable speculation, both at the time and later. *Time* claimed it came from Godfrey Thomas, but Thomas denied being the source—nor was he a likely source, unless somebody had eavesdropped on a private conversation. In any case there was little in the story that Hearst could not have formulated by putting two and two together from society gossip he had heard. Why else, after all, would Wallis have been getting a divorce, at this time? If they were not contemplating marriage, it would have been much simpler for her to remain Mrs. Simpson, at least until after the coronation. What was generally thought to have been inside knowledge, therefore, may have been hunch, reinforced by conversations with people who knew Wallis.

Anyway, the secret was out, and the impact was not confined to America. What should an editor do—Arthur Christiansen of the *Express* asked himself—when he knew that the author was William Randolph Hearst and knew (or thought he knew) that Hearst had recently visited the King at Fort Belvedere? There was nothing Christiansen could do in his newspaper, because of the compact his proprietor had entered into with the King. Still, the rumour that the New York *Journal*'s story was straight from the royal mouth, not just another example of press speculation masquerading as fact, quickly spread through Fleet Street to pubs where journalists and barristers congregated (occasionally, when there was gossip to retail, they actually mixed), and thence to wider circles.

To many people it came as a revelation. There had been little suspicion, up to this point, that the King wanted to marry Mrs. Simpson. The King had not told Baldwin of his intentions, nor had he confided in Beaverbrook. Beaverbrook, in fact, was to insist that he had been told by Goddard that the King did *not* intend to marry Mrs. Simpson. Even if he had known the King's real intention, Beaverbrook thought, he would still have done what he did. But would the other newspaper proprietors have accepted the gentlemen's agreement without Beaverbrook's assurance that marriage was not contemplated? It seems unlikely that Layton of the *News Chronicle,* for one, would have accepted. The prospect of a marriage automatically brought the King's relationship out of his private life, converting it into a matter of public interest. The gentlemen's agreement, in short, was based on a false premise, though Goddard presumably was not aware that it was false.

This would have mattered less if the gentlemen's agreement had terminated after the divorce hearing, as had originally been intended. But the silence continued, because of Goddard's assurance that though Mrs. Simpson was giving her husband his freedom, her relationship with the King would remain unchanged. The silence, however, extended only to the press. By the beginning of November, society could talk of nothing else but Edward and Mrs. Simpson. It was *the* news, according to Tom Jones, and Geoffrey Dawson noted in his diary, "No talk anywhere but of the King." This was not good for the reputation of the press, which, people began to think, must have been muzzled. But it was far worse for the reputation of Wallis, because, with every day that passed, the rumours about her grew more rancorous. So long as she had been regarded simply as the King's favourite, even as his mistress, she had aroused no great antipathy, except among those who were easily shocked. But now that the rumour began to gain ground that she was going to become Edward's wife, resentment spilled over. She must, it was assumed, by a designing adventuress, and scandal began to tailor grotesque stories around her—one of the commonest being that she had prepared for her forthcoming occupation of the royal bedchamber by having her linen monogrammed with the royal coat of arms. Such gossip was to be damaging, because those who spread it began to acquire a kind of vested interest in its being proved correct. Scores of people who knew nothing of the real Mrs. Simpson heard, and began to pass on, information (usually attributed to some servant who had worked for her) about her ambition, her Svengalian hold on Edward, and her character, and they wanted it to be proved true. The truth, being more prosaic, could not compete.

Another rumour, this one damaging to Edward, also began to spread: that he was not really interested in being King. There is no need to read malice into it. It represented the view of those in or close to the court, who frequently saw or heard of Edward behaving in ways that suggested to them that he was profoundly bored with the business. Not being in his confidence, they did not realize he would no longer be bored—or so he assumed—if he was allowed to recreate the monarchy to his own specifications. So his courtiers often received and passed on the impression that he would not be sorry to escape the responsibilities of kingship.

And Edward sometimes acted in ways that appeared to confirm this diagnosis. Although he had moved into Buckingham Palace, he was in effect camping there. He hardly even attempted to rearrange his suite to his liking, and what few changes he had made to it—putting in a shower as well as the bath and installing a personal switchboard with a private line to the Fort—encouraged the belief that he felt himself a transient occupier.

From the King's point of view, therefore, it was desirable that the full story should now be told. Beaverbrook and Rothermere had befriended him by obtaining the gentlemen's agreement. They could now do him an even greater service by introducing Mrs. Simpson to their readers in a sympathetic light. Admittedly there was a difficulty: until the divorce decree had been made absolute, convention and caution demanded that Edward's relationship with Mrs. Simpson should not be trumpeted abroad. But the main reason why the King shrank from allowing Mrs. Simpson to be introduced to the public appears to have been simply distaste for the idea of having pictures of her and her life story spread all over the popular newspapers— however sympathetically they did it. So no signal went out from the palace that the silence could be ended.

"Britannicus in Partibus Infidelium"

But not all newspapers and magazines came under the control, direct or indirect, of Beaverbrook and Rothermere. Why was the

story not broken by—say—some editor craving a scoop to put his
paper on the map? The temptation must have been considerable,
particularly for papers that needed a circulation boost. But for once
their managerial sides were not keen on the idea. They were afflicted
by fear of the unknown. What would the reaction be, should a paper
take a chance and spring the story? Obviously its sales for that issue,
and probably for the next few issues, would be prodigious, but what
thereafter? Suppose the public, though avid for the story when it
appeared, thought badly of the paper for having printed it—on the
same principle that a man who goes to a brothel may later register
his disapproval of prostitution? And what of advertisers? The weight
of official and unofficial disapproval at such an act of *lèse-majesté*
might well lead to the withdrawal of promised advertisements.
What, too, of the legal position? A single false step, a misstatement,
an unguarded innuendo, and swingeing damages could be expected
against the transgressor. No, on the whole it was safer to wait.

The position of the "quality" papers, London and provincial, was
rather different. Their silence—Tom Jones claimed, in mid-November
—"is not enforced by the government, but by a sense of shame." The
idea of the King's private life being held up to public scrutiny was
uncongenial to many editors. As the *Manchester Guardian* was later
to claim, they "did their duty by reticence while reticence could be
maintained." But reticence was not being maintained in America,
and the absurdity of continuing to maintain it in England was becoming every day more apparent. A single issue of the magazine
Liberty containing an article on "The Yankee at King Edward's
Court" sold two and a half million copies, and although British
newsagents were declining to distribute magazines with stories
about Mrs. Simpson and the King, the service to subscribers who
received mailed copies was uninterrupted. Yet no quality newspaper
cared to be the first to break the story. And their reluctance to take
the risk can only be attributed to the prevailing belief that on this
issue, the lead should be given by the government—or by the *Times*,
as it could be assumed that the *Times* would not pronounce without
government sanction.

If anything should have warned the King that the continued
press silence on Mrs. Simpson was a fatal mistake, it was the fact
that Baldwin was himself imposing it. Geoffrey Dawson was later
to be at pains to dissociate the *Times* from collusion with the government, but his own diaries make it clear that he allowed himself to be

restrained from broaching the issue by Baldwin. Even before the divorce hearing, Dawson had told Tom Jones that the *Times* would have to do something about the King and Mrs. Simpson and that the Prime Minister should indicate what he would like the *Times* to do. The answer came back that the Prime Minister would like the *Times* to continue to do nothing. And such was the awe in which the *Times* was held that the other quality papers would be unlikely to make any move until the *Times* gave the signal.

It hurt Dawson, as a good newspaperman, that what was being said could not be reported and commented upon in the *Times*. Yet he did not care to move without a go-ahead from Baldwin, and he recognized Baldwin's difficulty, which was also his own. As *The History of the Times* put it, "As long as the King had not definitely committed himself to the projected marriage, the Editor did not feel justified in publishing comment that would inevitably embarrass the Royal Family, and might finally wreck the Prime Minister's delicate negotiations." But among the letters on the subject pouring into the *Times* from different parts of the world, one had arrived that struck Dawson as particularly significant. Even if he could not publish it, he realized, he could still make use of it, and he decided that he would.

The letter came from a Briton who had lived several years in the United States. He had always done his best, he claimed, to further good relations between the two countries. "It has therefore been with great regret, and even with dismay, that I have watched in the course of the last few months the development of a situation that gravely lowers British prestige in American eyes. I refer to the poisonous publicity attending the King's friendship with Mrs. Simpson." The American public, he went on, had been titillated for months with rumour about Mrs. Simpson, "but in the course of the last three or four weeks there had come a perfect avalanche of muck and slime," including such assertions as that Queen Mary had been ousted from Buckingham Palace in order to clear the way for Mrs. Simpson's installation as the King's official hostess. The hoardings were full of advertisements promising the full inside story, and "distinguished Britons landing on American shores are beset by pressmen who ask them what the British people think about it all; and the next day appear accounts describing with malicious glee how the distinguished Britons struggled amid confusion and embarrassment to evade the question." This was not merely embarrassing.

British prestige was suffering—and after the humiliation over Italy and Abyssinia "it can ill afford to sustain additional shocks that are all the more intolerable in that they are so gratuitous, so unnecessary, and could easily have been avoided by a little more self-discipline on the part of one individual." The letter concluded:

It may be presumptuous, and even impertinent, for a person far removed from the centre of events to suggest a remedy; but I cannot refrain from saying that nothing would please me more than to hear that Edward VIII had abdicated his rights in favour of the heir presumptive. . . . In my view it would be well to have the change take place while it is still a matter of individuals, and before the disquiet has progressed to the point of calling into question the institution of monarchy itself.

Dawson was much impressed with the letter, which could hardly have been clearer, more pungent and more to the point if it had been written on his instructions in the *Times* office—as rumour was later to suggest it had been. It was not: the writer's name and New Jersey address were on it, though he signed it *"Britannicus in Partibus Infidelium."* The letter put the affair on a new footing. It was not simply a question of the King's relationship with Mrs. Simpson, but of the deplorable effect that it was having in the United States. What people in the United States thought or did was not then so much a matter of concern to Britain as it was later to become. The isolationist tradition worked in reverse: in Britain, not much store was set by trends of American public opinion. Nevertheless a situation in which the American press was full of spiteful gossip about the King could hardly fail to have repercussions, particularly in Canada. Surely the King should be able to realize this, and let himself be persuaded to exercise the necessary self-discipline? If not, he should go.

Up to this point the word "abdication" had not entered into the controversy. But after all, why not? Especially if—as rumour now persistently claimed—he did not really want to be King? Some time was to pass before the idea of abdication really sank in, but at least it had been implanted.

Copies were typed of the letter, and on October 26—the same morning as Hearst's assertion that the King was going to marry Mrs. Simpson appeared, doubtless bringing further embarrassment to "Britannicus" in New Jersey—Dawson took one to Buckingham Palace, where he saw Hardinge and asked him to put it before the

King. Hardinge, he realized, was in a difficult position. As the King's private secretary, he was bound by loyalty to him. But one of a private secretary's duties to the King—as the Duke of Windsor was himself to describe it—is to be "the only channel of communication between the Sovereign and his ministers." To perform this function, he is expected to keep the King informed of developments in Whitehall of a kind not to be found in state papers—"the falling out of a member of the Cabinet with the Prime Minister or an imminent attack by the Opposition on some point of Government policy." And beyond this, "The Private Secretary is responsible for the good public relations of the King. In that sense he is the Monarch's contact with the world beyond Whitehall, and should keep his ear to the ground so as to advise his master in the moulding of royal policy."

For these functions, Hardinge had some useful qualifications. As the son of a viceroy of India and the stepson-in-law of Lord Milner, he knew the Establishment and moved in it. Naturally he knew the editor of the *Times,* though they were not close friends—he still began his letters, "My dear Dawson." Hardinge was not cut off from the rest of society, as some courtiers were. On the contrary, though he was a simple and unpretentious man with no political guile, he was in quite a good position to be his master's public-relations officer and keep him well-informed. He did not need Dawson to tell him what people were saying. He knew.

Dawson found him depressed, worrying about what he should do. Up to this point Hardinge had thought it best not to mention the subject to the King, preferring to maintain relations with him as his private secretary "and thus be able to facilitate the access of ministers and other more weighty advisers." But already, Hardinge explained, he had been "bringing in big guns to bear on his master," including Baldwin.

This appears to have been the first Dawson knew about Baldwin's meeting with the King, and naturally his curiosity was aroused. The "Britannicus" letter was the perfect excuse to bring up the subject. He brought another copy to Downing Street that evening and there heard from Baldwin what had happened at the Fort, though "with what results he did not know." One result was obvious the following day. The fact that the divorce case was heard at Ipswich intimated that the King had not changed his mind and decided to intervene. Still, until the King had definitely stated his intention to marry Mrs. Simpson, Baldwin did not see how he could formally object, and in the meantime, he thought it best that Dawson should continue to exercise restraint.

Dawson was uneasy, but he had another reason for maintaining the silence. At this point, affairs of state were about to intervene. On November 5 there was the opening of Parliament, where the King would read his (in fact, his ministers') speech. On the 11th, Armistice Day, the King would be going as usual to the British Legion Rally at the Albert Hall. The following day he was to pay a visit to the fleet. Then, the week after, he was to tour South Wales. As Dawson later explained in his abdication memorandum, "If newspaper criticism were to begin before these engagements, it might be taken as an attempt to undermine His Majesty's popularity in advance; if immediately after them, as an attempt to minimise his influence." Baldwin accepted the force of these arguments, but declined to give advice. "The press," Dawson commented with a touch of exasperation, "is a closed book to him." All things considered, Dawson thought, it was safest to wait—and to restrain anybody else who might look like jumping the gun.

On November 10, Arnold Wilson, a Conservative MP, told Dawson that he felt so strongly about the press silence that he was determined to break it in *Nineteenth Century*, an old established monthly (as its name implied) that he edited. He had waited for the *Times* to give a lead, but if the *Times* wouldn't, *Nineteenth Century* would. Dawson managed to calm him down. A few days later he was able to reassure the editor of the *Morning Post*, H.A. Gwynne, who was also growing restive, and had written to the Cabinet asking for guidance—the *Morning Post* had no love for Baldwin, but Gwynne was an elderly man of unimpeachable respectability. In mid-November he asked Dawson around to the Bath Club for a talk, suggesting to him that the government should direct what should be done and that the newspapers should take simultaneous common action. Dawson pointed out the objections to "this sort of official press phalanx" (though he did not point out the chief one, from his own point of view: that he wanted the *Times* to take the lead when the moment came). But the main point of interest of the conversation, he thought, "was the certainty that the *Morning Post* was going to do nothing without a lead."

After the divorce hearing, though, the Establishment also began to grow worried at Baldwin's inaction. At a lunch Tom Jones attended at the beginning of November various possibilities were

canvassed to stir the sluggish Prime Minister into action, one suggestion being that the press magnates should form a deputation to
see him. Lord Willingdon, a former viceroy of India, thought Baldwin should call together half a dozen elder Privy Councillors, decide
on a policy, and send for the King. On November 17 Baldwin received a deputation on the subject, including among others Lord
Salisbury, Lord Derby, Lord FitzAlan, Herbert Samuel and Austen
Chamberlain. (Winston Churchill had been asked, but had refused.)
How uniform this attitude was can be judged from a letter that
Lord Linlithgow, then viceroy of India, wrote to Dawson from New
Delhi. He urged that matters should be brought to a head. "I think
you should see S.B. and push him into calling into counsel Neville,
Halifax, Hailsham, Simon, Sam Hoare by way of providing S.B. with
support on which he can fall back when he is driven out of the
Palace, on the occasion of the first assault."

Baldwin's way

But Baldwin had already, by this time, called some of his colleagues into counsel. On November 11, after the Armistice Day
service, he conferred with his Cabinet "inner ring"—MacDonald,
Halifax, Simon and Walter Runciman, President of the Board of
Trade, telling them what had been happening. Chamberlain could
not restrain his impatience. At the beginning of November, with the
help of senior civil servants, he had begun to draft a formal sub-
mission to the King "advising him to reorder his private life"—the
phrase is Iain Macleod's, but it has a Chamberlain flavour; and at a
second meeting of the inner Cabinet two days later he produced
copies of two documents he had brought with him: "The first was
formal advice to the King from the Prime Minister to put an end to
his association with Mrs. Simpson; the second was an informal letter
saying that the formal document was ready and that, if it were
tendered and the advice not taken, it would mean the resignation
of the cabinet."

It was typical of Chamberlain that he should approach the problem as if the King were a refractory company chairman, needing to
be disciplined by his directors. Nothing could have been better
calculated to put Edward in the mood to fight; and if Chamberlain's
ultimatum had been published, G.M. Young thought, "the country
would have been swept with a wave of sympathy for the King." But

Baldwin astutely avoided a decision, or even a discussion, by saying he would have to take the documents to Chequers for the week-end, to consider them. It was the last that was heard of them.

Before he consulted his inner Cabinet, though, Baldwin had not been idle. If he had given that impression, it was because he had hardly bothered to consult people whose views were predictable, like the members of his cabinet. Had he consulted them earlier, they might have pushed him farther or faster than he wished to go. It was more important, he had decided, to canvass the doubtfuls. What, for example, would be the attitude of the Dominions—particularly of Canadians, who had been subjected to a barrage of gossip about the King and Mrs. Simpson from over the border?

It happened that Mackenzie King, the Canadian Prime Minister, was on a visit to London at this time, and Baldwin took the opportunity to discuss the subject with him. So did Dawson, when they met at a banquet on October 21. Hearing that King was going to Buckingham Palace on the day of the divorce hearing, Dawson went to lunch that day at the Canadian High Commissioner's expressly to find out from King what had happened. King's account disappointed Dawson. He had told Edward of the reserves of affection and loyalty felt in Canada for the crown—and for him. But he had been unable to bring himself to the point of saying, as it had been hoped he would, that these reserves were now being squandered. Although he was particularly well-placed to give a warning, he had failed to do so. He had even made matters worse, Dawson thought, by reminding the King of his popularity in the Dominions. A valuable opportunity had been missed. Still, whatever impression Mackenzie King might have left on Edward, he at least made it clear to Baldwin that opinion in Canada would be hostile to the King's marrying Mrs. Simpson.

Where Baldwin showed himself at his shrewdest, though, was in sounding out men who were not in his political camp but who might make valuable allies. One was Clement Attlee, the leader of the Labour Party. He heard of the impending crisis a little belatedly and came to ask Baldwin what was happening, and although Baldwin appears to have given little away, he went off satisfied. And a few days later Baldwin took Sir Walter Citrine, the general secretary of the Trades Union Congress, into his confidence. Citrine had got the job as a relatively young man—at thirty-nine he was, in fact, the youngest ever. The power wielded by a TUC secretary was not great. He was the servant of the council of the TUC, and the council members were themselves the servants of their individual unions. A capable secretary, however, could often get his way, by tact, and at the time of the abdication Citrine had had ten years in office to learn it.

Early in November Horace Wilson telephoned Citrine on the Prime Minister's behalf to say that Baldwin would like a talk "as he had not seen me for over twelve months"—a characteristically indirect Baldwin approach. And on November 7 Citrine went down to lunch at Chequers, where the two men talked for a while on this and that and the state of affairs in Russia, about which Citrine had recently written a book. Over lunch they discussed Lloyd George, and it was not until after it that Baldwin brought up the subject of the King and Mrs. Simpson, explaining what had been said at his meeting with the King and asking for Citrine's opinion.

Citrine had recently been in America, so he was aware of the gossip, and his attitude to it ("I felt a sense of personal humiliation at the scurrilous allusions to the King's alleged carryings on with a married woman") reassured Baldwin. So did his reaction to the news—which Baldwin said he had not heard from the King himself, but from another source—that the King "might marry her before the Coronation, and think he can get away with it." Citrine agreed that the King would *not* get away with it and told Baldwin that in thinking so, he was undoubtedly interpreting the minds of most people in the Labour movement. Baldwin, satisfied, promised to keep him informed on what happened.

But what was perhaps Baldwin's most important discussion of the subject was with Stanley Bruce, later to become Lord Bruce of Melbourne, and at that time high commissioner in London for Australia.

Dominions high commissioners were not always men of influence, but Bruce had exceptional qualifications for the post. Although born in Australia, he had lived in England during his formative years, winning a rowing blue at Cambridge, and—according to his biographer, Cecil Edwards—coming to regard the mother country as his home. Yet when he returned to Australia, it had taken him only six years to reach the top of the political tree: he became Prime Minister while still in his thirties. "After that he was to be a world figure; an aggressively Australian voice in international affairs, heeded and respected by Chancellors of the Exchequer, Governors of the Bank of England and the great financial world of the City of London."

He was also heeded and respected by Baldwin, who invited him to lunch on November 15. Bruce's notes of the conversation reveal that Baldwin gave him much the same account of his meeting with the King at the Fort as he was later to give Parliament. But this was not enough for Bruce. He wanted to know what Baldwin proposed to do. Would the government resign to prevent the King marrying Mrs. Simpson? Or to force him to break off all relations with her? Baldwin did not seem to have worked this out: "It was clear his mind was fairly confused and that he had not got the whole position in proper perspective."

Bruce decided there and then to remedy this deficiency, and in his notes he claimed, "This was roughly how I put it:"

The alarming and devastating possibility is that the King should marry Mrs. Simpson. Should he do so it is impossible to calculate the consequences. The people of this country and the Dominions would never accept her as Queen, quite possibly the House of Commons would cancel the Civil List, the Throne would be imperilled, the Empire would be endangered, there would be a demand for the King's abdication, the Government would resign and it would be impossible to get an alternative Government. There would be no way out of the position save that the King must go, and clearly he would be forced to. As there is the possibility that the King is contemplating marrying Mrs. Simpson, as Prime Minister I would feel it my duty to put the question straight to the King as to whether he had any such intention. If his answer was that he had . . . then I should draw the picture of what the consequences would be and tell him that unless he was prepared to abandon such an intention I would be compelled to advise him to abdicate and unless he accepted such advice I would be unable to continue as his adviser and would resign. (With this divorce under way which, if the decree is made absolute, would make it possible for the King to marry Mrs. Simpson, I do not think the Prime Minister can delay insisting on a complete clarification of the King's intentions. Resignation in these circumstances would command universal support.)

If the King's reply was that he had no intention of marrying the lady, the Prime Minister's job is more difficult in some respects because . . . it has to be rendered impossible for the King to go back on his word. . . . On such an assurance, the Prime Minister's job was to do everything possible to break the entanglement and to get Mrs. Simpson out of the country, by appeals to the King's patriotism, sense of duty, etc., but if, as I imagined was almost certain, it was impossible to induce the King to go as far as that, then, with the same arguments, to do everything possible to induce him to behave with more discretion. . . .

Bruce's biographer emphasizes the fact that the following day, when Bruce sent Baldwin an *aide mémoire* of their conversation, was the same day that Baldwin went to the palace for his second confrontation with the King. Perhaps Bruce did clear Baldwin's mind for him, but there is always the possibility that Baldwin was less confused than he appeared—that he simply did not care to disclose what was in his mind.

A matter of great urgency

During the early part of November the King came nearer to being a king, in the sense he craved to be, than at any time since his accession. True, the opening of Parliament was a little disappointing. It rained, and instead of driving through the streets in a state coach, Edward went to Westminster unromantically in a closed car of old-fashioned make, so that the drenched onlookers scarcely caught a glimpse of him. He also had qualms about the oath he was required to take, promising to maintain the Protestant succession. He felt it "inappropriate to an institution supposed to shelter all creeds." But he took it, and his speech from the throne was a success: "The sound of my own voice in my ears was strong and vigorous; as I read on there welled up inside me a feeling almost of defiance." The speech was favourably received, even in the *Times*.

Then, on November 11—Armistice Day—there was the usual ceremony at the Cenotaph, the most moving of any since the first— underlined as it was by events in Spain, where Madrid was being besieged, making it painfully clear that the "war to end wars" theme was no longer realistic. That evening, Edward went as usual to the Albert Hall, there to join the British Legion in community singing of the songs of the Great War, and to read to the audience Laurence Binyon's "The Trust":

> They shall not grow old, as we that are left grow old
> Age shall not weary them, nor the years condemn
> At the going down of the sun and in the morning
> We will remember them . . .

The occasion—though not the recital of "The Trust"—was broadcast, and the enthusiasm for the King among the ex-servicemen was tremendous. He stayed at the Albert Hall until the Armistice night gathering broke up, but before dawn the next morning, he was at Southampton to embark on his inspection of the fleet. Commander Kenneth Edwards, who was present, later described in the *Saturday Review* how the way that the King carried out his exhausting programme went straight to the men's hearts—particularly the fact that he would not wear a waterproof while inspecting men in the rain, whereas the First Lord of the Admiralty, Hoare, wore his—"a small thing, but sailors take note of small things, and in this they saw the real difference between the Politician and the Monarch." It was by such small things that Edward could have, and to some extent had already, won confidence and loyalty.

That the visit to the fleet was an outstanding success was also to be attested by Hoare himself. The King seemed, Hoare recalled, "to know personally every officer and seaman in the Fleet . . . in my long experience of mass meetings I never saw one so completely dominated by a single personality." Edward mingled with the ratings on the huge underdeck of the aircraft carrier *Courageous* (destined to be the first major naval casualty of the Second World War), opened the community singing to the accompaniment of a mouth organ, and "made an impromptu speech which brought the house down. Then, a seaman in the crowd proposed three cheers for him, and there followed an unforgettable scene of the wildest and most spontaneous enthusiasm. Here, indeed, was the Prince Charming, who could win the hearts of all sorts and conditions of men and women, and send a thrill through great crowds." And tired though he must have been, the animation, the vivacity, Hoare added, lasted throughout the journey back to London, where they parted, the King driving out to the Fort.

Wallis had been invited to the Fort for the week-end, and she had arrived looking forward to it, as unsuspecting as Edward was himself of what was awaiting him there. Since the divorce, Wallis had been living in London in a new house in Cumberland Terrace, where she had been able to celebrate the successful outcome by giving Edward the kind of intimate dinner that they had so often enjoyed before he had become King. Edward had broken the news of his interview with Baldwin to her, and for the first time, she became frightened: "Don't be alarmed," he reassured her: "I am sure I can fix things."

It was a phrase she was often going to hear from him again, during coming weeks, and it carried more significance for her than might appear. In their ordinary social relations Wallis was, in a sense, the dominant partner. Edward trusted her good sense, her taste, her judgment. In matters pertaining to the monarchy, though, she accepted *his* judgment, and this meant more than simply accepting that he knew more about affairs of state than she did. One of the things that attracted her to him, she was to admit in *The Heart Has Its Reasons*, was his unmistakable power and authority: "His slightest wish seemed always to be translated instantly into the most impressive kind of reality. Trains were held; yachts materialized; the best suites in the finest hotels were flung open; aeroplanes were waiting"—and all this was done with no apparent effort, but in "the calm assumption that this was the natural order of things." So it was, but what Edward had failed to realize was that it was the natural order of things only so long as he kept his part of the constitutional bargain. He had grown so accustomed to the possession of royalty's magic lamp, with its attendant genie offering instant service, that he had begun to think of it as his—to forget that the genie's ultimate master was really Stanley Baldwin. And because Wallis knew so little about the workings of the Constitution, she had never grasped this either.

So far as she was concerned, then, all was still going smoothly when she arrived with her Aunt Bessie, who had come over to stay with her, for the Fort week-end. It was Friday the 13th—truly, she later recalled, a day of ill omen. When Edward arrived soon after, he was still in the high spirits Hoare had observed, delighted with his reception by the fleet. A dispatch marked urgent, however, was awaiting him, and he went to another room to read it. When he returned, "all the upwelling of joy that he had brought back from the Fleet was gone."

Since Dawson had shown him the "Britannicus" letter, two weeks before, Hardinge had been turning over in his mind how he could convey to the King what so many of his subjects were now feeling, and on November 13, when Dawson came to see him at Buckingham Palace, Hardinge showed him ("since I happened to be there," Dawson was later to recall in his memorandum) the draft of a letter to the King "which he had felt impelled to write after a sleepless night." Dawson thought the letter admirable—"respectful, courageous and definite." Hardinge had it sent to the Fort where the King now found it. It ran:

Sir

With my humble duty:

As your Majesty's private Secretary I feel it my duty to bring to your notice the following facts which have come to my knowledge, and which I *know* to be accurate.

1. The silence of the British press on the subject of Your Majesty's friendship with Mrs. Simpson is *not* going to be maintained. It is probably only a matter of days before the outburst begins. Judging by the letters from British subjects living in foreign countries where the press has been outspoken, the effect will be calamitous.

2. The Prime Minister and senior members of the Government are meeting today to discuss what actions should be taken to deal with the serious situation which is developing. As Your Majesty no doubt knows the resignation of the Government—an eventuality which can by no means be excluded—would result in Your Majesty having to find someone else capable of forming a Government which would receive the support of the present House of Commons. I have reason to know that, in view of the feeling prevalent among members of the House of Commons of all parties, this is hardly within the bounds of possibility. The only alternative remaining is a dissolution and a general election in which Your Majesty's personal affairs would be the chief issue, and I cannot help feeling that even those who would sympathise with Your Majesty as an individual would deeply resent the damage which would inevitably be done to the Crown—the cornerstone on which the whole Empire rests.

If Your Majesty will permit me to say so, there is only one step which holds out any prospect of avoiding this dangerous situation, and that is for Mrs. Simpson to go abroad *without further delay*—and I would *beg* Your Majesty to give this proposal your earnest consideration before the position has become irretrievable. Owing to the changing attitude of the press the matter has become one of great urgency.

Coming as it did after the success of his naval visit, the contents of the letter shocked the King, and the tone angered him. He did not question Hardinge's right to give the warning. What hurt him was "the cold formality with which so personal a matter affecting my whole happiness had been broached." In this he was being unfair to Hardinge. The letter was anguished, rather than cold. But phrases like "I have reason to know" gave the King the impression, and rightly, that Hardinge had been put up to it by Baldwin, which in a sense was true, as Baldwin had told Hardinge the inner cabinet had discussed the subject—the reason for Hardinge's sleepless night, and for his decision that the letter must be written.

In his *Reign of Edward VIII*, Robert Sencourt was to defend Hardinge on the ground that the King himself had made the crisis inevitable by refusing to confide in his secretary, leaving Hardinge no alternative but to put his views in writing—which he might have wished to do anyway, for the record. But equally it could be argued that if Hardinge did not have the courage to bring up the subject face to face, knowing what he did, he ought to have resigned. He did not have the equipment to deal with a situation of this kind, and he would have been better out of it. Had he tendered his resignation with the letter, he might have been spared his subsequent humiliation, but as things were, the limitations of both men were now to be exposed. The King made no allusion to Hardinge's letter, either then or later—in spite of the fact that, according to Hardinge, they continued to see each other for the conduct of ordinary government business for another three weeks. Why, in those circumstances, did Hardinge stay on? Presumably he had allowed himself to be persuaded by Dawson and others that he was a necessary channel of communication. But the channel was now blocked.

Still, Hardinge had played his part in the story. Ill-advised or not, his letter was crucial. It smoked the King out into the open. Edward could no longer hope that, if he simply waited long enough, matters would sort themselves out. If he did not act, the government would, and this could put him at a disadvantage. He must call their bluff. "They had struck me at the roots of my pride. Only the most fainthearted would have remained unaroused by such a challenge!"

Lord
Rothermere

Sir Walter
Citrine

Aneurin Bevan
and Jennie
Lee on their
wedding day

Ernest Bevin

Herbert
Morrison

PHOTOS, ABOVE, COURTESY
RADIO · TIMES HULTON PICTURE
LIBRARY; RIGHT, CENTRAL
PRESS PHOTOS LTD.

Pierre Laval

Sir Kingsley Wood

CENTRAL PRESS PHOTOS LTD.

RADIO TIMES HULTON PICTURE LIBRARY

Sir Samuel Hoare

The Archbishop of Canterbury,
Cosmo Gordon Lang,
leaving Downing Street
during the crisis

RADIO TIMES HULTON PICTURE LIBRARY

CAMERA PRESS LTD. (BASSANO)

The Bishop of Bradford,
the Rt. Rev. A. W. F. Blunt

Sir Thomas Inskip
and Lord Halifax
leaving Downing Street
after a meeting

PHOTOS COURTESY RADIO TIMES
HULTON PICTURE LIBRARY

Oswald Mosley,
Lloyd George, and
James Maxton; Sir
Stafford Cripps is
seated on right

CENTRAL PRESS PHOTOS LTD.

The director-general of the B.B.C.,
Sir John Reith

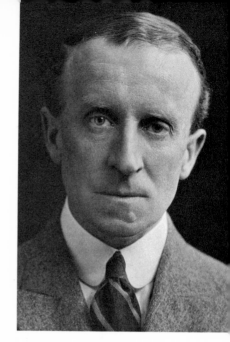

John Buchan, Lord Tweedsmuir

Anthony Eden in Downing Street going
to one of the crisis talks

RADIO TIMES HULTON PICTURE LIBRARY

The leader of the Labour party,
Clement Attlee, in Whitehall

RADIO TIMES HULTON PICTURE LIBRARY

The editor of
The Times,
Geoffrey Dawson,
with his assistant
editor, R. M.
Barrington-Ward

PHOTOS COURTESY RADIO TIMES
HULTON PICTURE LIBRARY

The Prime Minister,
Stanley Baldwin,
at the Degree Day
ceremony at
Cambridge, June 1936

Neville Chamberlain
in Downing Street

Winston Churchill
in his constituency

PHOTOS COURTESY RADIO TIMES
HULTON PICTURE LIBRARY

Walter Monckton
leaving 10 Downing
Street during the
abdication crisis

Minister of
War, Alfred
Duff Cooper

PHOTOS COURTESY RADIO
TIMES HULTON PICTURE
LIBRARY

Max Aitken,
Lord Beaverbrook

RADIO TIMES HULTON PICTURE LIBRARY

The Prince of Wales

With Crown Prince
Hirohito in Japan
in 1922

With Stanley Baldwin
in 1926

RADIO TIMES HULTON PICTURE
LIBRARY

At Brigade of
Guards point-to-point
meeting

PHOTOS COURTESY RADIO TIMES
HULTON PICTURE LIBRARY

With Wallis Simpson
at a race meeting

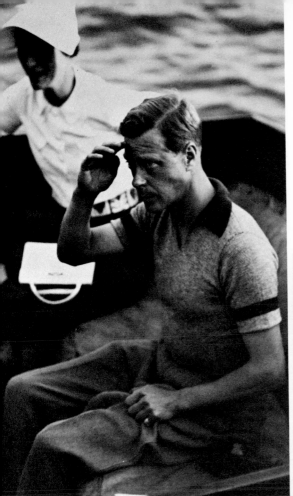

On the *Nahlin* cruise

TOPIX

The Home Secretary,
Sir John Simon, with
Queen Mary and King
Edward VIII on their way
to the Armistice Day
ceremony in 1936;
behind them are other
members of the royal family

"From light into darkness"

RADIO TIMES HULTON PICTURE LIBRARY

A Cecil Beaton portrait of Wallis Simpson

During the crisis

RADIO TIMES HULTON
PICTURE LIBRARY

The Duke and Duchess at
their wedding in June 1937;
with them are Mr. Herman
Rogers and Major "Fruity"
Metcalfe

PHOTO, ABOVE, COURTESY
RADIO TIMES HULTON PICTURE
LIBRARY; RIGHT, THE PRESS
ASSOCIATION LTD.

Ernest Simpson in 1937

SECOND CONFRONTATION—NOVEMBER 16

The form the King's reaction to the challenge took could hardly have given more satisfaction to Baldwin if he had arranged it himself. First, Edward summoned Walter Monckton. He had known Monckton since his Oxford days, when Monckton had been president of the Union. In that capacity—or so Union legend and Monckton's *Sunday Times* obituarist were to claim—he endeared himself to the Prince, who had come to a meeting as part of his training: Monckton, "noting how bored the Prince was by the tedium of the debate, sent him a note saying that no one would mind if he slipped away," which the Prince gratefully did. The story certainly rings true—even if the obituarist's belief that from this kindly thought "a lifelong friendship was born" was an overstatement. The two men lost touch with each other during the First World War and did not come together again until several years later, when Monckton became Attorney General to the Prince and to his Duchy of Cornwall.

Monckton—the obituarist continued—"was a man of his generation; born into the prosperous Edwardian upper middle class, educated at Harrow, he enjoyed hunting, cricket, wine. . . . It was said of him that he received more confidences than any man in London. They were never broken." He was much better qualified in these circumstances to give advice, and to give it in such a way that it would be accepted, or if rejected, would not give offence. Where Hardinge was an army officer and courtier transplanted into a job for which he had neither the skill nor the subtlety, Monckton was the go-between of Beaverbrook's dreams—except that he lacked Beaverbrook's restless ambition to utilize the power he won.

At this stage, though, it was not Monckton's advice that the King wanted but simply his consent to act as a liaison officer with the government, which he gave. The next step was to summon the Prime Minister to the palace, on the evening of Monday, the 16th. And this time the idea of the King's marrying Mrs. Simpson, not previously mentioned between them, was at last discussed.

Again, Edward's recollection of the conversation in A *King's Story* tallies with Baldwin's later account of it in the House of Commons. The marriage, Baldwin claimed, would not receive the country's approbation—and this was not simply his personal view: "I did tell his Majesty once that I might be a remnant of the old Victorians, but that my worst enemy would not say of me that I did not know what the reaction of the English people would be to any particular course of action; and I told him that so far as they went, I was certain that that would be impracticable." (Baldwin, Edward tartly commented, "might have been the Gallup Poll Incarnate.") The position of the King's wife was different from the position of other wives. "It was part of the price which the King had to pay. His wife becomes Queen; the Queen becomes the Queen of the country; and, therefore, in the choice of a Queen the voice of the people must be heard."

Listening to Baldwin, Edward became aware that his discourse was spiced with paradox. If his argument was carried to its logical conclusion, it would mean—although "no idea would have been further from Mr. Baldwin's wholly respectable mind"—that the King should have taken a mistress, "a discreet house nearby, a key to the garden door, decorous associations—the relationship might be privately deplored, but it had had notable precedents." Yet here was the King, who had acquired a reputation for paying insufficient attention to religious observances, spurning the proposal. He told the Prime Minister bluntly that he intended to marry Mrs. Simpson. If he could marry her as King, well and good, "but if, on the other hand, the Government opposed the marriage, as the Prime Minister had given me reason to believe it would, *then I was prepared to go.*" The King's face, Baldwin afterward told his son, when speaking of Mrs. Simpson wore such a look of beauty as "might have lighted the face of a young knight who had caught a glimpse of the Holy Grail." Baldwin, in the Duke's recollection, simply looked startled. Saying that it was most grievous news, he excused himself, asking for time for reflection.

On Baldwin's departure, the King began to act with greater decisiveness than he had yet displayed. The first necessity was to tell his family, of whom he had been seeing little. Even before talking to Baldwin, he had proposed himself for dinner that evening with his mother; and with her, at Marlborough House, he found his sister Mary. For the first time he told them of his love for Wallis and his determination to marry her, even if it meant leaving the throne. They sympathized with him, he thought, over his love, but not over his threat to abdicate. And on this issue they were never to be reconciled.

Queen Mary's views on divorce, according to Pope-Hennessy, were clear and strict: "One divorce could seldom or never be justified, and to divorce twice, on any grounds whatsoever, was to her unthinkable." And what weighed even more, perhaps, with Queen Mary and those who thought like her was that the two divorced husbands were still living.

To Queen Mary, too, who had accepted an arranged marriage and then, after the death of her fiancé, acquiesced in the decision that she should marry his brother, the idea of Edward's marrying for love was almost indecent. He must, she felt, be prepared to sacrifice his own feelings. After all, she pointed out, many of Edward's contemporaries had made a far greater sacrifice for their country, by laying down their lives in the Great War. A king's duty was to his country, which meant that he must give up his love or anything else that threatened to interfere. Edward argued that it was impossible to do his duty properly by his country if he could not have Wallis as his wife and companion. If they would only consent to meet Wallis, he urged, they might understand the reasons for his feeling. But this they would not do. It was too late. Now that the constitutional issue had arisen, Queen Mary felt that she had no alternative but to refuse, for fear that if she gave any encouragement to Edward, his choice would be made harder.

The King also saw his brothers and told them of his decision. None of them was happy about it. The Duke of Gloucester feared it would mean the end of his army career—he would have to undertake more royal duties. The Duke of Kent was sorry at the prospect of losing his brother, for whom he had so strong an affection. The Duke of York was appalled at the thought of having to become King. Edward, however, made it clear that his mind was made up, and from that time until the abdication, he saw little of his family.

The meetings, though, were not unproductive. They cleared the air. For the first time the members of the royal family were able without embarrassment to discuss the prospect of the King's abdication. The Duke of York had been in a particularly embarrassing position. Should Edward leave the throne, or be compelled to leave it, he would become King; yet until there was some intimation that Edward might leave the throne delicacy prevented him from discussing, almost from thinking about, the prospect. After Edward had himself broached the subject, it was no longer taboo, and a week later the Duke was writing to his brother's former private secretary, Thomas, that "if the worst happens and I have to take over, you can be assured that I will do my best to clear up the inevitable mess, if the whole fabric does not crumble under the shock and strain of it all." The very fact it could now be discussed, though, meant that the chance of the fabric crumbling was diminished. The royal family, the court, the government all had time to prepare their dispositions—and the very act of preparing them made the idea of abdication seem less terrifying.

Before he left for South Wales, too, Edward at last did what he might have been expected to do long before. He sought advice. There were two members of the government to whom he was close enough to have consulted them unofficially before. Now he felt it wise to obtain Baldwin's permission first. Baldwin gave it, and Samuel Hoare, who had been with the King so recently on the visit to the fleet, and Duff Cooper, his guest on the *Nahlin* and at Fort week-ends, were formally summoned to Buckingham Palace.

Samuel Hoare

At first sight, Hoare was a curious choice. He was a politician's politician, not at all the kind of man that Edward would have been expected to find congenial. "Intensely serious and desperately sensitive," "Watchman" described him, "the soul of care and caution." In the Commons, and frequently out of it, he had a schoolmarmish manner. His colleagues thought of him as a maiden aunt—"As he has severely plied his horn-rimmed spectacles, the irreverent have muttered, 'What's troubling Prunes and Prisms Hoare?'"

Gunther, too, thought Hoare "rather arch, rather delicate," neither of them a quality likely to appeal to the King. But Gunther added that the inner character belied the impression of primness, and in fact Hoare had shown quite a knack for getting to know, and be liked by, the right people. Perhaps they were surprised to find that he did not really resemble his rather unsympathetic public image. For one thing, he was quite a good conversationalist and well-read—he even startled the Commons once by quoting Proust, an author then considered by most MPs as not merely *avant-garde*, but rather disreputable. Alone of all the older generation of ministers, Hoare is referred to in *A King's Story* as "my friend"—though the friendship was not, it can be surmised, very close: the first reference to him in the book concerns the Prince of Wales going to the peers' gallery to hear his resignation speech in December 1935.

The occasion, though, was significant. With King George's health deteriorating, some ministers had been taking the Prince into their confidence, and Hoare, apparently, was one of them—to judge from Edward's claim that he knew much of what had gone on behind the scenes over the Hoare-Laval pact. He felt sorry that Sam Hoare "had been made the scapegoat for what was, in the last analysis, Mr. Baldwin's own policy," a view that may have owed much to briefing by Hoare, and it suggests that there was at least a theoretical possibility that Hoare might have been an influential ally. But again, the crisis precipitated by his pact with Laval was to be decisive. It wrecked the King's only chance of having a senior member of the Cabinet on his side.

By virtue of seniority, experience of office, and administrative ability, Hoare had contrived to establish himself in 1935 in the inner Cabinet circle, with, it seemed, a good chance of the succession to the premiership, after Chamberlain. Up to that time his career had moved with gratifying smoothness. Baldwin, perhaps influenced by the fact that he was a fellow Harrovian, had given him his first ministerial opportunity as Air Minister. But he owed even more to Chamberlain. In the summer of 1931, when the Labour government was collapsing, it was to Hoare that Chamberlain turned for help and advice—Baldwin having holed himself up at Aix, showing no desire to return and deal with the crisis himself. It was the kind of situation Chamberlain revelled in. He was virtually his own master, and he could approach the subject as a businessman or efficiency expert. But he liked to have somebody to talk to—or soliloquize at, as Hoare, without rancour, recalled. Their town houses were shut for the summer, so they had to stay at the Carlton Club, having their meals together in restaurants. That Chamberlain should have chosen him as his confidant, and as his right-hand man in the conferences that were held with the leaders of the Labour government, clearly marked him out for important office if the Labour government should fall.

It turned out to be more important than it sounded: he went to the India Office, there to pilot through the Government of India Bill—a performance by which Baldwin and his colleagues had good reason to be impressed. And as Foreign Secretary, in succession to Simon, Hoare had been responsible for the final stages of the Anglo-German naval pact, at the time accounted as an achievement, particularly by the Treasury, which would be spared the alarming cost of a naval building race.

It was characteristic of Hoare, though, that even with the assistance of hindsight he was unable to realize that he had been duped. In his autobiography he defended the treaty on the ground that the German navy was inadequately prepared when war broke out. As things turned out, it was, but this was nothing to do with the treaty. Where it suited Hitler's purposes, he broke it—as with the construction of the pocket battleships, exceeding the treaty limits. But Hitler did not plan to fight a war at sea, so German war production concentrated on aircraft and tanks and artillery rather than on warships—German naval strength never even reached the thirty-five percent allowed. What Hitler wanted was the agreement for its own sake—partly because of its prestige value, with the British government condoning the breach of the Versailles terms, and partly for the implicit snub to the French and to the League of Nations. The French government was not greatly perturbed (as Laval was Prime Minister, this was not surprising), but the French press reflected the wave of indignation that swept the country, reviving the old cry of *Albion perfide.*

Hoare, though, had a consummate ability to close his eyes to anything he did not wish to see. Not only did he remain unaware of the damage he had done, but he plunged into his next diplomatic adventure with sublime confidence in his own capacity.

It had been recognized by the Conservatives that to make sure of winning the forthcoming general election they must go forward as the party dedicated to the League of Nations. Hoare was ready to do his bit. On September 12, 1935, he ascended the Tribune of the League Assembly Hall at Geneva—and a sympathetic audience saw that he was limping, supported by a stick, owing to an arthritic foot. He spoke of the League as an ideal: "It is the fashion sometimes in the world of today—a foolish fashion, like many others in the world of today—to scoff at such ideals." And he went on to tell the delegates that in practice, the League was what its members made it—if risks were to be run "they must be run by all." On behalf of his own government, he could say that "they will be second to none to fulfil, within the measure of their capacity and the obligations which the Covenant lays upon them." The British government, he concluded, had already demonstrated its adherence to the principles of the League. Now, "in conformity with its precise and explicit obligations, the League stands, and my country stands with it, for the collective maintenance of the Covenant in its entirety, and particularly for steady and collective resistance to all acts of unprovoked aggression."

Hoare was not being hypocritical. He was simply indulging in one of the stock techniques of British political speakers. In Britain, references of this kind to the League would have attracted no more attention than a reference to God, or to His Majesty King George V. It would have drawn a polite ripple of clapping, and desultory "hear hears." Hoare expected nothing more. To his astonishment, he found himself rapturously acclaimed. He was not a good speaker. He had what "Watchman" called a governess-type voice, interrupted sporadically by the need to clear his throat, "a peculiar and most alarming sound, for all the world as though a spinster is flying into a passion of rage. Many members of the House of Commons lolling slumberous on all sides have been startled out of their post-prandial dreams by this clap of thunder interrupting the slow and measured progress of the painstaking Secretary of State." Nor was Hoare effective, as some speakers are, outside the House. His recorded voice on radio and on the newsreels was harsh, and his phrasing unsympathetic. It was a pleasant surprise, then, to feel that he had captured his audience—so great a surprise that he began to wonder whether he might have said something he hadn't intended to. He read through what he had said again, but could find nothing of significance that he had not said time after time in the Commons, without making any impact.

The reason for the delegates' excitement was simple. By this time it had become obvious that Mussolini intended to invade Abyssinia, and until that moment, doubts had remained whether, if that invasion started, Britain would fulfil her commitments to the League and help to deal with the aggressor. Now these doubts could safely be laid aside. The British Foreign Minister had made his country's position absolutely clear.

But Hoare never had any idea of his words being taken literally. During the days immediately before the speech, he had in fact been planning with Laval to secure a settlement that would award enough of Abyssinia to Mussolini to keep him happy—and keep him out of Hitler's embrace. It happened that Hoare had had past dealings with Mussolini, which made him assume that he was in a position to exercise influence. At the disastrous battle of Caporetto, vividly described in Hemingway's *Farewell to Arms,* Hoare had been a staff officer on the Italian front. Alarmed at the possibility that pacifism and defeatism would spread in Italy, Hoare had got in touch with Mussolini, then editor of the Socialist paper *Avanti* in Milan, to try to persuade him to exercise his influence in the other direction. "Leave it to me," Mussolini had said. "I will mobilize the militia in Milan, and they will break the heads of any pacifists who try to hold antiwar meetings in the streets." They did. Later, when they met, Mussolini reminded him of the episode. "No doubt," Hoare was later to explain, "I was foolish to imagine that an almost forgotten incident of many years before would influence the dictator. Yet, as almost anything was worth trying, I did my best in the personal letters that I sent him to remind him of my work for Italy during the First World War." It *was* foolish; Mussolini required a subtler type of flattery. And it led Hoare to make the fallacious assumption that deals might be done with Mussolini on a personal basis.

Laval had the same idea. He had told Hoare at their meeting that France simply could not risk driving Mussolini into the arms of Hitler, and for that reason she could not carry out her obligations— or what might be expected to be her obligations—to the League. There could be no question, for example, of closing the Suez Canal. That need not even be discussed, because he had already assured Mussolini that France would not stand for it. Hoare had gone on to Geneva, therefore, knowing that League action against Mussolini would not be effective—and knowing that Mussolini knew it.

Nevertheless Hoare went ahead with his speech, prepared before he had left England, unchanged. The thought did not cross his mind that in view of his agreement with Laval, reached only the day before, what he said was double-dealing. But inevitably, this was how it was interpreted by Mussolini. Laval had passed on what had been agreed between him and Hoare before the speech. Mussolini was therefore confident that the speech need not be taken seriously. He felt safe to go ahead with his plans, and three weeks later, the invasion of Abyssinia began.

There had never been any question of the League powers immediately going to war with the aggressor as part of their obligations under the Covenant. The principle upon which the League was supposed to work was that the member states would begin to impose sanctions, notably an embargo on exports to the aggressor. War was envisaged only as a last resort if the aggressor should retaliate. In the meantime, there would be negotiations, and the British and French governments got together to produce peace proposals that, it was hoped, the combatants might accept. For a while, attention in Britain was distracted from the war by the general election, which the Conservatives, pledged to stand by the League (and, therefore, by Abyssinia), contested and won. Then, when it was over, Hoare was told by his doctors that the state of his health made it essential for him to have a holiday. In his youth he had been a skating champion, and he welcomed the opportunity to see if he could recover some of his old prowess in Switzerland. It was with some irritation that he acceded to Laval's urgent entreaties for a meeting on the way. But at the meeting they naturally picked up where they had left off before Hoare's speech to the League.

To Hoare, it was now simply a question of doing a deal with Mussolini. How lucky it was, he thought, that he should have Laval, also a friend of Mussolini's, with whom to arrange it! When he had first met Laval, at their September encounter, he had been put off by "his greasy hair, dirty white tie and shifty look," but impressed by his quickness of mind. "Everyone knew him to be a cunning intriguer, but at the time there seemed a good chance of his wits once again being useful to us." Hoare learned with no surprise, therefore, that Laval had already given Mussolini a rough idea of what they were going to propose, and together with Vansittart, they sat down to redraw the map of Abyssinia, pausing from time to time so that Laval could consult Mussolini on the direct, secret telephone connection he had with the Duce. From their week-end sessions came the Hoare-Laval proposals—leaked on the Monday by the French press—to hand over a substantial segment of Abyssinia to the aggressor, Italy, with a further zone over which Italy would have economic development rights, Abyssinia being "compensated" by an outlet to the sea.

Hoare was to relate all this in his memoirs as if the way the negotiations were conducted was the most natural and sensible in the world. The end results, he thought, were what mattered. Abyssinia would benefit by the outlet to the sea—and by retaining her independence, which she would not do if conquered. Italy would get the territory Mussolini wanted. Mussolini, grateful, would stay in the Alliance. Peace would be restored. What more could anybody want?

Hoare was not being deliberately treacherous. He was not a devious man. Even Gandhi had been impressed by his trustworthiness. But he was a politician, and he thought in narrow political terms. It never occurred to him, either then or later, that the idea of himself and Laval sitting down to make a bargain with the aggressor, to enable Mussolini to get what he wanted as the price of halting his invasion, was not in the spirit of the League Covenant. Still less did it occur to Hoare that in the light of his League speech of a few weeks before, the proposals would make him appear to the world as a consummate hypocrite. He went on to his holiday in Switzerland in the happy conviction that he had done a very effective week-end's work.

Although his colleagues could blame Hoare for having committed them to too much, they did not at first feel that the proposals contained in his pact with Laval justified their making a scapegoat of him. When he returned from Switzerland—nursing his nose, broken in a fall—he assumed that they would back him, and Baldwin actually assured him, "We will all stand together." In Baldwin's mind, however, this was not quite the same as saying they would all fall together. Later the same day, Chamberlain came to tell Hoare that the Cabinet had changed their mind, and that what they now wanted of him was that he should say that he had changed *his* mind: that he now realized it was a bad plan, and that he had withdrawn his support for it. Hoare preferred to offer his resignation. Baldwin, unhappy at the possibility that the resignation might bring further obloquy down on the government, pressed him to stay. Hoare refused.

Perhaps because he was a good shot, and better company than most Cabinet ministers, Hoare had got on well with George V— though he gave a bleak reception to the King's quip about the meeting with Laval: "No more coals to Newcastle: no more Hoares to Paris." More surprisingly, he also got on well with Edward, and there is every reason to suppose that had the Hoare-Laval pact not been prematurely leaked—had it been discussed, and amended, by the governments concerned, and presented with greater subtlety; or even if they had decided discreetly to drop it—Hoare would have remained Foreign Secretary, and he would have been a great deal closer to Edward during his reign than any of his senior ministers were destined to be. The revulsion of feeling against the pact, therefore, and the Cabinet decision to make Hoare the scapegoat, was a severe blow to Edward's chances of winning influential support within the government. But what followed was to destroy the hope of having Hoare even as a friendly adviser.

Hoare had every justification for feeling angry with his colleagues, and at first he did. Chamberlain, going to say goodbye to him after his resignation speech, "found him more emotional than usual and, as I thought, a little inclined to bitterness"—as well he might be, after being callously sacrificed.

Most men, in his position, would have stood for a while on their dignity. In spite of the fact that he had to appear wearing sticking plaster over his broken nose, Hoare won sympathy from the House with his resignation speech, and though it was aroused less by the feeling that he deserved it than by the knowledge that he had been let down by his colleagues, at least attention was distracted from his own unfortunate part in the deal. With his inside knowledge of the Cabinet, and his parliamentary experience, he could have made himself a man to be watched, especially if he had linked up with the government's critics within the Conservative Party—Austen Chamberlain, Churchill, Amery and some of the disgruntled younger MPs. In due course, he would probably have been able to dictate his own terms, if asked to return to the Cabinet. But he was too impatient. He wanted to return at once. His only thought was that fate, rather than Baldwin, had been unfair to him, and for this to be remedied he must be received back quickly, in order to show that it had all been a silly mistake, that he really was an invaluable minister after all.

As things worked out, Hoare's hopes were soon fulfilled, but the circumstances of his return were such as to preclude any prospect of Edward's being able to exploit their friendship. Chamberlain, among others, had assured him he would be brought back as soon as the fuss over the pact had died down, and the opportunity presented itself, or so Hoare believed, with Hitler's re-occupation of the Rhineland. A Minister for the Co-ordination of Defence was needed. Who should be the minister? Hoare was certain that he himself was the most suitable candidate, and he went about canvassing himself with a zeal and indiscretion that embarrassed even those who were, or might have been, his supporters. Although the *Times* had been hostile to his pact with Laval, Dawson admired Hoare's qualities. But he was not impressed when, early in March, he met Hoare at a lunch and found him "feverishly anxious to get back into the government." Eden was also irritated, particularly when Hoare made a speech in the House so adulatory of Baldwin "as to be embarrassing to all who heard it." Neville Chamberlain, too, recorded his annoyance at what "sounded like an obvious and clumsy bid for power, and created a thoroughly bad impression."

Another man might have regarded the appointment of Inskip as a stinging rebuff. But such was Hoare's obsession with office that he continued to press his claims, and in May, Baldwin made him First Lord of the Admiralty, in spite of objections not only from Eden but from Halifax, who complained that Baldwin had yielded to Hoare's importunities. Baldwin, though, was only doing what he had done successfully so many times before: removing a possible source of danger to himself. The Admiralty was nicely calculated to satisfy Hoare, making him feel that he was back on the ministerial ladder, yet at the same time leaving him longing for the time when he could put his foot on the next rung and return once again into the inner Cabinet circle. Corroded by ambition, Hoare would not merely be safe—he could be exploited.

Nothing could have suited Baldwin better than for the King to continue to think of "my friend, Sam Hoare" and to seek his company. When Hoare received the invitation to the Sandringham house party in October, he did not at once accept, as in the past he would have done. He asked Baldwin's permission, on the pretext that his presence might be required at a Cabinet meeting. Baldwin, knowing his man, told him to go ahead and even suggested that he might be able to pour discreet words into the King's ear about the desirability of his giving up Mrs. Simpson. (Either Hoare decided that a confrontation with the King on the subject would be too risky, or the opportunity did not present itself.) And so confident was Baldwin of Hoare's reliability that he actually began to use him in what promised to be the tricky business of dealing with the popular press, and particularly with Beaverbrook. Characteristically, Beaverbrook had befriended Hoare when he was down, after the pact. Hoare was grateful, and Beaverbrook was willing to confide in him.

This was precisely what Baldwin needed. It meant that Baldwin had on call—in the words of the *History of the Times*—"a member of the Cabinet more than ordinarily capable of acting for him with the leaders of the press."

So when the request came from the King to be allowed to talk with Hoare, Baldwin had no worries. In his memoirs, Hoare quoted the Duke of Windsor's version of what happened at their meeting. Presumably it was substantially accurate. By this time the King had already realized that Hoare's temperament was "not such as to encourage the belief that I might convert him into a champion of my cause"—a notable understatement. The most he hoped for was that he might enlist Hoare's sympathy, so that when the Cabinet discussed the question, Hoare would at least be prepared to put the case for his right to marry. But even this hope was to be disappointed. Hoare was sympathetic, "but he was also acutely conscious of the political realities."

Edward could not, in fact, have selected a member of the Cabinet more acutely conscious of them. If Hoare had a principle, it was enshrined in the remark attributed to Charles II, on the restoration of the monarchy in 1660, when he intimated that he would take no rash actions: "Brother, I am too old to go again to my travels." Hoare had good reason to believe that he had worked his passage back into the party's confidence. Had not *Time* magazine, at the end of October, said that he was "increasingly often named as one of two or three statesmen with a real chance of becoming Prime Minister"? Some of his colleagues might sneer at *Time*, but they could hardly dispute that it was a useful sounding board for political gossip. Hoare was friendly, but he would hold out no hope. Baldwin, he told the King, was in complete command of the situation, and his ministers were solidly behind him.

Duff Cooper

From Duff Cooper, the King had a much better chance of getting both a sympathetic hearing and detached advice. They were of the same generation—Edward was four years the younger. Both had served in the army during the war, both had enjoyed to the full the London life of the twenties. They had first met in 1924 on the *Berengaria*, where they pulled together in a British tug-of-war team organized by Lord Louis Mountbatten. It was humiliatingly defeated by the American team—not surprisingly, as neither the Prince nor Duff had the appropriate physique. Later they had met fairly often—the Coopers had occasionally been his guests at the Fort. They spoke the same language. Duff Cooper might be worried at what was afoot, but he would not be shocked. And, as a man of the world, he would be more likely to come up with some solution than Hoare, or, for that matter, any other of his Cabinet colleagues.

Duff Cooper's father had been a successful London surgeon. His mother was descended from Mrs. Jordan—one of the ten children she had by the Duke of Clarence, later to be King William IV—and his uncle was a duke, the last to be created outside the royal family. Duff went to Eton, and enjoyed it. In *Old Men Forget* he was to speak of "the emotion which Eton stirs in the hearts of her children and which can best be likened to love." From school he went to New College, Oxford, and then to the Foreign Office. He was no rebel. In ordinary circumstances he would probably have ended up as a senior ambassador somewhere. But he entered the Foreign Office in 1913. War broke out a year later, and almost all his closest friends were killed. The generation contained an unusual crop of young men of great promise, and Duff Cooper, recalling gay parties, would sometimes realize that he was the only survivor. Eventually he managed to escape from the Foreign Office and go to the western front himself. Before the war ended he had won the Distinguished Service Order. By this time the prospect of a career in the Foreign Office no longer attracted him, and it became even less absorbing after his marriage to Lady Diana Manners, daughter of the Duke of Rutland and one of the celebrated beauties of her time, soon to win international fame for her performance in Reinhardt's *The Miracle.*

Duff Cooper decided to enter politics. Naturally he was a welcome recruit, with his connections, his Foreign Office experience, his good war record and his impeccably Conservative views. He was adopted as a candidate for Oldham, a Lancashire constituency, and won the seat in the general election of 1924.

His apprenticeship in the back benches was uneventful and brief; by 1928 he was financial secretary to the War Office. But his political reputation was made by a set of fortuitous circumstances. Although the Labour victory of 1929 cost him his Oldham seat, he had no difficulty in finding another and safer constituency: Winchester. While he was "nursing" it, the quarrel arose between Baldwin and the press barons, Beaverbrook and Rothermere, culminating in their decision to run an Independent Conservative candidate in the by-election pending in the St. George's division of Westminster. On an impulse, Duff Cooper decided to stand as a Baldwinite—in spite of warnings that it would be a rough and tough campaign.

It was. "Watchman" described it as "one of the most unpleasant by-elections which has ever blotted even our variegated democratic record." A subtle, and sometimes less than subtle, smear campaign was waged against Duff Cooper as a socialite and a "softy." It was diligently spread around that he was weak on the chief issue dividing Conservatives at this time—that he supported Indian aspirations for self-government. Rothermere produced cards containing the warning, "Gandhi is watching St. George's," and his candidate's followers trundled a life-size effigy of the Mahatma through the streets to show people whom they were really voting for.

The election had only about a fortnight to run when Duff Cooper entered the lists, but he quickly showed that whatever else he was, he was no softy. He knew Beaverbrook through Lady Diana, and had at first liked him, only to find that Beaverbrook "rightly admired Diana, and rightly thought I was unworthy of her." The fact that Beaverbrook might be right on both counts did not induce Duff Cooper to be gentle to him. He was if anything ruder about the press barons than they were about him. And when he won the seat, Baldwin showed his appreciation by walking up the Commons gangway as one of the two sponsors of the new member—an honor that Prime Ministers infrequently bestow. When the national government was formed shortly afterward, Duff Cooper found himself back as financial secretary to the War Office. Soon he was promoted to be financial secretary to the Treasury, and in 1935 Baldwin brought him into the Cabinet as Secretary of State for War.

Duff Cooper was a good deal more than a promising politician. From the start of his career, as Lady Diana Cooper recalled in her autobiography, "all doors were open to him"—her sister's, the Montagus', the Wimbornes', the Wallaces', the Ednams', Belvoir and Wilton, and Cliveden on political Sundays. He was also a *littérateur*—the author of a still-standard biography of Talleyrand, and a poet, the friend of Maurice Baring, Hilaire Belloc and other literary lights of the period. To all appearances, he was ideally suited to be the King's adviser—and ally.

But Duff Cooper's political situation was not as assured as it seemed. As Chamberlain had reminded him when he became financial secretary to the Treasury, he had a reputation for indiscretion. It was not undeserved. He had been a spoiled child, as he was to admit in his autobiography, and throughout his life continued on occasion to behave like one. From Eton, he recalled, he narrowly escaped being expelled by a reforming headmaster. At Oxford he was banished from New College to lodgings following a bonfire that he and his friends, having burned most of their furniture, decided to replenish from the rooms of one of the dons, which happened to be adjacent. In the process they destroyed not only the don's table, but also his research notes, which happened to be in a drawer. Expulsion in either case might have cost Duff Cooper his career, but authority was disposed to be lenient.

So far from settling down into respectability after the war, Duff Cooper, like the Prince of Wales, found the twenties a time of release. When he came to the point of asking for his Diana's hand in marriage, he was shocked at his future mother-in-law's angry reaction—partly caused, admittedly, by the fact that he was not well off, but also, he realized, by his reputation as "a wild young man who played too high and drank too deep." The playing too high was a reference to his addiction to gambling, which he found hard to shake off. From time to time the craze took hold of him again. "I cannot forgive myself," he wrote to his wife ("like a shamefaced child," she noted), "for my two mad nights at Cannes . . . I meant so firmly to do nothing of the kind." At thirty-eight, he thought, he really ought to have known better, "and what makes it more maddening is that I was sure I did."

In the circumstances it was not surprising that some of Duff Cooper's more staid colleagues thought of him as a lightweight. Even "Watchman," who was an admirer, admitted three years later that "A short time ago, he was treated as a promising but indiscreet young politician"—treatment for which his appearance ("He carried about him the look of a young soldier, almost a drummer boy") might have been partly responsible. People also thought his wife was indiscreet, and she could be. She herself recalled the occasion when she persuaded Duff to invite the Baldwins to lunch at Annecy in 1931, after the national government had been formed but before the election that was to give the Conservatives their huge majority. Baldwin was just back from London, where he had been to find out

how the crisis was evolving. Diana had promised to be totally discreet, provided she was allowed to wear trousers—still, at that time,
frowned on as "fast." They had hardly sat down to lunch before she
was begging Baldwin to tell them every word Ramsay MacDonald
had said, "for my husband tells me nothing." Mrs. Baldwin was
horrified—"My husband tells me nothing either, but then I would
never ask him." Duff Cooper feared his political career might be
jeopardized. Perhaps it was, but not in the way he thought: Baldwin,
susceptible to the charms of his hostess, was amused. It was Mrs.
Baldwin and her like—and this meant most of the Conservative
Cabinet ministers, as well as their wives—who were ill at ease with
the Duff Coopers and their social set and who came to feel that he
was not "safe."

For all his connections and his abilities, too, Duff Cooper was
inherently self-conscious. As he was to admit, he was frequently
overcome by shyness, from which he suffered "great misery." This
was reflected in a curious deference to those in authority. As his
wife put it, he "never lived down his schoolboy's bashfulness before
masters." Even Baldwin, though he owed much to Duff and was very
fond of him, had his doubts. He expressed them to Tom Jones in
September 1936: he would try Duff out for a year, he said, "and
then Neville can decide whether to carry him on." Duff, therefore,
was in no position to exert real influence over the Cabinet.

But he could still give the King the benefit of his advice, and
it was not encouraging. Although he had known the King for so
long, and realized his affection for Mrs. Simpson, Duff had remained
unaware of their plan to marry. He heard of it only the day before
the summons to Buckingham Palace, when Baldwin called him
into his room to tell him that the King meant to abdicate in order
to marry and had asked to be allowed to see the two Cabinet ministers with whom he was on friendly terms. Strictly speaking it was
correct, then, for Edward, recalling their meeting in his autobiography, to say that the facts came as no surprise to Duff Cooper.
But this was not, as Edward believed, owing to the closeness of
their association. Nor, if Duff's version is correct, was he as "encouraging and optimistic" as the Duke recalled. On the contrary, he
began by asking whether it was any use trying to dissuade him from
marrying Mrs. Simpson, only to be assured that he would be wasting
his time.

At this point, though, Duff Cooper propounded a plan of cam-

paign that was to win several allies. He suggested simple postponement. Again, there is a discrepancy between his version and Edward's. According to *A King's Story*, Duff pointed out that there was
no hurry, as the divorce would not become absolute for another five
months, and the government could not press him into a decision
"on a constitutional issue that did not exist." If, therefore, Edward
was patient, he could go ahead with the coronation, "and in due
time, after the people had become accustomed to see me as King,
raise in a calmer atmosphere the question of my right to marry
whom I pleased." And this, the Duke thought, was the counsel of a
sophisticated man of the world.

It was not, though—to judge by *Old Men Forget*—quite what
Duff Cooper had in mind. He thought, though naturally he did not
say so, that as time went on the King would be more reluctant to
step down from his throne, and that he "might in the interval meet
somebody whom he would love more." Either way, postponement
was the best, and indeed the only, way out for Edward.

Probably it was already too late: if Edward had suddenly at
this moment announced that he was not going to carry out his
threat to abdicate but simply carry on as he had been doing for
the past year, the Cabinet's suspicions would certainly have been
aroused. They might have found some way to force his hand. But
in any case it was not a solution that commended itself to the King.
Here the two accounts agree. He felt it wrong, Duff recalled, "to
go through so solemn a religious ceremony as the Coronation without letting his subjects know what it was his intention to do." Edward's own version put his case more emphatically. It would, he
wrote, have meant being crowned "with a lie on my lips."

It may seem odd that Edward, who ordinarily paid so little
regard to religious observances, should have worried. But although
he was not in the strict sense a religious man, he had a measure of
religious awe. On great occasions, such as a coronation, he wanted
to be able to enter into the spirit of the ceremony. At ordinary times
he would have been delighted to score off the Archbishop, but if
he had to resort to a lie in order to qualify to be crowned, there
was a sense in which the Archbishop would be scoring off him. His
decision to make his determination to marry Mrs. Simpson known,
therefore, was perfectly consistent. And it made the eventual abdication inevitable.

"Something must be done"

By this time, though, the King was not expecting much from his government. He was not greatly cast down by his failure to enlist his two friends in the government more firmly in his cause. It was more important to him—both from expediency and to renew his self-confidence—that the impending tour of South Wales, the first that he had undertaken since he came to the throne, should demonstrate once again the hold he had over the hearts of the people of Britain, for such a demonstration was more likely to move Baldwin than the advice of his ministers.

The King's visit to South Wales was not, he was later careful to insist, a device he had thought up "to curry favour with the Opposition, and to use whatever good feeling accrued therefrom as a shield between me and Mr. Baldwin." Like most royal occasions, it had been planned months before, its intention being to mark the resumption of the tours he had undertaken as Prince of Wales.

The idea of royalty concerning itself with social conditions was not new. While still a prince, the future Edward VII had actually been encouraged by Charles Dilke, then president of the Local Government Board, to serve on a commission concerned with working-class housing. In 1884 he had even made a speech on the subject in the House of Lords. George V had toured mining and industrial areas before the war, including a visit with Queen Mary to South Wales—which, she was assured on all sides, "would do more to bring peace and goodwill into the district than anything else." Royal visits of this kind were, in fact, recognized government emollients for industrial unrest. They had not reflected royal radicalism. Nor did they when Edward, as Prince of Wales, began to undertake them after his return from his Empire tours.

Edward's introduction to the forces of social unrest, at first hand, had been in 1919 when he went with his father to attend a parade of ex-servicemen in Hyde Park. Something, they sensed, was wrong. It turned out that the men had not just come to be inspected, to wear their medals, and to give three loyal cheers. They suddenly unfurled banners with such slogans as "Where is this land fit for heroes?" ("A land fit for heroes to live in" had been one of Lloyd George's wartime promises about peacetime Britain.) The men soon made it clear they felt no animosity to the King, only to his ministers, but the fact that they had demonstrated at all disturbed him. It disturbed Edward, too, but—he was later to claim—for different reasons. His father thought it was just a phase the country was going through, owing to the disillusionments of peace. Edward realized that the trouble went deeper and that Britain would not be the same again.

He therefore dedicated himself to promoting a new Britain, an idea that was to be the theme of a speech which he made at the Guildhall, on December 18, 1919. Britain's duty, he said, was

to show the world that we can work on our social, economic and industrial problems with a general fairness and sympathy, striving wholeheartedly towards one goal. That goal is happier conditions of life, to ensure that every man and every woman may enjoy the just proceeds of their labour, and that every child born into the country may have a sporting chance.

In some of the speeches he made on his tours, he had developed this theme—for example, in Montevideo in 1925:

In the realm of statecraft Uruguay appears to have devoted much thought and labour to the universal problem of providing the greatest happiness for the greatest number. In matters relating to labour, the administration of justice, suffrage, relief for old age, and kindred questions, her laws and practices have reached an advanced stage. The recent revision of the Constitution and the new electoral law mark another step in the direction of making the people's voice effective in determining the destinies of the country.

In *The Windsor Tapestry* Compton Mackenzie cited this as an example of the Prince's democratic ambitions: "We can be certain that the profoundest effect of the South American visit on the Prince himself was to confirm his determination to do everything he could do to secure to his own future realm 'the greatest happiness for the greatest number.' " But visionary statements of the kind that the Prince made were no different from those that Conservatives like Baldwin—or even Neville Chamberlain—were constantly making. At this time the test of an individual's political sympathies was not the end—a democratic, prosperous country—but the means, and here the Prince stood closer to Baldwin than to the Socialists.

Unintentionally, the Prince became identified with what to many workers, and all Socialists, was the wrong, the capitalist way of palliating unemployment. In his autobiography he was to describe how he went early in the Depression to Tyneside, where he met a skilled worker who had once earned good wages, but had now been out of work for five years. "What response," Edward asked, "could I make to that tragic disclosure? That the Monarchy was not responsible for his plight? That the Government was doing all it could? That he only had to be patient? What possible solace would that have given to a man who had been on the dole for five years?" The rhetorical questions reflect the Prince's very real dilemma. He felt deeply about the injustice of unemployment, and he wanted to do something about it. But his position precluded him from advocating political or economic remedies. All he could do was assist charitable enterprises, such as the scheme for setting up social centres for the unemployed, under the National Council of Social Service.

But schemes of this kind were regarded with mixed feelings by the Labour movement. The left-wing—and Communist Party—line was that these were part of society's desperate efforts to shore up the collapsing structure of capitalism. Most Socialists, George Orwell claimed in *The Road to Wigan Pier,* "say that occupational centres are simply a device to keep the unemployed quiet and give them the illusion that something is being done for them," and he thought that this undoubtedly was the underlying motive. It was far from always being a conscious motive. Many of those who were involved in the establishment of social centres, including the Prince of Wales, were moved by a genuine desire to ease the hardships of the families on the dole. But whether he was aware of it or not, Socialists (and many trade unionists) considered he was playing the capitalists' game—and Baldwin's.

Baldwin always used to insist that he stood for industrial peace. "We want to create a new atmosphere," he said in one of his speeches in the 1924 general election campaign, "in which the people can come together," and he recalled that when a coal strike had thrown men out of work in his family firm, through no fault of their own, he had made a small allowance to them "because I looked upon them as my own family." Chamberlain was a paternalist, too, but he was more of a technocrat: he liked to believe that if the state and industry were run efficiently, things would be better for everybody because the country could then afford better social and welfare services. But both repudiated the doctrine, prevalent on the left, of the inevitability of the class war, and Edward was on their side.

The only reason they had for worry, in fact, was his popularity among the workers. They became alarmed that the Labour Party might find some way of exploiting him for its own purposes. In the late 1920s stories began to get around of the astonishing effect the Prince sometimes had even on rabid left-wingers. Bolitho, in his biography, recounted an example. The Prince had made an appeal over the radio one Christmas night on behalf of the miners, and A.J. Cook, the miner's leader—generally regarded as a dangerous revolutionary—happened to be listening in with a couple of Communist friends. They had scoffed at the idea of a Prince making the appeal, but—Cook told the Prince—"they listened to what you had to say and when you finished, with tears in their eyes, they put their hands in their pockets and gave what money they had on them to the fund."

As a consequence of such stories, some of them doubtless myths, the Prince began to project the image of a man of leftist leanings, and this had disturbed Baldwin. Following the General Strike, coal mining became a depressed industry, with massive unemployment, and early in 1929 Sir Alexander Leith, an industrialist with business interests in the northeast, asked the Prince to come on a tour of the mining areas of Durham and Northumberland, with a view to showing the miners that people still cared about them—that they were not entirely forgotten. Edward, regarding the project as simply an extension of the kind of social work he had long been doing in connection with ex-servicemen, accepted. To his surprise, he learned that the Prime Minister had raised objections. The visit, Baldwin feared, would have political repercussions. With a general election due in the spring, "unemployment may well be used as a stick with which to beat my party." Therefore, he did not wish attention to be drawn to it, as it obviously would be if the Prince went on his visit. But— the Prince replied—the idea for the trip had originated with a Tory pillar. It was Baldwin's turn to be surprised. As soon as he heard that it was Leith who had organized the visit he immediately withdrew his objections. "Of course, this information puts quite a different face on the matter," he said, ushering Edward out. "I hope you have a succcessful trip, and don't find the cold too trying."

The Duke of Windsor's recollection of the occasion may have

been coloured by his subsequent experiences, and Leith later repudiated the account. But it is certainly true that Baldwin did not think of conservatism as a party creed. The Conservative Party had to exist *as* a party, because such was the logic of the English political system, which had developed out of her democratic institutions—then generally claimed to be the best in the world. As its leader, therefore he had to be a politician, and watch out for what the other parties might be planning. If the Labour Party had managed to persuade the Prince to go up to visit the depressed area in the northeast —or if he had decided to do so himself, thereby giving the Labour Party the opportunity to make capital out of his visit—then he would have to be stopped, because this would be using the royal family for political purposes. If, on the other hand, the Prince was going up at the invitation of Alexander Leith, that was a very different matter. It ceased to be a political issue. True, Leith was a member of the Conservative Party, but it was not the essential point. He was a respected figure in the region. His sponsoring of the trip took it out of politics and made it respectable.

This was an attitude of mind that infuriated Socialists, particularly in connection with local government. When they put up candidates for local urban and rural councils between the wars, they were told that they were dragging party politics into issues where party politics had never had, and never ought to have, any place. But—the Labour candidates protested—the councils were dominated by Tories. They were, but the Tories on them did not think of themselves or call themselves such. They were often members of the local Conservative Association and worked for the Conservative candidate at general elections, but for local issues they believed themselves capable of putting political considerations aside. They called themselves Independents or—to rile their opponents still further—Progressives, and pretended to be politically non-partisan.

It is never possible to be sure how far Baldwin deliberately exploited this non-partisan concept of Conservatism with the deliberate intent to assist the Conservative Party and himself. That he did exploit it is beyond doubt. Whether he was always or even usually aware of what he was doing is less easy to assess. But it is reasonable to suppose that when the King's visit to South Wales had first been mooted, he had looked upon it as being potentially useful to the government. A minister, after all, would be accompanying the King, and government officials. It would appear to be government-sponsored. By the time Edward was to go to Wales, though, circumstances had changed. Baldwin had good reason to fear that if it were a rousing success, the King would be tempted to believe that his reception reflected his own popularity, and the government's enemies might then be encouraged to propagate the idea that the trip was the King's idea and that he had goaded his torpid ministers into reluctant action.

This was what happened. What more prophetic place for him to make this personal appearance, the King felt, than the principality that had given him the name by which he had become so famous, and so popular? He spent two days, November 18 and 19, among the mining villages, and the press reports indicated that his reception was everywhere cordial, and often enthusiastic. One pledge he gave, in particular, caught the public imagination. "Something must be done," he told Allan Harris, an unemployed Blaenavon miner, "to meet the situation in South Wales, and I will do all I can to assist you." In the Labour *Daily Herald,* Hannen Swaffer said that the King got down to it, with his ministers and their advisers, at dinner the same night—he could be seen "banging his fist on the table with insistence." And "Something will be done," the newspaper headlines echoed the following day.

It was a popular pledge—except with those who would now be expected to implement it, the members of the government. In *A King's Story,* the Duke recalled his ministers' reaction, still with some mystification, as revealing "the unfathomable complications that the economic issues of the twentieth century have introduced into the technique of kingship, rendering it almost impossible for a monarch to continue to play the role of the Good King, free to move un-hindered among his subjects and speak what is in his mind." In it-self, "Something must be done" need not have been construed as a rebuke to the government, let alone as a formal declaration of war on them. Nor would it have been, at any other time. But now, how could the words be construed in any other way? It had not passed unobserved by reporters, American as well as British, that the King had dined in the company not only of the government's chief commissioner for the Special Areas, Sir George Gillett, but also of Gillett's predecessor, Percy Malcolm Stewart. Stewart's report on the Special Areas had been such unpalatable reading for the government —as were the measures it recommended, because of their expense— that it had been hastily shelved; and Stewart, exasperated, had resigned. Taking everything into consideration, the *News Chronicle* was in no doubt that Edward had dissociated himself from his government. "The King is above and outside politics. What he has done is in the sole interest of truth and public service. . . . The man in the street feels that Whitehall stands condemned." And in the House of Commons, the rumour spread that the King had decided to use the Welsh trip to test out his popularity before making an appeal to the country over the heads of his ministers.

Even if this had not been in Edward's mind when he went on the trip, he could hardly escape speculating on it when he returned to find some of his friends delighted with what they took to be his manifesto—and respected journals like the *News Chronicle* taking it for granted that what he had done was right and proper. Why, then, did the King not make a concerted effort to exploit the situation, by cultivating the left? Conversely, why were the workers, the trade unionists and the Socialists not drawn to his side, under the impression that he was on *their* side, in the critical three weeks that followed?

"A First-class show"

The answer is that the King was incapable of identifying himself with the left. The picture of Edward as a man of leftist leanings, which has lingered on in spite of the evidence from many sources, including his own books and articles, is a myth. He was by temperament and training a Tory. He was on the progressive rather than the reactionary side in home affairs—he was a do-gooder, concerned about the poor and needy, and about getting to know them through boy's clubs and charitable ventures—but had none of the deeper democratic instincts, of the kind that help a man to shed his class prejudices and enable him to see society through the worker's eye.

How far Edward was from being or becoming a rebel against the society in which he lived is illustrated time and again in his memoirs. There was, for example, his attitude to Oxford. Certainly he disliked the snobbishness he encountered there, particularly in his own college. He was disillusioned to discover that what the president of Magdalen, Herbert Warren, "appeared to value most in the world was his connection with a certain baronet, a fact he managed to insert into every conversation," and as it was believed he cherished an ambition to fill Magdalen with titled undergraduates, Edward was never quite certain whether Warren regarded him "with a teacher's benevolence, or from a collector's secret satisfaction with a coveted trophy." But for men already on the peaks of social eminence, this kind of social climbing is always irritating. There are few signs that the Prince's dislike of snobbery extended further—to questioning, let alone rejecting, the social standards he found at Magdalen, standards Warren and his like had established.

The main influence of Oxford on Edward, as on so many undergraduates before and since, lay in teaching him how the upper-class Englishman should choose his clothes, smoke, and drink. The Bullingdon Club, where the horsy undergraduates (as their contemporaries thought of them) used to congregate, initiated him into the pleasures of communal inebriation. Edward described one of their dinners in a letter to his father, saying that he had gone home early because his fellow guests had got "rather, not to say very excited" on the champagne they had drunk, but excusing himself for staying as long as he did on the ground that "it is interesting for me to see the various forms of amusement that undergraduates indulge in." The real reason for his leaving early, he was to disclose nearly half a century later, was that "I was no longer so steady on my feet or so clear in my speech as I was when we sat down to dinner"—the state that such occasions were designed to promote. There was amusement to be obtained from watching what freshmen (particularly a Prince) did when unable to hold their liquor, and also from the saturnalia that usually followed—vividly recalled a few years later by Evelyn Waugh at the opening of his *Decline and Fall*, where he described the aftermath of a "Bollinger" dinner: "A shriller note could now be heard rising from Sir Alastair's rooms; any who have heard that sound will shrink at the recollection of it; it is the sound of the English county families baying for broken glass."

It was to be the same during the war. The Prince liked to be able to talk with, to get along with, members of the forces from all social classes and of all nationalities. But for his friends, he preferred people of his own background, his own set. As he wrote to his father, he liked serving with the Guards Division "where are all my friends, and what is more the friends of my friends at home." Recalling this in *A King's Story* he defended the Guards Division as "a great club; if tinged with snobbishness, it was the snobbishness of tradition, discipline, perfection, and sacrifice." His later rejection of the court circle was based not on any egalitarianism, but because it was stuffy and boring. Given the opportunity, he would have liked to throw open windows, thrust out old musty furniture and pension off old courtiers, but the people with whom he would have replaced the old courtiers would have come from the same social class.

Not that Edward had any deep-rooted belief in the value of the English class system. On the contrary, he chafed under it. His liking for Americans appears to have arisen, in part at least, because of their relative immunity from the symptoms of class consciousness that his own countrymen tended to display. But among his own countrymen, he could not escape his class conditioning. He did not really feel at ease for long with people of different social standards, however much he would have liked to. The reason was that at this time the English upper class had social hackles that rose on encountering "non-U" individuals—to use the term later popularized by Nancy Mitford in her revealing essay on the subject. How a "non-U" (non-upper-class) man dressed, his accent, the way he used words or pronounced them, was sufficient, as it often still is, to give a sense of actual discomfort—sometimes conscious, sometimes unconscious, but either way effectively barring social intimacy. For the Prince and his associates to mix socially with English men—or women, unless their beauty was sufficient compensation—of a different class was difficult.

When the Prince moved out of his class, then, it was rarely in English company. The Scots and the Irish were easier, their accents and idioms being sufficiently removed to avoid causing embarrassment; and better still were the Americans, who presented all the advantages of egalitarianism with none of the social embarrassments.

It might have been expected that mixing so much as he did with Americans would have helped the Prince of Wales to shed his identification with his class. But Americans sometimes encouraged it. Bolitho quoted a writer in the New York *World* who complained about the way that the Prince's visits to the United States had provoked an exhibition of social climbing and went on to make the point that the visit had "managed to demonstrate to Americans, grown tolerant of the business of royalty, that it is, whatever his personal democracy may be, in fact a pyramid of snobbery." The Prince was democratic in the choice of his friends in the sense that their precise position in the aristocratic hierarchy meant nothing to him, but what he could not do was to take the monarchy out of its hierarchical upper-class cocoon.

And his American friends did not necessarily want him to. There is an instance of this in the contrast between his recollection and Wallis' of the company at the last Balmoral holiday. Since the time of Queen Victoria, Edward recalled, "the guestbook at Balmoral had annually recorded the descent of a succession of Cabinet ministers, archbishops, admirals, generals, and so forth," but because he regarded himself as still on holiday, he decided to confine his first house party there to friends, and "none of my guests, except my brother George and his wife Marina, had ever been to Balmoral." But though the archbishops and the admirals were excluded, the guests were not exactly newcomers drawn from the highways and byways. Wallis recalled that they included the Duke and Duchess of Marlborough, the Duke and Duchess of Buccleuch, the Duke and Duchess of Sutherland, and the Earl and Countess of Rosebery, "who, like their ancestors before them, had been perennial guests there."

It was Wallis, too, who had unwittingly encouraged him to begin to act out of his earlier democratizing character. One of his most engaging traits during the war had been his refusal to accept the advantages that would have naturally come his way, as heir to the throne, because he realized that to accept them could easily breed resentment. It was for this reason that he had taken to bicycling. Staff cars, he found, were resented: "The cars of the brass hats honked infantrymen off the road into ditches, splashed them with mud, and even under the best of circumstances, were an irritating reminder of the relative comforts of life on the staff." So, when he went to collect material for a report or to make an inspection, he went on an army bicycle. He even rode several miles to attend dinners—to the chagrin of Oliver Lyttleton, later Lord Chandos, who once had to accompany him and had hoped for a lift in a car. Chandos, recalling the episode in his autobiography, thought that the Prince at the time was "the most charming and delightful human being that I had ever known." No doubt thousands of soldiers coming out of—or, worse, going up into—the trenches, who would have been irritated to see a young pipsqueak (he would have looked the part) riding in comfort in a limousine, were similarly impressed when they saw the Prince sweating it out on two wheels. The word got around: the Prince was all right.

Had he been younger when he met Wallis he might have appealed to her in the same way. But in the meantime, bicycles—or their equivalent—had lost their charm for him. He had ceased to care so much what people thought. The first signs began to show themselves when he became frustrated for the lack of sufficiently absorbing occupations in the late 1920s. In *The House Is Sitting*, Arthur Baker, who was to be chief of the *Times* parliamentary staff at the time of the abdication, recalled in circumstantial detail a visit the Prince paid to his Duchy of Cornwall in 1927. When he arrived in Exeter, it had begun to rain, and students who had laid on a quaint fancy-dress ceremony for his benefit heard the Prince say, "Cut it short." The ceremony over, he drove through the city streets, but although they were lined with thousands of drenched spectators, "he went so fast in a closed car that many of them barely caught a glimpse of him." Two days later, it had been arranged that he would visit some of his duchy farms. At a village nearby, the annual church fete was in progress, and crowds waited there, along with the secretary of the duchy. The Prince did not arrive. It transpired that he had decided to have a round of golf instead. On the last day he made more of an effort, but when he left from Exeter station, only a handful of people were there to see him off. "It took a long time for the people of Exeter to forget."

By the time Wallis met him, the Prince had grown accustomed to the staff car way of life. When she admitted that his ability to summon it was one of the things which had attracted her—the way trains and boats and planes would wait, and hotel suites open, for him and for his party—she had not realized that his changes of plan might mean that other passengers were kept waiting for the trains and boats and planes, perhaps missing their connections, that other people arriving at their hotel would be told that their bookings had mysteriously not been received, and they would have to look elsewhere. Edward might want to remove the court's stuffiness, but he had no intention of abolishing his own precedences and privileges.

Perhaps he thought that people would not mind, because they were inconvenienced for royalty. If so, he was mistaken. They were not necessarily mollified by the news that it was the Prince of Wales who had inconvenienced them. If it were some statesman, late for a conference, the excuse would have been more acceptable. The Prince and his entourage began to arouse hostility—on a small scale, but such things get around. And still more important was the effect it had on him. He began to share the staff officer's mentality, expecting comfort and punctuality, forgetting the infantryman by the roadside.

Even Edward's often reported liking for informality has to be qualified. Many of the examples quoted at the time now suggest nothing more than the capacity to use his common sense. It was the fact that the Prince behaved as anybody else would do—instead of like his father, who always behaved as a King would do—that was seized upon and quoted as evidence of how he had the common touch. Thus, Bolitho solemnly recorded how on a visit to Oxford, Edward went to see his old college and, while there, went to the porter, "without a fuss, to ask if he could use the telephone." And later, when he was King, the director of a London hospital who was ringing Buckingham Palace got through direct to him by mistake. Edward said, "Tell me what it's about, I may be able to help you." Bolitho—and it is clear that he was not trying to be funny—actually believed that those who loved Edward "recognised his true nature in these incidents," so "hope became high again."

Edward liked informality only on his own terms. On one of the Prince's visits to Magdelen, according to Compton Mackenzie, he went to the Junior Common Room, and when the company assembled stood up, he begged them to sit down again, because he wanted to be treated simply as a Magdalen man. The next time he went into the J.C.R. nobody stirred. He asked sharply if that was the way to treat an heir to the throne. This, Mackenzie thought, might sound inconsistent, "but surely the instinct of those undergraduates should have led them to pay him the courtesy of rising and allowing him to put them at their ease a second time." But surely—it could also be argued—Edward should have had enough of the politeness of princes to realize that the undergraduates were respecting his wish expressed on the earlier occasion—or, if they weren't, that his rebuke to them would in any case be pointless. Such stories, admittedly, always tend to circulate about all members of the royal family who mix with the public, but the fact that this story should actually have been produced by one of his defenders, the first author to spring to Edward's defence after the abdication—himself a Magdalen man—suggests that it may have had a basis in fact.

In any case, there is ample evidence of the way that even in the most informal circumstances, Edward still insisted on certain observances. On the *Nahlin* cruise he might go around shirtless, as happy as a sandboy—he might even, for a time, *become* a sandboy. He found a shrimping net and—looking, Diana Cooper recalls, like a child of eight—set about catching jellyfish, "while we all leant over the ship's side shrieking, 'There's a big one, Sir.'" Even when His Royal Highness was catching jellyfish, they still remembered the "Sir."

A strict, even tiresome regard for court punctilio would not, of course, necessarily have prevented Edward from admiring and sympathizing with the British workingman, in preference to the British capitalist. But although Edward admired the workingman as an abstraction and sympathized with the unemployed and the afflicted, at no time does he seem to have been tempted to share the aspirations and aims of the politically conscious section of the working class.

The test of his sympathies came, as for so many, with the General Strike of 1926. Many Socialists opposed the strike, either because they thought it tactically ill-timed or because they had heeded the advice of economists (and of Bernard Shaw) that it was bound to fail: the workers would starve long before the employers. But it was one thing to oppose it, another to join the flock of upper- and middle-class strike-breakers who came out to drive trains and buses and perform other tasks to keep the economy going. Recalling the occasion in *A King's Story*, the Duke left no doubt where his sympathies had lain. "The people I knew felt they were putting down something that was terribly wrong, something contrary to British traditions. And they put on a first-class show."

Although he was in Biarritz at the time, convalescing after an operation, the Prince returned as soon as he realized what was happening, arriving as the strike began—only to be instructed by George V not to comment on what was happening, not even to appear in public, so far as possible, while the strike lasted. For the Prince, this was "like asking a man in a burning building to retire to his room while the firemen coped with the blaze." It irked him to obey his father's command, and he departed from it to the extent of lending his car and chauffeur to transport the government "scab" newspaper —the *British Gazette*, which Winston Churchill edited—to South Wales. And when the strike collapsed, he shared his friends' feeling that all had stood up well to the test, that "a dangerous social crisis had been overcome in the traditional English way, without blood-shed or reprisals and leaving no lasting scars."

That the Duke should have been able to continue to believe this itself gives some indication of how remote he remained, in spite of his concern for the poor, from the British worker. True, there was no bloodshed. Nor—thanks to the timely intervention of his father—were there reprisals on any serious scale. But the General Strike did indeed leave deep and lasting scars—not so much in politics as in the trade-union movement.

Surrounded by sycophants

It was not just what the King felt about the left that mattered. More significant was what the left felt about the King.

In its early days the Labour Party had been mildly republican. Its founder, Keir Hardie, had actually treated the House of Commons to a remarkable piece of fortune-telling at the time of Edward's birth. There was no knowing, he complained, how the child, who would some day be called upon to reign over the Empire, would turn out:

From his childhood this boy will be surrounded by sycophants and flatterers by the score, and will be taught to believe himself as of a superior creation . . . in due course, following the precedent which has already been set, he will be sent on a tour round the world, and probably rumours of a morganatic marriage will follow. And the end of it will be that the country will be called upon to pay the bill.

But later, republicanism began to die out, except among intellectuals: H.G. Wells wrote to the *Times* to urge that republican societies should be set up. The project elicited no enthusiasm. And although two republican motions were put forward to the Labour Party conference in 1923, both based on the argument that the monarchy was an anachronism, George Lansbury had carried the delegates against the motion by saying that though he too was a republican, there were differences of opinion on the subject within the party, and "why fool about with an issue that has no real importance?" The conference agreed, and thereafter republicanism had ceased to be a serious issue within the party.

The main reason why it did not revive was the skill with which

George V won the Labour government's confidence when it came to power in 1923. He had the dual task of inviting Ramsay MacDonald, a Socialist—worse, a wartime conscientious objector—to form a government, and of helping the ministers with the new homework to which fortune's wheel—as J.R. Clynes put it in his memoirs—"had brought in MacDonald the starveling clerk, Thomas the engine driver, Henderson the foundry labourer, and Clynes the mill hand." The King put the ministers at their ease. He was all kindness and sympathy, relaxing cherished protocol and etiquette so as to avoid embarrassing them—even over court uniform, about which he was ordinarily so pedantic. The ministers refused to wear knee breeches, because they thought to do so would make them look silly (and possibly expose them to the charge of having become "courtiers," a term of abuse in Labour circles). The King grudgingly intimated he would not mind what they wore so long as they all wore the same, and Lord Stamfordham found that Moss Bros., then beginning to win their reputation as a firm that rented clothes to fit all occasions, actually had "a few suits of Household Second Class Levee Dress" for hire. The Labour leaders, instead of laughing at the King for his pedantry, thanked him for his conciliatory behaviour. From that time on, they were devoted to him.

George's attitude to the new political left was what could have been expected of a man brought up in his tradition. The British people, he assumed, were fundamentally good, and loyal. Where they went wrong, and indulged in strikes or demonstrations, it was because they had been misled by agitators—usually "Bolshies," the standard term of political abuse at the time. From the start, George differentiated between "Labour" and "Socialists"—a distinction that those referred to might resent, but which soon was from his point of view to be proved valid. When he met J.H. Thomas, the railwaymen's leader, in 1919, he at once recognized "a good and loyal man" —as he turned out to be. And with "Labour," George established excellent relations. At the time of the General Strike in particular, George behaved with a detachment not shared by his ministers (or by his elder son). Tempted though he was to regard the strike as a revolution in embryo rather than an industrial dispute, George never lost his head. When Churchill's *Gazette* announced that the armed forces would be supported by the government in any action they might take "in an honest endeavour to aid the Civil Power,"

George made an immediate protest to the War Office about this "unfortunate announcement," and he warned the government against provocation—a warning that was needed, and heeded. In the circumstances, it was not surprising that the Labour ministers began to think of King George almost as an ally and to regard him with even more veneration than did Conservatives.

Not all Labour members shared this view. The maverick Josiah Wedgwood, later to become Lord Wedgwood, complained that the Labour Party around the throne had behaved exactly as any other party: "Their knees trembled, and they confined their conversation entirely to 'Yes, Sir' or to 'No, Sir.'" Wedgwood thought that a Scandanavian-style monarchy was more suitable, and he hoped Edward was going to provide it. But the great majority of Labour MPs realized that behind all the royal formality, George was more of a constitutional monarch, by training and temperament, than his son. Citrine was probably right when he claimed that the Labour movement, though "republican at heart," had come to realize that a limited monarchy, as it operated in George V's time, was "probably about the safest system in present circumstances."

This was the trouble: what was liked about the monarchy in Labour circles was that it was safe—predictable. Under Edward, it seemed much less safe. Attlee had hinted at this, perhaps meaningfully, in the Commons after Edward's accession. King George, he claimed, had succeeded where others failed "because he was a democrat." Edward was not really a democrat at heart. Like Neville Chamberlain, he was impatient with democracy—it was too inefficient. Edward loved people, provided they were prepared to love him, but this did not mean that he was prepared to respect their political judgment.

Labour MPs had heard stories about Edward's high-handed ways with his ministers. They had also heard of his indiscretions. As Beaverbrook was to recall, "He made enemies among politicians by his habit of discussing them in free and unflattering terms with no regard as to who might be listening." The King's admiration for Mussolini, too, was notorious. So was his Germanophilia, so was his contempt for the League of Nations. The Labour Party, deeply hostile to Fascism and deeply committed to the League, could not but fear the consequences if Edward was allowed to have his head. And rumour was now exercising its influence. "From the working-class point of view," the Labour MP Fenner Brockway told *Time*, "the only issue which is relevant is the rumour that Mrs. Simpson has Fascist sympathies. We do not know whether this is true or not, but it may be of significance in the development of events." It was not true; but it was indeed of significance.

It proved to be unfortunate, too, that Edward, unlike his father, had made so little effort to win the confidence of Labour politicians or trade unionists. To some extent it was his father's fault, but Edward's lack of personal contact with opposition leaders was seriously to diminish his chances of winning their sympathy. In his speech following the abdication, Lord Snell observed that the peers on the Opposition benches had had no hope of interpreting what was in the King's mind: "We know him only in his official capacity and we have had no closer contact with him than has been enjoyed by the general public. We do not complain of that, but it does lessen the opportunity to offer him understanding assistance in this, the great crisis of his life."

The contrast here with Baldwin was marked. The Prime Minister had devoted years of time and effort to winning the confidence and respect of his political opponents, and with remarkable success. It is not unusual for politicians who have the art of winning the public's confidence to be mistrusted by their political opponents. But Baldwin's political opponents did not mistrust him. "Let me say," Asquith wrote to him—in reply to a letter from Baldwin on the occasion of his retirement in 1926—"that I have never found, and could never desire, a more straightforward and scrupulously honourable opponent, or one who more completely satisfied my ideal of an English gentleman."

The leaders of the Labour Party, though they had more to fear from Baldwin, took a similar view—at least until the Second World War threatened, when Baldwin in retrospect became a rogue who had sacrificed country for party. Up to his retirement in 1937, Baldwin had the confidence of Opposition members to an extent rarely if ever approached by a Prime Minister. And this was to be vital to his peace of mind when the abdication crisis threatened. Whatever views the Opposition leaders might hold, he could be confident that they would not oppose him merely for party gain, or from faction—as they would have been much more inclined to do had Neville Chamberlain been Prime Minister. And in particular, Baldwin had won the grudging respect of the leader of the Labour Party, Clement Attlee. Baldwin, Attlee once asserted, was more at home with Labour MPs, particularly trade unionists, than "with his own lot."

When Baldwin retired, a respected Labour MP, David Kirkwood, wrote to him giving him the credit for banishing the class war and for improving relations between employers and trade unions, tracing this back to a speech Baldwin had made that "made flesh the feelings of us all, that the antagonism, the bitterness, the class rivalry, were unworthy, and that understanding and amity were possible." Though Baldwin was in retirement, Kirkwood assured him that "your name is often on our lips, and thoughts of you in our hearts." That Baldwin should have discussed the King with the leader of the Labour Party and the general secretary of the Trades Union Congress was not, then, a sign of weakness—an admission that there might be a risk of Edward's exploiting them against the government. On the contrary, it was an intimation of his confidence in them, and theirs in him. Knowing them, he sensed that all he needed to do was to keep them informed of what he was doing and why. He could then count on their support. Events were to show that the confidence was not misplaced. The Labour Party as a whole was predisposed to be sympathetic to him rather than to the King.

And whatever they might think of Edward, Labour politicians in general were even more strongly disapproving of Mrs. Simpson, when they heard about her, than Conservatives. This was partly for personal, partly for electoral reasons. Many Labour MPs belonged to the Nonconformist churches, and Nonconformity, still assumed to be a powerful political force, was generally considered to be politically linked with Labour. The strength of the Nonconformist churches, as measured in attendance, was admittedly on the decline. But the hard core remained, becoming more restrictionist and puritanical, and Labour MPs, particularly those in marginal constituencies, were terrified of losing it. Clearly, Nonconformists were going to be more shocked at the King's relationship with a divorcée when they heard about it, and they would regard with horror the notion that he might marry her.

The Labour Party and the trade-union movement, therefore—it could safely be predicted—would be antagonistic to the King's project. But there was another reason why it would annoy them, which was going to prove important. It can be summed up in a word: Spain.

"Yes, I am Spain"

Until the 1920s Spain had been a monarchy under the last of the Bourbons, Alfonso XIII. Alfonso looked the part—he almost parodied it—and had he been a constitutional monarch in the sense that George V was, he might have survived and flourished. But he was expected to rule, and in spite of having the support of the aristocracy, most of the bourgeoisie, the army and the Church, he was unable to make the semi-feudal, inefficient and corrupt society work. For a time in the 1920s Spain had flirted with Fascism under the dictator Primo de Rivera, but he too proved unable to administer the system efficiently. He resigned in 1930, and when elections revealed the extent to which republican feeling had begun to spread, Alfonso sensibly departed too. "I could very easily find means to support my royal power against all comers," he explained, "but I am determined to have nothing to do with setting one of my countrymen against another in fratricidal strife."

His abdication, however, only revealed that it was the system, not the king, that had been at fault. Gradually, Spain began to slide into anarchy. The Spanish left was not, as in Britain, concentrated largely into a single party. It consisted of a remarkable amalgam of Radicals, Liberals, Socialists, Anarchists, Syndicalists, Trotskyites and Communists, whose internal squabbles effectively prevented them from co-operating to form a stable administration. Their very diversity, however, meant that they were watched with particular interest and concern in other European countries and in the United States. Political feelings in and about these different groups were strong the world over at this time—and yearly becoming stronger, as the Stalinist regime in Russia began to act in ways that made it difficult for any but the most politically obtuse, or the most abject party-liner, to remain an orthodox card-carrying Communist. What was to happen in Spain therefore carried far wider implications than anybody suspected when the army staged its rebellion in July 1936.

The rising did not at first arouse strong feelings in other countries—people had become inured to Spanish *coups d'état*. Atrocities were reported, but they appeared to be evenly balanced between either side. It all seemed uncivilized and a little remote. Louis MacNeice was to recapture the feeling in his *Autumn Journal:*

> And the next day took the boat
> For home, forgetting Spain, not realising
> That Spain would soon denote
> Our grief, our aspirations
> Not knowing that our blunt
> Ideals would find their whetstone, that our spirit
> Would find its frontier on the Spanish front
> Its body in a ragtag army.

For a few weeks, the left's ideals remained blunt. The first event of the war to capture the public imagination abroad, in fact, was the rebel stand in the Alcazar, an old fortress on the Tagus, against republican besiegers, particularly when the story was told how General Moscardo, in charge of the fortress, reacted to the news that his son would be executed if he did not surrender—his son being brought to the telephone to give the news himself. "Commend your soul to God," was Moscardo's advice. The son was duly executed, but the Alcazar held out. But the glamour that the rebel (or "nationalist," as right-wing papers preferred to call them) forces acquired from the defence of the Alcazar was quickly dissipated. The government had been duly elected, and fairly elected: if they were to be overthrown by a military coup, how would any democratic government anywhere be safe? Gradually, during the summer, public opinion in Britain began to harden against the rebels, and in favour of the government; a feeling that was to develop, at least on the left, into passionate support when the government forces began the defence of the capital, Madrid, there to be joined by the first units of the International Brigade, recruited from countries all over Europe.

Madrid was indeed the whetstone. By the end of the summer of 1936 Spain was beginning to preoccupy the minds of politically conscious men and women in Britain. Some—George Orwell was one—volunteered for the International Brigade, others were attending meetings urging help for Spain, and the poets took up the cause, W.H. Auden among them:

> Death? Very well, I accept, for
> I am your choice, your decision, Yes, I am Spain

But the British government was pledged to non-intervention, by international agreement, and for a while non-intervention was also a left-wing policy too. Léon Blum, the Socialist leader of the French popular-front government, argued that if arms and men were allowed to be sent to Spain, the chances were that Franco would benefit by German and Italian aid much more extensively than the government. As things worked out, though, Hitler and Mussolini simply ignored the non-intervention agreement, so the Spanish government had the worst of both worlds—and the clandestine supplies that came in from Russia were insufficient to turn the scale. The feeling began to spread on the left in Britain that not enough was being done to help the Spanish government, and this was reinforced by the news that Franco had sent planes over to bomb Madrid.

Although the bombing raids on London during the First World War had been puny affairs, they had given some indication of the shape of things to come, and H.G. Wells' book of that name, his vision of the future, had appeared in 1935, giving a graphic description of how cities would be destroyed by this means. Now it was happening; and, worse, it was a Spaniard who had given the orders for the bombing of his own capital city. Worse still, the planes and the pilots were from Nazi Germany. Goering made no secret of the fact that the Kondor legion was being used experimentally, to test out the possibilities—to try to find out, for example, whether the bombing of civilian objectives would prove a useful military expedient, by creating terror among the population.

At the time of the Labour party conference, in October 1936, the national executive was still committed to non-intervention, and at first it looked as though they were going to persuade the delegates to accept it. Aneurin Bevan, just beginning to emerge as the young white hope of the left, spoke against the official line, but a resolution to support non-intervention was passed by a huge majority. At this point, however, something happened that was to change the course of the Labour movement in Britain. Two Spanish delegates had come to the conference, and one of them was Señora Isabel de Palencia, whom Michael Foot in his biography of Bevan was to recall as "a proud Amazon straight from the Spanish battlefields, speaking perfect Scottish and recalling her own Scottish childhood when she walked the streets of Edinburgh." No one who heard her speech, Foot claimed, was ever likely to forget it. It was a marvel of calculated passion. "Let me tell you," she concluded, "if you wish this atrocious war to end soon, come and help us as you have been asked whenever you can. Think of the precious gift that is being wasted—of the lives of our youth. Do not tarry. Now you know the truth. Now you know what the situation is in Spain. Come and help us. Come and help us. Scotsmen, ye ken noo!" The conference, deeply moved, rose and sang the *Red Flag*, and Attlee went to London to confer with Chamberlain (Baldwin was still convalescing) to find if anything could be done.

In fact, nothing effective could be done, and the party's formal decision on non-intervention remained unchanged—to the despair of some delegates: Jennie Lee, Bevan's wife, described in her autobiography how they emerged from the conference "the most unhappy, guilty-looking collection of people I have ever seen." Nor was this gap between sentiment and action ever bridged, during the civil war. George Orwell, arguing that the British working class never really thought or acted internationally, complained that "for two and a half years they watched their comrades in Spain slowly strangled, and never aided them by even a single strike." Nevertheless, Spain now began to dominate political thinking and activity on the left to the point of obsession. Rallies were held, sales of work, whist drives —every fund-raising device in the book was employed to obtain money for republican Spain. And in the process, something resembling a popular-front movement, including Communists and Liberals as well as Labour Party members, began to develop in Britain.

The aid-for-Spain movement happened also to fuse in well with the hunger marches, a device invented by the Communists in the early days of the Depression to draw attention to the plight of the unemployed—and also to the virtues of Communism. The most striking of them, however, was led by a Labour MP, Ellen Wilkinson, from the Tyneside town of Jarrow. Jarrow had had a shipyard. In the slump it was allowed to go derelict, and with characteristic inhumanity the national government allowed the breakers to come in, thereby banishing hope of the town's recovery. But in 1935 Ellen Wilkinson—"small, pretty, redhaired and crackerjack with vitality," as Ronald Blythe described her in his account of the episode in *The Age of Illusion*—became MP for Jarrow, and she determined to bring its misery to the attention of her fellow members of Parliament. On October 5, 1936, two hundred men set off to march to London, led by Ellen, and they finished the three-hundred-mile journey by November 1, four days before the state opening of Parliament. An even bigger hunger march from Wales also arrived at this time, and on November 8 a massive demonstration was held in Hyde Park with members of the Labour Party, the Co-operative movement, the Communist Party and many left-wing splinter groups all, for the first time, represented on the platform. At long last, it seemed, causes had emerged that could reunite all the disparate elements on the left, and that could lead (and eventually did lead, but not until after the war) to the emergence of a restored Labour Party—a party capable not merely of winning an electoral majority, but also of carrying out the Socialist project to nationalize the means of production, which Ramsay MacDonald had so humiliatingly failed to achieve.

For men and women of the left to concern themselves with the King's infatuation for a twice-divorced American woman seemed, in these heady times, an irritating irrelevance. Just how irrelevant can be gauged from the memoirs of the time. Many left-wingers, like Fenner Brockway, did not mention the abdication at all, or dismissed it with impatience. Sometimes this is even true of the memoirs of Conservatives—particularly those who, like the Duchess of Atholl, became involved in Spain. The Duchess went to Madrid during the siege and later helped to get thousands of Basque children out of the war zone to England. She had been a friend and admirer of the Prince, but in her absorption with Spain, she appeared not to have noticed his departure from the throne.

There is no indication that Edward was aware of the significance of Spain. In *A King's Story,* he was to make only two references to the civil war. When he came back from the *Nahlin* cruise, he had a call from Anthony Eden, who brought him up to date on the troubles in Palestine and in Spain and informed him that the government "after many vacillations" had decided to remain aloof from the Spanish civil war. "In my turn," the Duke recollected, "I gave the Secretary of State for Foreign Affairs the benefit of my conversations with the monarchs and statesmen of the countries I had visited." Later, after Baldwin put to his ministers the proposal that the King should marry Mrs. Simpson morganatically, "I waited anxiously for the arrival of the red box containing the secret minutes of the Cabinet meeting. I opened it myself with the gold key that had been my father's. The solitary paper I found inside, purporting to describe the momentous discussions of that day, was blank except for a perfunctory paragraph relating to the carriage of arms to Spain. . . . "

Labour and the King

The leaders of the Labour Party were not entirely happy about the hunger marches, which were permeated by Communist influence. Nor were they quite sure whether they would be right to abandon non-intervention in Spain. The exhilarated mood of the rank and file had not spread to them. But this did not make them any more likely to be sympathetic to the King. The Opposition shadow cabinet might have little in common with the actual Cabinet, but they were at one on the subject of Mrs. Simpson.

The leader of the Labour Party, Clement Attlee, had a public-school and Oxford education and had been an officer in the war. As chancellor of the Duchy of Lancaster and, for a short period, Postmaster General in the second Labour government, he had established a reputation for soundness, but little more. In the landslide of 1931, though, he was one of the very few previous officeholders to retain his seat, and when Lansbury resigned the leadership in 1935, Attlee succeeded him.

Attlee was conventional, respectable, a believer in the sanctity of the home, and he believed that the great majority of party members would feel, as he did, that a twice-divorced woman could not be Queen. (The fact that she was technically the innocent party on both occasions meant even less to the working class than it did to the Establishment.) The risk, Attlee realized, was not so much of a split in the party between pro- and anti-Edward, as that a constitutional crisis might encourage the party's factious elements, on the extreme left, who would certainly want to exploit it. He had no desire to give them the opportunity. The party, he felt, had nothing to gain by the monarchy being dragged into politics. His instinct was to keep the affair hushed up as long as possible, and in the meantime to assure Baldwin of his support.

At this time Attlee was still looked on as a stop-gap leader. His most likely successor, it was thought, was Herbert Morrison, boss of the London County Council, where Labour had managed to fight off the massive Conservative advance of the early 1930s. "The rising hope of the Labour Party," A.J. Cummings, the best-known poltical commentator of the time, called him. "One might say its only hope. He is a comparatively young man with a political future that holds out the dazzling promise of the premiership as its crown and climax." John Gunther agreed, naming Morrison as one of Labour's two most interesting personalities. If Lansbury's resignation had been deferred until after the 1935 election, it has often been surmised, Morrison might well have succeeded him, but as he was not an MP he was regarded as temporarily out of the running.

Morrison had a great feeling for Londoners, which they reciprocated. They liked his bantam-cock look with his quiff of hair— the cartoonist's delight—and they admired his self-assurance. He would have been a useful ally. But he had met the King over one of the King's pet social projects, and they had not hit it off together. The King had been anxious to introduce a low-priced-housing scheme, which he had heard about, on a site that had belonged to his Duchy of Cornwall, but that he had sold to the London County Council. He managed to interest a group of financiers in the project, but first they had to persuade the LCC to re-lease the land. Morrison himself turned up at a conference on the subject at York House, with his officials, and it quickly became clear that they were not interested. To the King, who hated having his brain children aborted in this way, Morrison's decision was simply a matter of "the expediences of party politics," but the LCC's opposition was more probably based simply on traditional bureaucratic irritation at amateurs coming in trying to teach professionals their business.

Morrison, too, with his keen interest in constitutional problems— he was to write a book on them—was already concerned about the monarchy. He had seen, and been impressed by, Londoners' reaction to King George's jubilee. If the monarchy was capable of arousing such enthusiasms, he realized, it was important that the holder should recognize its constitutional limitations. Edward had several times shown a reluctance to accept them, and now, to Morrison, the "Something must be done" line in South Wales, though acceptable to Labour, could be construed as critical of the government. "I did not think well of it," Morrison recalled in *Government and Parliament*, "for it was a case of a sovereign publicly expressing views on matters which were the subject of political controversy."

The elder statesmen of the Labour Party were also for Baldwin, and this applied whether they had gone over under Ramsay Mac-Donald to the national government or stayed in opposition. J.R. Clynes, who in 1923 had been defeated by MacDonald for the leadership of the Labour Party by a handful of votes, was prepared to concede that if the King had chosen an *un*attached American girl, he might have got away with it, but although he admired the King, and was sorry for a young man of "such sincere and definite feelings regarding peace and war, unemployment, slums and other problems," he found the idea that the King should want to marry Mrs. Simpson distasteful. As soon as it became a choice between Edward's abdicating or seeking support against the government, Clynes came down on the side of abdication, and he later expressed relief that Edward had faced a difficult situation "like a true son of that fine gentleman, his father."

Both the senior members of the party who had joined the national government shared Clynes' view. Lord Snowden, MacDonald's Chancellor of the Exchequer, had retired. He made no public expression of his opinion, but at the end of the crisis he was to write to Geoffrey Dawson to say how wholeheartedly he approved of the *Times'*—and, presumably, of Baldwin's—handling of it. J.H. Thomas' attitude was characteristic. He had still been in the Cabinet when Edward came to the throne, but had unwisely disclosed some budget secrets to friends. Their attempt to profit from the inside knowledge was traced to Thomas, and he had to resign. He forthwith began to write his autobiography, in which he sang Edward's praises: his love of the people, his democratic tendencies, his understanding of the people's needs, even "the keen and intelligent interest King Edward displays in foreign affairs." The King's "noble pride in his Empire, his great qualities as a sportsman, his insistence on 'playing the game' in all his manifold duties," Thomas felt sure, justified his people's looking forward to a great and glorious reign.

This chapter had been written before the abdication crisis, and after it, his publishers tactfully suggested that Thomas might wish to revise it. To his credit Thomas decided he would not: what he had written should be allowed to stand. But even Thomas, for all his enthusiasm for Edward, could not bring himself to take the King's side in the abdication dispute. Public opinion, he insisted, would never have allowed the King to marry Mrs. Simpson and retain his throne.

If Edward was going to win support in the Labour movement, it was more likely to have come from the men of his own generation or younger—Hugh Dalton, perhaps. Dalton had been to a public school—Winchester—and thence to Oxford, where he had a distinguished academic career. One of his books on economic theory became prescribed reading for university examinations. He had held junior office in the MacDonald Labour government, becoming a member of the Labour Party shadow cabinet in opposition, and it happened that in 1936 he was chairman of the party's national executive, a position which, as he realized, was of great potential prestige and influence. For all his academic background, too, Dalton was far from being stuffy. He was gregarious, enjoyed parties, and relished backstairs intrigue. The King and he could have enjoyed each other's company. But they had not come together, and now, to Dalton, it was unthinkable that he or his party should take up Edward's cause. The idea of the King marrying Mrs. Simpson, let alone making her his Queen, was simply unacceptable.

In his autobiography, Dalton commented that on this, "Roman Catholics and Free Churchmen, as well as Anglicans, were agreed." The attitudes of Catholics, Nonconformists and Anglicans were important to Dalton, in his party-chairman role. But other party intellectuals who did not have to worry about them shared his view—notably Harold Laski, who regarded himself as the party's Socialist conscience. Like Morrison, Laski was concerned with the constitutional aspect. If Labour were to return to power, he believed, it would have to be much more ruthless in dealing with the City and other vested interests, and it therefore required a genuinely constitutional monarch—which Laski feared Edward VIII was not. During the crisis, according to his friend and biographer Kingsley Martin, Laski was to be "the strongest and most unhesitating of Baldwin's supporters," and after it was over he explained to his American friend Judge Felix Frankfurter that the new King would find it difficult to interfere in policy, and "that, after all, is the main thing."

Among the younger members of the parliamentary party, Aneurin Bevan was already regarded as outstanding. Gunther—in a typical phrase—singled him out as the most interesting of the younger Socialists: "Vital, ambitious, magnetic, with an immense Welsh laugh, he is one of the attractive characters in the Commons." Bevan had already indicated what his attitude would be. Among the places which Edward visited on his tour of South Wales was a social centre in Bevan's constituency, and some of his constituents felt that he should be present. Bevan replied that he could not associate himself "with a visit which would appear to support the notion that private charity has made, or can ever make, a contribution of any value to the solution of the problem of South Wales." Bevan's view—

according to Michael Foot—was that for an expedition of this kind to be organized to Wales as if it were an unknown barbarous and distant land, "much in the same way as you might go to the Congo," was an affront. He thought that the King was being used by Baldwin and his Minister of Labour for political ends—the inevitable fate, he considered, of the monarchy. Just before the King left for South Wales, Bevan had sent him a warning in a speech made in Trafalgar Square: "Our message to King Edward is that the people cannot rejoice, they are sad at heart. We could bring to London next year a poverty army that could make the coronation look like a hollow sham. We are not here just to give honour to the dead, but to bring life to the living." Edward could hardly expect support from that quarter.

As for the Trade Union Congress, closely linked to the Labour Party, there was no risk of its general secretary, at least, backing the King. Gunther, again, expressed the common view of Walter Citrine —that he was a bureaucratic machine, living on files—and he quoted A.J. Cummings: "For my part I would rather rely on Sir Walter Citrine, archpriest of British Trade Unionism, than on Mr. Baldwin, the Conservative Prime Minister, to keep the present system intact. There is to-day no Toryism more fearful and immovable than that which is enshrined in the ideals and practice of Trade Union leadership." Of all the men of the left, Citrine was the one on whom Baldwin could most confidently rely.

An even more influential figure in the TUC, though, was Ernest Bevin. Bevin had created, and now led, the massive Transport and General Workers Union. He was not in Parliament, but at party conferences he was the most powerful single individual—it had been his brutal attack on the pacifists in 1935, for "hawking their consciences around on their sleeves," that had driven Lansbury from the leadership of the party.

The disparity between Bevin's views and the King's can be gauged by a speech he made at the Labour Party conference in 1936, when he praised Czechoslovakia as "one of the most glorious little democratic countries, hedged in all round, in danger of being sacrificed tomorrow." Bevin went on to issue a warning: "I want to say to Mussolini and Hitler, if you are banking on being able to attack in the East or the West, and you are going to treat the British Socialist movement as being weak—and are going to rely on that at a critical moment—you are taking us too cheaply." This was precisely the kind of provocative talk that irritated Edward, feeling sure as he did that British relations with Mussolini and Hitler could be restored to cordiality, with the exercise of a little restraint. And Bevin, for his part, had no sympathy for the King's attitude to social problems. Over the visit to South Wales, he was reported as saying that though he did not hold it against the monarchy, a royal visit would not take the place of government action, "and I am sorry that the King has been brought into this business."

This was particularly unlucky for the King as, apart from his influence in the TUC and in the Labour Party, Bevin—according to his biographer, Alan Bullock—was the key figure among the trade-union directors of the *Daily Herald:* "Bevin was proud of the *Herald,* referring to it as 'my paper.'" As the editor, Francis Williams, was to testify, Bevin never interfered with the day-to-day running of the paper, but his views were always treated with respect.

Among the ex-leaders, leaders and aspiring leaders of the Labour Party, in fact, Edward was able to muster only two allies, and neither was of a kind to bring him any comfort. George Lansbury was one of the party's patriarchs. He had actually led it in opposition after 1931, but only because he alone of MacDonald's Cabinet—other than those who went over with MacDonald to the national government—had survived the landslide of 1931 and retained his parliamentary seat. But in 1935 his pacifist views had been repudiated by the party. He had been ousted from the leadership and from his place in its councils. He wanted the party to support Edward—according to Laski, he was only just prevented from pronouncing a "Salute to the Democratic King" when the crisis broke. But even if Lansbury had gone ahead with his salutation, he would not have been taken seriously.

Edward's other support in the party was to come from an even more suspect source. As a young man, Stafford Cripps had been an extremely successful barrister, and he took a heavy loss of income in order to become Solicitor General—and consequently a knight—in Ramsay MacDonald's second government. It gave him a reputation for austerity, and he looked the part. The comedian George Robey used to call him, expressively, "Sir Stifford Crapps." Cripps' political stock in trade, as "Watchman" put it, was "to utter lamentations, anguish and foreboding, to resurrect and revitalise Jeremiah, Job and Cassandra." What his colleagues were not prepared for was the course on which his forebodings were going to set him, in opposition to the national government. Like Laski, he had moved to the left—convinced that MacDonald had sold out to the City. He began to see the City's malign influence everywhere, and among Labour's worst enemies he included the court. "There is no doubt," he had warned in a speech in 1934, "that we shall have to overcome opposition from Buckingham Palace." In the summer of 1935 he went further, accusing the City of having got rid of the last Labour government by using "the Buckingham Palace influence."

This was not a popular line in the party. Every time Cripps opened his mouth, it used to be said, he lost Labour 100,000 votes. Unpopularity only made him more unpredictable. He opposed sanctions on Italy, recommended co-operation with the Communists in a popular front, and took other courses that the party disapproved of and for which it was soon going to expel him. That he should support Edward, then, was regarded by his colleagues as only another sign of his irresponsibility.

And Cripps' support was equivocal. He asserted that Edward was being denied the right to marry for the wrong—social—reasons: "I cannot help feeling," Cripps argued, "that if the lady in question had been a member of the aristocracy, under precisely similar circumstances, quite a different decision would have been come to by the Government." He felt, therefore, that the government had no reason to compel the King to abdicate. But this, he stressed, was only his personal view. In his capacity as a lawyer, he had been asked by some of the King's friends whether, if the King married, his wife would be Queen. Cripps' advice was that she would be, and that consequently the King was bound to accept his ministers' advice —wrong though it might be—on the matter of his choice. This was not much consolation to Edward, as it was Cripps' advice as a lawyer that Edward's supporters valued. His opinions as an individual—or as a politician—did not interest them. They knew that as an ally, in those capacities, he would only be an embarrassment to the King.

THIRD CONFRONTATION—NOVEMBER 25

A morganatic marriage?

In ordinary circumstances Baldwin would now have been in a
very strong position. What he had been fearing was a constitutional
crisis arising from the King's determination to go his own way,
without heeding his ministers' advice. But now the King had said
that he was prepared to go if he could not marry Mrs. Simpson, and
the implication was that he would go quietly. Alternatively, he
might decide to give Mrs. Simpson up. But that decision, although
it would keep him on the throne, would be an admission of defeat so
that if he stayed, there should be less trouble from him afterwards.

The King's choice of advisers had also been a relief. If he could
do no better than Hoare and Duff Cooper, there could be little to
worry about. As for Monckton, Baldwin knew him well. They had
been governors together of Harrow School. If Baldwin had been
left to make the choice of a go-between himself, he could not have
chosen better—from his own point of view.

Baldwin now had reason to hope that the whole Mrs. Simpson
issue could be settled without fuss or clamour. The chief danger was
Geoffrey Dawson, whom he had told of the summons to Buckingham
Palace and who would want to know what happened there. Dawson
had been around to see Hardinge that morning, only to discover
that there had been no reaction to his letter to the King. Now, late
in the evening of the 16th he received a call from the House of Commons, and went there expectantly—to find Baldwin uncommunica-
tive ("His lips were sealed," was Dawson's rather curt comment).
All that Dawson could gather was that the King was in the grip of
an obsession, that there was to be a further meeting within a week,
and that in the meantime, "Public comment would weaken his
[S.B.'s] influence." Dawson found that his second-in-command, R.M.
Barrington Ward, had been able to obtain more definite information.
He had seen Monckton, who had given him the impression that

things were moving toward abdication. But with Baldwin's request in mind, Dawson could do nothing in the *Times*.

Baldwin's other confidants were also left in the dark. When he got back that night to 10 Downing Street, he confessed that he was temporarily at the end of his tether. "I have heard such things from my King tonight," he told the Conservative Party's chief whip, "as I never thought to hear. I am going to bed." And to bed he went, to the disappointment of those who had been waiting for his account of what had happened. The next day he had left to make a speech in Scotland, and as the King was in South Wales, London gossip was left to its own devices.

"Appalling frankness"

But Baldwin's position was, in reality, very far from secure. He was suffering from the after-effects of a political gaffe. On November 12, while the King was with the fleet, the Commons had been debating disarmament, and Baldwin, aware that he had a poor case, decided to do what he had previously done with such effect, and tell all. But this time, candour did not work.

"I put before the whole House my own views with an appalling frankness," Baldwin asserted. It certainly appalled many supporters. Baldwin now confessed that he had been deeply shocked by the Fulham by-election result in 1933. He could not, he had realized, ask for a mandate for limited rearmament of the kind he eventually asked for, and received, two years later. "Supposing I had gone to the country," he asked his hearers, "and said that Germany was rearming and we must rearm: does anybody think that this pacific democracy would have rallied to that cry at that moment? I cannot think of anything that would have made the loss of the election from my point of view more certain."

Never in history, G.M. Young thought, has a statesman made a confession more fatal to his good name: "Baldwin puts party before country" was to be the index reference to the episode as described by Churchill in *The Gathering Storm*. His defenders were later to argue that Baldwin had been referring only to a hypothetical election, which was never held. But if he had really believed in 1933 that rearmament was desirable, to meet the threat of a resurgent Nazi Germany, then he ought to have warned the country, and if necessary asked for his mandate, even at the risk of losing the election. Admittedly this might have meant that the Labour Party, pledged to disarmament, would have been returned, with possibly even more dire consequences. But the Labour Party's opposition to rearmament was based on its mistrust of a Conservative government's indulging in an arms race to gratify their capitalist backers. The outright pacifist element of the party was relatively insignificant.

Baldwin's admission was gleefully seized upon by the Opposition. NEVER AGAIN WILL THE NATION TRUST HIM, ran the headline given by the Labour *Daily Herald* to an article by Harold Laski—all the more effective because Laski had been an admirer of Baldwin. Laski now claimed to be disenchanted—Baldwin himself, he wrote, "has torn away the mask from the popular portrait of the simple, honest man, deserving of confidence. He makes treachery the essence of leadership." The political commentator of the *News Chronicle* reported that the "Tory ranks were in dismay." Baldwin, he thought, had finally wrecked his reputation with his followers, he couldn't last much longer.

Many Conservatives were indeed dismayed—Amery, for one. Baldwin's admission, he thought, instead of educating the public to the realities and "exposing the delusions of the pacifists, professed its devoted belief in these delusions." It was also recalled that in a debate on armaments in 1934, Baldwin himself had said, "The greatest crime to our own people is to be afraid to tell the truth." Yet here he was admitting that he had been afraid to tell it in 1933, and already some Conservatives had begun to believe that the fear might ultimately prove to be criminal in its consequences. To add to the hostility, many people believed that Baldwin had been referring not to 1933 but to 1935—a misunderstanding that was to persist, further damaging his reputation.

A surge of resentment went through that section of the party which, though not followers of Churchill on other issues, believed he had been right about the need for rearmament. Baldwin's betrayal of the League through the Hoare-Laval pact was recalled and execrated, and "Arms and the Covenant"—a movement designed to bring together men of all parties who believed in the League of Nations, but who realised that to be effective its member states must be both armed and resolute—began to attract members and funds. Once again, Baldwin found himself facing a threat to his authority.

And as it was attracting support in the political centre, as well as among the politically uncommitted, it promised to be more dangerous to him than earlier threatened rebellions from the right.

Once again, as after the Hoare-Laval pact, Baldwin's confidence in his ability to gauge public opinion had been shown to be overconfidence. The King's reception by the ex-servicemen, by the fleet and in South Wales had made it obvious that he had not lost his appeal to the masses. Suppose he decided to exploit it? Or—and this was more likely—suppose the enemies of the government, with or without the King's collusion, decided to exploit it? There was no need for the King to break out of his constitutional trappings in order to appeal to the country over his ministers' heads. The popular press could do the job for him, leaving him in the position where he could still claim that he himself was doing nothing unconstitutional.

From the moment Baldwin realized this, it became even less in his interest to work for a compromise that would keep the King on the throne. But it was important to continue to appear to be working for one. If the government showed its hand, the King might decide to fight—or, worse, to reassess his prospects and to adopt more subtle policies, with the idea of gradually winning the public around to acceptance of his marriage to Wallis. The better policy would be to convince Edward that every avenue would be sympathetically explored in order to find some way to keep him on the throne—while in fact confining the exploration to cul-de-sacs.

But this would take time, and time might not be on the government's side. On the morning of Monday, November 23, Rothermere's *Daily Mail* confirmed Baldwin's fears of the popular press. The *Mail* had been prominently featuring the King's recent activities. Now it came out with a leading article "splashed" under the heading "The King Edward Touch," describing how the King had gone to see for himself what was going on in South Wales and had then called for all the evidence available. The contrast, the *Mail* claimed,

to the way in which national questions are customarily approached can escape nobody. There is consultation, committees are appointed, and conference takes place in the solemn apartments of Whitehall; but how often does a Minister, as a preface to this consecrated and lengthy procedure, go boldly forth to see for himself and measure a problem by independent judgement, following this with immediate action?

To Geoffrey Dawson, this was "a monstrous attempt to contrast

His Majesty's solicitude for the unemployed in South Wales with the indifference of his Ministers." Dawson had been growing more and more impatient as the days went by. He was willing to go along with Baldwin and avoid public comment, but it irked him that he should be in possession of information that he could not use in the *Times*—especially as the risk remained of some other paper breaking the story. The suppression of the facts, too, was having some embarrassing side effects, such as the censoring of American newspapers and periodicals by newsagents, afraid of the possibility of libel actions. Rather than forego sales, importers had begun to cut out stories that referred to Mrs. Simpson before sending on the papers to the bookstalls. Naturally, readers were irritated. Some of them complained to their MPs, and on November 17, Walter Runciman, president of the Board of Trade, was called upon to answer a parliamentary question on whether there was any special scrutiny of books and printed literature imported from other countries. When he replied that he was not quite sure what the question meant, a Labour MP, Ellen Wilkinson, threw in a "supplementary":

Can the Right Honourable Gentleman say why, in the case of two American magazines of high repute, imported into this country during the last few weeks, at least two and sometimes three pages have been torn out; and what is this thing the British public are not allowed to see?

Runciman could only reply that it was nothing to do with his Department.

Runciman, as it happened, was himself perturbed about the spread of the Mrs. Simpson scandal, which was now beginning to seep down into the provinces. A Methodist, he was a power in the Nonconformist world. He and Dawson had met, during the weekend when Dawson was waiting to hear what had been the King's reaction to the Hardinge letter. Runciman told Dawson that he was having difficulty in holding back local preachers, "who were showing signs of wanting to fulminate from the pulpit." Baldwin, too, brought Runciman into the Cabinet inner circle—less for the benefit of his experience (he had been president of the Board of Trade once before, during the First World War, but, like Simon, had gone into the Liberal wilderness after it) than to exercise more effective control over him and, indirectly, over his preachers. But it was not possible to be sure that he would be able to keep them quiet.

Dawson knew, too, that other editors were becoming increasingly restive—Wilson Harris, for one, editor of the weekly *Spectator*. The *Spectator* had existed for over a century as a journal of opinion. It had first made its name as the passionate advocate of the Reform Bill of 1832 and after that time had frequently demonstrated its left-of-centre independence. Harris felt the time had come to speak out. But he was sufficiently unsure of himself to ring up Barrington Ward to ask him what the *Times* was going to do, and he was grateful when Barrington Ward "promised to let me know when they decided to break silence, so that the *Spectator* might speak at the same time." As the *Spectator* appeared only weekly, the chances that it would speak "at the same time" as the *Times* were clearly small, but "it was not for us," Harris thought, "particularly as a weekly, to attempt to give the lead."

But what hope could Dawson have of restraining his fellow editors if the Rothermere press opened what was, in effect, a campaign to rouse public support for the King and to cast discredit on his ministers? Dawson set to work to compose an editorial blasting the *Mail* for its impropriety, and then used it as an excuse to go around to have a word with Baldwin on the subject. He found Baldwin worried, speculating on the various possibilities and the popular reaction to them. The trouble—he confided to Tom Jones, who had dropped in to find out what was happening—was that the King had agreed to go quietly, and had told his mother and brothers as much, but now had gone back on his pledge. The week-end with Mrs. Simpson at the Fort, Baldwin surmised, must have been responsible for his change of mind. Whatever the reason, the success of the policy of masterly inactivity, which had appeared to be giving such promising results, was now threatened.

Baldwin's chopping block

For the first (though not the last) time, then, Baldwin was perturbed by the course events were taking. The very day he confided his worry to Dawson, though—November 23—they suddenly took a new course, much more favourable to the government. And the man responsible was Lord Rothermere. He had decided to intervene, and in doing so, just as he had done five years before, he presented Baldwin with the lever with which, a few days later, he was going to prise the King off his throne.

Rothermere used an intermediary, his son Esmond, who asked to see the Prime Minister that evening. Uneasy both about the *Mail* article and the prospect of the press silence being broken before he was ready, Baldwin agreed to the meeting, hoping to tackle him on these subjects. But Esmond, he found, had not come to talk about the press. He had a proposition to put to the Prime Minister. A crisis, he suggested, could be averted if the King was allowed to contract a morganatic marriage—to marry Mrs. Simpson without making her his Queen, and depriving their children, if any, of the rights to the succession to the throne.

While the King was in South Wales, Esmond Harmsworth had invited Wallis to have lunch with him at Claridge's, to ask her if the King had given any thought to the idea of a morganatic marriage. It was a term that—she was to recall in *The Heart Has Its Reasons*—she had come across in history books, "something romantic, having to do mostly with the Hapsburgs." Esmond, she found, had done research on it, discovering that it was an expedient quite frequently used by foreign royalty. It was not, he admitted, very flattering to her, but it might be the only way of keeping the King on his throne. Would she suggest the idea to him? She agreed to do so.

The idea had come to Esmond from his father, Lord Rothermere, who had himself heard it, according to the journalist John Connell, from the editor of his *Sunday Dispatch*. What Rothermere did not realize was the connotation the term "morganatic" had acquired. To Wallis there might be something romantic about it. To the English, "morganatic" had an under-the-counter, rather sleazy connotation, the kind of thing that Balkan royalty might do—and Balkan royalty "didn't count." Edward sensed this, when Wallis brought up the idea that week-end at the Fort, after he had come back from Wales. His face, she was to recall, showed his distaste.

Edward was versed well-enough in the history of his family, though, to be aware that there was a precedent from the life of the Duke of Cambridge, the eldest grandchild of George III, and second only to Victoria in the line of accession, until she bore children. Sent into the army at the age of eighteen, the Duke became attached to an actress, Louisa Fairbrother, and desiring to marry her, he requested permission of the Queen, as he was bound to do under the Royal Marriage Act of 1772. The consent was refused, presumably on the ground that George was too close to the succession. He chose to go on living with Louisa anyway, and she had two sons by him before in 1847 they married without royal permission.

Whatever its legality, as Compton Mackenzie noted, it was an extremely happy marriage, lasting until her death in 1890—only four years before Edward was born. No attempt was made by Queen Victoria to punish the Duke for his disobedience of the royal edict. On the contrary, she treated his wife with "the greatest kindness and consideration." The sons had reasonably successful careers in the services, and George himself, after commanding a division in the Crimean War, went on to become commander in chief of the army, a post which he was to hold until he retired in 1895—nearly forty years. Clearly, his marriage made no difference to his career. When he died, he could have been buried in Westminster Abbey—had he not preferred to be beside his wife in Kensal Green.

The marriage of the Duke of Cambridge could not be regarded as a direct precedent for Edward, because the Duke did not become King. But had Victoria died before giving birth to any children, the Duke would have become King, and the situation would then have arisen where either his wife would have become Queen, or she would have had to be given some other—morganatic—status.

King George IV's marriage to Mrs. Fitzherbert could also be described as, in effect, morganatic. His open marriage to Princess Caroline was bigamous, except on the assumption that royalty had a special dispensation to have one formal and one informal wife. But these precedents were from the previous century, and in the interim, "morganatic" had become almost the equivalent of "un-English."

However little Edward cared for the morganatic-marriage idea, it did at least offer a possible way out, and by this time, as his and the Duchess' accounts agree, he realized he needed one. He was getting desperate. He saw Esmond Harmsworth and agreed that the idea should be put forward to Baldwin. It was only at this point, by her own account, that Wallis grew alarmed. The project, she began to think, though well-meaning, might simply lead Edward into a trap —"He would be putting his head on Baldwin's chopping block." Edward would not listen. "I've got to do something," he replied. "At the very least I'll get my head in a more comfortable position on the block."

This was what he now did. Baldwin did not rush things. He was due to see the King on the 25th, and he was prepared to wait until then. In the meantime, Harmsworth had begun lobbying among the Establishment. He met Lord Lothian for lunch, telling him about his interviews with Mrs. Simpson and with the King, assuring him that

Mrs. Simpson had no desire to be Queen, and saying that she would accept being Duchess of Cornwall or some such alternative. She would be a peeress, but she would not attend formal court functions, and her children would not succeed to the throne.

Lothian went to Tom Jones to ask him how the plan would be regarded by Baldwin. In Lothian's view the compromise was a possible one—and he stressed the point that the working classes would not take so severe a view of it as would the middle class and the Empire. Jones arranged to have breakfast the next morning with Baldwin and put the idea to him. Baldwin was not impressed. He could not, he insisted, carry the Commons on that. "Is this the sort of thing I've stood for in public life? If I have to go out, as go I must, then I'd be quite ready to go out on this." Clearly, his confidence was returning.

That day—November 25—Baldwin had his audience with the King. At this meeting, he later told the Commons, the King asked whether the morganatic-marriage proposal had been put to him. "I said, yes. He asked me what I thought of it. I told him that I had not considered it. I said, 'I can give you no considered opinion.' If he asked me my first reaction informally, my first reaction was that Parliament would never pass such a bill. But I said, if he desired it, I would examine it formally. He said he did so desire." Baldwin then gave the King what amounted to a last chance, pointing out that "formally" meant not only putting it before the whole Cabinet, but also communicating with the Prime Ministers of the Dominions. Was that the King's wish? "He told me that it was. I said that I would do it."

Now, indeed, the King's head was on Baldwin's block. By the Statute of Westminster any change that concerned the crown would have to be enacted separately by each Dominion. Even if no legislation had been required, it could have been—and certainly would have been—argued that the King's choice of a bride concerned the crown and, therefore, the Dominions. But an act enabling the King to marry morganatically clearly fell into the category covered by the statute, and if the King was anxious to marry morganatically, Baldwin was right to insist that he must find out what the Dominions' reaction would be.

Constitutionally, too—as Edward realized—the word "advice" now assumed a particular significance: "Whenever the Prime Minister 'advises' the King, he is using a respectful form of words to express the will and decision of the Government," and the King is virtually bound by it. So far, the King had only received "advice" in the colloquial sense, committing neither him nor the government. But if Baldwin now formally advised him that the government could not accept the morganatic proposition, the King could not go ahead with it, even if the Dominions expressed themselves willing to accept it.

Alternatively, Edward could go ahead with his plan to marry Wallis as soon as her divorce was through, in the knowledge that the government would resign. But in that case, he must be able to call on an alternative Prime Minister. The obvious choice would have been the leader of the Labour Party. But Baldwin had taken the precaution of sounding Attlee out on what the Labour Party's attitude would be. Attlee was in no doubt. The party, he said, would have no objection to an American becoming Queen, but in his view Mrs. Simpson was out of the question, and though there would be sympathy for the King, he was sure that the party, "with the exception of a few of the intelligentsia who can be trusted to take the wrong view on any subject," would take the same view as he did. When Baldwin advised the King that the government would not pass the legislation necessary for a morganatic marriage, he also—according to Beaverbrook—intimated that it was no use Edward's hoping that the Opposition would lend a more favourable ear to the proposal.

By his own account, Edward realized as the door closed behind the Prime Minister that he had gone a long way toward sealing his fate. Baldwin must have realized it too. If he had been really anxious to keep the King on the throne, he would have urged informal consultations with the Dominions first, in the hope of showing Edward that the morganatic proposal was madness. But Baldwin chose to take the King up on his request for formal consultations, and no doubt he did so with relief. His worry, so far as the Dominions were concerned, had been about what their reaction would be if they were *not* formally consulted, and soon. Now, the excuse had been provided. And by this time, Baldwin no longer had any incentive to waste time seeking ways to keep the King but lose Mrs. Simpson. Unwittingly Rothermere—by the infelicitous combination of the Monday morning's leading article, and the morganatic proposal presented by his son later in the day—had first alarmed Baldwin, and then given him the opportunity he had needed to bring the King's matter to a head. He had not trapped the King—the trap had been presented to him, ready-baited, by the King's friends.

There are occasions when the King's actions, in retrospect, seem to suggest not rashness or thoughtlessness, but a desire—not necessarily conscious—to have done with the whole business. This was one of them. True, he still had faith in the support of the people of the Dominions, but even he can hardly have believed in the likelihood of a massive irresistible upsurge of public opinion behind him, sufficient to topple any government that tried to resist it, simply because he wanted to marry Mrs. Simpson, and the British government objected. Nor did he have to rely on Baldwin's word alone that neither government nor Parliament would approve. He had already heard as much from Monckton. Yet he had now insisted that the proposition be put, formally. It was as if the strain had been too great and he had made up his mind that he would rather chance the impossible odds of having the morganatic proposal accepted, in the certainty that if it was not accepted the affair would drag on no longer. He was later to insist that he had never regretted the decision: "I am sure it was the only one for me." And in retrospect it was; for by this time, his chance of finding a way to keep his throne and Wallis had vanished.

The Dominions reply

Once again, Baldwin was in control. Although he was still preoccupied with the subject, Tom Jones now felt that he was no longer worrying about it—he was "in a much more decisive mood about this than about other political questions." The inner circle of the Cabinet discussed the morganatic marriage proposal on November 25, and when, two days later, it was put to the full Cabinet, Baldwin's only worry was that the press might be tempted to hint at the reason for the meeting. The story was put out that ministers had been recalled because of events in Spain—an explanation that most papers accepted, either from gullibility or from a willingness to be co-operative. The *Manchester Guardian,* however, as if belatedly mindful of its fourth-estate duties, declined to go along with the hand-out. Its "London Letter" said bluntly that the Cabinet had met to discuss a domestic, not a foreign issue. But as it did not say what the issue was, its readers were none the wiser.

While the government awaited the replies from the Dominions, Baldwin put Sir John Simon onto the task of exploring the con-

stitutional issues, for use when the time came. He left no account
in his autobiography of the events that led up to the abdication.
Its intimate details, he explained, came to him "in discharge of his
duty in a situation of special confidence"—the Home Secretary being,
as George V had long ago pointed out to him, in a special sense the
sovereign's secretary, too. But from the comments Simon makes on
the abdication, the lawyer in him was dominant. He was fascinated
by the constitutional problems raised by the abdication. His knowledge of history was sketchy, and the wider constitutional issues
seem hardly to have concerned him. What intrigued him was the
absence of any precedent for voluntary abdication and the possibility that the King's Act of Abdication would not of itself bar his
descendants, without parliamentary confirmation. There was also the
Statute of Westminster to consider. It was a complex, if not a
particularly complicated, process, and it gave Simon a lot of work of
the kind that he was good at and enjoyed.

Baldwin might again be serene; it was the King's turn to be
worried. Wallis had begun receiving abusive, and sometimes threatening, anonymous letters, and when a rumour spread that her house
would be blown up, Edward decided that she and her Aunt Bessie
should move to the Fort. Her lawyers had advised her to avoid
seeing him until her decree was made absolute, for fear that someone should take advantage of the *nisi* rule—an intervener might
allege that her continued association with Edward was evidence of
her unworthiness to get a divorce. But he assured her this would
not happen, and again Wallis assumed he would be able to arrange
things so that it did not happen. She and her aunt went to the
Fort. He could now see her whenever he wanted to, but there was
no longer the old atmosphere. "It was no longer the enchanted Fort;
it was the Fort beleaguered."

At this point, Beaverbrook came back into the reckoning. Had
he been consulted at the time about Rothermere's proposal for a
morganatic marriage, he would certainly have condemned it; but
he was by then on his way to Arizona on the liner *Bremen,* ostensibly to throw off a bout of asthma. According to Driberg, Beaverbrook's bouts of asthma were related to his state of mind—so much
so, that they appeared to be a protective mechanism by which he
unconsciously avoided difficult situations. But they were also the

excuse Beaverbrook deliberately grasped at to escape the English winter, which he detested.

Hitherto the King had turned to Beaverbrook only for help, not for advice. So casual was their relationship, in fact, that until he rang up at the week-end after getting the Hardinge letter, he was unaware that Beaverbrook had left the country. Beaverbrook by his own account had not been sorry to slip away unnoticed. The King, he had found, appeared to be interested in him only as a way of keeping information out of the papers—which naturally irked a man whose delight was to get information into them. The King had also wanted him to try to curb the American papers, and that promised to be both difficult and tedious. Beaverbrook felt "glad to be out of the affair."

On his arrival in New York, though, Beaverbrook had found a message begging him to come back. At first he thought of ignoring it, but it was followed up by a telephone call from the King. Beaverbrook took it reluctantly—partly because he was in the offices of the New York *Daily News,* which might monitor the call and publish any indiscretions, but chiefly because it would be hard to refuse the King's plea, if it were made, to return at once. It was made. With grim humor, Beaverbrook announced his health had so improved as the result of his sea voyage that he was determined to repeat the dose and return to Britain on the *Bremen.*

Immediately after the liner docked at Southampton, Beaverbrook went to the Fort to learn what had happened in his absence. The King tried to impress him with the advantages of the morganatic marriage proposal. It had the pledged support of Lord Rothermere, he pointed out, and although, according to Baldwin, Attlee had expressed his opposition to it, Edward believed that Labour MPs would not be hostile in the long run and that there would be a good deal of support for it among the younger members of the Conservative government. Beaverbrook was skeptical. He did not believe the Cabinet would accept the proposal, and he counselled delay while he rallied supporting forces— including, as he hoped, Samuel Hoare.

But Hoare, when he saw him that evening, was evasive. Beaverbrook by his own account tried to persuade him that simply to put the case for a morganatic marriage to the Cabinet would not imply his approval. Hoare replied that he was the wrong man, as he was against the idea of the King's marrying Wallis, whether morganatically or otherwise. Some other approach, Beaverbrook realized, was required. He even thought of invoking the assistance of the Lord Chief Justice, Gordon Hewart—not so much from any idea that Hewart would convince Baldwin, as to gain time, in the hope that the King himself would realize before it was too late that the project was impracticable.

But it was already too late. With Beaverbrook back, Baldwin—to whom Beaverbrook's views were presumably passed on by Hoare—could risk no further delay, and too late, Beaverbrook heard that the morganatic-marriage proposal had been discussed by the Cabinet. Only Duff Cooper spoke up for the King, and he was not in favour of the morganatic marriage. He suggested simply that the proposal be dropped until after the coronation. But this was precisely what the Chamberlain wing of the Cabinet most feared. Once Edward was formally crowned, with all the attendant euphoria, he would be in a much stronger position to introduce Mrs. Simpson as his in-tended—perhaps even as his wife, if he chose to follow George IV's example and marry her in secret. "I have no doubt," Chamberlain wrote in his diary, "that if it were possible to arrange the mor-ganatic marriage, this would be the prelude to the further act, of making Mrs. Simpson Queen with full rights." Duff Cooper was overruled, and the decision was taken formally to consult the Dominions' governments on the proposal.

As soon as Beaverbrook heard what had happened, he realized all was lost. He hurried around to Buckingham Palace, according to Edward, in a state of unusual agitation, to echo Wallis's warning: "Sir, you have put your head on the execution block. All that Bald-win has to do now is to swing the axe." The government, Beaver-brook knew, had no power in law or in precedent to prevent the King from marrying whom he chose. Edward was therefore in a strong position to choose whomsoever he wished—provided he did not formally ask the government's consent. But a morganatic mar-riage, because it would confer a special status on Wallis, required legislation. By putting it up formally to the Cabinet, therefore, the King had handed Baldwin, in effect, the power of veto. Worse, he had allowed Baldwin to extend that power of veto to the Do-minions. And the questions to the Dominions, Beaverbrook had gathered, really boiled down to the simple proposition, "Do you recommend the King's marriage to a woman with two husbands living?" According to Edward, Beaverbrook made it clear that in this form, there was no doubt what the replies would be. "I am a Canadian. I know the Dominions. Their answer will be a swift and emphatic No."

It might still have been possible for Edward, if he had acted immediately, to withdraw the morganatic-marriage proposal, before it had been sent off. But he still clung to what had all along been his belief that the Dominions, at least, would prove to be on his side. He had never lost the feeling of closeness to their peoples that he had acquired on his world tours, and because of that, he could not believe that they had lost their affection for him. "The die was cast," he felt. He was impatient for their answer.

But Baldwin's questions were not being put to the cobbers that the Prince of Wales met on his voyages. They were being put to Premiers, who had already been briefed from London on what was happening. On the day the Cabinet met to agree on the questions, Geoffrey Dawson visited Bruce, the Australian high commissioner, who was ill but said he had given his views. "To judge from his conversation," Dawson noted with satisfaction, "they were refreshingly robust." As it happened, Bruce's Prime Minister had no need of such prompting. Stanley Lyons later gave an account of what had happened to his Commonwealth Parliament. The British government's questions, he said, had come in the form of a secret and personal cable from Baldwin:

informing me that he had had conversations with his Majesty the King about Mrs. Simpson, and that his Majesty had stated his intention of marrying Mrs. Simpson, but that at the same time his Majesty had said that he appreciated that the idea of her becoming Queen and her children succeeding to the Throne was out of the question, and that consequently he contemplated abdication and leaving the Duke of York to succeed on the throne. His Majesty had subsequently asked Mr. Baldwin's view on a new proposal, namely, that special legislative provision should be made for a marriage to Mrs. Simpson, which would not make her Queen and would not entitle her issue to succeed to the Throne. Mr. Baldwin informed me that he had advised his Majesty that he did not think there was any chance of such an arrangement receiving the approval of Parliament in Great Britain, also that the assent of the Dominions would be essential to the carrying out of such an arrangement. He invited my personal view.

Baldwin, in short, had been careful first to put into the Premiers'

minds the idea that the King was willing to abdicate—thereby relieving them of any fear of a constitutional crisis of the kind that
might have been expected to arise if Edward had not been prepared
to be co-operative. Baldwin had also intimated that the Parliament
at Westminster would not agree to the proposal that the King
should make Mrs. Simpson his wife, but not his Queen—thereby
relieving them of any fear that if they rejected the proposal, they
might be left out on a constitutional limb.

There was no doubt what Lyons' view would be. He was a devout Catholic. According to his wife, he had found himself a
fellow guest at a banquet in 1935 with Lord Craigavon, Prime
Minister of Northern Ireland, an Orangeman of traditional hue.
How many Roman Catholics, Craigavon asked, were there in Australia? About one in five of the population, Lyons replied. "Well,
watch 'em, Lyons," Craigavon warned: "watch 'em. They breed
like bloody rabbits." Lyons had twelve children, six boys and six
girls, and he had a Catholic's strict views on the subject of divorce.
His reply to Baldwin, he told the Australian Parliament, was that the
proposed marriage, "if it led to Mrs. Simpson becoming Queen,
would provoke widespread condemnation; and the alternative proposal, or something in the nature of a specially sanctioned morganatic marriage, would run counter to the best popular conception
of the Royal Family." It is possible that his message to Baldwin
was more vigorously phrased than he disclosed. Lyons' draft was
"even stiffer," Bruce found, than the one he had recommended; and
Baldwin later confirmed to Dawson that the Australian message was
the strongest.

It appears to have been taken for granted that New Zealand's
Premier would give the same opinion as Lyons; and Joseph Michael
Savage—a Catholic, as his Christian names suggested—did. According to Beaverbrook's account, he needed some prodding, because his
reply failed to express positive disapproval of the morganatic-
marriage idea. Baldwin had to take steps "to secure a reply favourable to his own designs"—so a New Zealand minister who happened
to be in London was interviewed "and asked for an answer hostile to
the King." But in any case the general sense of the New Zealand
reply was unfavourable to the project. All that Baldwin wanted,
apparently, was to make it more specific. From De Valera, premier
of the Irish Free State, with its population ninety percent Catholic,
there could be no doubt what the answer would be, and the South

African premier was also safe. General Herzog's comment in public a few days later was characteristic: When asked by a heckler at a meeting, "What's going to happen to our King?" he replied, "If your father or your mother did wrong, you would not refer to it publicly. Let us show delicacy by not discussing this matter publicly." The only doubt concerned Canada. Mackenzie King, it was felt, had not displayed on his visit to London the determination required if Edward was to be brought to his senses—or to his knees. And on November 23, Dawson, lunching with the Canadian high commissioner in London, Vincent Massey (brother of the film star, Raymond Massey, then at the height of his career) found him still hoping for a compromise. But now the Establishment came into its own, in the person of the Governor-General of Canada, John Buchan, Lord Tweedsmuir.

John Buchan had come from a background similar to Cosmo Gordon Lang's. His father was a Scots Calvinist minister, and John went to school in Scotland and to Glasgow University before going up to Oxford. There he became president of the Union and was believed to be a certainty for an All Souls fellowship. Perhaps he was over-confident—he was not chosen, much to his disgust. In 1901, however, his feet were set firmly on the upward path again when Amery, unable to go out to join Milner's Kindergarten, recommended Buchan in his place.

Buchan was to become best-known to the public as an author, but he also had a conventional career as an administrator and, later, as a Conservative MP. He had a wide range of influential friends: When he married, Lang—then a bishop—conducted the ceremony. After the war, Buchan became one of the country-house circuit, and revelled in it, so much so that a newspaper found his "rich vein of self-complacent snobbery" hard to take. The heroes of his novels were Milner Kindergarten types—the villains tended to be over-rich aliens, and anti-Semitism was never far below the surface. So enamoured did Buchan become of Eton, where he sent his sons, that he actually said about his own admirable Scots education, "I never went to school in the conventional sense"—meaning that he had not been sent to a boarding school. Like most of the Establishment men of his time he was much more agreeable—kindly, friendly, hospitable—than all this would make him seem, but he was very much a man of the Establishment.

When he entered Parliament for the Scottish Universities in

1927, Buchan became a friend of Baldwin's. According to his biographer, Janet Adam Smith, "When Baldwin was at No. 10 Downing Street Buchan was often summoned by a note in the Prime Minister's own hand, or invited to dine quietly at St. Stephen's ('I want a chat with you on certain things American. Give me a quarter of an hour on Monday afternoon or evening')." According to Baldwin's son, his father was closer to Buchan than to his Cabinet colleagues such as MacDonald or Chamberlain. When the Pilgrim Trust, of which Tom Jones became secretary, was founded in 1930, Buchan and Baldwin were both trustees.

Buchan had originally been suggested as high commissioner for Canada in 1925, and in 1934 the Conservative and Liberal leaders there agreed on him as their nomination. The Liberal Prime Minister, Mackenzie King, did not see eye to eye with Buchan—now Lord Tweedsmuir—on all matters, but their relationship remained close, and it fell to Tweedsmuir to handle the delicate business of the King's matter. He was brought into it formally in mid-October—even before the first confrontation between Baldwin and the King—when Hardinge wrote to inquire about the Canadian reaction to articles on Mrs. Simpson then circulating in *Time* and other American magazines. The situation, he replied, was disquieting, and on November 9, he elaborated on the theme in a letter to Baldwin:

Canada is the most puritanical part of the Empire, and cherishes very much the Victorian standards in private life . . .

She has a special affection of loyalty for the King, whom she regards as one of her own citizens. This is strongly felt particularly by the younger people, who are by no means straitlaced; and they are alarmed at anything which may take the gilt off their idol.

Canada's pride has been deeply wounded by the tattle in the American press, which she feels an intolerable impertinence. She is very friendly to America, but she has always at the back of her head an honest chauvinism.

Surely, Tweedsmuir argued, the King could be brought to see this? But only Baldwin could do it—"The Archbishop," he sagely advised, "should be kept out of this." His wife, who was in London during November, saw Baldwin at Chequers, and added a further point about the French Canadians' disapproval of divorce. And in the final phase of the crisis, according to Janet Adam Smith, Tweedsmuir was in daily contact not only with Baldwin but with Mackenzie

King. King kept on arriving agitatedly "like a wet hen" to consult the Governor-General. And although the Canadian reply was the least downright, the fact that Tweedsmuir subsequently praised Mackenzie King for his handling of the affair suggests that King took his advice.

On November 30, Dawson saw Baldwin again and heard that "the Dominion replies are coming in, and very strong, especially Australia (as Bruce rang up to tell me)." The crisis, he considered, could not long be postponed. Two days later, Baldwin formally put the morganatic-marriage proposal to the Cabinet. It was unanimously rejected. Baldwin went to the palace, and the look on his face when he was announced was enough to warn the King what he was going to say. Inquiries by the party whips, Baldwin announced, had ascertained that Conservative MPs were generally, and the Labour MPs almost entirely, unanimous against the proposal, and although the replies from the Dominions were not yet quite complete, it was clear that they would also be hostile.

Formally, Baldwin outlined the three courses that the King could now take. He could give up the idea of marriage, he could marry in defiance of his ministers' advice, or he could abdicate. The second of these courses, he pointed out, was manifestly impossible. But this, the King pointed out, left him with no choice at all. As he was determined to marry Wallis, and could not get his ministers' consent, abdication was in fact the only course left open to him. Baldwin—with undeniable earnestness, Edward conceded—insisted that he did indeed have a choice: "Believe me, Sir, it is my sincere hope—and the hope of the Cabinet—that you will remain our King." The King replied that he was determined to marry, even if it meant abdication, and the conversation ended.

That night, Dawson found Baldwin looking very strained: "He was getting worn out, and sat with his head on his hand, propped up by the table." But it was weariness, not nerves. "He was quite clear about his course, and reported a solid front in the House of Commons and in the Dominions." And he had good reason to be pleased with himself, for he had succeeded by means that would restore the confidence of his colleagues and the wholesome respect of his political opponents. Assuming that nothing now went wrong, the King would formally agree to abdicate, and Baldwin would be able to present Parliament and the country with a *fait accompli—*

arrived at with a dexterity that would banish the memory of his disastrous political year and reinstate him as the undisputed leader not only of his party but of his country. And then, after seeing the new King settled in and crowned, Baldwin could retire, sure of the plaudits of friend and foe.

And this was what was to happen—though not quite so easily as Baldwin had hoped. Friend and foe did indeed praise him unreservedly for his handling of the affair. True, the cables to the Dominions could be criticized for their rather loaded presentation of the issues. When Lord Avon claimed in his memoirs that they were "worded with a scrupulous impartiality, which would have defied the reader to guess the judgment at home in Britain," his recollection was at fault. But Avon's verdict was to be generally accepted:

> Baldwin had at once sensed the dangers for the country and Empire of any action by the Crown which might divide its peoples. All through the sad crisis he understood the instinctive reactions of the British people at every stage of a very human problem. From first to last, he never had any doubt as to what they would think. I do not pretend to have had any such infallible instinct, as events unrolled which made many of us very unhappy. There can, however, be no question that the decision taken was inescapable.

Pebble and avalanche

And so it came about that the abdication of King Edward VIII was virtually settled before millions of people in Britain were aware that it was even contemplated, or that there was a crisis of any kind. But Baldwin and his Cabinet, meeting on December 2 in order formally to reject the King's proposal, must have realized that they had left things just too late to avoid publicity. That morning, the first break came in the newspaper silence, in a few northern provincial papers.

The pebble that started the news avalanche rolling (commentators understandably found the metaphor irresistible) had been thrown the day before by the bishop of Bradford, Dr. A.W.F. Blunt. Blunt was an obscure figure at the time, nor was he ever again to attract attention—though "in the light of the historical consequences of his sudden action," the Duke of Windsor was to say in *A King's Story*, "it was perhaps noteworthy that the next time Blunt was in the news was in 1950, when he was attacked in the House of Lords as a leading personality in a strange organisation called 'The Council of Clergy and Ministers for Common Ownership,' which was said to be an instrument for Communist infiltration into the Church. Of such material is history made." Blunt himself, though, was no Communist—indeed, in 1937 he was to tell a Quebec audience that he had felt bound to speak out because Communists had been making trouble by handing around cuttings from the American newspapers. He was a Christian Socialist, inclined to air his political views from the pulpit—and in print: He was the author of several books, most of them treatises such as *Israel Before Christ*. His *Our Need for God* had just been published in 1936.

Blunt had been attending a conference in London called by the Archbishop of Canterbury. Lang was in a difficulty. At the beginning of November he had met Baldwin at a house party at Hatfield, the Salisbury home, and Baldwin had told him of the first discussion with the King at Fort Belvedere. Baldwin had not seemed perturbed, and at their next meeting on the 19th—at the time the King was on his tour of South Wales—had appeared confident that the King was going to abdicate. But a week later, according to his biographer Lockhart, the Archbishop found that "all was uncertainty." Baldwin feared that the new morganatic-marriage proposal "if put forward with the King's approval might be strongly supported by a section of the press."

This news confronted Lang with a dilemma. He was very anxious to launch his projected "Recall to Religion" campaign, and the obvious peg to hang it on would be the coronation. It would have been a tricky enough exercise to try to relate it to King Edward at the best of times, considering his known views. But if the news were to get around that Edward had even contemplated morganatic marriage—or, indeed, marriage of any kind to Mrs. Simpson—the campaign would be made a laughing-stock. Uneasy, Lang called the bishops together to discuss the subject and explain the difficulties to them.

Blunt then went back to Bradford, where he was due to address his diocesan conference on the subject of the forthcoming coronation—and the Recall to Religion campaign. It may well be, as Sencourt suggested, that the responsibility for what was to happen should be put on the shoulders of the provocative Bishop Barnes of Birmingham, who had actually urged that the coronation should be secularized, at least to the extent of separating it from the administration of Holy Communion. Barnes' views used frequently to enrage his episcopal colleagues, and Blunt went out of his way, at the diocesan conference, to refute them. The coronation, he insisted, was not simply a piece of national "Pageantics," like the state opening of Parliament, and coming as it would at a critical period in history, it must be a recall of the state to religion. Its benefit, though, must depend on the faith, prayer and dedication of the King. He should, therefore, be commended to God's grace, which he would abundantly need if he were to do his duty faithfully. "We hope," the bishop added, "that he is aware of his need. Some of us wish that he gave more positive signs of his awareness . . . "

Blunt subsequently insisted that he had prepared his speech weeks before and that although he had seen cuttings from the American papers he was not concerned with Mrs. Simpson, merely with the King's irregular churchgoing. But inevitably the fact that he had been at the Archbishops' conference was noted in the American press and formed the basis of the broad hints that were to be dropped, in British newspapers as well, that Lang had put him up to it. On the contrary, Lang's biographer insisted, the Archbishop was not privy to the Blunt speech and certainly had not instigated it: "He was extremely annoyed by it, since it looked as though the leakage had come from Lambeth." Lang's irritation was to be justified—the suspicion aroused was to be damaging to him. When "Cassandra," the *Daily Mirror* columnist, came to write his *"J'accuse!"* a few days later, he was to put the leaders of the Church even before the Prime Minister on his charge sheet, claiming that they had placed the King "in a position from which it was impossible for him to retreat."

Intimidation in code

Before Blunt had spoken, however, there had been many signs that the press silence could not last. The *Mail* editorial a week before, praising the King and disparaging his ministers, was responsible for a marked change of atmosphere. It showed how hostilities could be conducted without any formal declaration of war, and Geoffrey Dawson, chafing under Baldwin's restraint, gratefully seized the opportunity. What he had to find was some suitable excuse to put the opposite case, in favour of representative government against irresponsible monarchy, but in such a way that it did not appear, outwardly at least, to have anything to do with Edward VIII. The day after the *Mail's* comments, a *Times* editorial pompously castigated them as mischievous, but the following morning there was a much more subtle onslaught, which Rothermere—and the King—must have thought more mischievous still.

A new Governor-General had just been appointed for South Africa: Patrick Duncan, one of the Milner Kindergarten. Surprisingly, the *Times* editorial criticized the choice. Duncan, it said, possessed in full measure the qualities and the experience required, but he had been deeply involved in South African politics, and this would make it difficult for him to remain above the political battle there. The circumstances of his appointment might weaken even the best of men: "It is the position—the position of the King's deputy no less than that of the King himself—that must be kept high above public reproach or ridicule, and that is incomparably more important than the individual who fills it . . . the King's deputy, like the King himself, should be invested with a certain detachment and dignity, which need not at all preclude his contact with all sorts and conditions of people, but which are not so easily put on as a change of clothes."

So, to the last, the Kindergarten played its part. Dawson was delighted with his ruse, and he had no fear that it might not be noticed, as he had lunch the day he wrote it with Lady Milner, Neville Chamberlain, Alec Hardinge and others. Dawson wrote in his diary, "I had some talks with A.H. on the overshadowing topic and saw N.C. again in the evening in the House of Commons." And the editorial was shrewdly timed; it appeared on the 25th, the day the King was to ask Baldwin to put the morganatic proposal formally to the Cabinet and to the Dominions. Already, Edward was nervous of the *Times*. And now Dawson had found a way—as Beaverbrook was characteristically to describe it in his BBC review of the *History of the Times*—of "intimidating the King in code." This was the effect it had on the King. "The bombardment appeared imminent," he assumed, and "because of the intimate association of Mr. Baldwin, the Archbishop of Canterbury and Mr. Geoffrey Dawson, editor of the *Times*, we had instinctively braced ourselves for an opening salvo from 'The Thunderer.'" It had now come—not a salvo, but an underwater torpedo attack. As Beaverbrook described it, "Dawson conducted a campaign in the *Times* advocating the importance of keeping the Crown and its representatives remote from glaring personal scandal," and that it was intended as a war of nerves is clear from Dawson's diary, in which he was gleefully to note that the significance of his editorial had not been lost on the American press, "or indeed on many people in England."

Encouraged by the results, Dawson continued with intimidation in code. On November 30, for example, an editorial ended with a plea to the House of Commons to preserve the steadiness and balance it had shown in recent months: "Given the continuance of this spirit—and it shows no sign of weakening—the House of Commons may well prove itself what the country has required in similar times during its long history, but has seldom been given—namely, a Council of State which is able to demonstrate its solid strength in any crisis that may arise, whether foreign or domestic."

By this time, even the sober weekly *Church Times* had joined in. Its issue for November 27, commenting on the war between the *Times* and the *Mail*, came down apparently on the *Mail*'s side: The King, it claimed, could legitimately criticize and "ginger up" his ministers. It added, though, that "for him there is no escape from constant circumspection, self-sacrifice and self-control, if he is to maintain the prestige of the monarchy at home, and the prestige of the nation abroad."

There was also the risk that the independent magazines might take a chance and run the story without disguise. In mid-November the *New Leader,* the weekly organ of the Independent Labour Party—formerly influential, but now a dwindling group of Socialist diehards—included an article criticizing the continued press silence, under the title "How Long Will Censorship Be Maintained?" The King's personal relations, the writer claimed, were his own affair, "but when the press of the whole world outside Britain is discussing at length whether King Edward is going to marry Mrs. Simpson, and when the whole of London is debating the likely developments, it is ridiculous that, under the influence of high circles, no word should appear in the British press." The influence of high circles extended to the firm that printed the *New Leader*. Its Tory owners— the editor of the *New Leader*, Fenner Brockway, complained to *Time*—refused to print the article, first claiming it was a breach of faith, and then insisting that it was a seditious libel. And the *New Leader* bowed to their command. (The *New Leader* eventually ran the article, which was quite mild in tone, during the crisis.) *Caval-cade* had also, for some reason, become more circumspect.

In Fleet Street, the atmosphere became tense. The tabloid *Daily Mirror* all but broke the silence with a reference to stories in U.S. newspapers of an impending outrage in Mayfair. The next day a retraction appeared:

U.S. reports unfounded

NO GUARDS FOR SOCIETY WOMAN

On further enquiry yesterday, the *Daily Mirror* learned that there is no truth in the reports appearing in American newspapers of threats against the life of Mrs. Simpson, a former U.S. society woman, now living in London, or of special guards having been engaged for her protection.

We regret having given publicity in our later editions yesterday to these reports, for which there is no foundation.

At the *Express,* Christiansen was constantly worried by the possibility of being scooped by some rival, not necessarily because his rivals were less scrupulous, but because the story might begin to break at any moment in some unexpected fashion—as indeed it eventually did—leaving editors uncertain whether to suppress or ignore the signs of the breakage or to go ahead and tell all. Christiansen also had to contend with the whims of his proprietor, Beaverbrook, and, on occasion, to circumvent him by ingenious ruses. When Beaverbrook went to the palace for a consultation, he used to enter by a back door to avoid been seen. But he was seen, and the *Express* was duly informed. Christiansen knew he could not print the information without risking trouble, but he could, and did, persuade the International News Service—who had tipped him off—to include Beaverbrook's visit in their story to New York, so that it would appear on the tapes there—and enable the *Express* to give it, quoting the INS as its source.

It was a ridiculous situation, and even Baldwin, according to Tom Jones, expressed his regret that the press silence was still continuing. It was ceasing to be to his advantage, now that the popular press was staging a campaign for the people to rally behind their King. On November 28 the *Mirror* had joined in, with a new feature designed to appear every Saturday, entitled "Our King This Week"—billed as "a running record, told week by week, of the life of our beloved monarch." It followed up the by now familiar thesis that the King's reaction to South Wales had at last goaded his weary-brained ministers into action.

Wednesday—the Cabinet of a wisely unconventional monarch became unconventional itself. Altered its agenda, distressed itself about the distressed. For just over sixty minutes.

Wednesday night—a further to-do.

Mr. Baldwin postponed his dinner, hurried in his car from No. 10 to Buckingham Palace, and for a long time talked with his Majesty about the people who have no dinner at all.

He reported progress, words which fell sweetly upon the ears of the King.

The *Mirror*'s words were unlikely to fall sweetly on Baldwin's ears. Its readers could not be expected to realize how comically inaccurate the story was. Probably Baldwin would have relaxed his opposition to the *Times* breaking the story, but for his antipathy to reaching positive decisions. Had Dawson simply sent a message to say that his Mrs. Simpson article was going to appear the next morning whether the government approved or not, Baldwin would probably have been relieved. But perhaps he also still hoped that the King's matter might be settled before the story broke. That would have been a notable achievement. So he held his hand.

Forecast: thundery

By the end of November there was probably only one person who could not see that the press silence was disastrous: the King. He continued to fear the deluge of publicity that inevitably would engulf him and, worse, Wallis. But a few of his friends realized, even if he did not, that the only chance of persuading the people of Britain to accept the morganatic marriage project was to explain what it was for and to make it sound reasonable and practicable. They had begun to put out feelers among editors who might be expected to be sympathetic, to see what could be done—giving the impression that the initiative had come from Edward.

When Bishop Blunt retired, nearly twenty years later, Kingsley Martin wrote in his "Critic's Diary" in the *New Statesman and Nation* that he owed Blunt a grudge, though the fault was none of his. Like many editors Martin had thought, in November 1936, of telling the story in the independent Socialist weekly the *New Statesman*, but he had decided not to on the ground that the King, like any other citizen, was entitled to have a private life. "Then, a message reached me: the King, I was authoritatively told, had irrevocably decided to marry Mrs. Simpson, and would be quite pleased if some serious discussion of the constitutional issue involved could be begun in a responsible paper like the *New Statesman and Nation.*" The theory, as put to Martin, was that this would "forestall scandalous headlines," and this removed Martin's doubts about publicizing the story, as the choice of a queen was a matter of public concern. Martin thereupon wrote an article arguing that the King had a right to marry the woman he loved, but that Parliament would have to deal with the constitutional aspect, presumably by authorizing some form of morganatic marriage.

As the information about the King's intentions had been passed on to Martin as coming from the King himself, he decided that the King ought to see the article before it was published, and he transmitted it through D.N. Pritt, QC, a barrister on the far left of the Labour Party. Pritt described in his autobiography how he put Martin in touch with Monckton, "whom I described as the only honest and loyal friend the King had." Monckton passed the article on to the King, and it came back to Martin with a message "that he would be glad if I went ahead and published it." Before the article had gone to the printer, though, Martin was asked to hold up publication. "Not too happily, I decided to hold up the article for a week. Then came 'a blow with a Blunt instrument,' as jesters said at the time, and my article died a natural death."

Another editor had been having a similarly frustrating experience. Claud Cockburn's *The Week* had been founded to provide subscribers with stories that did not ordinarily appear in the press—inside information, rumour, gossip, scandal—and with their help had become, to quote Cockburn's own enthusiastic but justified verdict in his autobiography, "one of the half-dozen British publications most often quoted in the press of the entire world"—read avidly in ministries and embassies, banks and business houses, with a mailing list that included "a dozen members of the U.S. Senate, twenty or thirty members of the House of Representatives, about fifty members of the House of Commons and a hundred or so in the House of Lords, King Edward VIII, the secretaries of most of the leading trade unions, Charlie Chaplin and Nizam of Hyderabad." *The Week* had repeatedly infringed the laws of libel and the Official Secrets Act, but it was not worth suing for money, as it had none, and many of those disparaged were reluctant to have the whole matter thrashed out in open court. It collected much of its material from disgruntled civil servants, anxious to expose what they felt to be injustice, and as a consequence, unsavoury episodes that might otherwise have been hushed up received an airing. The King's matter was made to measure for Cockburn—or should have been.

The Week's performance and attitude during the period when the crisis was developing illustrated both the virtues and the vices of the methods that Cockburn employed. He had sensed that something was happening as early as the beginning of October, when the King returned from Balmoral: a social bomb, *The Week* forecast, would be exploded after the coronation by elderly peers disgruntled with the King's "conduct and constitutional practice," and they were hoping to enlist the Archbishop of Canterbury on this side. Cockburn was to pat himself on the back for this forecast, but it was couched in very vague terms.

The Week for October 14 was more specific. It drew attention to the significant absence of any reference in the newspapers to the impending Simpson divorce case, asserting that one respectable newspaper that had planned to splash the story had been deterred from doing so by the threat to cut off one of its most useful sources of tittle-tattle; and it argued that the effects of this unofficial censorship would be disastrous, giving the impression abroad that there was something to hide and thereby encouraging the spread of unfounded allegations.

This line, which *The Week* adhered to throughout, could hardly be criticized. The trouble was that Cockburn remained under the impression that the evidence for the stories in American newspapers about the King's determination to marry Mrs. Simpson was "extremely slender." He put the blame for them on disgruntled courtiers, whose gossip had been taken up and garbled in the American press. Cockburn was hardly the man to be so censorious. The exploitation of gossip had been the making of *The Week*. Rumours, he used to insist, were in the last analysis just as important, just as valid, as "facts."

There was a sense in which he was right—as the November 4 issue showed. Because of the rumour that the King would marry

Mrs. Simpson, "and that the opposition of the Bishops, Nonconformity and the Conservative Party generally will force him from
the throne," insurance premiums against the risk of the coronation
being postponed had risen to the high rate of eight percent. *The
Week* was able to cite this as justification for its warnings about the
futility of trying to keep what was common gossip in the United
States out of the British press. But Cockburn still clung to the belief
that it *was* gossip—that there was no evidence that the King wished
to marry Mrs. Simpson. As for the American press stories that the
royal family had set their face against her, *The Week* brushed them
aside by pointing out that Mrs. Simpson had had lunch with the
Queen at Marlborough House. The Queen had not, in fact, entertained Mrs. Simpson at Marlborough House, or anywhere else. Some
American reporters, it was later disclosed, had thought they had
seen Mrs. Simpson entering, but it had been somebody else. But
The Week, picking up their rumour, had presented it as fact, as it
did with the story, also false, that the Archbishop had called on the
King at Buckingham Palace, presumably to discuss Mrs. Simpson.

By November 25 *The Week* was on the right track again, pointing out how much more there was than met the eye in the *Times'*
editorial on South Wales. This, *The Week* claimed, represented a
clear threat: "It has to be stated that the atmosphere around the
whole controversy has become definitely more thundery over the
week-end." The accuracy of the prediction was quickly confirmed
when Cockburn was visited by a left-wing Labour MP and author,
John Strachey (this was Cockburn's version, not confirmed by
Strachey), who said he had been asked by Lord Louis Mountbatten
to find whether he would be willing to help the King, by giving his
side of the case in *The Week*.

What had happened—according to Mountbatten—was that in
a discussion among a few friends, it had been suggested that an
attempt be made to circulate a sympathetic version of the position
of the King, and *The Week*, with its select influential readership,
seemed to offer a means of doing it. Although Mountbatten was not
the moving spirit, he agreed to his name being used because he
feared that the popular press would make a sensation of the whole
news story unless it was circulated among thinking people in a non-
sensational manner. John Strachey's help was enlisted, through a
mutual friend, to sound out Cockburn.

According to Cockburn's account in his autobiography, Edward

knew *The Week* because Mountbatten had been trying to awaken
the King to the dangers from Nazi Germany and had used information in the newsletter for that purpose. "You are asking me," the
King had replied, "to prefer the information of an obscure political
scandal sheet, run by somebody I never heard of, to that of all my
ministers?" But he had to admit that *The Week's* advance inside information on German moves had been proving more accurate than
the advice of his ministers. He may also have been pleased with the
fact that *The Week* had been on his side—or at least against his
adversaries, the court and the Archbishop, the government and the
Times. He had therefore consented to Cockburn being approached.

The results, Cockburn was warned, might be catastrophic, with
denials by the Cabinet—but that was unlikely to deter him. Nor
was the fact that he was "rather far from being a passionate champion of the monarchy." The opportunity was too good to miss, and
he accepted. It was agreed that a special edition of *The Week*
would be printed, and circulated by hand in case the police tried to
hold it up. On the afternoon of the 26th—the date of Beaverbrook's
return from the United States—Cockburn was told that the material
would be in his hand in a few hours. His staff assembled to handle
it. At eleven P.M. there was a telephone message, announcing a brief
further delay. It was after midnight when a dispatch rider arrived.
Cockburn ran down the office stairs to meet him. "He handed me a
small unaddressed envelope, and I knew from the size of it that
it was going to be no good . . . inside the envelope was a single
sheet of plain paper with this typewritten line. It read, 'The situation has developed too fast.' "

The reason given appears to have been the correct one. By the
time *The Week* (and the *New Statesman*) were ready to publish,
negotiations with the government had progressed too far. In Pritt's
opinion, the reason why the *New Statesman* article did not appear
was that "the oligarchy had heard of the project, and had brought
pressure too strong to be resisted—not on Martin, but on the King."
More probably, the King's advisers felt it would be foolish to irritate the government at a critical stage in the negotiations by what
might appear to be an underhanded appeal to the left.

Apart from all these pressures in and around Fleet Street, the
contents of other American newspapers and magazines was in any
case beginning to make the British press silence farcical. While the
presidential elections were in full swing there had been a lull in

the stream of gossip, but after Roosevelt's crushing victory early in November, the centre of news interest shifted back to London. Although magazines were often rejected or cut, they were still coming unscathed through the mails, and the New York newspapers were still arriving uncensored. *Time* ran current Simpson gags for Broadway: one of the mildest, it said, was, "Have you heard that her husband is writing a play called *The Unimportance of Being Ernest?* In it, the hero cries, 'My only regret is that I have but one wife to lay down for my King.' " Nor was it only the gutter press that concerned itself with the relationship between the King and Mrs. Simpson. After the divorce case, even the *New York Times* discussed the implications and criticized the British press for its continued silence. In her monograph *American Public Opinion and the Windsors*, Stella Sutherland could name only one American newspaper that refused to mention the story: the Lancaster (Ohio) *Eagle-Gazette*. Walter Winchell also declined to mention it on the radio. Otherwise, *The New Yorker's* verdict stands: "the greatest conglomeration of ensilage ever dumped."

The Crystal Palace burns

By the end of November the tension in and around Fleet Street was formidable. Then, on the last day of the month, the Crystal Palace, a famous South London landmark closely associated with royalty—it had been originally put up in Hyde Park as the showpiece of the Exhibition of 1851, and much admired by Queen Victoria—was burned down. It was later to be regarded as yet another omen, but so far as Fleet Street was concerned, the news came as a relief—at least it *was* news. The next day, Bishop Blunt's words to his diocesan conference came over the tapes—"The leakage," as the Archbishop of Canterbury described it, "which at last burst the dam."

There was only a trickle, at first. The press silence had been kept for so long that editors were inhibited when the time came to break it. But later in the day the tapes carried the text of a long quotation from an editorial that the *Yorkshire Post* was to print the following morning. After referring to what had been said, the editorial commented:

Dr. Blunt must have had good reason for so pointed a remark. Most people, by this time, are aware that a great deal of rumour regarding the King has been published of late in the more sensational American newspapers. It is proper to treat with contempt mere gossip such as is frequently associated with the names of European royal persons. The Bishop of Bradford would certainly not have condescended to recognize it. But certain statements which have appeared in reputable United States journals, and even, we believe, in some Dominion newspapers, cannot be treated with quite so much indifference. They are too circumstantial and have plainly a foundation in fact.

Arriving in the *Times* office after dinner, Geoffrey Dawson found the text of the *Yorkshire Post* editorial, and soon comments began to come in from other northern newspapers. It happened that some of the editors of northern papers had conferred together shortly before, coming to the conclusion that the press silence could not last much longer. When the excuse came to break it, they were ready. Dawson was not. Three weeks before he had confided to his diary his plan that the story should first appear in the *Times* and had prepared an article on that assumption. But because of the King's visits to the fleet and to South Wales, and also in deference to Baldwin's wishes, he had held back. Now his nerve failed him.

"I had always felt very strongly that we must be the first to speak," he wrote in his diary. "The rest of the press had quite openly been looking to us for a lead. And now the floodgates had unquestionably been opened . . . the problem, so far as the *Times* was concerned, was whether to begin to-night or to leave it till to-morrow." Previously the other editors had come to him. Now Dawson sought guidance from them. Gwynne of the *Morning Post* had gone to bed, giving instructions that nothing was to be published. Camrose of the *Telegraph* told Dawson he was reluctant even to report Blunt's address. Dawson decided the *Times* must print the address—"It was quite impossible in my opinion to withhold publication of a pronouncement which would certainly become historic" —but he decided to refrain from comment: "Anything else would look too like collusion."

He could not, however, resist one final piece of intimidation in code. In the *Times* the next morning, a leading article was devoted to the Duke of York, then on a visit to Scotland. "That loyalty," it ran, "which has always been part of the fiercest pride of Scotland, and which overflows so spontaneously from the Sovereign to all his kin, is combined with a special affection for the Prince in whose posterity another race of Scottish descent may someday be called to the Imperial Throne." It went on to refer to the royal regalia in Edinburgh—castle, crown, sceptre and sword of state—before concluding:

This visit of the Heir Presumptive to the great fortress that now stands aloft as a symbol of indissoluble union, instead of an object of endless border strife, encourages the speculation whether a time may not some day come when these historic "Honours" may be used again, with the free consent of the Scots, in the crowning of a King of Scotland on the Stone of Destiny.

But the time for such subtleties was past. In histories of the period it was to be the *Yorkshire Post*, not the *Times*, that occupied the niche reserved for the paper that broke the news. Ironically, its editor had called in to see Dawson earlier in the week, and in his diary, Dawson—with the mildly patronizing air he tended to adopt toward fellow editors—described how he had "brought him up to date." Mann, he thought—although rather worried about the affairs of his own paper—was "perfectly sound." Now it was Mann, not Dawson, who had given the signal for the last act to begin.

NINE DAYS' WONDER

THURSDAY, DECEMBER 3

The King awaited Thursday morning's papers with trepidation. Wednesday's comment in the northern papers had been guarded. No comment had appeared in the London dailies, and the early editions of Wednesday's evening papers were also cautious. But in their later editions, something of the prevailing unease crept through, with the news of a heavy fall of prices on the Stock Exchange—it was the worst day's trading of the year. The restraint obviously could not last, and during the afternoon Beaverbrook rang to warn the King that the last vestiges of the gentlemen's agreement were "about to go with a whoop."

What—Edward wondered—would Geoffrey Dawson's "fluent and pitiless pen" concoct? So worried was he at the prospect that he asked Baldwin to try to find out what Dawson was going to say, and if necessary to stop him. Baldwin, Dawson noted in his memorandum, rang twice during the evening ("the only time, I think, that I ever heard his own voice on the telephone"), first to say that he had tried to persuade the King—without success—that he had no power to censor the *Times*, then to report that the King would be satisfied if the leading article were read over to him. Would Dawson mind letting this be done, for the sake of peace? Eventually Dawson sent the editorial around to Downing Street, but by that time it was late, and he heard no more about it.

The King's fears were groundless. The *Times* took the line that the institution of the monarchy was more important than the individual, and made clear that if any constitutional contest arose, it would be found on the government's side. But it made no direct reference to what the crisis was about, except to say that the American press had "gone to the length of predicting a marriage incompatible with the throne"—and, worse, had claimed that Queen Mary approved of it. The editorial's main purpose was to express concern at the effect of such scandal-mongering on the monarchy, and Runciman wrote to Dawson to congratulate him on an editorial "perfect in argument, temper and historical sense"—an indication that the government was pleased, too, that the temperature had been kept down.

The other quality papers, the *Telegraph* and the *Morning Post,* were similarly restrained.

So were the popular newspapers. The *Express* was now boasting that during the month of November its circulation had reached just under 2,200,000—the biggest, it claimed, in the world. But as if determined to show that this commercial triumph had not been won by any lowering of standards, it contented itself with a modest reference to a constitutional crisis that had arisen because the King wanted to make a marriage of which the Cabinet disapproved. It did not mention Mrs. Simpson by name and made no attempt to editorialize. The *Mail,* too, emphasized the constitutional-crisis aspect and did not introduce its readers to Mrs. Simpson. The *Mirror,* however, was unable to resist the temptation to secure a scoop. Priding itself on its outspokenness, it had chafed under the gentlemen's agreement. Now it decided to bring Mrs. Simpson out into the open.

But there was a snag. The system of staggered edition times in Fleet Street—the first editions had to be printed early in the evening, to enable the Scots and the Irish to have their newspapers with their breakfast—had led to the growth of a system whereby each editor was supplied every evening with the early editions of every other newspaper, so that what might be one paper's scoop for Edinburgh readers would be "lifted" by rivals in time for their London editions. To avoid this risk, the *Mirror* in its early editions on this Thursday did no more than hint at the grave issues, but in its late editions, for London consumption, it revealed the facts, together with a portrait of Mrs. Simpson.

Hugh Cudlipp, the editor of the *Mirror,* was to be understandably annoyed when, years later, he read in *A King's Story* that Edward had commiserated with Wallis because "the world can hold few worse shocks for a sensitive woman than to come without warning upon her own grossly magnified countenance upon the front page of a sensational newspaper." The "grossly magnified countenance," Cudlipp tartly pointed out, was in fact a studio portrait "posed by the lady herself and taken by a photographer of her own choosing."

The *News Chronicle,* though it did not carry a picture of Mrs. Simpson, named her, and it also brought up the idea of a special marriage. The King, it suggested, might marry Mrs. Simpson in his capacity as Duke of Cornwall, and "his wife's position would then be that of King's Consort, not that of Queen of England." In his diary, Dawson singled the proposal out as "particularly mischievous"—his favourite term for ideas that ran counter to his own—but otherwise there was little in the popular press to which even he could have taken exception, and the line taken by the Labour *Daily Herald* was very much to his, and the government's, satisfaction. It carried no editorial comment, but Harold Laski's feature article, setting out the constitutional issues, concluded that the King must take the advice of his ministers: "Nothing save the formation of a new Government able to secure a majority in the House of Commons can justify the King in refusing to do what his ministers advise him to do."

The reason why the *Herald* took Baldwin's side was to be the subject of much speculation. In *The Long Week-End* Hodge and Graves attributed the decision to commercial promptings: its readers, particularly in the north, were assumed to be jealous guardians of the Nonconformist Conscience and would be "shocked at the idea that the King proposed to marry not only a commoner, but also a foreigner and a divorced woman." But years later, Julius Salter Elias explained that it was his decision. Ordinarily he was content to run the commercial side of the paper, leaving policy to Bevin, Attlee and the editor—Francis Williams. On this occasion, according to his biographer R.J. Minney, Elias decided to intervene. His personal feelings were mixed: "His deep and innate sense of loyalty made him inclined to support the King, but his own feelings on divorce and on the sanctity of marriage were shared, he felt sure, by large numbers of people who had not yet had an opportunity to express themselves. They would be outraged if the King, to whom the entire nation had to look up, married a woman who had twice been through the divorce courts." Elias therefore decided to oppose the King's wishes and informed the other directors, including the representatives of the Labour Party and the Trade Unions, of his decision.

Beaverbrook was to tell a different story. On Thursday, by his account, he and Churchill went to see Elias. "He was personally favourable and gave us reason to hope that he would support the King. But his Labour Party colleagues who dictated policy overruled Mr. Elias and supported the abdication." Elias appears to have had one overriding consideration. Newspaper proprietors of his standing had usually in the recent past received titles, and he had done much to earn one by his generosity. He had undertaken to do all the printing for the King George's jubilee trust fund, and had given back the profits, amounting to over one hundred thousand pounds, to the fund; and he had published volumes like *His Majesty's Speeches*, which had come out in 1935. It would be a shame if an unguarded decision should spoil his chances. At the time when Beaverbrook and Churchill came to see him, it may have looked to him as if their cause was likely to prove successful. Later, when it was clear their cause was not going to succeed, it became desirable to indicate that he had been for Baldwin all along. In any case, whatever his views, it is clear that Bevin, Attlee and Francis Williams had already agreed on the paper's line, and the *Times*—not ordinarily given even to naming other newspapers, let alone praising them—signified its approval of the *Herald*'s "admirable words."

Although the rest of the mass-circulation dailies now ranged themselves on the King's side, they obviously found a difficulty in deciding quite what line to take, for a reason that was to become clear later. The King himself had rejected Beaverbrook's appeal to be allowed to strike back vigorously against the government. His main desire at this period, by his own account, was to "dampen the uproar," to avoid splitting the nation, and to protect Wallis from sensationalism. But there was an additional complication. Although the popular papers were on his side, they were not on Wallis'. Their aim was to keep him on the throne. If he insisted on marrying her, they would have to put up with her, but they would much rather she got out. And now, she did get out—of the country, at least. They assumed that this was the beginning of the end of the crisis. They were right—but for the wrong reasons.

By her own account, Wallis had wanted to leave the country from the moment, over a fortnight before, that she had seen the Hardinge letter, which had advocated that she should. She let herself be persuaded to stay because she failed to understand the constitutional position of the monarchy: "The apparent deference to his every wish, the adulation of the populace, the universal desire even of the most exalted of his subjects to be accorded marks of his esteem—all this had persuaded me to take literally the ancient maxim that 'the King can do no wrong.'" And the King—she added rather pointedly in her autobiography—"did nothing to disabuse me of these misconceptions." It seems unlikely that it would have made any difference to the ultimate result if he had disabused her, and if she had left there and then. But now, her departure meant that he lacked her presence when he most needed it—which fatally weakened his resolution. It also meant that his supporters, hoping to save him from himself, pursued, without telling him, their own project, to persuade Wallis to give him up—wasting their time and energy on it, and, for the last time, helping to make Baldwin's task easier than it would otherwise have been.

The conspirators

Events delivered Wallis into the hands of "the conspirators"—a term by which Edward was later to describe them, without rancour. As soon as she heard the press silence was to break, she again said that she must leave the country, and this time, Edward did not oppose her wishes. It was arranged that she should go to stay with her old friends from her China days, the Rogerses, at their villa near Cannes, and for her escort, Edward picked on his lord in waiting, Peregrine Brownlow—a near contemporary and an old friend, one of the Fort circle. What Edward did not know was that "Perry" was also in Beaverbrook's confidence. The evening before Beaverbrook had entertained him at dinner, along with Walter Monckton, Esmond Harmsworth, and George Allen (the King's solicitor), to try to persuade him to use his influence on Wallis to leave. Now, to his astonishment, the King himself was asking him to leave with her.

The conspiracy had been organized by Beaverbrook in the days at the end of November, while the King was waiting for news of the Dominions' reactions to the morganatic-marriage proposal. It was essential, Beaverbrook felt, to gain supporters for the King's cause— something that Edward had so far conspicuously failed to do himself. Beaverbrook did not share Edward's illusions about winning over the younger members of the government, or Labour MPs. But there were still the Liberals to be accounted for, and Beaverbrook determined to try to enlist them.

Since the rise of the Labour Party in the 1920s, the Liberals had declined catastrophically in numbers and in influence, and they were too rent by internal dissensions for much confidence to be placed in their potential strength as allies. Certainly no support could be expected from the Simonites, now Tories in all but name. But though there were only twenty Opposition Liberal MPs in the

House of Commons, at least they were a nucleus around which a party of King's friends might be constructed, and they were led by Archibald Sinclair—"universally respected for his high gifts of mind and character," as Beaverbrook knew. He had a host of friends, "and, what was more important, he had no enemies."

That Sinclair had no enemies was indeed significant but it ought to have warned, rather than encouraged, Beaverbrook. Sinclair had no enemies because he was essentially a man of the Establishment: Eton, Royal Military College Sandhurst, a Guards officer in the First World War, Lord Lieutenant of Caithness. He had become leader of the Liberal Party only because Herbert Samuel had lost his seat at the 1935 general election, and although, as "Watchman" noted, he could be "so furiously and attractively eloquent" that he had worried some of the leaders of the other parties, his charm and eloquence were Sinclair's only real political assets. He had little political dynamic, and there is no evidence to substantiate Beaverbrook's claim that if he had consented to lead an all-party government, he would have commanded wide support. In any case, as Beaverbrook soon found, there was never the slightest chance of obtaining his consent: "Sir Archibald Sinclair had a strong bias towards the Nonconformist Conscience and he, like Mr. Attlee, had joined the 'no marriage' front." So had Samuel. His memoirs revealed his attitude: "There were no two opinions as to the injury to the public interest of the marriage that was contemplated."

The other Liberal alternative was Lloyd George. Such was the power of his name and his past record that during the 1920s it had been difficult to believe he could be kept out of office indefinitely, even though his party was disintegrating. But during the second Labour government, Lloyd George's political manœuvres—flirting on the one hand with Churchill, on the other hand with Ramsay MacDonald—proved too much for his party followers, and he ended up without any, except his own family. The Simonites went one way, and the Samuelites another, leaving Lloyd George with a family group of four MPs. Nevertheless it could have been argued that he alone had more potential influence than the entire Liberal rump under Sinclair. In spite of misgivings about him, he would certainly have been included in the national government when it was formed had he not been ill, and in 1936 his views still commanded attention—though not always respect: when he paid a visit to Germany, the adulatory article he wrote about Hitler for the *Daily Express* had not enhanced his reputation.

Lloyd George would have been delighted to join, preferably to lead, a party of King's men. He had felt Edward to be in a sense his protégé, having been in part responsible for the idea of the world tours, and in any case the conflict offered the hope of a political comeback. But for the second time in his career, poor health removed him from the scene at the critical time. When the crisis arose, he was in the West Indies—escaping, as Beaverbrook had wanted to do, from the November London fog.

Lloyd George did not know of the impending constitutional crisis until it was too late—December 3. He had no doubt Edward should be supported: "A nation has a right to choose its Queen, but the King also has a right to choose his own wife: if Baldwin is against them, I am against Baldwin." And he instructed his son and daughter, both MPs, to be against Baldwin too. But, just as he was preparing to return and throw himself into the struggle, he was told that it was over. In a letter a few weeks later, Geoffrey Dawson was to express the opinion that providence had undoubtedly watched over Britain, "most notably in the present case by deciding that Lloyd George should have sailed for the West Indies." According to von Ribbentrop, Churchill was to claim that "they would not have been able to depose Edward VIII had Lloyd George not been abroad. I alone was too weak." The two men together would have been a formidable proposition.

In desperation, Beaverbrook even turned to Aneurin Bevan. He had adopted Bevan as a political protégé in spite of their divergent political views—or because of them: Beaverbrook liked nothing better than to attract into his company and his newspapers young men of strong left-wing views—Percy Cudlipp, Michael Foot, Tom Driberg, and many more. And where Attlee had been insisting that a constitutional king must accept the advice of his Cabinet, the real point, Bevan insisted (according to Michael Foot, his biographer), was whether the Cabinet had given the right advice.

When his point of view became known, Bevan received a message inviting him to go around for consultations to Stornoway House, Beaverbrook's London home. There he was introduced to an equerry, "a slight little figure in satin breeches with a toy sword at his side," and asked what the reaction of the Parliamentary Labour Party would be if His Majesty went ahead and married Mrs. Simpson. Bevan professed neutrality, but suggested that the best way to find out would be to ask himself what would be the reaction of "a typical middle-class woman in Surbiton." Bevan was then taken upstairs to find "a single figure walking up and down under a brilliantly lit candelabra—tears streaming down his cheeks into his whisky—Winston Churchill." "I never thought the time had come when a Churchill must desert his king," Winston Churchill said. "Oh, it is only the second occasion in history," Bevan answered —tactlessly recalling "the far-off day when the great Duke of Marlborough had marched out of London at the head of King James' troops and returned at the head of King William's."

Winston Churchill

Of the men brought into the conspiracy, Churchill was undoubtedly the most formidable. With the exception of Lloyd George, he had had the longest and most eventful political record of any British politician of the era. Yet as the record stood at that time, there could have been no more unfortunate choice as the King's last champion—unfortunate both for the King and for Churchill himself.

His career had had some curious similarities with that of his father, Lord Randolph Churchill. Randolph's brilliance as a young man had led to a general expectation that he would become a Conservative Prime Minister, but he had overplayed his strong hand. He had resigned once too often, hoping to get his way. He had not got his way, and disappointment and illness had removed him from the political stage. He might have been better off, he sometimes thought, in the Liberal Party, and his son had not been long in Parliament as a Conservative when he did what his father had only contemplated and crossed to the more congenial Liberal benches. His move brought him ministerial posts before and during the war, but it also brought him the hatred of Conservatives. Thereafter they had not trusted him.

After the collapse of the Lloyd George coalition, Churchill had eventually returned to the Conservative Party, and Baldwin, feeling it was safer to have him as a colleague than a critic, made him Chancellor of the Exchequer in 1924. For a time, his career looked settled. But during the second Labour government of 1929 to 1931, Churchill began to show signs, as the older Conservatives had warned that he would, of "re-ratting"—as one of them called it.

Labour's victory had left the Conservatives with two choices. They could assume, as most did, that the Labour government would collapse from its own incompetence, and in the meantime they could concentrate on trying to rebuild Conservative morale. Or they could argue, as Churchill did, that the Socialists were too dangerous to leave in office. Taken together, Conservatives and Liberals held a majority in the Commons. Churchill wanted to get together again with Lloyd George to throw the Socialists out as soon as possible. He was not alone in this opinion. Austen Chamberlain shared it. But the majority of the Conservative Party wished no further truck with Lloyd George. That Churchill should be flirting with him was regarded as yet another proof of his political irresponsibility. "It would be an immense accession of strength to us," Neville Chamberlain told Amery, "to get rid of Winston."

But it was to be Churchill who broke with his colleagues—over India. He was an irrational but fervent imperialist, and although he did not dispute the need for a greater measure of Indian self-government, he thought it was madness to let it appear to have been won by the campaign of Mahatma Gandhi. Churchill could not reconcile the weird, loin-clothed figure of Gandhi with his romantic notions about India, and when he heard that a conference was to be held, with Gandhi, "lately released from commodious internment," as the central figure, he could bear it no longer. "On the release of Mr. Gandhi in order that he might become the envoy of nationalist India to the conference, I reached the breaking-point in my relations with Mr. Baldwin . . . I felt sure we should lose India in the final result and that measureless disasters would come upon the Indian peoples. Therefore after a while I resigned from the Shadow Cabinet on this issue." This was in January 1931. In his letter to Baldwin, he said that he would of course continue to oppose the Socialists in the House of Commons and in the next general election, and Baldwin, he found, "seemed quite content with these developments." Well he might be—he had at last got rid of a man whom he, and most of his colleagues, now felt was an encumbrance to the party.

For many of his admirers, Churchill's decision to leave the shadow cabinet was a grievous mistake. Duff Cooper, for one, although he disagreed with Churchill on India, regarded it as "the most unfortunate event that occurred between the two wars." Churchill's resignation on the issue simply lent justification to the

mistrust Baldwin felt for him, and it left him out of the national
government. Young once asked Baldwin whether it would not have
been safer in the thirties, as in the twenties, to have had Churchill
inside the government. Baldwin replied that Churchill's attitude to
India made it impossible: "He had gone about threatening to smash
the Government on India; and I did not mean to be smashed."

Soon, Churchill was to give Baldwin grave reasons for resentment. Even before 1933, Churchill had been uttering warnings of
what was likely to happen if the Nazis came into power, and when
Germany began to rearm, his forebodings were shown to have been
justified. No government likes to be reminded "I told you so," particularly if, for electoral reasons, it still does not wish the warning
to be heard. "As surely as Germany acquires full military equality
with her neighbours," Churchill told the Commons, "while her own
grievances are still unredressed, and while she is in the temper
which we have unhappily seen, so surely shall we see ourselves
within a measurable distance of the renewal of European war." The
reaction, Churchill was later to recall in *The Gathering Storm,* was
depressing. "When one considers that the facts were hardly in dispute, the actions of a responsible government of respectable men and
the public opinion which so eloquently supported them are scarcely
comprehensible. It was like being smothered by a feather bed. I
remember particularly the look of pain and aversion which I saw on
the faces of members in all parts of the House when I said, 'Thank
God for the French army.'" "Pain and aversion" accurately expressed
the general feeling: Churchill had become the best-hated man in
British politics. Such was the feeling against him that he even began
to encounter hostility on a social level. Wallis first met him at a party
given in honour of the American journalist H.R. Knickerbocker, who
had been touring Europe. Churchill exploded at Knickerbocker's
opinions, effectively demolishing them, and then told Wallis that he
didn't get a chance to do that sort of thing very often since his
break with the Tory leadership: "As a matter of fact, this is the
first time Clemmie and I have been invited out this year."

The course of events since the Baldwin government's return
to office in 1935 had done nothing to make Churchill any less unpopular. On the contrary, the vindication of his prophecies by the
German re-occupation of the Rhineland only made ministers more
angry with him, and the appointment of Inskip as Minister for the
Co-ordination of Defence was about as effective a way of showing

their irritation as they could have found. The less charitable of them were also delighted when, by September, the Churchill name was brought into derision in the foreign press. The newspapers reported that Churchill's son Randolph, then twenty-five years old, had had to be dispatched in pursuit of his sister, because she was eloping with the comedian Vic Oliver. She had taken the *Bremen* to New York. Randolph, the papers claimed, had followed on the *Queen Mary*, which was faster, to try to bring her back to her senses. It was the kind of story that ordinarily might have brought a parent sympathy, but to some of his enemies it gave only malicious pleasure.

Still, Churchill was not the kind of man to be thrown out of his political stride by such episodes, and Baldwin—who had had to listen to himself being described by Churchill in the Commons as "decided only to be undecided, resolved to be irresolute, solid for fluidity, all-powerful to be impotent," and had been compelled to realize that many Conservatives, even some of those who feared and disliked Churchill, agreed with him—knew that Churchill was potentially his most dangerous adversary. The news that he had been enlisted into the King's camp was consequently a good reason for expediting the processes which were already leading inexorably to abdication.

In fact—though in all probability Baldwin did not know it—Churchill had not been formally enlisted. According to Beaverbrook he had been "specifically and positively banned by Baldwin from audience of the King," but this is not confirmed by his own account, which claimed that although he had been aware all summer of what was happening, he had made no attempt to intervene, feeling that the initiative should come from the King. Again, nothing could better illustrate the King's fatalism than his failure to consult the two men—Lloyd George and Churchill—who, in spite of their unhappy political records, at least were public figures. If they had both come out decisively in the King's favour, the impact could have been considerable, particularly as their views would have been given extensive publicity in the Beaverbrook and Rothermere papers. As things were, Churchill heard what was happening only at second hand, through Beaverbrook. Though he felt bound to place his loyalty to the King "upon the highest plane," he was unable to give his views to Edward in person.

Voilà la dame!

For a brief moment on November 30, by Beaverbrook's account the conspirators were given a gleam of hope. Monckton came to report that he had received fresh instructions from the King: his plea for formal advice on his marriage from the Cabinet and the Dominions was to be withdrawn. But this time Baldwin was in no mood to listen. Did the request imply, he asked, that the marriage was to be abandoned? Monckton did not know, and Baldwin ignored the request. Members of his Cabinet had already voiced their suspicions that the King might pretend to back out of the marriage only to go through with it later, and Baldwin was not prepared to take the risk—particularly as he must have known of the "conspiracy" from Hoare, and probably from other sources.

But now the conspirators had the opportunity they had been hoping for: Wallis was in their hands. They were not very happy, though, at the idea of her going to France. Their plan had been to keep her in England, so that they could work on her—and so that there would be no risk of the King leaving the country to follow her, which they realized would be fatal. In the car, on their way to the coast, Brownlow begged Wallis to change her mind and to go to stay with friends in Lincolnshire instead. But she could not bring herself to agree, and later on the Thursday evening, they caught the cross-Channel boat at Newhaven, as planned.

Again, by this time it was too late for her decision to make any difference—except to the timing of Edward's final capitulation. But their voyage through France did add something to the gaiety of nations. The Duchess' account of the drive down through France remains grimly hilarious. The aim had been to keep her destination secret, but if she had been deliberately leaving clues, she could hardly have made their journey more conspicuous. They travelled as "Mr. and Mrs. Harris"—but they had forgotten to change the name on her car's papers, so her identity was unmasked immediately when they landed at Dieppe. At Rouen, the detective who was with them gratuitously drew attention to their departure by knocking a camera out of a girl's hands. They went by a roundabout route, but Wallis could not resist telephoning the Fort at their break for lunch and she had to shout, as the connection was so poor. She had written down what she wanted to say—urging the King on no account to do anything precipitately—and she left the notes in the telephone booth. (The proprietor later gave them to Harold Nicolson, when he happened to pass that way, and he returned them to their author.)

At Blois, where they stayed the night, the reporters caught up with them, and though Wallis and Brownlow shook them off by getting up in the small hours, they soon caught up again. The weather was dreadful, and to add to the discomfort, a flask of whiskey which Brownlow had brought along, for fortification against the cold, broke in his pocket. The contents seeped down through his clothes onto the car upholstery, and the bouquet pervaded the interior. They were recognized at Lyon, where a man shouted, "*Voilà la dame!*" And by the time they had lunch at the famous Pyramide restaurant in Vienne, a concourse of reporters was with them, grateful for what would clearly be an unprecedented expense-account meal.

Again, the fugitives managed to elude their pursuers by climbing out of a small back window, but they could have saved themselves the trouble. Their destination had been guessed, and when they arrived early on the morning of December 6, Wallis had to crouch under a rug on the floor to keep out of sight of the reporters and photographers assembled around the villa gates.

Now that Wallis was safely out of the way, the conspirators decided, the line to take with the King would be to urge the need for patience. He must make no hasty decision—and this, of her own accord, Wallis was also urging, whenever communication by telephone proved possible. Their line with *her* would be that she should use all her influence to persuade the King to renounce her until after the coronation. By that time, the people of Britain might have come around to accepting the match—or (though naturally this was not stated) the King's affections might have been transferred elsewhere. Either way, the King would be kept on his throne, and Baldwin humiliated.

This was to become the line of the Beaverbrook-Rothermere newspapers, and of the *News Chronicle*. They did their best to present the crisis as if it were something that could be resolved with a little patience. The word "abdication" was avoided, wherever possible. The Paris *Figaro* claimed perceptively on the Friday morning that abdication was certain but few people reading the English dailies would have realized, at this stage, that it was more than a remote possiblity. The popular papers avoided it because they did not want people to get the idea it was even being considered. The quality papers avoided it because they did not wish to be accused of seeking to push the King into it. The public did not realize how far the King had committed himself to go, and Beaverbrook was now engaged, with enormous relish, in deploying his forces so that the King would be heartened by the signs of support for his cause, and would be encouraged to turn and fight—no matter what he might have told Baldwin.

The talking mongoose

Edward later came to think that Wallis' decision to leave the country was the turning point: in agreeing that she should go, he believed, "I must have unconsciously made up my mind that the struggle to save my Throne was hopeless." It would be closer to the truth to say that her departure confirmed his defeat. He had not lost all hope, but she had by this time become so essential to him that he was incapable of sustaining the campaign without her. The issue had already been settled. All her departure did was to confuse it for a while, because it gave Beaverbrook and the other conspirators grounds for hope.

But at the time, the King was far from discouraged. Before she left, Wallis had put an idea into his head. Now that the story had come out in part, why not spell it out in detail—tell the whole of it, from their point of view, in a broadcast to the nation? His father had made excellent use of the radio in his Christmas messages. So had Roosevelt with his fireside chats. Impressed, he began to write a draft script even before Wallis left, and after her departure it began to be his preoccupation. He would tell the nation that *he* would never make a marriage of royal convenience. It had taken him a long time to find a woman whom he wished to make his wife, but now that he had, he was determined to marry her—though it was not necessary she should become Queen.

Edward knew the constitutional proprieties involved. He could not broadcast without the government's consent. There was also a technical problem: the broadcast ought to be made, for maximum effect, from Windsor Castle. This, at least, could be fixed direct with the British Broadcasting Corporation, and on Thursday Godfrey Thomas put through a call to the director-general, Sir John Reith.

Reith was one of the most remarkable men in public life between the wars. A deeply religious Scot in the John Knox image, he had been put in charge of the British Broadcasting Corporation when it had been given its monopoly in the twenties, and he had moulded it into what he hoped was a great educative force, with himself as headmaster and the listening public as pupils. It was not fully realized then, though it was beginning to be suspected, how much potential power the BBC wielded. Under Reith it became massively single-minded, as a description of it given by Stuart Hood—who rose in it to the position of third in the corporation hierarchy before leaving in 1964—was later to reveal. Just as you can spot a Communist or ex-Communist, Hood claimed, by the way he talks about "the Party," anybody who referred to the BBC as "the Corporation" was, or had been, its servant: "What the verbal habit reflects is the same in both cases: the sense of belonging to a closed community; of having received certain truths about the nature of politics or of broadcasting; of subscribing to the same ethos; of sharing with all other members certain attitudes of mind." And like the Communist Party, Hood went on, the BBC was run on a system of democratic centralism. "There is a line formulated at high level and passed down."

Reith's political opinions were far removed from Stalin's, but his will was as rigorously enforced. His aim, he stated, was that the BBC should provide "all that is best in every department of human knowledge, endeavour and advancement." Entertainment was not on his list of priorities. A characteristic rule, dating from the BBC's earliest days, was that the announcers reading the evening news should wear evening dress. Such was the insistence on keeping the Sabbath holy that no dance music was played on Sunday—only music of a Palm Court variety, along with church services, organ music, classical music, chamber music, and the occasional uplifting talk, usually on some religious topic (though in abdication-crisis week Alastair Cooke was actually billed to discuss the current cinema). As Low satirized in a cartoon of the period, doubts had even been expressed whether gardening talks should be permitted on Sunday. And on divorce, Reith's attitude was notoriously stern. One of the themes of A.P. Herbert's *Holy Deadlock* had been the need of the wife who was divorcing her husband to keep her lover's name out of the proceedings, because he worked for the BBC. Had he been cited as co-respondent, he would have been fired.

Reith, then, was not a man to whom the King could have

turned in any confidence of winning his sympathy. Edward had not made real contact with Reith before—though they had some points in common. Both craved occupations that kept their talents at full stretch (Reith was to complain in a broadcast years later that his own never had been, after he left the BBC). Edward, too, enjoyed broadcasting, and Reith would have been delighted to cater to his interest in the new medium. They had once met, and Edward remembered the meeting, because Reith had told him an odd fact that stuck in his mind—that the consumption of water fell when there was something especially interesting being broadcast, but that immediately after it there would be a sudden, sometimes alarming, peak load. But the only indication that Reith recalled in his autobiography of the King's interest in broadcasting was the occasion when the London representative of the National Broadcasting Company of America had rung up from Fort Belvedere to say the King would like the BBC dance orchestra to play a certain tune. Henry Hall had duly played it and had received a royal message of thanks at the end of the programme.

The two men had something else in common: Reith cared as little for the Establishment as the King did. As Hood recalled, he fought resolutely for the independence of the corporation, being courageous enough in 1926 to insist—against the wishes of Churchill, Home Secretary at the time—that the General Strike should be reported fairly, with the views of both sides given. He also fought against the government's desire to prevent the BBC from broadcasting topical controversy. Reith, however, resisted governments and politicians not because he had any rebel leanings, but because he suspected them of being all too frequently swayed by party or personal considerations. He regarded his position as roughly equivalent to that of a judge, set up to enforce standards applying to all, ministers and governed, alike.

However much he disliked government intervention, though, Reith would have been poorly placed to defy it at this time even if he had wished to. The BBC was in serious trouble. It had managed to make itself unpopular not only with those who objected to Reith's relentless nannying, but with influential political and commercial interests who were beginning to speculate how they could deprive Reith of his most precious possession: the BBC's monopoly of sound broadcasting.

It was not an absolute monopoly, because of the existence on the

Continent of Radio Luxemburg, which beamed lucrative sponsored programmes to Britain—they were mainly of dance music, with a little light comedy, but they attracted big audiences away from the BBC. This infuriated Reith, particularly on Sundays. He had once persuaded the International Broadcasting Union to pass a resolution that the systematic diffusion of programmes intended for listeners in another country, where it had been the object of protest by the broadcasting organization of that country, constituted an "inadmissible act from the point of view of good international relations," and on the basis of that resolution, the Postmaster General had been asked to "interfere with the stations in question." The jamming of Radio Luxemburg, however, proved impracticable.

The success of Radio Luxemburg encouraged the development of a commercial radio lobby. The House of Commons had discussed the BBC's future in April 1936. Many speakers were critical of Reith's dictatorship, but the one who most disturbed Reith was Richard Law, son of the former Prime Minister, who asked whether it was really necessary, in the interest of good, balanced programmes, to have them all put out by the corporation. And to add to Reith's difficulties, the BBC had then become involved in a ludicrous court affair. It was particularly important that the corporation should preserve its dignified image, but here was a case that gave the popular newspapers a chance they had not had since the affair of the rector of Stiffkey. They seized on it with delight, all the greater because they still regarded broadcasting with suspicion, as an interloper; and it became known as "the case of the talking mongoose."

At this time, there was considerable interest in the examination of psychic phenomena, and probably the best-known investigator—though doubts were later to be thrown on his integrity—was Harry Price. He used to be called upon to investigate hauntings, or poltergeists, and one of his cases concerned a house in the Isle of Man where it had been reported that a mongoose had learned—like Saki's cat Tobermory—to talk. Price went to have a look, along with another investigator, R.S. Lambert. The investigators were unable to locate the mongoose, but this did not deter them from publishing a book on the subject, *The Haunting of Cashen's Gap*—their conclusion being that it might be a poltergeist.

Although the talking-mongoose story aroused some interest, it would have been quickly forgotten had it not been for a quarrel that arose between Sir Cecil Levita, a member of the London County

Council, and Lambert. The quarrel had nothing to do with the mongoose. It arose out of the affairs of a film institute in which both men were concerned. Levita, however, suggested that Lambert's credulity about the talking mongoose demonstrated that he was not a fit person to be a director of the film institute. More unwisely, he began to lobby his acquaintances on the BBC to discredit Lambert. This was a serious matter for Lambert, because he was editor of the *Listener*, a BBC publication, and he decided to take legal action.

The BBC, anxious to avoid what they rightly guessed might be undesirable publicity, advised Lambert not to proceed with the case, and when he rejected their advice, he was warned that his position might be prejudiced if he persisted. Lambert persisted. He was awarded seventy-five hundred pounds damages—a very large sum for those days. The BBC, displaying better sense than it had hitherto, did not carry out the implied threat to remove him from his editorship, but the fact that it had been made was enough. MPs, angered, called for an official inquiry, the Government accepted their demand, and a commission was set up in November 1936 to investigate the corporation's internal structure. The inquiry was therefore in progress when the abdication crisis broke. The BBC could hardly expect that its report would be other than critical (critical it duly was, though only mildly), but in the meantime it had every incentive to be on its best behaviour.

Baldwin probably realized this. He knew Reith, and knew how to handle him. As far back as 1924 he had impressed Reith on the occasion of the first party political broadcast at a general election. MacDonald and Asquith had both asked for the broadcast to be relayed from one of their public meetings. Baldwin preferred to come to Reith for advice—which he took: he spoke from a studio. Baldwin does not seem to have worried about what the BBC might do with the Mrs. Simpson story. There was no need. As the *News Chronicle* critic was to complain, when the story broke the BBC handled it gingerly, discussing only the constitutional issues, without mentioning Mrs. Simpson.

Reith, though, was flattered to have a visitor from Buckingham Palace. He was to recall in his autobiography that Thomas' impending arrival "made me do what I had never done in office hours before. I got a whiskey and soda sent up for him; he needed it." Thomas had come to ask if the King could broadcast from Windsor, at short notice. Certainly, Reith replied—if the Prime Minister agreed. Thomas said that would be arranged the following evening, and Reith went ahead with the preparations—to the alarm of Horace Wilson, who heard about them and rang Reith to find out what was happening. Reith was able to reassure him that no broadcast would be made without Baldwin's dispensation.

Reith must have been amused to find that the government was worried, and pleased to be able to show that it could have confidence in him. But the King was not contemplating going on the air without Baldwin's permission. As soon as the draft was completed, he sent for Baldwin and showed it to him. He also asked whether he might consult Winston Churchill about it. The Prime Minister appeared startled, as if, Edward recalled, he was saying to himself, "Damn it, what will this young man be thinking up next?" He agreed, though, to call a Cabinet meeting to discuss the broadcast project, and, he also agreed, though without enthusiasm, to allow the consultation.

"We are the people of England"

Churchill's name was later to become so identified with the abdication that it still comes as a surprise to realize that he had not yet been consulted by the King. He had known Edward as Prince of Wales. There was no reason, at an earlier stage, why he should not have been consulted informally—Churchill, indeed, was later to express regret that they had not talked the subject over. But at this stage, so as not to lend countenance to a charge that he was acting unconstitutionally, Edward felt bound to apply formally to see Churchill, and Baldwin was caught unawares.

The two requests brought a new element into Baldwin's calculations. The King had earlier promised to go, and go quietly. Now, it looked as if he might be reneging on his pledge. What if Mrs. Simpson's departure was only a blind, to give the impression that she was a noble-hearted woman who would not stand in the King's way? What if the move to bring in Churchill was an intimation that a King's party was now covertly being established, with the idea of making a fight of it? Baldwin had to consider what the prospects would be if war were to be declared on him. And the prospects, he must have felt, were not nearly as satisfactory as they had seemed the day before.

Public opinion was now having a chance to display itself, and it was less hostile to the King than the government had expected. It was not yet realized that Edward was contemplating abdication. As the *Times* was later to recall, when the story broke, "scarce one subject in ten thousand could have heard the very word 'abdication' without a sense of incredulity and outrage." The general assumption was that the government—or, more commonly, "they," implying those in authority, whoever they might be—were trying to get rid of the King. When the first letters began coming into newspaper offices in Fleet Street, they were overwhelmingly on Edward's side. Reporters, too, came back with stories of signs of popular feeling in favour of the King—or against his ministers. The United Press, claiming that the British masses, "from the cockney bootblack on Ludgate Hill to the bowler-hatted clerks scurrying along Barrister's Row, stood staunchly with King Edward VIII," suggested that this was not from any sympathy with Mrs. Simpson, but because the masses wanted him to win out over "the grey-beards."

This was precisely what Baldwin had most reason to fear. Not merely could he no longer be sublimely confident of his sure "feel" for public opinion, after the rebuffs it had received in the past twelve months. He also had to reckon with the possiblity that the public might react illogically to the situation and accept the presence of Mrs. Simpson, even if they shared his dislike for the idea, simply to demonstrate their antagonism to the government. Nor was it only uninformed mass opinion, perhaps deceived by the poplar press, that the government had to worry about. There were also a few signs of cracks in what had appeared to be the solid Parliament-Establishment front.

Baldwin had left the King a glimmer of hope when he admitted that the Conservative Party was not unanimously against the morganatic proposal—a "significant reservation," Young thought, "which meant that some elements might hope to form a King's party in the House." They did. On Thursday morning, the Labour MP Josiah Wedgwood—who had been divorced himself—gave notice of a motion he was going to propose:

that in the opinion of this House the Oath of Allegiance which they have already taken to King Edward VIII is unaffected by any form of Coronation ceremony, or by the presence or absence therefrom of any dignitary or personage whatsoever; nor will they substitute any other for the King of England.

The phrasing was designed to encourage people to believe that the crisis had arisen, as rumour had been insinuating, because the Archbishop of Canterbury had said he would refuse to crown the King. And when Churchill got up in the Commons that afternoon, to plead that no irrevocable decision should be taken without the House having a chance to discuss it, he was cheered. Outside Parliament, too, efforts were being made on the King's behalf. Field Marshal Sir Ian Hamilton sought out Baldwin to say that there would be an ex-servicemen's revolution if the King abdicated.

And Baldwin had another reason to regret acceding to the King's request to consult Churchill. Churchill that evening was due to speak at a mass meeting at the Albert Hall in connection with the campaign that, if it got under way, might constitute a serious threat to the government. It was described in some newspapers as being for "the defence of freedom and peace." Churchill described it as "Arms and the Covenant," its aim being to give teeth to the League of Nations, teeth that Britain could provide only by more resolute diplomacy and by rearmament. But what disturbed the government was that it was an all-party affair. As well as Churchill and other Conservatives, the Liberals were billed to be represented on the platform by the party leader, Archibald Sinclair, and by Lady Violet Bonham Carter, Asquith's daughter. And the chairman was to be Sir Walter Citrine.

Citrine might be conservative, by Socialist standards, but the fact that the chairman of the TUC should be willing to appear on the same platform as Churchill was significant. If anything, dislike of Churchill had been stronger among Labour MPs than on the Conservative side. He was remembered as one of the backers of the White Russian counter-revolution, as the chief advocate and exponent of a tough line at the time of the General Strike, as a reactionary Chancellor of the Exchequer, and as a Gandhi-baiter. Citrine himself was to recall, of this period, that Churchill was regarded as "an active Tory politician whom few people in the Labour movement either trusted or admired."

But now, they were to appear together in the Albert Hall. Citrine knew that Churchill had strong feelings about the crisis. They had met for lunch a few days before and, when the subject of Mrs. Simpson came up, Citrine had repeated what he had earlier said to Baldwin, stressing that the trade-union movement would back the government even if it meant the King abdicating. Churchill had replied that he felt it was *his* duty to defend the King, irrespective of what the King might do. "Winston looked grave, and, putting his hands on his breast, said with emotion, 'he feels it here.'"

When Beaverbrook telephoned to deliver the King's request for assistance and to read over the draft of his proposed broadcast, Churchill immediately agreed to co-operate. It was irritating not to be able to get down straightaway to revising the King's speech—a job so much after his own heart—but he was committed to the Albert Hall meeting. Why not, he thought, use the meeting to express his view? On the spur of the moment, he was to recall in *The Gathering Storm*, he reminded the audience:

There is another grave matter which overshadows our minds to-night. In a few minutes we are going to sing *God Save the King*. I shall sing it with more heartfelt fervour than I have ever sung it in my life. I hope and pray that no irrevocable decision will be taken in haste, but that time and public opinion will be allowed to play their part, and that a cherished and unique personality may not be incontinently severed from the people he loves so well. I hope that Parliament will be allowed to discharge its function in these high constitutional questions. I trust that our King may be guided by the opinions that are now for the first time being expressed by the British nation and the British Empire, and that the British people will not in their turn be found wanting in generous consideration for the occupant of the Throne.

In Citrine's autobiography, though, there was to be a very different version of what happened. When Churchill arrived at the Albert Hall, Citrine recalled, he announced that he proposed to bring the matter up. The audience, he asserted, would expect it of him. Citrine replied that the audience would expect nothing of the kind—they had come to hear how to stand up to Hitler, and if Churchill was going to insist on dragging in the King, he would refuse to take the chair. Lady Violet Bonham Carter, in her memoirs, confirmed the Citrine version: Citrine, she recalled, was backed by Sinclair, and Churchill gave way. The audience, however—estimated at from 7,000 to 10,000—gave vent to their feelings in the enthusiasm with which they sang the National Anthem, and responded at the end of it to a call for "Three Cheers for the King."

When Monckton arrived at Fort Belvedere that evening, he too was the bearer of good tidings. The *New Statesman* had appeared with a sympathetic editorial, arguing, "We should have thought it possible, indeed not difficult, so to alter the law that the King's wife should not be Queen of England." More surprisingly a Catholic weekly, the *Tablet,* had urged that a Protestant king's marriage was his own affair, and that though it hoped Edward would change his mind, Parliament had no right to compel him to do so. And crowds outside Buckingham Palace had been singing *God Save the King* and *For He's a Jolly Good Fellow.* According to Edward, "Chesterton's prophetic lines came irresistibly to mind:

> Smile at us, pay us, pass us; but do not quite forget
> For we are the people of England, that never have spoken yet."

Something, Edward believed, was stirring. "There is no want of evidence," he was to claim, "that a multitude of the plain people stood waiting to be rallied to my side."

FRIDAY, DECEMBER 4

It had been arranged that Churchill should visit the King on Friday evening, and that morning Baldwin wished he could have retracted his permission. At the Cabinet meeting he reverted to an old expedient. He had, he admitted, made his first blunder. According to Young he explained to one of his staff that this was "the only way to carry it off—owning up to a mistake." But the mistake could not now be undone.

"Another very trying day," Geoffrey Dawson wrote in his diary. "New efforts in the baser press at a King versus Baldwin issue—pleas for delay, for reference to the people, for a way out which would keep our beloved sovereign." (In his memorandum on the abdication he was to add, "and, it was not obscurely hinted, get rid of a bad Prime Minister.") Already in that morning's *Times*, however, Dawson had launched a counterattack. An editorial dealt with the Mrs. Simpson issue direct—though still cautiously referring to the affair as "such a marriage as the King has been understood to contemplate." The trouble did not lie, the *Times* insisted, "in old-fashioned conventional dislike of the King marrying a commoner, or an American." Nothing could be further from the truth. There were "many daughters of America" whom he might have married with approval and rejoicing. It would have been an innovation, but by no means an unwelcome innovation, in the history of the Royal House, "which is under no obligation in these days to look for a bride in what is described across the Atlantic as some 'hand-picked princess.'" The only objection to "the marriage which rumour has so freely projected" was "that the lady in question has already two former husbands living, from whom in succession she has obtained a divorce, on the last occasion at a recent date and in circumstances which are matters of fairly common knowledge." As for the idea of a marriage that would enable Mrs. Simpson to become the King's wife without becoming Queen, the *Times* dismissed it as a Continental device—adding the ingenious explanation that it had only had to be employed because the Continental monarchs were constitutionally bound to marry within circumscribed family limits, whereas no such restraint lay on an English king.

But as well as the editorial, there was also a commentary by "Our Parliamentary Correspondent," which was the furthest that the *Times'* tradition of anonymity allowed its staff to identify themselves. On this occasion, the protection was useful to Dawson, for "Our Parliamentary Correspondent" that morning was Dawson himself. He was particularly concerned to challenge the implication that the King had intimated his intention of marrying and that his ministers had objected. "A more accurate version, as it will probably be found when the issue is made public—and the importance of clearing it up rapidly by an official statement can hardly be exaggerated —is that the King has expressed his desire to contract such a marriage as would require a special Act of Parliament; that he has himself taken the initiative in asking whether such a measure can be passed; and that Ministers, after full consideration and consultation, have replied that in their opinion it is impossible."

Dawson's aim was clear; he wanted the ministers, and Baldwin in particular, to be exonerated from the charge of interfering with the King's private affairs. But what was interesting was the way in which—in his capacity as "Our Parliamentary Correspondent"—he put on once more the mantle of Delane. He wanted to demonstrate that the *Times* knew what was happening, but he had at all costs to avert suspicion of collusion between the *Times* and the government. He therefore put forward what he knew from Baldwin and others as if it were speculation—well-informed, of course, and almost certainly correct, but still speculative. The course events had taken was related knowledgeably, but always with such cautious phrases as "A retrospect of the past week suggests that . . ." and "The interval, it may be assumed, was occupied by . . ." and even "That there was no material difference in the result of all these inquiries is sufficiently indicated by the belief that . . ." And the injunction "the importance of clearing it up rapidly by an official statement can hardly be exaggerated" was pure Delane: Baldwin was due to make the official statement that afternoon.

But skilful though Dawson's technique was, it would not reach a mass audience as the popular papers were doing. And the trouble was that the popular papers' line sounded so reasonable. Did not everybody—well, almost everybody—want to preserve Edward on the throne? Surely the people ought to be consulted? Why not, then, permit delay?

One reason, the government could have claimed, why there should be no more delay was the effect on the American press, which had bubbled over with mirth at being proved right about the King and Mrs. Simpson. It now devoted more space than ever to what H.L. Mencken that morning described as "the best story since the Resurrection." The American papers had no reason to be sympathetic to Britain in her predicament, and they revelled in such tidbits as the story that a hotelier in Fremont, Ohio, had cabled the King offering him employment if he abdicated ("LIKE YOUR DRIVE STOP COULD USE MAN WITH YOUR INDEPENDENCE STOP JOB AWAITS").

But apart from this humiliation, it was not easy for the government to justify its now obvious desire for Edward to leave quickly, except on the ground that support for the King appeared to be growing. The crowds outside Buckingham Palace, which according to the *News Chronicle* had been small the day before—about forty people had assembled, but had meekly allowed themselves to be moved on by the police—now began to increase. The Associated Press reported sizeable demonstrations, orderly but noisy, parading with banners—one of them, composed of women, chanting, "Flog Baldwin, down with the bishops." And when that afternoon the Archbishop of Canterbury saw the moderator and the secretary of the Free Churches, he was disconcerted to find that though they believed the mass of the people would support the government, they admitted that many, particularly the young, felt strong sympathy with the King. The Archbishop set down their contentions in his diary: "He is doing the honourable thing. He wants to marry the woman he loves. Why shouldn't he? etc." To people like himself, Lang ruefully concluded, who had been involved in the affair for two years, it was hard to grasp the impact of the crisis "on minds wholly unprepared for it and ignorant of all that had led up to it"—an ignorance that correspondence and conversations had revealed to him to be widespread.

The popular newspapers—except the *Herald*—were also now doing what, if Beaverbrook had had his way, they would have begun to do weeks before: they were introducing their readers to Mrs. Simpson, and placing her in a very favourable light. In the *Mail,* for example, Margaret Lane—daughter-in-law of the thriller writer Edgar Wallace and winner, the year before, of the Prix Femina Vie Heureuse—devoted a long article to her, concluding: "a most attractive woman, a vibrant personality," and the *Express* described in detail how she had conquered London as a hostess. If the public could be persuaded that in spite of her two divorces, Mrs. Simpson would make Edward an admirable wife, public opinion might become attracted to the idea of an act enabling her to become the Duchess of Cornwall—or whatever title might be chosen.

There was even a minor setback for the government from the Dominions that day. It was reported that Mackenzie King had defended himself in Ottawa from the charge that Baldwin had acted at the instance of, perhaps on the insistence of, the Dominions—and particularly of Canada, because of Canadian irritation at the Mrs. Simpson stories in the U.S. newspapers. The initiative, Mackenzie King insisted, came not from him, but from London.

Whatever worries Baldwin might have over the course public opinion was taking, there was one place where he could still feel confident: the House of Commons. Any risk that the Labour Opposition might desert him had been removed by the editorial in that morning's *Herald,* which had lined up with him: "Sad as the consequences may be, we cannot see how the Cabinet could have done other than tender the advice which seems to it right." The atmosphere in the House that afternoon might be tense. When MPs bobbed up to catch the Deputy Speaker's eye, he inadvertently named "Mr. Simpson," and although there was a Labour MP of that name, he was not among those wishing to speak. But Baldwin was unruffled. In reply to a question from Attlee, he at last clarified the government's position.

Suggestions had been made, he said, that if the King married, his wife need not be Queen. "These ideas are without foundation. There is no such thing as what is called a morganatic marriage known to our law." If, therefore, the King married, his wife would become Queen, and her children would be in direct succession to the throne. "The only way in which this result could be avoided would be by legislation dealing with a particular case; His Majesty's Government are not prepared to introduce such legislation."

The crucial point in Baldwin's speech, though, was his reference to the Dominions. Their assent was also required, he said, to a morganatic marriage, and "I am satisfied, from inquiries I have made, that this assent would not be forthcoming." When Baldwin sat down, the whole House—according to Dawson—cheered him, "and Winston, who was out for mischief, looked very glum." Relieved of any fear he might have had of a revolt in the Commons, Baldwin could now deal with the King, and he had decided to allow the King no further rope. On arrival at the palace that evening, Edward recalled, he was "brisker" than he had been before. The Cabinet had decided, Baldwin said, that the broadcast project was unacceptable, and the replies from the Dominions were fully confirming his forecast: they were hostile to the morganatic-marriage project.

This Edward already knew. That day he had received from a friend in Reuters its correspondents' dispatches from the Empire capitals, describing public reactions and quoting newspaper editorials. The verdict, though not quite unanimous, was overwhelmingly against the King. As the Melbourne *Argus* put it that morning, however much Edward was admired, he could not dissociate his personal life from his royal responsibilities, because the throne's march "must be continuously on a high level of conduct ever illumined with the burnished light of sacrifice." Not all the editorials were couched in such incandescent prose, but their message was similar.

According to *A King's Story*, it was at this point that Edward finally made up his mind to capitulate. He had placed much reliance on the verdict of the Dominions, and now it had gone against him. The rejection of his planned broadcast, too, would prevent him from putting his case directly before the public. And perhaps—though he did not mention it in *A King's Story*—there was another incentive to end the affair quickly.

According to Young, Baldwin had realized the possibility that as Mrs. Simpson's decree *nisi* would not be made absolute until May, there was always the chance "that some muddle-headed busybody would seek to delay the proceedings by an unjustified intervention." But it did not necessarily have to be a muddle-headed busybody. There were some respectable citizens who felt that the Ipswich divorce had been obtained by collusion and ought to be re-investigated. A young barrister, John Foster—later Sir John Foster, QC— had been briefed before the end of November by a potential intervener, to investigate the possibilities, and the longer the crisis dragged on, the more risk there was of the divorce being challenged.

Edward had understood that it could not be challenged—not, at least, with any hope of impressing the King's Proctor that there was a *prima facie* case for intervention. This also appears to have been the view of the Solicitor General, Sir Terence O'Connor. Esmond

Harmsworth discussed the subject with him on the day the press silence broke and reported O'Connor as saying that "if the King remained on his throne, the King's Proctor or any private complainant would in law find it impossible to raise objections to the divorce case"—because the only person who would be likely to be cited by any intervener would be the King, and in law, the King could not be cited. If Edward were a private individual, though, he could be cited, and this, Beaverbrook thought, was another good reason why he should at all costs cling to his throne. But whether by accident or design, the King appears to have been advised at this time that an intervention was likely on other grounds, even if he remained King. Nothing could have been better calculated to shake his confidence. Again, his too ready assumption that "the King can do no wrong"— and Wallis' too ready acceptance that he knew what he was doing —had proved destructive.

Now that he had intimated to Baldwin that a decision would soon be reached, Edward decided, he must break with Beaverbrook; and he sent him a message saying that for the time being communication between them must be suspended—as it had already been between Beaverbrook and Monckton—in case it should be misunderstood. If he had sent a similar message to Churchill, a great deal of unnecessary trouble might have been averted. But although Edward felt "wearied to the point of exhaustion," he did not cancel his invitation to Churchill, who arrived out at the Fort that evening for dinner. By this time the King's circle of trusted advisers had contracted to three: Monckton, Ulick Alexander, and George Allen. Churchill treated them to one of his soaring disquisitions on the constitutional issues involved. Edward listened entranced: "When Mr. Baldwin had talked to me about the monarchy, it had seemed a dry and lifeless thing. But when Mr. Churchill spoke it lived, it grew, it became suffused with light." The King should never have allowed himself, Churchill insisted, to be subjected to an ultimatum from the government. It was contrary to the spirit of the Constitution. He proposed, therefore, to recommend a pause for reflection, and the following day he would issue a statement to the press, explaining why the respite was essential.

On the way home Churchill called upon Beaverbrook, hoping to lay plans how best to utilize whatever respite might be obtained. Beaverbrook, who had heard of the King's decision from Sir John Simon, told him that he was wasting his time. But Churchill would not listen, and went off to put the finishing touches to his appeal. And certainly in London, there were still indications of growing support for the King. According to Hodge and Graves in their *The Long Week-End,* the feeling that he was getting a raw deal from his ministers was openly expressed: "That night diners rose at restaurants and addressed the tables proposing a loyal toast which nobody could refuse." At the St. James's Theatre—the *Mail* reported the next morning—after the National Anthem had been sung, "the distinguished audience broke into spontaneous applause, which continued for some time." Crowds lingered outside Buckingham Palace; they might be disappointed by the absence of the King, but there was no feeling, as yet, that the tide had turned against him. Had the King been in residence at the Palace he might, after listening to Churchill's eloquence, have been tempted also to listen to the pleas of the crowd. But he was isolated, at the Fort. "It was a night of soul-searching," he recalled. But, pacing his bedroom floor, he decided that the risks of calling a King's Party into being were too great. "I felt I had come to the limit of man's powers to shape events and fend off catastrophe. Were I to wait longer I might indeed reap the whirlwind. And so in faith and calmness, not unmixed with sorrow, I resolved to end the constitutional crisis forthwith."

THE WEEK-END: DECEMBER 5-7

On Saturday morning the King told Walter Monckton that he had finally made up his mind to abdicate, and that Baldwin should be told of the decision. Monckton, who by this time was growing uneasy about the possibility of intervention in the Simpson divorce, had an idea. Why not ask the government, when they put forward the Abdication Bill, to present another bill at the same time, making Wallis' divorce absolute forthwith? Such legislation might be unusual, but there was precedent for it. Certainly it was within Parliament's powers. Edward gratefully accepted the proposal as "a lifeline thrown across a crevasse," and Monckton and George Allen went off to discuss the idea with Sir Horace Wilson and Major Thomas Dugdale, MP, Baldwin's parliamentary private secretary.

They realized what they were up against: the High Churchmen Halifax and Hoare, the Free Churchman Simon, the Low Churchman Inskip, and the Nonconformists MacDonald, Kingsley Wood, Chamberlain and Runciman. Nevertheless they felt the force of Monckton's plea. So, by Edward's account, did Baldwin, for when he came to the Fort that afternoon it was to say that he had summoned a special Cabinet meeting for the following morning—Sunday—to discuss the abdication, and that he would resign if the Cabinet refused the second bill. Sir John Simon was put to work as draftsman, and the King—and, presumably, Baldwin—retired that night satisfied that the crisis was over. All that remained now was to get the Cabinet's consent, and the complex legal and constitutional processes could be set in motion.

But members of the Cabinet did not see things that way. They had gone to their homes or to their constituencies for the week-end, unaware of what was happening. And Saturday morning's newspapers were—from their point of view—more disgraceful than ever.

True, the quality papers emphasized the "danger of delayed decision"—as the *Telegraph*'s main headline put it. At Westminster, the *Times* editorial explained, the feeling was one of anxiety that "so disturbing a factor should have come into public affairs at a moment when the need for national calm and national unity was

(3 2 5)

never greater. A prompt decision, which would put an end at least
to the major elements of disturbance and distraction, would not
therefore be the least service to the nation which His Majesty could
render." The *Herald*, too, showed no signs of wavering: it reported
hardening of opinion in the Labour Party "that the authority of
Parliament must be upheld against the personal wishes of the King."
And the provincial newspapers remained firm. The *Manchester
Guardian*, in fact, thought that Baldwin's intervention in the Commons to explain the government's attitude to a morganatic marriage
marked a turning point. The issue was now clear. "Laying aside our
own feelings about the dignity and status of the Crown as we would
have it—and for long, had it in fact—would it be right or fitting to
send on State Visits (or, it might well be, leave behind in the purely
English background) a consort who was doomed to play no part,
or a much reduced part, in the monarch's public life? That does not
seem to be a role which should, on reflection, commend itself to
King or people."

In this, the *Guardian* was getting to the heart of the matter, but
like the rest of the quality papers, it was preaching, presumably, to
the converted minority. In the long run, it might be the majority who
read the Beaverbrook and Rothermere papers who were going to
matter, and it was on Saturday, as Dawson noted in his diary, that
the agitation in "the Simpson press," as he had begun to describe it,
reached its climax: "The *Daily Mirror*, which for some reason seems
to have been selected by Rothermere as the spearhead of his attack,
was particularly outrageous." The *Mirror* had led with the plea
"TELL US THE FACTS, MR. BALDWIN!" And its able young columnist
"Cassandra"—William Connor—had denounced Baldwin in a forceful
article for failing to trust a loyal nation. The people of Britain, he
complained, had been kept in suspense, barred from the truth—"The
cancer of rumour has undermined their confidence."

Worse was in store for Dawson later in the day in Beaverbrook's
Evening Standard, for which George Bernard Shaw had written one
of his "fictitious dialogues" from "The Country of the Half-Mad"—a
fantasy about a King who wanted to marry Mrs. Daisy Bell, an
American divorcée. Shaw's King was visited by his Prime Minister
and the Archbishop of Canterbury, who expressed their disapproval
and asked what he proposed to do. He proposed, he replied, to do
nothing. "I shall be crowned in May; in April I shall marry Daisy."
When the Prime Minister threatened to resign, the King replied that

in that case, he would form a King's party to carry on, a prospect the Prime Minister clearly did not relish. And when the Archbishop said he would refuse to officiate at the coronation, the King pointed out that as only eleven percent of his subjects were Christians, he would be happy if the religious part of the coronation ceremony were omitted altogether. There was just enough basis of fact behind the fantasy—including the point that as the Royal Marriage Act did not apply to the King, the government could not advise him on his choice —to be irritating, apart from the defiance of accepted canons of good taste.

The evening papers also carried Churchill's appeal. When Beaverbrook heard that the Cabinet had been notified of the decision to abdicate, he went to Churchill's Westminster flat to warn him, "Our cock won't fight." But the King had neglected to inform Churchill of his decision, and Churchill would not listen to Beaverbrook. "I left him with the parting words, 'No dice,' but he simply would not believe my miserable news." So the appeal duly went out to the newspapers, and appeared in them that day.

It began, "I plead for time and patience." The King, Churchill pointed out, had been under great stress: surely, if he asked for time for further consideration, that should be granted? But time was precisely what most members of the government were now reluctant to give—particularly in view of what could be thought of as an implied threat at the close of Churchill's pronouncement. The King, Churchill said, "has no means of personal access to his Parliament or his people. Between him and them stand in their office the Ministers of the Crown. If they thought it their duty to engage all their power and influence against him, still he must remain silent." This, obviously, would be the line, if the King allowed himself to be persuaded at the last moment to turn and fight. The King, the public would be told—and how the *Express* and the *Mail* would love to tell it!—was being prevented from explaining his position to his people by a small, selfish clique of discredited politicians. If only he was allowed to explain, all would be clarified, and the crisis would vanish. Why not, then, let him be heard?

The Cabinet meets

To ministers reading Churchill's appeal in their evening papers, or at their homes on Sunday morning before the Cabinet meeting, it appeared to be a direct appeal to the people over their heads. All the old resentment against Winston came surging back, and ministers arrived for Sunday morning's meeting in no mood for sympathetic compromise. The two bills had been drafted and had passed the scrutiny both of the Attorney General and of Sir John Simon. Baldwin told Monckton, who had come to 10 Downing Street to await the Cabinet's answer, that it should not take long. It took two hours, and the answer to the request for a bill to grant Mrs. Simpson her divorce forthwith was no. The Cabinet had decided, Monckton was informed, that it would smack of an under-the-counter bargain —it would affront the moral sense of the nation, and it might be interpreted as an abandonment of the moral position the Cabinet had taken up.

So Monckton had to report failure when he returned to the King. The surrender must be unconditional. And, for the first time, Edward began to feel he was not a negotiator, but the helpless victim of inexorable pressures, ruthlessly applied—"the static yet implacable grip of a vise which, having fastened about an object, never relaxes . . . how lonely is a Monarch in a struggle with a shrewd Prime Minister, backed by all the apparatus of the Modern State!"

But in fact, the Prime Minister had not been shrewd enough. He had made what might, if he was not careful, be a serious mistake. He had realized that there would be difficulty with some of his ministers, but he had assumed that he would be able to handle them. Now he had lost control.

Predictably, ministers had advanced the arguments of their respective creeds. By Beaverbrook's account, Inskip said that the Church—by which he meant the Low Church—would not tolerate a bill that in effect facilitated the remarriage of a divorced person. Halifax spoke up for the High Church, which regarded divorce as an abomination, and the Methodist Kingsley Wood said simply that "the bill would lose votes." But religious scruples were not the only, perhaps not the chief reason for their resistance. Returning after the failure of his mission, Monckton reported that when he said the King would need time to think over the implications of the rejection, he had been told there must be no delay. One minister had complained that "the continued uncertainty had already hurt the Christmas trade"—Chamberlain, Monckton thought. And Chamberlain it probably was.

By this time Chamberlain was impatient to get the business finished. The "time and patience" plea exasperated him. He was appalled at the waste of government time which would have been better spent on public affairs—the crisis, he complained in his journal, was "holding up business" and "paralysing our foreign policy." Whatever sympathy he might have for the King in such a predicament, he had none at all with Edward's efforts to extricate himself. And consequently—as Chamberlain's biographer, the historian Keith Feiling, commented—"his impatience to make men, even kings, face reality, his instinct against procrastination, did not make him an ideal counsellor in this intertwined mass of pathos, folly and ambition."

What had most infuriated Chamberlain was the press insinuation that the crisis had resulted from a government attempt to push Edward off his throne because his progressive views were unpalatable. The public was being told, he complained,

that we are engaged in a fight with the King because we have advised him to abdicate and he has refused. That is quite untrue, and we must say so. He asked us to examine the morganatic marriage proposal, we told him we could have nothing to do with it, and he has accepted that view. The public is also being told that we are trying to rush the King into a decision that he has not had time to think over. That is equally untrue. He has been thinking it over for weeks, though he has been unwilling to face up to realities.

Unlike Baldwin, Chamberlain was not troubled by any feeling that everything possible should seem to be done to keep the King on his throne. He simply set out the issues in the way he customarily did:

There are only three alternatives before him:
(1) Marriage with Mrs. Simpson as Queen;
(2) Abdication and marriage;
(3) Renunciation of this marriage altogether.
Now, (1) is already barred, because apart from feeling in this country, the Dominions have plainly said they won't have it. The choice is therefore between (2) and (3). The general public will prefer (3) but if the King is not prepared for (3) there remains nothing but (2).

In ordinary circumstances, ministers would have been prepared to follow Baldwin in any clash between him and Chamberlain, if only out of deference to his experience and his guile. But by this time they were growing impatient. Baldwin had given too many hostages to fortune in the past twelve months. He must not be allowed to make one mistake too many. What was the point, now that the King had agreed to abdicate, of incurring odium by appearing to have won his consent only by what would certainly be construed as a bribe? How could ministers face their constituents, let alone their local clergy, with the admission that they had broken their principles for the sake of an easy way out of a difficult situation?

In any case, did they know that the King would keep his word? Here were Beaverbrook and Rothermere, and now Churchill, asking for more time. But if the King had decided to abdicate on Saturday morning, as Monckton claimed, why had he not called off the press campaign and silenced Churchill? Presumably because he was trying it on—bargaining with the government as a delaying tactic, but really waiting to see how the King's party developed. If so, that would explain why—when they turned down the project of a bill to expedite Mrs. Simpson's divorce—Monckton had said the King would require still more time. It was all exceedingly suspicious. Chamberlain, they decided, was right. Henceforth there must be no further shilly-shallying. Let the King set his name to the Instrument of Abdication as quickly as possible, with no strings attached—or else.

Their obstinacy must have put Baldwin in a dilemma. If he carried out his threat to resign, ministers would presumably simply accept his resignation, and Chamberlain would take over the leadership of the party. The King would be no better off—having gone so far, he could hardly step back now. But even if he did, and announced his determination to continue to reign, Baldwin would still be out. Either way, in fact, he would be made to look ridiculous.

Tom Jones was later to recall that Saturday was a bad day for Baldwin. He had tried out a legalistic escape, "but it got jammed." This was true, but when Jones went on to assert that he recovered his full authority in Sunday morning's Cabinet, he was wide of the mark. All that Baldwin could do was accept the Cabinet's decision and try to work out how to reconcile it with his promise to the King. He could see no immediate way out. But he knew, none better, the value of waiting, and watching, until a suitable opportunity presented itself.

"The man who objects"

One other step that Baldwin had taken was also later to have its repercussions.

During the weeks of mounting crisis, the Archbishop of Canterbury had decided it would be wise to remain in the background. He made no attempt to see the King, later excusing himself on the ground that when Edward had admitted his determination to marry Mrs. Simpson, he had also made clear his determination to deal only with the Prime Minister. Lang wondered whether he ought to have written to the King: "Yet almost certainly this would have invoked, if any reply had been given, the sort of slight which *I* personally might have understood, but to which the Archbishop of Canterbury ought not to be exposed." The argument was typical of Lang. Another man might have asked himself whether the slight was not worth risking, particularly as it would not be made public. But Lang was in no mood to take any risks for the sake of a reconciliation that he could not really have desired. The King, for his part, assumed that although Lang avoided him until the crisis was over, "from beginning to end I had a disquieting feeling that he was invisibly and noiselessly about." Invisibly and noiselessly was right. Except with Halifax, Lang had no close relations with any member of the Cabinet. But close relations were not necessary. Baldwin knew his man. He had no difficulty in guessing how Lang would react in any given circumstances. If Lang had been less predictable, Baldwin would have paid attention, possibly court, to him. It was not necessary. All that Baldwin had needed to do, during the crisis, was to keep Lang informed—and that not very often.

Even his old friend Geoffrey Dawson saw little of Lang in the critical weeks. On November 11, when Dawson decided the *Times* ought to speak out after the King's return from the tour of South Wales, he had lunch with Lang at Lambeth Palace and showed him the article, but that was all. On November 29, when Dawson went to Lambeth again, he noted in his diary that Lang "was right out of things (wisely) and had seen no one lately but Queen Mary."

When the crisis broke, Lang became more active. On the Friday, after conferring with the moderator and the secretary of the Free Churches' federal council, he issued a message to Church of England clergy, urging "those who have a duty to speak to the people from the pulpit or otherwise" to refrain from discussing the subject: "Words spoken with imperfect knowledge of an extremely difficult situation can give no helpful guidance, and may only mislead or confuse public thought and feeling. Silence is fitting until the ultimate decisions are made known." But the fact that he communicated with Dawson by letter in this period—thanking him for the *Times* editorial of December 3—hardly suggests that they were busy at the time conspiring together, and the letter's contents—a hope that the government would stand firm—indicates that he was not privy to the government's doings.

The Archbishop was not consulted formally or informally by Baldwin until on the Sunday, when he was brought back from Canterbury, where he had been holding a confirmation service, because—his biographer explained—"the King had put forward a new proposal on which Mr. Baldwin desired his opinion." The new proposal was to speed up Mrs. Simpson's divorce, and inevitably, Lang took the same view as Chamberlain and the rest of the Cabinet. Probably Baldwin had originally asked him to come to London on the assumption that, having won over the Cabinet, he would also have to win over, or at least mollify, the Archbishop. Having failed with the Cabinet there was no longer any point in trying to persuade Lang, but by that time it may have been too late to rescind the request for him to come to London—or the fact that he was coming may have slipped from Baldwin's mind.

The effect of his appearance was unfortunate—as the *Times* later that week, in defending him, was to concede. The crowd outside 10 Downing Street was hostile, and according to the New York *Herald Tribune* correspondent there was an attempt to "rush" the Archbishop as he was getting back into his car. Next morning his picture appeared in the newspapers with such captions as "The man who objects." The Sunday excursion was to be responsible for some of the odium in which the Archbishop later found himself.

Baldwin did not, however, send for Geoffrey Dawson. Dawson had spent the week-end at Eton, where Founder's Day was being celebrated with the assistance of over fifty Old Etonian MPs, answering their names at a roll call conducted by the Speaker of the House of Commons and planting commemorative trees. To Dawson's annoyance, one of his companions at dinner on the Saturday evening was the economist J.M. Keynes, whose views on the crisis—he

thought ministers were ganging up on the King to push him out—
Dawson thought "mischievous." After calling on the Wigrams the
next day, Dawson came back to Printing House Square to find "no
definite development" in the crisis—in other words, no inside information from any of his sources, and as he "saw no one outside the
office," the *Times* the next morning gave no clue to what had
happened.

Talking to the station master

Baldwin had more to worry about than the Cabinet's rejection of
the Monckton plan. There was the possibility that the King, exasperated, might be thrown into the arms of Beaverbrook and Churchill.
In that case, everything would depend on how public opinion was
moving. During the week-end, many MPs were down with their
constituents, and as it was unlikely that there would be any other
topic of conversation, they would presumably come back to Westminster on Monday with some idea of how the constituencies were
reacting. If there was a widespread desire to keep Edward on the
throne, even at the price of his marrying Wallis, they could hardly
miss it. When they came back on Monday morning, therefore, the
government might be confronted by back-benchers who, whatever
their personal views, would be influenced by what they had heard
and—if it was favourable to the King—reluctant to follow the course
the Cabinet had now set. Should this happen, there was no knowing
what the King and his friends might decide to do.

During the week-end, there were some intimations that the
King's party was growing. On Sunday night Dawson reported "the
mischief makers getting very busy." The crowds on the streets were
bigger than before—three thousand people, it was estimated, outside
Buckingham Palace. Even more serious, there were reports of a
King's-friends movement among the Conservative back-benchers.
Sir Reginald Blaker, Conservative MP for a Middlesex constituency,
told a meeting on Sunday that a group of Conservative MPs had
been formed with the object of keeping the King on his throne, and
in his *Modern British Monarchy* Sir Charles Petrie recalled how
early on Monday a meeting of the King's supporters was held at
Westminster attended by some forty Conservative members of the
two Houses, and a few others: "Although there was considerable
difference of opinion as to the course to be pursued, there was gen-

eral agreement that the Government was using Mrs. Simpson as an excuse to avenge itself on the King for his attitude in the matter of the distressed areas." But the meeting adjourned until the evening, and in the meantime, Baldwin's Fabian policy had once again paid off—helped by, of all people, Lord Rothermere.

On Monday, a letter from Rothermere appeared in his own *Daily Mail*, asking whether Britain could afford to lose a sovereign of "such superlatively splendid" qualities as Edward VIII, and urging that the issue should not be approached in the narrow spirit of a constitutional lawyer, but through human sympathy. So why not a morganatic marriage? "When it was declared in Parliament that morganatic marriage was unknown to the law of England, it should have been remembered that also unknown to the law of England is a constitutional situation similar to the present and the legislation which abdication would necessitate." Thus far, the argument was familiar enough, but Rothermere proceded to elaborate on it. The King, he said, was essential to the country, because "now that the shortage of recruits has become a grave national emergency, the King is the only human agency to whom we can look to make the voluntary system a success. If he goes, conscription will be inevitable."

Possibly the absurdity of the idea was pointed out to him, or possibly Rothermere suffered from the congenital disease of writers of open letters—dissatisfaction with what they have written when they see it in print. The *Evening News* that same day carried a different letter over his name. It once again urged, with greater brevity and pungency, that a morganatic marriage was the common-sense solution, enabling the King to live privately and unostentatiously with the woman he loved as his wife, and it went on to cite the Continental precedent of the Emperor Francis Joseph of Austria, morganatically married to Frau Schratt. But again, Rothermere fell into the trap of being unable to close his letter without an additional punch line. The Cabinet, he claimed, had acted too precipitately. It "must guard against the suspicion—completely unfounded as it is— that, in resentment of the King's strong words about the depressed areas in South Wales, it has seized upon this pretext to encourage his Abdication."

For an editor to change the words and even the sense of his editorial is not uncommon, but for a correspondent to change letters is unusual, except on legal advice or to correct error. The switch simply gave Rothermere's adversaries the chance once again to deride him. But the reference to South Wales, in spite of the "unfounded" admission, infuriated them. Rothermere's intervention provided precisely what Baldwin needed to help restore unity in the Conservative Party—and, as things turned out, in the Commons as a whole.

If MPs, returning that morning from the constituencies, had brought with them a consensus of opinion hostile to the government, not even Rothermere could have made any difference. But it turned out that the feeling they had encountered had been overwhelmingly against the morganatic-marriage proposal—particularly in Labour constituencies. Even in South Wales, Owen and Thompson reported in their account of the abdication, "the King's popularity had gone. Cinema audiences saw in cold silence the films of his recent visit to the valleys where they had all cheered themselves hoarse. Lancashire and Yorkshire members found those counties solid against the marriage, whether the King abdicated or not. Scotland was dead against the King."

Hugh Dalton's experience over the week-end confirms this view. He was staying in South Wales, in one of the towns the King had passed through on his tour, where his "Something must be done" had "kindled fresh hope in hearts long cold with despair." But speaking with the unemployed, some of whom had even seen the King, Dalton found they all deeply disapproved of the proposed marriage. A gathering of local notables—councillors, civil servants, and trade-union leaders—"were unanimously and most emphatically against the marriage, morganatically or not. Many strong words, even some jeering words, were spoken against the King." The wives, Dalton added, were even more bitter than the men: the King, they felt, was letting them down by wanting to marry a woman like Mrs. Simpson. And another Labour MP, Jack Lawson, reported the same feeling from his mining constituency in northeast England.

From left to right of the parliamentary spectrum—except at the very extremes—the verdict was conclusive. There was no doubt, Amery wrote in his diary, "that over the week-end opinion in the country had settled down steadily behind the Government, and that outside the London area—less Puritan, perhaps, and influenced by the Harmsworth and Beaverbrook press—the country as a whole was getting progressively more shocked at the idea that the King could hesitate between his duty to the Throne and his affection for a woman." And Kingsley Martin wrote in the *New Statesman's*

"London Diary," later that week, "that one of the most important influences which affected the House of Commons over the week-end was the flood of evidence which reached MPs from their constituencies, showing that amongst the rank and file in all parties in the provinces the feeling against this marriage was overwhelmingly strong."

By the time the Commons met, Baldwin was confident again. Young later suggested to him that he had been the only man who, the previous Friday, had known what the Commons would be thinking on the Monday, and Baldwin replied, "half shyly, half triumphantly, 'I have always believed in the week-end.'" He added a delightfully wry comment on the way MPs had tasted public opinion: "How they do it I don't know. I suppose they talk to the station master." Baldwin had once again demonstrated his "feel" for how MPs would react. He had acquired it the boring way—by sitting through debates even when he had ample excuse to escape from them. Once, when he complained to Tom Jones about being badgered in the Commons, Jones asked him why he attended so much. "It is very important," Baldwin replied, "that I should do so. The House is very jealous. You remember how Lloyd George lost touch with it." Baldwin might be indolent, as Simon observed, but "his habit of sitting for long hours on the Front Bench listening to a tedious debate gave him an exact appreciation of the political atmosphere . . . there have been Conservative statesmen in the past who in their heart of hearts fought shy of democracy, but Baldwin paid more than lip service to it."

That afternoon, when Baldwin entered the House, Josiah Wedgwood rose to ask if the motion standing in his name could be heard at the earliest opportunity. Baldwin, immediately sensing the House's mood, replied simply, "No, Sir." Wedgwood tried to pursue the point with a supplementary, his intention being to ask the Prime Minister if he would at least give an assurance that the fatal step of abdication would not be accepted without parliamentary approval, but immediately on hearing the word "abdication"—the first time it had been used in the House—MPs howled him down.

Then, in reply to a question from Attlee, Baldwin explained to the House that the reason for the delay was that the decision now rested with the King. When he had made up his mind, he would doubtless communicate it to the government and to the Dominions' governments, and "it will then be for those Governments to decide what advice, if any, they would feel it their duty to tender to him in the light of his conclusion." An unsympathetic House might have dismissed the explanation as stalling, but MPs were obviously impressed.

There followed the saddest episode of the whole crisis. Churchill had been to an Anglo-French Club luncheon, at which he had proposed the loyal toast. Refusing to listen to friends who begged him not to intervene, refusing to be warned by the hostile reception accorded to Wedgwood, he rose to make the same request, the request that the Commons had cheered him for making only four days before —a plea for assurance that no irrevocable step would be taken before the House had an opportunity to discuss it. But the House did not want the opportunity for such a discussion. Members did not even want to hear it advocated. Angry cries of "Shut up" and "Sit down" assailed Churchill, and though for a while he remained standing, as if hoping to be allowed to continue, he eventually put out his hands in a gesture of helplessness and resumed his seat—"the most striking rebuff," as the *Times* described it, "in modern parliamentary history." A National Liberal rose and proposed what was, in effect, a call for a vote of confidence by acclamation in the Prime Minister, and the House gave it. The King's-friends movement had collapsed.

All the King's men

But how could so massive a swing of public opinion have come about? There is plenty of evidence that when the news of the constitutional crisis broke in the middle of the first week of December, popular feeling was against the government. "There appeared to be a tide," Beaverbrook recalled, "now running with immense and gathering force in favour of the King. If the hearts of the King's supporters were uplifted, there was good reason for it." Even the letters to the *Times* were overwhelmingly on the King's side. They were not printed. In the first days of the crisis Kingsley Martin found the mood in London tolerant: the usual comment was that the King "ought to marry anyone he likes, the same as anyone else," and a friend of Martin's whose work brought her in contact with the poor said the general opinion was summarized in the phrase, "He's a naughty boy, but we don't want to lose him." An aspiring young Conservative politician, Roger Falk, was nursing a South London constituency at the time. Full of ardour, he was systematically canvassing a working-class district, and until the week-end he found the great majority of householders and housewives supported the King.

But after the week-end, to his surprise, Falk found the great majority of the people he canvassed were on the side of the government. With each day that passed, Hugh Dalton noted, public opinion turned against the King, and the swing was reflected in newspaper correspondence. In *The Modern British Monarchy*, Sir Charles Petrie recalled that it was said that of the letters received in the more responsible papers at the beginning of the crisis, ninety percent were for the King, and ten percent critical, but "by the time it ended the positions were reversed." And at Printing House Square, Dawson noted the trend with relief, ordering that an editorial should be written "giving the points of our 'fan mail.'"

As the days went by, clearly, the public learned what the real issue was. Their first instinct had been to assume that the King, whom they liked, was being got at by his ministers, whom they did not like, and it was this, rather than any sympathy for the King's project, that gave the appearance of wide-spread support for him.

Discussing attitudes to monarchy in his *The Uses of Literacy*, Professor Richard Hoggart admitted that it was difficult, with all the publicity surrounding the institution, to make an accurate assessment, but in his own experience members of the working class (which he came from himself) rarely think about the subject. They are neither monarchists nor antimonarchists—"they either ignore it, or, if they are interested, the interest is for what can be translated into the personal." Colourful members of the royal family arouse more attention, not always favourable, than members of the government. But although the working classes are disinterested, Hoggart continued, they distinguish the royal family from its advisers, and they sympathize with individual members of it as "caught up in a big machine manipulated by 'them.'" People will sympathize with royalty: "It's a rotten job . . . they get pushed around as much as we do." And Hoggart has clear memories "of the emotional atmosphere in our street. Everybody was strongly pro-Edward: Baldwin was seen as a grim-faced Machiavellian who, aided by the Church or aiding the Church, was prepared to do violence to true love to save appearances . . . There was very strong feeling also against the Bishop who blew the gaff first. The public figure-heads came together to close the ranks too neatly to do other than provide a splendid set of stage villains. This really was 'them' in action."

It took a little time for this attitude to change, because the real issues were not immediately made clear. On the Thursday, when the story broke in the national dailies, Mrs. Simpson herself was featured only in the last edition of the *Mirror,* and only the *News Chronicle* put forward the marriage proposal. Not until Baldwin's Commons speech the following day was the nature of the constitutional crisis formally clarified. But as soon as it was, people began to realize that Baldwin had a case. The project of a morganatic marriage made no appeal. As if sensing this, the *Mail* on Saturday put its chief foreign correspondent, Ward Price, onto explaining that a morganatic marriage was not necessarily sinister or disreputable. But it was no use. The King, people felt, was behaving out of character. He had stepped out of his fairy tale: Prince Charming might marry a princess, or he might marry a Cinderella, but he could certainly not marry a Mrs. Simpson. And by this time the rumours about her, which previously had not spread far outside the capital, were surging through the provincial towns, gathering ugly and hostile accretions as they went.

Christiansen of the *Express* had been under no illusions. He was a technician whose genius lay in presentation and lay-out, and he was ordinarily content to leave policy to his proprietor. But Beaverbrook respected his judgment of what people were thinking (as distinct from what Beaverbrook thought they should be thinking) and was dismayed when Christiansen reported that the people would be on Baldwin's side—quoting, as typical of provincial Englishwomen, the view of his mother, who "called Mrs. Simpson 'that *woman*' with a ferocity which astonished me." Women, in fact, were particularly hostile, because of a feeling that Ellen Wilkinson expressed in the *Herald* that a morganatic marriage was an affront to women's dignity—as well as being contrary to Socialist ideals about women's rights. As the *Manchester Guardian* remarked, the King could not really have much confidence in the propriety of his marriage, "for otherwise he would never have seen any reason to consult his ministers as to the possibility of some lowered and incomplete status for the lady he had in mind as wife."

The other provincial newspapers were almost unanimously hostile to the project. By Friday, their attitude was consistent: that the King must be prepared to give up Mrs. Simpson or his throne. "It will be the devout hope of all," the *Western Mail* claimed, "that a monarch who has already won the hearts of his subjects will be able to make whatever personal sacrifice is necessary to comply with the traditions of his position," and the *Scotsman* agreed, hoping that the King would "put the interests of the nation before any personal feeling, however strong."

What was decisive, probably, was that people—even those sympathetic to the King—could not see Mrs. Simpson in the role of a consort of any kind. In his *Ordeal in England*, Sir Philip Gibbs—a prolific author-journalist, delighted to be able to draw on such material—went around sampling people of different classes to see if he could arrive at any consensus. The professional, upper middle class, he found, were not moved by any moral indignation, but most of them felt that Mrs. Simpson was not the right woman for the King. The artisan class, however—craftsmen, bricklayers, mechanics—were unanimously hostile, out of a kind of class consciousness. "It did not occur to them that they were talking 'class stuff' and acknowledging the caste system," but planted in their minds was "the conviction that a Queen of England should belong to the old 'Quality.' They expected a high standard of selection."

To some extent, the image of King George V as King had faded, but the image of Mary as Queen was as strong as ever, and it was heightened when, soon after the news of the constitutional crisis broke, she went out to look at what remained of the gutted Crystal Palace. On the 30th she had noted in her diary her sorrow about "a great landmark gone," and on the afternoon of the Thursday on which the story of the crisis broke, when she might have been expected to seek seclusion, she decided to drive out to see the ruins— a visit which, according to Pope-Hennessy, was intended to have a salutary effect on public morale, and did.

Beaverbrook suggested another reason for the failure of the King to retain public support. He blamed the King himself. "Throughout all the days of public controversy he shackled the press that was favourable to himself. He would allow us no liberty in expressing our views, or in arguing strongly for his cause." Undoubtedly, Edward's reason for this decision—his desire to protect Wallis from publicity—was tactically a mistake. If she was ever to be made acceptable to the public, her qualities had to be made known. But Beaverbrook was not really interested in the King's cause. The cause he wanted to fight was his own—against Baldwin. The King wanted to marry Wallis and keep his throne if he could. Beaverbrook wanted him to keep his throne whether he married Wallis or not. They were allies, but they did not really have a common purpose.

The King's Party

But who, then, formed the "King's Party," which, in *A King's Story*, Edward described as "a rocket, not a very big rocket, but for a moment it hung brilliantly in the sky"? Who were the individuals and groups who demonstrated noisily for him at the week-end, with their processions, their banners urging "God Save the King—from Baldwin," and their sporadic choruses of *For He's a Jolly Good Fellow* outside the gates of Buckingham Palace?

No political party tried to exploit the crisis—though on its left wing, there were a few members of the Labour Party who felt that the opportunity was too good to be missed. Baldwin, they felt, had often cheated them by exploiting national crises for political ends—they should have no compunction about exploiting this one to revenge themselves on him.

Typical of this attitude were letters which two rebel Fellows of All Souls, G.F. Hudson and A.L. Rowse, wrote at that time urging the Labour leaders to back the King, even to the extent of offering to form an alternative government if Baldwin resigned. The party would then, they suggested, be able to demand a general election, but they need not fight it on the constitutional issue. Whether the party decided to back the morganatic-marriage proposal, or not interfere with the King's choice at all, was unimportant. The essential point was that the party's election platform should concentrate on the wretched record of his government in both domestic and foreign affairs.

The recipient of one of the letters—the party chairman, Hugh Dalton—admitted later that for a time in the early stages of the crisis he held similar views, but he soon changed his mind, because he realized that it would split and smash the Labour Party: "Even in the early days of the crisis I was satisfied that the great mass of men and still more of women, outside London and perhaps the colleges of Oxford and Cambridge, were anti-Simpson." But even if the leaders of the Labour Party had believed that opinion in the party as a whole favoured the Hudson-Rowse line, they would not have accepted it, because of their mistrust of the King.

This was partly because of the mistaken notion that he and Mrs. Simpson had Fascist sympathies. *Cavalcade* that week actually claimed that this was the reason why the Labour Party "had turned suddenly round to Baldwin." But the main reason for the mistrust was the fear that the King had unconstitutional leanings—a suspicion which had been intensified by the reaction to his visit to South Wales in the popular press. This meant that to some Labour leaders, the issue was not King against government, but King against Parliament. Herbert Morrison later described how the Commons had come together "following their traditional policy of unanimity in time of major constitutional trouble," and even before the week-end, Ernest Bevin was reported in the *Mirror* as insisting that the trade-union movement could not allow anything to take the place of or weaken the power of parliamentary government: "However mighty or difficult the problem, we cannot forget the supremacy of Parliament."

It was galling for Bevin to have to sit back and watch Baldwin, so lately discredited, recovering his authority with Labour's help. Better than anybody else, probably, he realized that what the Labour Party was doing was going to entail grave political risks. "We cannot forget," he wrote to Attlee on Monday, "that old Baldwin did us over the Trades Union Act, over Abyssinia, over rearmament, and over peace at the last general election . . . the risk of personal government is great; on the other hand, so is the risk of backing the Government without the facts." Nevertheless, Bevin felt that they had no alternative but to continue to give Baldwin their support.

For many in the Labour Party, the predominant feeling was mounting irritation with the King for having precipitated a ridiculous constitutional diversion at this time. On the day Blunt spoke, Madrid was heavily raided by the bombers Hitler had loaned to Franco. The *Telegraph*'s lead story on Thursday was headed, "More Germans arrive to support Franco," and its correspondent described goosestepping and Nazi songs at the bar of the hotel where the Germans had their headquarters. It was infuriating to those who cared deeply about the agony of Spain to have the news and pictures from Madrid driven into corners on back pages to make room for protracted accounts of ministerial comings and goings and speculation about Mrs. Simpson.

There was also a fear that the dictators were deliberately exploiting the crisis. In the Co-operative Society's Sunday paper, *Reynolds News,* the respected commentator H.N. Brailsford warned that while Britain was absorbed in Mrs. Simpson, "Germany marches forward to the conquest of Spain," and the following day the *News Chronicle,* although it remained sympathetic to the King, protested at the way the Germans and Italians were taking advantage of the situation to ignore the non-intervention agreement and reinforce Franco: "Nothing could better illustrate the disastrous results abroad of the crisis in this country than the news from Spain."

Any lingering doubts there might have been about the party's line were finally removed on Monday morning by the *Daily Herald.* In an article entitled "This is the real issue," Harold Laski emphasized the grave risk of personal rule undermining democratic institutions: If the King's party succeeded, "a blow would have been struck at the roots of Parliament's authority from which it would not easily recover." An editorial warned those left-wingers who were taking the King's side and accusing Labour of "supporting the Government." If they felt that taking the same attitude as the government necessarily implied support for it, they should "take a look at their own bedfellows and see how they like them." And their bedfellows were not a very attractive bunch.

In one sense, the Communist Party—small in numbers, but more of a threat to Labour's peace of mind than it was soon to be, when the Moscow trials, the Nazi-Soviet pact and the invasion of Finland brought it into discredit—took the King's side, but it was chiefly concerned to torment the *Daily Herald,* making fun of it for toadying to Baldwin. The Communist Party leader in Britain, Harry Pollitt, argued that instead of displaying solidarity with the supporters of reaction, the Labour Party ought to exploit the occasion in the hope that Baldwin would resign, enabling Labour to take office. The crisis was a sham—it was ridiculous, while slums, poverty and malnutrition were widespread in Britain, to worry "because a rich young rentier wants to marry a divorcée." But as the Conservatives realized this and had manufactured a crisis for their own party political ends (to get a more docile king), the Labour Party should play them at their own game. Most fellow travellers were similarly cynical. In *The Week* Cockburn preened himself on the success of his "thundery atmosphere" forecast in the previous issue, but contented himself with speculation about what the King had said to the

Archbishop ("Please remember that *I* am the head of your organization") and to Baldwin ("If you go on in this way I just shan't come to your Coronation").

Most of the King's supporters were drawn, in fact, from the extreme right—from two different groups, though the distinction between them was often blurred.

First, there were the simple—usually in both senses of the word—royalists. The "pure" royalists were not concerned. They still stood faithful to the cause of the Stuarts, ousted by the revolution of 1688 —their royal line continuing in the person of Prince Rupert of Bavaria. But there were others who gave their loyalty unswervingly to whoever happened to be on the throne. Usually they mistrusted democracy and loathed all political parties, Conservative, Liberal and Labour, impartially. They were few in numbers but, in a crisis, energetic and vocal.

The most outspoken of them, in print, was the rich and rumbustious Lady Houston, whose *Saturday Review* was dedicated to the task of extracting Bolshevists from under every bed. Stanley Baldwin, to her, was a crypto-Communist—in much the same sense as General Marshall was to McCarthy. So was Ramsay MacDonald. Worst of all was Anthony Eden. In standing for sanctions against Italy, he was clearly working for Russia. And as the government was against the King, the King must equally clearly be in the right. Unfortunately for Lady Houston the *Saturday Review* had gone to press just before the Blunt story broke. The best she could do for the cause was a hurriedly printed pamphlet.

The organ of the British Union of Fascists, *Action*, was equally ill-served by its deadline. But at the week-end, it was the Fascists who provided the only organized support for the King.

The crisis was just what the leader of the British Fascists, Sir Oswald Mosley, needed, Six years before, if there had been a poll on the most likely future leader of the Labour Party, Mosley would have emerged at, or certainly close to, the top of the list. He was a baronet, rich, handsome and dashing. He had been educated at Winchester and Sandhurst, served in France during the war, and married Lord Curzon's daughter. Becoming a convert to Socialism in the 1920s, he had risen rapidly in the party, and MacDonald made him Chancellor of the Duchy of Lancaster in the 1929 government. Chafing at the government's lack of drive and purpose, Mosley had put forward a plan the following year for a new economic system (it bore some resemblance to what was later to emerge in the United States as the New Deal), based on expanding credit to end unemployment. It was turned down. Mosley resigned and formed his own New Party to fight his cause.

He impressed some Labour supporters and attracted some Conservatives. Amery recalled that his speeches in the period immediately after he left the Labour Party left a deep impression by their courage and originality, and Walter Elliott nearly put his career in jeopardy by praising their ideas. Mosley could, Lord Boothby thought, have become the most formidable political leader of the younger generation, but he was too impatient for power and too arrogant in his assumption that he could put it to better use. Attracted by Fascism, he began to shape his party along Mussolini's lines, and although this lost him all his responsible supporters, for a time the movement seemed to be catching on.

Mosley, however, made a fatal mistake: he imitated Italian Fascism—and later Nazism—too closely. Although he was later to insist that he himself had never been an anti-Semite, *Action* was full of snide anti-Semitic material—the issue just before the abdication crisis broke, for example, had a letter signed "Vicar" complaining about the way Jews changed their names, and another protesting about the degradation of "being dominated in our own country by an alien parasitic race." If this anti-Semitism had been more discreet it could have found more favour—there were many Britains who shared it but did not care to admit it. "Some of my best friends are Jews" became a national cliché, and clubs that blackballed all Jews used to pretend it was because "they wouldn't fit in here." But *Action* was too blunt.

More damaging was the adoption by the British Blackshirts of strong-arm methods, particularly the beating-up of hecklers at meetings. Mosley himself remained a draw: "Arrogant, supercilious, dressed in black like a skating champion, he puts on a superb show," Gunther wrote, even if "what he talks is mostly nonsense." But his lieutenants were too crude, too vulgar. And Mosley made foolish mistakes—such as writing an adulatory letter to Julius Streicher, a sadist who liked to carry a whip as another man might carry a walking stick, the publisher of the pornographic *Der Stürmer*, described by William Shirer as "one of the most unsavoury characters in the Third Reich." As a result, Fascism continued to be regarded in Britain as an alien creed, and the movement failed to put down roots.

In 1936, too, Mosley suffered two setbacks. In February he was made to look ridiculous in a court action he had brought for slander against a trade-union official. For the defence, D.N. Pritt was allowed to describe in detail the ugly course that Fascism had taken in Britain, in particular over a notorious meeting held at the Olympia Stadium in London in 1934, where the methods used by the Blackshirt stewards had been especially unpleasant. The jury delivered a verdict for Mosley—but awarded him one farthing's damages, which, as Pritt recalled with satisfaction, quickly wiped the beaming smile off his face.

In the autumn, such was the disrepute into which the Fascist movement had fallen that the Conservative government, tired of being attacked for being too gentle with thugs, introduced a Public Order Bill to restrain the activities of quasi-military organizations and in particular to restrict the wearing of uniforms. The bill had its second reading in Parliament on November 16, and Sir John Simon was able to cast more discredit on the Fascists by showing they were receiving funds from abroad. The bill ran into opposition, but not of a kind likely to please Mosley: its critics were mostly concerned with the liberty of the individual subject and with the rights of organizations who wore uniforms, like the Boy Scouts and the Girl Guides. For Fascism there was no trace of sympathy.

The constitutional crisis, therefore, gave Mosley his chance. At the week-end, Blackshirts and sympathizers were ordered out to distribute leaflets, to chalk up on walls "Stand by the King," and to tour the streets in cars or on foot shouting slogans. They were almost certainly the largest element in the King's party. But they hardly did his cause a service—or their own. The third reading of the Public Order Bill was heard on Monday, and the voice of its critics was henceforth muted, allowing the bill's later stages to be concluded without serious opposition.

There was one other element on the King's side—described by Geoffrey Dawson in his diary as "the mischief makers." They were out chiefly for the fun of it. The King meant little to them, and Mrs. Simpson less, but they disliked Baldwin and were delighted to add to his embarrassments.

A revealing portrait of a demonstrator in this category was to be given by Jessica Mitford in her *Hons and Rebels*. Then in her teens, she "didn't especially care one way or the other what the outcome might be: two middle-aged people with nothing in particular to recommend them, a good deal less interesting than the average film star." But she had a friend who insisted that they must have a demonstration, and on Sunday afternoon they met a few more friends, some carrying home-made banners calling on Baldwin to resign—or saying, "Long live Edward," which made Jessica uncomfortable, as she felt it smacked of royalism.

The procession did not collect the support its organizer had hoped for. Only about fifty demonstrators eventually ended up outside Buckingham Palace, shouting, "We want Edward" (they were unaware that he was at the Fort). When it became obvious that Edward was not going to appear, Jessica suggested they move, instead, to Downing Street, but they did not even know the way—they set off in the wrong direction, and eventually had to ask a mounted policeman, who redirected them. When they arrived it was to find Downing Street blocked off. "The demonstrators, murmuring that it was time for tea, gradually dispersed."

The "King's Party," in fact, never had any real existence. The pro-king demonstrations, as Dalton claimed, "were only froth." Edward's impression that a multitude of the plain people stood waiting to be rallied to his side had been justified only so long as the issues were not clear—so long as it was believed that the King was being bullied by "them." But as soon as it was realized that he wanted to marry a twice-divorced American woman, the mood had changed. "It wouldn't have done," as a taxi driver told Kingsley Martin. "It wouldn't have done."

MONDAY, DECEMBER 7—
WEDNESDAY, DECEMBER 9

The King's party might have appeared to Edward to go up like a rocket. It had now come down a bent stick. At Westminster his supporters melted away. The Conservative group that had met earlier in the day to pledge its support to him met again in the evening, much reduced in numbers. An effort had been made to enlist Labour support, but only two Labour MPs, Wedgwood and Ernest Thurtle, had been recruited. It was decided to send a deputation to see Monckton "and through him convey to the King an assurance of support in all circumstances, but combined with the hope that if at all possible he would see his way to give up Mrs. Simpson." According to *Figaro's* London correspondent that morning, the King's supporters had hoped, when Mrs. Simpson went to France, that he would publicly renounce the marriage project, and his failure to do so had been a help to Baldwin. Now, they felt, he must be persuaded to renounce her. There was no other course.

Or so it seemed, until late on Monday evening, when news came over the tapes from France. Until then, it had been a satisfying day for Dawson. He had lunched with Wigram and been interested to hear from him of a "curious approach to him by 'Ernest' (Simpson)." With his leave, Dawson passed it on to Halifax (what the approach was, has never been disclosed) and then went to Westminster to witness the "complete obliteration of Winston," before returning to Printing House Square to prepare for the following morning's paper. But late that night, before it went to press, he was confronted with a statement from Mrs. Simpson: she was "ready to withdraw."

In *The Heart Has Its Reasons*, Wallis was to describe how she had come to this decision. From the time she had reached Cannes, Wallis had tried, whenever the connection was good enough, to persuade Edward to listen to his friends—Beaverbrook and Churchill —rather than bow to the demands of his enemies, but she found that he had turned "remote and unapproachable." Had she been in

Lincolnshire, as the conspirators had planned, communication would have been less difficult. As things were, she became more susceptible to Brownlow's advice that the only way out of the situation was to "make a strong and unequivocal public statement" that she was going to give Edward up, in a way that would leave him no choice. With his help, she prepared a statement—though it was not strong enough for Brownlow, who would have preferred her to say outright that she had decided not to marry Edward. She felt that this would be too hurtful.

> Mrs. Simpson throughout the last few weeks has invariably wished to avoid any action or proposal which would hurt or damage His Majesty or the Throne.
>
> Today her attitude is unchanged, and she is willing, if such action would solve the problem, to withdraw from a situation which has been rendered both unhappy and untenable.

On Monday, Wallis read the statement over the telephone to Edward. At first, she recalled, he was unbelieving, "then, hurt and angry." But eventually he told her to go ahead if she wished—"it won't make any difference." And at seven o'clock that evening the statement was given to the press.

It was just what the popular newspapers, which were beginning to despair, were needing. To the King's supporters, the news from Cannes appeared decisive. The only obstacle to his remaining on the throne was now out of the way. To make sure, Christiansen rang Beaverbrook.

" 'What d'ya think of it?' he asked.

" 'Well,' I said, 'It could be a way out for the King, if he wants a way out.'

" 'You are entitled to take that view—if that is your view,' Beaverbrook advised."

It was Beaverbrook's standard formula of approval—leading Christiansen to wonder whether he might have been responsible for Mrs. Simpson's pronouncement. "Certainly the sonorous, almost Biblical phrase "unhappy and untenable" was typical of the Beaverbrookian style." The story was set up for the next morning under "END OF THE CRISIS" in the *Express*'s biggest headlines, and the editor went with some of his staff to celebrate in Soho.

The other popular papers, though less confident, agreed that Mrs.

Simpson's statement put a new complexion on things. Her renunciation, the *News Chronicle* thought, was the best way out: the King could now take up his responsibilities again. But for Geoffrey Dawson, Mrs. Simpson's statement was simply an irritant. Ordinarily the *Times* preferred to ignore the existence of the popular newspapers, but Rothermere's open letters in Monday's *Daily Mail* and *Evening News* were too much for Dawson. Two *Times* editorials had been prepared, to demolish them. The first Rothermere letter was mocked for its grammar, the second denounced for its content. He was accused of again giving currency, "in the sly form of a denial, to the abominable insinuation that the Government are pressing the King to abdicate because he was too sympathetic to South Wales." And by reviving the morganatic proposal (the *Times* was here echoing the *Manchester Guardian*) Rothermere was in effect demanding that the Empire Prime Ministers should accept and ratify "a permanent statutory apology for the status of the lady whom the King desires to marry. The Constitution is to be amended in order that she may carry in solitary prominence the brand of unfitness for the Queen's throne. Can anyone in possession of his faculties imagine any Prime Minister moving, or any Parliament undertaking to support, a proposition so invidious and so distressing?"

Put that way, no. But did it have to be put that way? In his broadcast review of the *History of the Times,* Beaverbrook clearly regarded the words as a calculated insult. Tom Driberg, discussing the review in his biography, took a kinder view. The *Times,* he thought, was protecting rather than denigrating Mrs. Simpson. The most likely explanation is that the *Times* was ingeniously having it both ways.

If Mrs. Simpson's renunciation was to be taken seriously, one at least of these editorials would have to be scrapped and a new one written, discussing the new situation. Better, Dawson thought, not to take it seriously. The *Times* contented itself with printing Mrs. Simpson's statement alongside a news item: "Thelma Viscountess Furness arrived at Southampton on the liner *Queen Mary* yesterday from New York." In later editions the two items were separated, but too late to save the *Times* from a charge of "feline malice and vulgar frivolity"—as Driberg put it—"that can scarcely have been paralleled in the worst of the gutter press."

Holy Deadlock

On Tuesday morning—"a foul, cold gloomy wet day," he described it in his diary—Dawson went round to see Hardinge at the palace, finding him "almost unemployed: all normal business suspended," and Hardinge agreed with him that Mrs. Simpson's dramatic offer meant "exactly nothing." They were right, but theirs was not the general view. At Westminster, MPs assembled in the morning wondering whether Mrs. Simpson's decision might not have changed the whole situation overnight.

Ironically, it happened that day that A.P. Herbert's bill to reform the divorce laws was in committee. By tact, assiduity and good luck, Herbert and the allies he had collected around him had been able to get it through its second reading—in which the main principles of the bill had been debated and accepted. But in committee, the clauses were being taken one by one, and it was consequently vital for Herbert to keep his supporters together, to prevent clauses that he regarded as important from being emasculated or rejected. This would have been difficult enough at the best of times, but as it happened, Herbert was also committed to writing the script for Charles Cochran's *Coronation Review*. "With appeals in my ear from a Hungarian composer, an American producer, and an English comedian to write more words or better words, I would hurry to the Treasury Solicitor to get the text of the new amendments, and to the House to confer . . . Then I would find an odd assembly of telephone messages. 'From Mr. Kent, insanity amendment on the way'— 'From Mr. Collins, please send second verse of *Twilight Sonata*'— 'Please ring Treasury Solicitor'—'Please ring Miss Binnie Hale'— 'Please ring Mr. Cochran'— Twice I woke up from a fitful sleep and found myself trying to set divorce words to one of M. Brodsky's tunes. A weird and worrying time."

The standing committee on the Matrimonial Causes Bill, as it was formally called, had met for the first time on Thursday, December 3, and it passed off satisfactorily, clause one being accepted without a division. Now, on Tuesday, the second day of the committee's deliberations was due, and this was nerve-racking. On the agenda was an amendment that, in the circumstances, was loaded. An opponent of the bill as it stood was objecting to divorce being granted on the ground that the respondent "has since the celebration of the marriage committed adultery." He wanted this altered to "has since the celebration of the marriage committed *persistent* adultery."

Obviously, the amendment was designed to put an end to hotel divorces of the kind Herbert had described in *Holy Deadlock*, where the decree was obtained on the ground of a single night with a girl hired for the purpose. But Mrs. Simpson's detractors—and even many of those sympathetic to her—assumed that Ernest Simpson's divorce had been obtained by the use of the *Holy Deadlock* technique, and, as Herbert put it, "the last thing that anyone wanted was to provoke discussion of these sad matters in the House."

What made it more embarrassing was the rumour, for once correct, that an intervener had at last presented himself. A solicitor's clerk, Francis Stephenson, had put in an appearance in the Divorce Registry in Somerset House, invoking the section of the act that allowed for intervention to "show cause why the decree *nisi* should not be made absolute by reason of the decree having been obtained by collusion or by reason of material facts not having been brought before the Court." For some reason, this was not made public until on Thursday the *Daily Worker* scooped the rest of the press by reporting the intervention. According to *The Week*, the other newspapers were unable to follow it up because when they arrived, they found the Registry mysteriously shut against them. Ordinarily, the intervener would have had until the following Monday to file an affidavit setting forth the facts on which he was basing his case, and Mrs. Simpson, or her lawyers, would then have been entitled to file a counter-affidavit answering the allegations made. The court could then either have rescinded the decree *nisi*, or ordered a fresh investigation, or dismissed the intervener's application. But by the Monday the crisis was over, and—for reasons that have not yet been disclosed—the intervention was later withdrawn.

On Tuesday morning, the standing committee assembled slowly. Herbert kept an uneasy eye on the clock. If members of the committee felt bashful about discussing such a subject at such a time, a quorum—twenty MPs—might not be available. If no quorum was available, the committee would have to adjourn till the next day, Thursday, and if they were still bashful on Thursday, the bill would go to the bottom of the list—which would destroy any chance of its passing. Ten minutes after the committee was due to begin work, only fourteen MPs had assembled. One of Herbert's allies

went out to scout around, returning to report that there were sufficient members waiting outside, but "they were reluctant to come in
and debate this particular amendment because of its possible
relevance to the constitutional crisis. It would be impossible, they
said, to avoid indiscretions." Herbert begged them to put their fears
aside. No reference, he assured them, would be made to individual
cases. No indiscretions need be perpetrated. At last they were persuaded to come in. The section was debated, and the clause of which
it formed a part was passed.

Interlude in Cannes

MPs were worried because they did not know what was happening. So was Baldwin. This was the only time, he told a friend, that
he was really frightened throughout the crisis. He feared that after
Mrs. Simpson's renunciation, the King might change his mind.

Baldwin's first thought was to find out what was going on at the
Cannes villa, and Horace Wilson was instructed to get hold of
Wallis' solicitor, Goddard, with the idea of flying him to the south
of France. Goddard consulted the King. Edward, his suspicions
aroused, instructed him not to go. But Baldwin was insistent. The
King rang the villa to warn Wallis of Goddard's impending arrival
and to tell her to pay no attention to anything he might say. The
villa household waited up, baffled, until 2:30, but Goddard did not
appear. Eventually it was reported that he had landed at Marseilles
—bringing with him "Dr. Kirkwood, the well-known gynaecologist,
and his anesthetist." (For the last time, when this was published,
rumour had its fling—until the explanation followed. Goddard had
a weak heart and the "gynaecologist" was a doctor who had been
engaged to travel with him—a precaution often taken in those days,
by those who were rich enough and who worried about travelling by
air. The "anesthetist" was a solicitor's clerk.)

When he arrived at the villa, Goddard disclosed his business: a
warning about the impending intervention in the divorce proceedings, and a positive proposal that Wallis should drop them. Wallis
turned to Brownlow for his advice. Brownlow was skeptical. If she
withdrew, only to find that the King was determined on abdicating
anyway, there would be a hopeless anticlimax. She decided to speak
to Edward, and he removed her last doubts, bringing his solicitor,

George Allen, to the telephone. The King, Allen told her, had "made up his mind to abdicate, and in fact was already in the process of doing so."

Precisely why Baldwin had been so insistent on Goddard's flying to see Mrs. Simpson has remained a matter for speculation. In *A King's Story*, Edward suggested that the visit had been inspired by Horace Wilson, "momentarily attracted by the possibility of breaking the abdication with a sudden and overpowering appeal to Wallis." According to Sencourt, Goddard was in any case planning to go in connection with the divorce, but, flattered to be approached by the Prime Minister and pleased to be offered a ride in a private airplane, he had agreed to undertake the mission on Baldwin's behalf, too. Baldwin's aim, Sencourt thought, was to make sure that Mrs. Simpson was not simply withdrawing for the time being "in order that she might again appear on the scene when she and her admirer should deem the chances more propitious." If she withdrew her divorce suit, she would remain the legal wife of Ernest Simpson, and the government "could face the future with comparative equanimity."

If all that the government wanted was to make it impossible for the King to marry Mrs. Simpson, this explanation would be plausible, but by this time they no longer cared whether he married her or not. What they wanted was to get him off the throne as expeditiously as possible. Why, then, should Baldwin risk encouraging him to remain King by putting marriage out of his reach? Beaverbrook thought it was because Baldwin now knew the King must go. His only remaining worry was the pledge he had foolishly given Edward that he would resign if the Cabinet did not agree to the second bill expediting the divorce. Here was the chance to ease his conscience. If he could pin Mrs. Simpson down to a promise to suspend the divorce proceedings, the King could no longer reproach him with failure to speed them up, and "Baldwin could escape from his dilemma."

Baldwin's friends, however, have since ridiculed this theory—even to the extent of questioning whether he ever gave the pledge. The most likely hypothesis was later to be put forward by Lord Brownlow: that Goddard was acting on his own behalf; that he had in mind, apart from his obligations to Mrs. Simpson—and to Baldwin—the possibility that he might win a crown of glory by solving the crisis, if he could persuade Mrs. Simpson to withdraw; and at the same time he would avert the risk of embarrassing disclosures about the Ipswich case, because withdrawal would eliminate the possibility of any intervener making a nuisance of himself. In his own statement, written to Beaverbrook fifteen years later, Goddard naturally did not elaborate on his motives, and perhaps he was not fully aware of them; but he could hardly have been unaware of the prestige that would have accrued to him if his proposal had been accepted, and proved to be the solution of the crisis.

In the meantime—even before Goddard left for the South of France—Baldwin had decided to sound out the King, to see whether Mrs. Simpson's statement had had any effect on his resolution to abdicate. Tactfully, Baldwin brought what on the surface was a polite request from the Cabinet that the King should reconsider his decision:

> Ministers are reluctant to believe that Your Majesty's resolve is irrevocable, and still venture to hope that before Your Majesty pronounces any formal decision, Your Majesty may be pleased to reconsider an intention which must so deeply distress and so vitally affect all Your Majesty's subjects.

In reality, it was a polite way of telling the King that if he had any intention of changing his mind, this was his last opportunity.

But Baldwin's fears were groundless: The King had no fight left in him. He was no longer in touch with the conspirators, and none of his friends at the Fort were in sympathy with the conspiracy's aims. For a week, too, he had been under constant strain. After Wallis' departure for France, Beaverbrook recalled, it had begun to tell on him. "He smoked incessantly, sometimes a cigarette, sometimes a pipe . . . sometimes he would sit with his head in his hands. Occasionally he would wipe the perspiration from his brow with an unfolded handkerchief, or hold the handkerchief against his head, as if to ease some hidden pressure or pain."

Over the week-end, the strain had intensified, and its effects were reflected in his relations with his brother, the Duke of York. According to the Duke's chronicle of the crisis, the King had asked him to go to the Fort on Friday morning.

> I rang him up but he would not see me and put me off till Saturday. I told him I would be at Royal Lodge on Saturday by 12:30 P.M. I rang him up on Saturday. "Come and see me on Sunday," was his answer. "I will see you and tell you my decision when I have made up my mind."

Sunday evening I rang up. "The King has a conference and will speak to you later," was the answer. But he did not ring up. Monday morning came. I rang up at 1:00 P.M. and my brother told me he might be able to see me that evening.

And that evening the Duke, unable to bear the "awful and ghastly suspense of waiting," went out to the Fort, to hear that his brother had made up his mind to go.

Perhaps the King delayed making his final decision known to the Cabinet out of curiosity to see what effect Wallis' renunciation would have. It had no effect. By this time, the public had ceased to care what Mrs. Simpson said or did. The change of mood was felt in and around Fleet Street. James Agate noticed it: at the week-end, he wrote in his diary, his impulse had been to hope that the King would tell Baldwin to resign and be damned. But on Tuesday, he realized, "I do not feel this now. I do not think anybody feels this now."

More probably the King's delay was due simply to a reluctance to take the irrevocable final step. When Baldwin arrived out to the Fort that evening, though, with the message from the Cabinet, the King replied that he had given the matter his further consideration and that he could not alter his decision. Baldwin, relieved, stayed to dinner. The Dukes of York and Kent were there, along with Ulick Alexander, Walter Monckton, George Allen, Thomas Dugdale, who had arrived at the Fort with Baldwin, and Sir Edward Peacock, receiver general of the Duchy of Cornwall. It was a meal, the Duke of York wrote, that "I am never likely to forget." The rest of the table were sad, but "my brother was the life and soul of the party, telling the Prime Minister things I am sure he had never heard before about unemployed centres etc. (referring to his visit to S. Wales). I whispered to Walter Monckton, 'And this is the man we are going to lose.' One couldn't, nobody could, believe it."

Edward was later to give a less roseate account of this, his last meeting with the Prime Minister. Baldwin, he was disturbed to notice, had arrived at the Fort with a suitcase—probably because when he came to describe the negotiations to Parliament "his story would sound much better if he were able to tell the country that he had spent a last night with the King in a humble and sincere effort to talk him out of his project." It was intimated to Baldwin that he would be welcome only to dinner. Still, it seems likely that the King did not at the time harbour the suspicions of Baldwin that emerged in *A King's Story*. In Colin Coote's biography of Walter Elliott, a junior minister in Baldwin's government at the time, Elliott was described as reporting on the Monday that the King had rejected the idea of a King's party because he realized that its aim would be to keep him on the throne "and let her be his mistress," which he could not accept: "Therefore, he has no animosity against ministers, who had not opposed his abdication. On the contrary, he is very matey with Baldwin." Admittedly, this was the impression Baldwin was anxious to give, but it seems to have been justified.

A lull

As the King had now pledged himself to abdication, making no further reference to Baldwin's pledge to resign if he could not persuade the Cabinet to accept the divorce bill, Baldwin no longer needed to worry on Wednesday whether Goddard succeeded in his mission. The government's only cause for concern was over the abdication procedure.

There was still a constitutional difficulty, of a kind to delight the mind of the Home Secretary. By the Statute of Westminster, the assent of each Dominion must be obtained for any law altering the succession. The Abdication Act, therefore, needed this sanction, and the timing was important, Simon explained, because "each Dominion had to receive the news through a cipher telegram to its Prime Minister before a cable from London could reach it, but not so early as to risk a reverse message being sent to London and made available in the 'stop press' before Baldwin made the announcement in the British House of Commons." Fortunately for the government, none of the Dominions' governments objected, and the time-table worked satisfactorily, but it meant a further day's delay, and until the Dominions' consent was obtained, Baldwin did not deem it wise to release the news. From his attitude, though, and that of his ministers, it was clear that a settlement was imminent, and there could be little doubt what it would be. The *Times* editorial on Wednesday morning was headed "A Lull," but it no longer protested at the delay. Dawson knew of the dinner party and realized its inevitable outcome, and his editorial was altogether gentler and more sympathetic than its predecessors.

Even the popular press was subdued. Tuesday's "End of the

Crisis" headlines turned out to be its last kick. On Wednesday, the *Express* ran a cartoon by Strube showing all the usual news subjects —Christmas shopping, the Spanish civil war, and the cricket Test Matches (the series was being played in Australia)—re-emerging as the crisis was ending, but it could be interpreted—just—as an indication that the *Express* realized all was over. Only the Houston and Mosley papers prepared to keep up the campaign—and once again, their printing deadlines mocked them. Theoretically, they were not due out until Saturday. In practice, they were to appear on Thursday. At the time they went to press the issue seemed still in doubt. The *Saturday Review* claimed that although Baldwin, "primed with instructions from Russia—to get rid of the King," had insisted, "Do my will or abdicate," the plot had failed. *Action* had an article by William Joyce—later to become notorious as Lord Haw-Haw, the war-time radio commentator from Germany, and to be hanged in 1945 as a traitor—saying, "Let the people now deliver their verdict." But by the time the *Saturday Review* and *Action* appeared on the streets, it was all over.

Nevertheless, the delay had its embarrassments. The crisis was still affecting business. Reports had been coming in of orders for coronation souvenirs being cancelled—before the week-end an official of the Birmingham Jewellers and Silversmiths' Association had told the press that in the event of abdication the loss to the trade would be "colossal." He was wrong. The trade simply sold two sets of coronation souvenirs, the one that happened and the one that didn't. But at the time this was either not realized or not mentioned, and in the Commons on Wednesday a Labour MP asked the Prime Minister whether he was aware of the grave financial inconvenience that was being caused by the delay. That point, the Prime Minister replied, had not escaped him.

So long as the crisis lasted, too, rumour continued to fly around. The most likely reason for the delay in coming to a decision, it was assumed, was that there was some hitch about who should be Edward's successor. On Friday the *Evening Standard* had hinted that the Duke of York might not be willing to succeed the King, and in a letter to Geoffrey Dawson on the same day, a peer had suggested that a regency should be established. Over the week-end rumour played around with the possibility that the Duke of York did not feel up to the job and that Queen Mary might take it on. On Tuesday, Tom Jones noted in his diary that there was much sympathy for her, "some going to the length of suggesting that she should act as Regent for Princess Elizabeth." The following day Sir Philip Gibbs heard this rumour in his club, and that evening *Figaro's* London correspondent, reporting that abdication was imminent, claimed in his message that the Princess Elizabeth would be proclaimed Queen, with a regency council presided over by Queen Mary. There was no foundation to the rumours—except, perhaps, that the Duke of York had been under severe strain for weeks, all the greater because of his brother's inability to confide in him; and at the critical time, his wife, on whom he relied, caught influenza and had to retire to bed. When, on Wednesday, he went to see Queen Mary to confirm that Edward's decision was irrevocable, he "broke down and sobbed like a child." But there had never been any question of his fitness to succeed, and he had been prepared for the eventuality for weeks.

The prolonging of the delay was also having unfortunate effects abroad—in the United States, particularly. So long as the papers and radio programmes there had simply been speculating, it had been possible to disregard them, but now that their speculation had been proved to be accurate, their criticisms and sneers redoubled, to the alarm of the Foreign Office. According to Asa Briggs in his history of the BBC, the monitoring of foreign programmes that was to play such a large part during the war went through a new phase of development at the time of the abdication crisis, "when Whitehall was especially interested in knowing what American stations were saying about the King and Mrs. Simpson."

What they were saying often hardly bore repeating. Two strands emerged, both hostile to Britain. On Friday, Upton Sinclair told the *Mirror* ("talking white-hot American over the transatlantic phone") that if the King of England did not marry Mrs. Simpson, America would feel it was an insult to an American citizen—"What's wrong with American women anyhow!" But the other kind of criticism was even more galling. On Sunday, complaints were heard from pulpits all over America of the way that the British monarchy was undermining moral standards. Dr. Frederick Harris, for example, a well-known Washington clergyman, spoke for his congregation of "barnyard morals" and a "trumped-up divorce."

The longer the crisis dragged on, the more contemptuous became the general tone. "The future will hardly believe," the *Washington Herald* claimed on Monday, "that the British Empire, at this moment in international, world-wide danger and uncertainty, could descend to such puerile foolishness as in the Mrs. Simpson–King Edward incident." And the following day, it switched to verse:

The King is in his palace, fighting many foes
Mrs. Simpson rests in sunny France, thinking of her woes
Queen Mary is at Marlborough House, crying in her knittin'
And the Duke of York is thinking that he'll soon be King of Britain.

Jests and lampoons of that kind proliferated, as did news stories related to the subject. INS reported that an English actor living in New York had been compelled to make a pledge in court, after his wife had had him arrested for striking her in a quarrel, that he "would not argue with her about Mrs. Simpson."

The possible effects of the crisis on Europe also had to be considered. Whether Hitler and Mussolini deliberately took advantage of the crisis to reinforce Spain is doubtful. They were quite capable, as events were to show, of going ahead with their plans whether Britain was in a state of crisis or not. But the Germans for a time had hoped to exploit the crisis more directly. Von Ribbentrop had arrived in London in October and presented his credentials at the palace. But the constitutional crisis broke before he had time to follow up his plan to establish contact with the King—they had met only on formal occasions. Ribbentrop realized he must act quickly. At his request, Hitler ordered that the German newspapers should play down the story and refrain from comment—presumably realizing that for the Nazi press to take the King's side could only help Baldwin. In Italy, Mussolini gave similar instructions. But as the days went by, Ribbentrop saw that the King was losing. "I was very depressed," he wrote in his diary, "and racked my brains for a possible way in which to influence the course of events . . . King Edward VIII had shown himself a potential advocate of Anglo-German undersanding, therefore it lay in our interests that he should remain King." He asked for an audience, but his request was turned down by a court official—probably Hardinge.

But there was not going to be much further delay. On Wednesday afternoon Baldwin told the Commons that he hoped to have a statement for them the following day, and it was clear that the difficulties were now technical. The King's friends resigned themselves to his departure. Only in the south of France did the conspiracy give one final feeble twitch, and, appropriately, it came from Rothermere.

His son Esmond Harmsworth was staying in Monte Carlo, and on Wednesday he telephoned to Wallis to come over and consider a fresh solution that, he claimed, was being canvassed: the creation of a council of state, enabling the King to withdraw to the Continent for a while. Even Wallis, desperate though she must have been for any grounds of hope, found this hard to believe, and driving back to the villa she decided instead to accept Brownlow's last-resort proposal, which she had resisted before. Renunciation having failed, Brownlow urged, she must simply remove herself from the scene. She would go, she decided, to Peking, and stay with some friends she had made there years before.

A final statement to this effect was prepared for the press, and she rang the Fort to tell Edward of her decision. Again, he referred her to George Allen. The King, Allen told her, had given his final decision to abdicate, the Cabinet had been informed of it, the Instrument of Abdication was being prepared, and he would be out of England within forty-eight hours.

THURSDAY, DECEMBER 10—
FRIDAY, DECEMBER 11

On Thursday morning Rothermere's *Daily Mail* virtually conceded defeat in its main news headline—"Abdication feared today"—and, for the first time, a rival claim to be the lead story threatened the abdication's paramountcy: a Dutch airliner had crashed in the previous day's fog near Croydon, with a heavier death toll than any previous air accident in Britain—fourteen, including a former Premier of Sweden and de la Cierva, the inventor of the Autogiro.

At ten o'clock the King's three brothers went to the Fort to join Peacock, Monckton, Alexander and Allen—the King's steady companions of the past few days—in witnessing the signing of the Instrument of Abdication:

I, Edward VIII, of Great Britain, Ireland, and the British Dominions beyond the Seas, King, Emperor of India, do hereby declare My irrevocable determination to renounce the Throne for myself and for my descendants, and desire that effect should be given to this Instrument of Abdication immediately.

In token whereof I have hereunto set My hand this tenth day of December, nineteen hundred and thirty-six, in the presence of the witnesses whose signatures are subscribed.

At Westminster, MPs were in no mood to transact routine parliamentary business—much to A.P. Herbert's alarm. His Matrimonial Causes Bill had provided a bizarre counterpoint to the crisis. Now it seemed possible that the King's choice of a day on which to abdicate might wreck the bill's chances. Two days before, Herbert had been worried by the reluctance of members of the standing committee to attend for fear of indiscretions. Now, with the Prime Minister's statement imminent, a quorum was hard to obtain for a different reason: MPs found it very difficult to think about anything except the impending abdication. When Herbert went out to find what was happening, he was told that "everyone was too much upset by the crisis to give his mind to the bill." What was worse, a Labour Party meeting was due to be held at 11:30, which would remove all supporters in the Opposition. In desperation, Herbert thought of a way out: he arranged that whenever his bill's critics called for a division, the Labour members on the committee would be called for, so that they could come running around to vote. By this means, two of the bill's reforms—granting divorce for desertion and for cruelty—were carried that morning.

For a while that afternoon, too, MPs had to contain themselves as best they could, knowing that the Prime Minister had the decisive announcement ready—but knowing also that he could not give it to the House until prayers had been said and Question Time completed, and over fifty questions were on the Order Paper for the day. Rarely had answers been listened to less patiently. But at last, the Prime Minister rose to announce that he held a message from the King, in the King's hand, and he presented it to the Speaker—who had some difficulty, observers noted, in keeping his own hand steady enough to read it.

After long and anxious consideration, the King's message ran, he had determined to renounce the throne, a decision which was now final and irrevocable. He did not propose to go into the private reasons for his abdication. Suffice it to say that he had come to realize that he could no longer discharge his tasks as King efficiently, or to his own satisfaction. Accordingly, he had signed the Instrument of Abdication drawn up by the government, and he wished to take leave of his people "in the confident hope that the course which I have thought it right to follow is that which is best for the stability of the Throne and Empire."

Baldwin then formally moved "that His Majesty's most gracious message be now considered," and he related to the House what had happened since he had had his first interview with the King on the subject of Mrs. Simpson nearly two months before. He spoke from notes, extempore, but as Sencourt claimed, "It was one of the most subtle and adroit presentations of the story that a trained experience could have devised." To his audience it seemed transparently honest and guileless. It explained what had previously been mystifying, and above all, it seemed to make very clear that the government had not been engaged in any scheme to get rid of the King or even been involved in any dispute with him. On the contrary, both had been striving for a way out of what had turned out in the end to be a hopeless impasse.

All through the speech, Baldwin slid in intimations of his affection for the King, and the King's for him. It was, he insisted, the King's own frankness, "one of his many attractions," which had made his abdication inevitable. "It would have been perfectly possible for His Majesty not to have told me [of his decision to marry] at the date when he did, and not to have told me for some months to come. But he realized the damage that might be done in the interval by gossip, rumours, and talk, and he made that declaration to me when he did on purpose to avoid what he felt might be dangerous, not only here, but throughout the Empire, to the moral force of the Crown." Baldwin concluded, "Let no word be spoken today that the utterer of that word may regret in days to come, let no word be spoken that causes pain to any soul . . . let us rally behind the new King—stand by him, and help him—and let us hope that, whatever the country may have suffered by what we are passing through, it may soon be repaired, and that we may take what steps we can in trying to make this country a better country for all the people in it." At the end of the speech, after a brief adjournment, Attlee gave the Labour Party's seal of approval, and Sinclair the Liberals'. Churchill, too—saying, "What is done, is done"—accepted wholeheartedly that the King's decision had been taken freely, voluntarily and spontaneously, "in his own time, and in his own way."

It was left to the members of the Independent Labour Party to try to shake the House out of its cosy self-congratulatory mood. The ILP had once been a power on the left: now it was reduced to a handful of Clydesiders who were regarded in the House with benevolence, as tamed tigers. One of them—John McGovern—was later to claim that he had been the first to bring up the subject in the Commons before the story broke. Following a question on Coronation arrangements, he had asked "if there is any use going on with these arrangements in view of the gambling at Lloyd's and elsewhere as to whether this Coronation will ever take place?" And when, after a silence, somebody asked what was the trouble, he replied, "Mrs. Simpson," before the Speaker hurriedly called the next business. But McGovern's recollection of the period in his autobiography was tinged with bitterness—he had become an active Moral Rearmament worker, and it is possible that the MRA doctrine of absolute purity coloured his recollections.

At the beginning of the crisis, a rumour had got around that the ILP had pledged their support to Baldwin, but on Friday it had been formally denied in a statment to the press: "This is not the case. The ILP remains absolutely uncommitted. The ILP is republican and anti-monarchical." And now, James Maxton rose to expound the ILP's line. He had once been feared as a redoubtable political demagogue, and he had made his mark at Westminster as an orator: Lord Boothby, recalling "the lean emaciated figure, the raven locks, the deep resonant voice, the stabbing forefinger, the swelling but always controlled passion, the flashes of humour that lit his bitterest speeches," thought him at his best an incomparable debater in the Commons. But "he never aspired to be more than an agitator, and the mellowing influence of Parliament blunted the edge of his attack." And on this occasion Maxton was careful not to offend susceptibilities unnecessarily: "I share with others in this House," he claimed, "the human sympathies that go out to His Majesty," and he shared the same human sympathies with the Prime Minister in his task. He felt, though, that the circumstances in which King and Prime Minister had found themselves had been bound to arise, in the nature of hereditary monarchical institutions, and he and his ILP colleagues felt that the lesson of the past few days was that the monarchy had outlived its usefulness.

George Buchanan, another ILP member, was more outspoken. He had listened, he said, to more cant and humbug than he had ever listened to in his life, about the King. "If he had not voluntarily stepped from the Throne, everyone knows that the same people in the House who pay lip service to him would have poured out scorn, filth and abuse . . . If he is a tenth as good as you say, why are you not keeping him? Because you know he is a weak creature. You want to get rid of him and you are taking the step today." But MPs, confident in their rectitude and once again mesmerized by Baldwin, did not take Buchanan seriously.

Thereafter, events moved rapidly. The Abdication Bill was prepared that evening. It went through all its stages in the Commons before lunch the following day—Friday. When Geoffrey Dawson looked in at Westminster, early that afternoon, everybody had left.

Edward had asked to be allowed to broadcast before he departed, and this time Baldwin did not demur. Churchill was invited out to lunch at the Fort to put the final polish on it before sending it to Baldwin for scrutiny, and to say farewell. Beaverbrook was not invited to lunch, but Edward telephoned to say goodbye to him, too. His toothache had returned—owing, he thought, to the abrupt transition from extreme activity at the heart of affairs to complete inactivity and isolation—and he was at the dentist's when the message came. "Buckingham Palace—no more" was his first reaction. "The fight had been lost and the most stubborn enemy of our plan for a United British Empire had scored his greatest triumph." But eventually he went to the telephone for a brief exchange of good wishes.

The new King—King already, though he would not be proclaimed until the following morning—came for a final talk. A title for Edward had to be decided upon, and it was agreed that the new King's first act would be to create his predecessor Duke of Windsor. Monckton, in charge of the farewell arrangements, returned to say that Baldwin's approval had been given, and the King left the Fort for the last time, to dine with his family at Windsor Royal Lodge before making his broadcast.

The cables had been laid into Windsor Castle the previous Monday. All that had to be considered was how best to introduce the King. Who should do it? Reith had been wondering: "If any consideration of courtesy was relevant, I naturally would; probably the personage concerned would not want anyone around." But Edward decided he would like Reith to be there, and Reith, feeling it was "interesting to assist in, or for the matter of that, *assister à,* historical occasions," needed no persuasion.

The civil war in Spain had not prevented Radio Madrid from ringing up to ask for permission to relay Edward's Abdication speech —which amused Edward, when Reith told him. A voice test followed: Edward, picking up a paper at random, found himself reading a speech by Samuel Hoare to a tennis meeting, noting that the new King (unlike the old) was a keen player. In suitably awestruck tones, Reith announced, "This is Windsor Castle. His Royal Highness, Prince Edward," and left the room. Edward, moving into the chair he had vacated, kicked a table leg—and gave rise to the legend that Reith, perhaps to show his contempt, had slammed the door as he left the studio.

The broadcast ran:

At long last I am able to say a few words of my own.

I have never wanted to withhold anything, but until now it has been not constitutionally possible for me to speak.

A few hours ago I discharged my last duty as King and Emperor, and now that I have been succeeded by my brother, the Duke of York, my first words must be to declare my allegiance to him. This I do with all my heart.

You all know the reasons which have impelled me to renounce the Throne. But I want you to understand that in making up my mind I did not forget the country or the Empire which as Prince of Wales, and lately as King, I have for twenty-five years tried to serve. But you must believe me when I tell you that I have found it impossible to carry the heavy burden of responsibility and to discharge my duties as King as I would wish to do without the help and support of the woman I love.

And I want you to know that the decision I have made has been mine and mine alone. This was a thing I had to judge entirely for myself. The other person most nearly concerned has tried up to the last to persuade me to take a different course. I have made this, the most serious decision of my life, upon a single thought of what would in the end be best for all.

This decision has been made less difficult to me by the sure knowledge that my Brother, with his long training in the public affairs of this country and with his fine qualities, will be able to take my place forthwith, without interruption or injury to the life and progress of the Empire. And he has one matchless blessing, enjoyed by so many of you and not bestowed on me—a happy home with his wife and children.

During these hard days I have been comforted by my Mother and by my Family. The Ministers of the Crown, and in particular Mr. Baldwin, the Prime Minister, have always treated me with full consideration. There has never been any constitutional difference between me and them and between me and Parliament. Bred in the constitutional tradition by my Father, I should never have allowed any such issue to arise.

Ever since I was Prince of Wales, and later on when I occupied the Throne, I have been treated with the greatest kindness by all classes, wherever I have lived or journeyed throughout the Empire. For that I am very grateful.

I now quit altogether public affairs, and I lay down my burden. It may be some time before I return to my native land, but I shall always follow the fortunes of the British race and Empire with profound interest, and if at any time in the future I can be found of service to His Majesty in a private station I shall not fail.

And now we all have a new King. I wish him, and you, his people, happiness and prosperity with all my heart. God bless you all. God Save the King.

"Take all the great speeches of history," Lowell Thomas, the American radio correspondent, wrote, "of the stage, of impassioned orators, of great statesmen—there is nothing approaching in poignancy that of the man who today spoke to the Empire for the last time." In fact, Edward spoke to the world: to wherever radio sets could be tuned in to him. One of the biggest telephone exchanges in New York reported that during the speech, not a single telephone call was received. In Jamaica, Lloyd George listened: he was observed by the people with him to be close to tears. T.R. Fyvel, an English writer, was in Zion Square in Jerusalem: traffic came to a standstill as Arabs in their burnooses, Jewish trade unionists in their blue tunics, British soldiers in uniform, civilians, and tourists stood in silence as the speech was relayed from a loudspeaker outside a radio shop.

In London, cinemas interrupted their programmes for the speech, and theatres arranged that it should coincide with an interval—or in the case of the Royalty Theatre, had it taken down in shorthand and read out when the next interval came around. Everywhere, people who had no set looked around for one to listen to. At Claridge's, Somerset Maugham borrowed a portable from one of the porters and listened with Graham Greene and Osbert Sitwell. And at the villa in Cannes, Wallis was to recall, everybody, including the domestic staff, gathered around the radio. Edward's voice "came out of the loudspeaker calmly, movingly. I was lying on the sofa with my hands over my eyes, trying to hide my tears. After he finished, the others quietly went away and left me alone. I lay there a long time before I could control myself enough to walk through the house and go up to my room."

The hostility that had arisen against the King in the previous few days was largely dissipated by the broadcast. It was finely spoken, Sir Philip Gibbs thought, with perfect timing and emphasis. Great numbers of people, he heard, wept when it ended. Richard Hoggart was to confirm that people had tears in their eyes in his working-class street. "There was a general feeling that 'they' had done him and that he had taken the only reasonable course, since love after all is the most important thing in the world." Geoffrey Dawson, who listened at home, thought the broadcast "very correct and rather moving." Even the Archbishop of Canterbury admitted it had real pathos—though, typically, one passage jarred on him, where Edward said he had been denied the happiness of his brother in having a wife and children—"as if he might not at any time have honestly possessed this happiness if he had chosen." But perhaps Lang, a bachelor, wanted to convince himself that he had remained one by choice. Beaverbrook also had a criticism. The broadcast, he thought, was a triumph of natural and sincere eloquence, but when the King spoke of Baldwin in terms of friendship, "I could not believe that I had heard rightly."

From Windsor Castle, Edward went back to Royal Lodge to say goodbye to his family—formally bowing to his brother as the new King—before driving down to Portsmouth with Monckton, to board a destroyer that the Admiralty had put at his disposal. "And so it came to pass that at two o'clock on the morning of December 12, 1936, HMS *Fury* slid silently and unescorted out of Portsmouth Harbour. . . . I knew now I was irretrievably on my own. The drawbridges were going up behind me. But of one thing I was certain: so far as I was concerned, love had triumphed over the exigencies of politics."

AFTERMATH

SUNLIGHT AND SHADOW

The abdication might have been expected to leave a wake of controversy. It did not. Edward's movements after the first few days of his exile scarcely rated a paragraph in the newspapers. Over the week-end, it seemed, the public accepted the new King as if he had been on the throne since the death of his father. His first act, the *Times* noted, was "to interpret and answer one hope common to most of his subjects by taking the significant title of King George VI." He meant to return to his father's ways. So close was the identification that the Archbishop of Canterbury, recording the arrival of a "most kindly" Christmas letter from the King, observed "that it would be difficult to see in his handwriting, and especially in his signature 'George R.I.,' any difference from that of his father. Prosit Omen!"

At court, there was a return to the values, and even to some extent to the habits, of George V. The new King invited each of his ministers to spend a night at Windsor, and in due course, the Duff Coopers received their invitation. They had been forewarned that knee-breeches would be worn, but it turned out that the King had changed his mind and that trousers were to be worn instead. Duff was offered a pair belonging to a secretary, but fortunately his servant had packed his own. Alec Hardinge arrived to give a briefing— Lady Diana recorded it in her diary: "Dinner at 8:30, leave dining room with gentlemen at 9:30, but gentlemen don't stop, they walk straight through us to the lu and talks and drinks. Girls gossip until 10:15 when the men reappear flushed and relieved, and at 10:30 it's goodnight." Through dinner, what appeared to be "an inferior make of loud gramophone" played airs from *Our Miss Gibbs* and *The Bing Boys:* it turned out to be an army band, muffled. Windsor Castle was itself again.

So far from embarrassment being felt at Westminster over what had happened, the general feeling was of self-congratulation—as it was in the country as a whole. There was little mockery. Hodge and Graves reported that an advertiser ran a campaign, "The King may abdicate, but with the love for Dixon's jams and pickles, the family sticks together like the Empire," but such jocosity was rare. The wind in the treetops, a *Times* editorial claimed on the morning of December 11, "strengthens and settles the roots of the tree . . . For a brief, bad moment it felt like an earthquake. It was only a storm. It has blown over, not without leaving its traces. But the black sky is now behind, and there is sunlight ahead."

By the following day, even this seemed too modest. "Not for the first time," the *Times* claimed, "a sudden emergency has enabled the British people to prove its native greatness." And, surprisingly, others accepted this interpretation. *Figaro* in an editorial contrasted the British morale, as demonstrated by the handling of the crisis, with French political indiscipline, which had left the state so fragile; and *Le Temps* took much the same line, arguing that Britain and her former King were giving a rare example of a political dignity to a world that "has lost faith in itself and is everywhere slipping toward moral and social disorders."

The fear that the arch of the Empire might be weakened by the discovery of the need to replace its coping stone proved unfounded. Only De Valera took the opportunity, which he had been awaiting since he came into power earlier in the 1930s, to remove his country a little further from the Empire. He did not declare a republic because he wanted to wait until it could be an all-Ireland republic, but he hurried through an act abolishing the office of Governor-General and retaining the crown as a symbol only for purposes of external relations—such as the signing of treaties. Some amusement was caused by the pronouncement of a legal luminary, Professor Berriedale Keith, drawing attention to one result of the act's hasty drafting. Under the new law the dissolution and summoning of the Dail, the Irish Parliament, was to be undertaken by the Speaker, in place of the defunct Governor-General. But in law the Speaker's office ceased to exist when the Dail was dissolved, so in law the Irish Parliament ceased to exist, as "the Dail cannot be summoned by a non-existent person." But the Dail was duly summoned, and met.

Although the affair had no obvious effect on Anglo-American relations, it is difficult to believe that it had no long-term effects. "We British are a very curious people," Hugh Dalton wrote to a friend in the United States, "but I think we have got out of this particular mess with characteristic skill. Some foreigners will be amazed, others amused." Americans, he hoped, would not feel affronted. A few

Americans did—or at least claimed that they did: Upton Sinclair said
that Mrs. Simpson was only a hypocritical pretext to get rid of the
King, and Sinclair Lewis, in an open letter, invited him to come and
live in America, "where we have a feeling that a man has a right to
his own private life." But in America, too, feeling had begun to
harden against the Duke. Old republicanism began to show through.
Senator Borah of Idaho announced that he was glad Parliament had
been victorious. Big Bill Thompson contented himself with a barbed
"No comment" to reporters: "The King's lady friends are no business
of mine or anybody else's."

But although there was little disposition when it was all over to
indulge in further sniping at Britain for having rejected an American
queen—H.L. Mencken actually blamed Edward, as a "poor fish"—
the weeks of gossip, much of it laced with anti-British feeling, cannot
but have had an effect. No comparable story has ever received such
attention. "In the whole history of the American people," a New York
correspondent, Nicholas Murray Butler, wrote to Geoffrey Dawson,
"no public event, whether domestic or foreign, has ever so seized
upon the interest and imagination of the people, or has occupied so
large a portion of the daily press, as the recent happenings in England." Nor was it only the popular papers that gorged their readers
on the affair. The New York *Times* gave the London *Times'* editorials, as well as those of the *Telegraph*, the *Morning Post* and the
Manchester Guardian, along with the debates in the Commons.
From her study, Stella Sutherland calculated that by the end of the
year 1936, there could not have been less than half a million press
clippings on the subject, and, as she went on to point out, the anti-
British attitude continued after the abdication. The American press,
she concluded, "remains unfriendly and even openly hostile to England a century and a half after the revolution. With a few noteworthy exceptions, both newspapers and periodicals from the highest
order to the lowest assume this attitude. No month passes without a
score of articles so acrimonious in tone as to persuade all but the
most optimistic of the imminence of a break in diplomatic relations."

Nor should the effect on Britain of what was published in America be underestimated. Every Cabinet minister and most members
of the Establishment saw some of the press cuttings—and it was
usually the more scabrous cuttings which were sent back to Britain.
And an event a year later that was to cause some stir in Whitehall
may have had some connection with the resentment aroused.

Roosevelt's victory in the Presidential election of 1936 put him in the strong position of a man who—as he then assumed—was in his last term of office, and could consequently state his own ideas, even if they were not electorally popular. He was well-disposed to Britain, and the abdication did not worry him, though he was full of curiosity about it. When Beaverbrook was next in America, according to Driberg, he was invited to Washington to be cross-examined by Roosevelt on what had happened. (Roosevelt thought the moral was that Edward should have remembered the maxim "Never resign.") It would not have been difficult for the British government to make use of the fact that for once, they had a sympathetic President. But Chamberlain was by this time infected by a deep, though not conscious, anti-Americanism, and when Roosevelt offered help, he was snubbed.

Lord Avon described the occasion in his memoirs. He was taking a January holiday in the south of France when the Foreign Office recalled him on urgent business: a message from Roosevelt to Chamberlain about the deteriorating international situation. At the risk of offending isolationists, still regarded as politically influential, Roosevelt announced that he was prepared to call a conference, to see whether it would be possible to reach agreement on the principles upon which international relations should rest. But before he did so, he would like to ensure that it had the cordial approval of His Majesty's government.

The British ambassador in Washington cabled an urgent plea that the government should accept Roosevelt's initiative: if they did not, it would create a deplorable impression in the United States. Eden, when he heard, was wholeheartedly in favour of acceptance, but Chamberlain, he found, acting on Sir Horace Wilson's advice, had turned the proposal down, on the ground that Britain was about to enter upon negotiations with Germany and Italy, and the President's plan might cut across them. "A douche of cold water," Sumner Welles commented, and Roosevelt was disappointed. Eden was furious. Not for the first time, he found it "difficult to escape the conclusion that the Prime Minister had deliberately withheld the information from me, sensing that I would disagree," and a month later, finally disillusioned by Chamberlain's abject appeasement of Mussolini, he resigned.

Naturally this helped to justify the suspicion and hostility in the United States even in circles that might ordinarily have been friendly. In *Harpers* for March 1938, Elmer Davis remarked that the present British government was an excellent argument for isolationism, not only because Britain's foreign policy for the past seven years had been "an almost unbroken succession of blunders," but because "it had proved its unscrupulousness by the way it got rid of King Edward (he had to be got rid of, but the methods employed were pretty dirty)." This disruption of amicable communication lasted up to the outbreak of war, with further snubs to Roosevelt. It was not surprising that in the summer of 1940 many Americans—including Joseph P. Kennedy, then ambassador in London—should have felt that Britain was not worth wasting arms and munitions on, that she was decadent and would soon collapse. But for the advent of Churchill, with his ability to establish rapport with Roosevelt and to arouse the admiration of the American people, the lend-lease help that came just in time might well have been withheld.

Winston Churchill

Churchill's own career was almost finally wrecked by the abdication. It was not his fault—as the King had neglected to warn him—that his plea for time and patience should have come out on Saturday morning, leading ministers to assume he was helping the King to play a double game, but as even Compton Mackenzie had to admit, its timing was unfortunate. And his attempt to repeat the plea in the Commons on the Monday, leading to the ignominy of being refused a hearing, seemed to many observers to mark the end of his career. "It was felt," Lord Kilmuir recalled, "no doubt unjustly, that his aversion towards Baldwin was at least as great a factor in his intervention in the abdication crisis as his admiration for the King." Above all, confidence in his judgement was shaken once again, a factor of great importance when his sombre warnings of the German menace began to become insistent. The "Arms and the Covenant" campaign on which he had set such store was shattered, and he was himself "so smitten in public opinion," he later recalled, "that it was the almost universal view that my political life was at last ended."

This was the *Spectator's* view. Only the week before, the *Spectator* had carried a sympathetic profile of Churchill saying that "as spearhead of a great popular movement for the defence at home and abroad of all that democracy cares for, he may achieve what he never could if checked by the trammels that accompany the authority of office." The following week, "Janus"—the editor, Wilson Harris —in his column had to admit sadly that such speculation, relevant when it was written, was now completely irrelevant because of his intervention in the constitutional crisis. "Mr. Churchill has hopelessly compromised not only himself but the cause for which he is working." Whether he would have been able to exert effective influence on the Chamberlain government if he had not compromised himself and his cause remains a matter for speculation, but his belated intervention in the abdication crisis certainly destroyed much of his potential authority in the next three years.

The effect of the crisis on the Establishment was also unfortunate, though for the opposite reason. Its members preened themselves on being victorious over what in their correspondence they sometimes referred to as "the powers of darkness"—embracing Mrs. Simpson, Beaverbrook and Rothermere. Having saved the Empire, as they thought, they were all the more convinced of their own rectitude and their capacity to run the country.

As things turned out, the abdication crisis was a kind of rehearsal for the Establishment's part in appeasement. On whether Hitler and Mussolini ought to be appeased, admittedly, the Establishment did not show quite the same consistency as it had over the abdication. But those who thought business could be done with Hitler were far more numerous and more influential than those who, like Robert Brand, thought Hitler and Mussolini should be resisted. Chamberlain—who succeeded Baldwin as Prime Minister after the coronation —Halifax, Simon, Inskip, Hoare, Geoffrey Dawson, Tom Jones and Horace Wilson were all to be men of Munich, as were their Cliveden hosts; and the fact that their chief adversary was the discredited Churchill only confirmed them in their assumption that they must be right. Eden's resignation early in 1938 did not disturb them, because he had been dragging his heels over the policy of appeasing Mussolini. Duff Cooper's resignation over Munich only made them feel they should have dispensed with his services earlier: had he not been Edward's friend? The Establishment became progressively more intolerant of criticism, managing to shut their minds to the fact that Hitler and Mussolini were doing precisely what Churchill had warned that they would do.

Geoffrey Dawson

There was a curious echo of the abdication crisis at the time of Munich. When Geoffrey Dawson wrote his article on the morganatic marriage and by-lined it "By Our Political Correspondent," nobody on the *Times* probably thought it odd. Editors were, in a sense, their own political correspondents, and they occasionally liked to break away from the limitations imposed by the editorial pattern. When Duff Cooper resigned after Munich, Dawson stepped out of his chair again—but with a difference. To those who were on Duff Cooper's side, his speech seemed outstanding. Churchill thought it one of the finest parliamentary performances he had witnessed, and Harold Macmillan rated it the finest. Anthony Winn, the *Times* lobby correspondent, was also impressed, and said as much in his report. But Dawson had also been in the House that afternoon, and he thought the speech was deplorable. When he saw the lobby correspondent's report he not merely suppressed it but substituted a derogatory report of his own, calling the speech "a damp squib," but he left the by-line "By Our Lobby Correspondent."

Technically, Dawson was within his rights. The *Times* boasted a tradition of anonymity: "Our Lobby Correspondent" could be held to refer to the job, not the man who undertook it. But in practice, the various *Times* correspondents inevitably became identifiable in Fleet Street and where they worked—in this case, at Westminster. Winn, finding in the *Times* an article giving views flatly opposed to those that he had expressed the night before, felt he had no alternative but to resign.

Nothing that Dawson did—not even his admission, later to be disclosed, that he "did his utmost, night after night, to keep out of the papers anything that might hurt German susceptibilities"—did more damage to his reputation. "A beloved creature in so many ways," Colin Coote, who was working under him at the time of the abdication, described him; "and yet, on this occasion, 'unprincipled.' Why?"

After Dawson's death, Bishop Headlam gave the sermon at a commemoration service in All Souls, saying of him, "He had a deeper sense of duty than anyone else I have known . . . it did not matter, he said, what your reputation was—it did not matter whether what you did was known or unknown, it did not matter whether you obtained any recognition for what you had done; what mattered was that you should be conscious yourself of having tried to do what was right." It was an accurate assessment, but the trouble with Dawson, as with Chamberlain, Lang, and other Establishment figures of the time, was that because they formed so tightly knit a clique, and because they were blinkered by their sense of rectitude, they assumed they were right politically, as well as morally, on the issues of the day, and they also assumed that anybody who disagreed was not merely wrong, but irresponsible—"mischievous." From this it was a short step to refusing to listen to their arguments and, where possible, actually suppressing them. The consequences were nearly disastrous. It is possible, though difficult, to make out a case that Britain gained time by accident from Munich, but nothing can justify the wilful blindness the Chamberlain government showed both before and after to the realities of Nazism. And for this blindness, the *Times* must take some of the responsibility. For all Dawson's virtues, Lord Boothby commented, "and they were many and great, he goes down to history as an architect of the Decline and Fall of the British Empire, to the service of which he dedicated his life."

Cosmo Gordon Lang

At the time, however, the only member of the Establishment to come badly out of the affair was the Archbishop of Canterbury. He was already under suspicion as the man chiefly responsible for pushing the King from his throne, and now, in a broadcast he made the day after Edward had left the country, he was unwise enough to express what many members of the Establishment felt but were shrewd enough not to say in public.

A few felt sympathy. "Seldom must any man," Lord Dawson, the royal doctor, wrote to the Duke shortly after Christmas, "have been faced with a more critical decision, and equally seldom has such decision been reached with equal quietude and strength." That this was not simply flattery was revealed in another letter he had written to the Princess Royal, commiserating with her on the trials she and her family had been through, but saying, in extenuation, "A *first* absorbing love coming after forty is apt to take possession. To have abandoned it would have spoilt life and work and therefore worth. To preserve it in marriage was impossible. Granted the dilemma, with what strength and dignity it was met!"

The more general Establishment's reaction, though, was compounded of relief at being able to speak freely without risk of *lèse-majesté,* and pent-up resentment at Edward for giving them such a scare. That he had behaved with scrupulous regard to his responsibilities mattered less to them than that he had appeared to be on the verge of behaving irresponsibly, and what a pit might have yawned in front of them if he had! They could not know how ineffective the King's party was doomed to be, even if Edward had encouraged its development, and they could not know—nor did they want to listen, if told—that Edward had rejected it. They preferred the story that more readily presented itself, that Edward, egged on by Mrs. Simp-

son and her raffish friends, encouraged by the gutter press and by
Churchill, had wanted a trial of strength, and that this had only been
prevented by the wise and conciliatory Baldwin, who had managed
to convince Edward of his duty to his subjects and to the institution
of the monarchy. In private, therefore, they spoke ill of the departed
King, and the campaign of snide rumour about him and his wife-
to-be continued.

Lang, however, felt it his duty to break the silence. He should
have known better: once, years before, he had made a similar error
with humiliating results. In 1914, recalling that he had seen the
Kaiser kneeling at the deathbed of Queen Victoria, he referred to it
as "a very sacred personal memory." The Kaiser was already an
ogre, and public opinion reacted so furiously that, according to
Sencourt, Lang suffered from a nervous trouble "which upset his
capillary glands and made him suddenly bald." But this reference to
the Kaiser, though tinged with his unctuous snobbery, had at least
had a kindly intent. The words which were to bring him into public
disfavour for the second time had not even Christian charity to recommend them. After remarking on the King's great gifts and wide
popularity when he came to the throne, Lang said:

> From God he had received a high and sacred trust. Yet by his own
> will he has abdicated—he has surrendered the trust. With characteristic
> frankness he has told us his motive. It was a craving for private happiness.
> Strange and sad it must be that for such a motive, however strongly it
> pressed upon his heart, he should have disappointed hopes so high and
> abandoned a trust so great.

Coming from somebody other than Lang, these words might have
made an impression. There were still people who thought of the
monarchy in those terms—Queen Mary, for one. According to Pope-
Hennessy, she greeted her son's decision to give up the throne "with
consternation, with anger and with pain." Nothing else in her life,
she was to insist, caused her so much distress, and so much humiliation. Even her pleasure and pride in the success of her second son as
King "failed to obliterate for her the memory of the shock which
King Edward VIII's abdication had caused." His inability to communicate to her the nature of his feelings, or indeed to mention the
subject at all, had left her with one hope: that he would grow bored
with Mrs. Simpson as he had grown bored after earlier attachments.
But failing that, Queen Mary had assumed that he would put his

duty to his country first and renounce his love. The realization that so far from contemplating renunciation he was actually prepared to give up his throne in order to marry Mrs. Simpson was a profound shock.

From Queen Mary, what Lang was saying might have been accepted, but not from Lang. And he went on to voice a more specific criticism.

Even more strange and sad it is that he should have sought his happiness in a manner inconsistent with the Christian principles of marriage, and within a social circle whose standards and ways of life are alien to all the best instincts and traditions of his people. Let those who belong to this circle know that today they stand rebuked by the judgment of the nation which had loved King Edward.

Not content with the criticism, the Archbishop proceeded to compound it with cant.

Yet for one who has known him since his childhood, who has felt his charm and admired his gifts, these words cannot be the last. How can we forget the high hopes and promise of his youth; his most genuine care for the poor, the suffering, the unemployed; his years of eager service both at home and across the seas? It is the remembrance of these things that wrings from our hearts the cry, "The pity of it, O the pity of it." To the infinite mercy and the protecting care of God we commit him now, wherever he may be.

Lang's excuse was that his task had been difficult; "I felt that I could not in all honesty and sincerity merely say kind, and of course true, things about the late King's charm and manifold services: that in my position I was bound to say something about the surrender of a great trust from the motive of private happiness and about the social circle in which he had thought that happiness could be found." He was incapable of realizing that though his feelings had been expressed in all honesty and sincerity, the fact that they were not in all charity was going to be destructive. The broadcast had the reception it merited—a "torrent of abuse" descended on him in his mail. This, he claimed, he had fully expected, and he consoled himself with the fact that there were "just as many letters of gratitude." In this, his biographer had to admit, Lang was deceived. The majority of the letters were critical or abusive, but they were tactfully withheld from him.

There were many people who, though they realized that the correct decision had been taken and that abdication had been the only possible solution, nevertheless vaguely felt that Edward had been badly treated. Until Lang spoke, they had been hard put to it to justify this assumption, except by arguing that "they" had it in for Edward. The Archbishop now presented himself as the perfect scapegoat. He was ideally suited to the part: a pliable, title-adoring courtier, head of a Church that had lost its hold over the imagination of the people. "Progressives," leftists, agnostics, Nonconformists and Catholics could join in execrating him. His attack on Edward and his circle came in for much criticism, but even more, the crocodile tears of "The pity of it, O the pity of it."

Even in the Establishment, irritation was felt with the Archbishop for reviving a cause that had seemed to have been by some miracle dead. Geoffrey Dawson had been delighted with his "fan mail," as he playfully called it—as well he might have been, for it contained high praise from many eminent people, including some who had no love for the *Times*. But after the week-end, he noted in his diary, the tone of his correspondence changed. It was "directed now against the Archbishop's broadcast." The common view—as Lloyd George expressed it, across the Atlantic in Jamaica—was that the Archbishop was "kicking his sovereign when he is down"—to the British, traditionally, one of the unforgivable sins.

By contrast, Baldwin's Commons speech had seemed admirably Christian—as was Halifax's in the Lords: "It is no part of his subjects' duty, even if their hearts allowed, to pass judgement upon the conclusion which His Majesty has felt impelled to reach." An author who took the same view, Gerald Bullett, was moved to compose a sour little epigram and offer it to the *News Chronicle*. Reluctantly the editor, Gerald Barry, turned it down, but it was short enough to acquire general currency by word of mouth.

> My Lord Archbishop what a scold you are
> And when your man is down how bold you are
> Of Christian charity how scant you are
> How Lang, O Lord, how full of Cantuar!

As the verse circulated, it acquired a more savage last line:

> And, auld Lang Swine, how full of Cantuar!

Even the *Daily Telegraph*, which might have been expected to take the Archbishop's side, came out against him. And later commentators who might have been expected to put in a word for him found it impossible to stand over him on this issue. Inevitably, too, some of the hostility to Lang rubbed off onto the Church of which he was Primate. The conclusion of Owen and Thompson's *His Was the Kingdom* expressed what had become a common attitude: "If nobody believes any more in the theory of the Church's anointed, do not blame the atheists or the anarchists. Send the Bill for that to the Archbishops."

This was particularly unluckily timed for the Church, because it badly needed the revival that the "Recall to Religion" campaign had been designed to provide. The Archbishop still hoped that the coronation of George VI would arouse it, but the coronation, when it took place, was accepted not as a religious rite but—as Bishop Blunt had feared—as a curious and colourful piece of historical pageantry. Millions saw it for the first time on film. But the Archbishop, playing a leading part, managed to muff his big moment.

The King had expressed understandable anxiety that the crown should not be put on back to front—easy to do, because there was no very obvious guide to which was front and which was back. To simplify the Archbishop's task, a small piece of red cotton was attached under one of the jewels in the front. But when the crown was handed to him at the service's big moment, he found to his horror that he was unable to locate the cotton. He turned the crown this way and that, without success, before taking a chance and placing it on the King's head. Some official, apparently, examining the crown, had noticed the thread, and, assuming it had got there by mistake, removed it. In ordinary circumstances the Archbishop's fumbling would hardly have been noticed—it might even have been regarded as part of the ceremonial—but such was the lingering feeling of resentment toward him that his predicament became the subject of popular jest. The "Recall to Religion" campaign, though duly launched, disappeared without trace.

That year, too, the rector of Stiffkey administered a last touch of ridicule to the Church for which he had once laboured so enthusiastically.

His presence in a barrel was no longer sufficient draw, and that summer he was billed to appear at Skegness to give a lecture from the cage of a lion called Freddie. And thus, as Ronald Blythe described it in *The Age of Illusion*, "in scarcely credible terms, the little clergyman from Norfolk and the lion acted out the classical martyrdom to the full. He fought wildly, gallantly, but Freddie killed him in full view of a gaping mob. Eventually the lion-tamer showed immense bravery and managed to get his body away from the animal and out of the cage. She was a sixteen-year-old girl named Irene."

At coronation time, A.P. Herbert's Matrimonial Causes Bill passed into law—no comfort to the Church, which the debates had shown to be hopelessly divided on the issue. It is possible to argue, as Anthony Howard did in his essay on the churches in *The Baldwin Age,* that the Anglican ecclesiastical authority during that period should be credited with one achievement: in spite of attack from without and erosion from within, "they preserved intact the institution which they had inherited and passed it on—buffeted but not broken up—as a perpetual trust to their successors." They did, but the question remains to be answered whether it might have been better for the community if the Church *had* been broken up, thereby compelling it to face the problems posed by Darwin, Marx, Freud and their followers—as eventually in the 1960s the "South Bank" movement, with the bishop of Woolwich, began to try to do—instead of retreating into its shell and playing less and less part in the life of the community. By the middle of the century the Church had begun to sink into obscurity. A public-opinion poll taken in 1965 revealed that although over ninety percent of the population of Britain continued to believe in some form of Christian religion—two-thirds of them "Church of England"—and although nearly half regularly prayed to their God, only thirteen percent claimed to go to church "most Sundays," and the proportion that had actually been to church the Sunday before they replied to the poll was seven percent. All the indications were that Britain had become a country where institutionalized religion had ceased to be relevant. Lang and his like, the administrators, had failed.

The press

The other institution to come badly out of the whole affair was the press. Throughout, its role was ignominious. Afterward, admittedly, excuses were found, mainly along the *Manchester Guardian's* "reticence while reticence could be maintained" line. But although the press had been silent "partly for a wholly reputable reason," the *New Statesman* admitted when the silence broke, it was also because of "very astutely managed official pressure." In the Newspaper Proprietors' Association, the popular papers were dominated by Beaverbrook and Rothermere, the quality papers by the *Times,* and the rest of the newspapers and magazines were too overawed—except *Cavalcade. Cavalcade* received a trouncing from the *Telegraph* as a "scandalmongering publication which has sought to thrive on extracts from the American press," but as it firmly replied, it had only presented the facts—and nothing but the facts.

Immediately after the abdication, the *Times* defended itself from charges that it had been wrong to withhold comment. This had had its disadvantages, an editorial admitted, but there must be few who would not agree that the advantages had outweighed them, "and that it was a true exercise of responsibility to spare elaborate or sensational publicity for the King's private affairs before they had reached the threshold of decision." With the development of the conspiracy theory, however, accusations began to be made that the *Times* had had some ulterior motive. According to Compton Mackenzie, writing a few months later, the belief had become general that when Baldwin made himself responsible for the handling of the King, "the editor of the *Times* made himself responsible for the handling of the people." When the volume of the *History of the Times* dealing with the 1930s came to be written, therefore, its authors felt it incumbent upon them to rebut the accusation in some detail. They were not particularly concerned to defend Geoffrey Dawson. On some issues, notably appeasement, they were critical of him—an attitude that might have been beneficial if it had been expressed more freely by some of those who worked with him at the time. Their chief aim was to defend the *Times* and the press in general from the charges that were levelled against them in the months following the abdication.

There were five main grounds of criticism.

1. *"That the long silence of the newspapers was due to some censorship or muzzling from outside."* This charge, the *History* asserted, "is easily disposed of. There was no official or unofficial censorship of the British press . . . the nearest approach to interference from high quarters was probably the customary request from Buckingham Palace (the precedent having originated in Victorian times) that the Sovereign's privacy should be respected by the press during his annual holiday."

This is demonstrably inaccurate. The popular newspapers were persuaded not to sensationalize the Simpson divorce by Beaverbrook and Rothermere, at the King's request, and the "gentlemen's agreement," in practice, continued to inhibit newspapers from referring to the subject after the King's determination to marry Mrs. Simpson had become common knowledge in Fleet Street. As for the *Times,* Dawson wanted to broach the story, but stayed his hand at Baldwin's request. There was no formal censorship—but informal censorship, of the kind that led the owners of the *New Leader's* printing house to reject Fenner Brockway's article, could be even more insidious.

2. *"That it was due to collusion—an agreement between themselves for common action."* There was collusion, the *History* admitted, about the reporting of the Simpson divorce. But otherwise, the silence was maintained "from the customary restraint and reserve that obtains in the British press towards the Sovereign and his immediate family . . . responsible proprietors and editors, therefore, were united in considering that the King's friendship with Mrs. Simpson, or with any other woman, did not offer a suitable topic for newspaper comment or gossip as long as it was only part of his private life."

But this was precisely the point: it was *not* part of his private life —not, that is, if the argument were accepted that eventually carried the day, with the *Times'* approbation, that a king's wife has to be approved by his government on behalf of his people. The *History's* argument also blandly assumed that the "customary restraint and reserve" toward the King were desirable. What happened in the autumn of 1936 showed that it was highly undesirable, because of the gossip flying around in the United States, in Canada, and to some extent in Europe, and the rumours in London. Whatever the justifications for restraint in ordinary circumstances, they were not applicable here.

3. *"That this arrangement was shared by the Government, who used the press for their own purposes."* Not so, the *History* replies: Baldwin and Dawson were old friends, who for years had discussed public affairs together. "But the Prime Minister committed no impropriety whatever in his talks with the editor. Neither did the editor."

The writers of the *History* here fell into the old fallacy of assuming that for an impropriety to be committed, it must be committed consciously. There was nothing wrong with the editor discussing affairs with the Prime Minister, so long as he did not allow his independence to be compromised. But Dawson certainly allowed himself to be influenced by Baldwin—as did Camrose of the *Telegraph*, through Baldwin's friend Davidson. Baldwin was too astute to give orders—he knew his men too well. He also knew that Dawson could be relied upon to try to keep the other quality papers in line if they threatened to break out, and Dawson did.

Only the last two charges, in fact, were satisfactorily disposed of in the *History:* that the conspiracy included the heads of the Church, "who deliberately selected the Bishop of Bradford to break the silence," and that the *Times* was guilty of "hitting a man when he was down."

On reflection, many people in Fleet Street felt ashamed that the press had been so timid. Arthur Christiansen of the *Express*, though prepared to defend his reluctance to print pictures of Mrs. Simpson on the *Nahlin* cruise, concluded his account of the period with the injunction, "There is one rule that should never be broken. Tell the people!" Wilson Harris of the *Spectator* agreed. At the time, he wrote that although there was "something professionally galling in the reticence that has been uniformly observed, without a shred of authority to enforce it, month after month by every paper in the country," he thought this reticence was much to their credit. After second thoughts, though—a week later—he was not so sure. It might have been well-intentioned—and, as it involved sacrifice, creditable —but "it was thoroughly mistaken." It was also unintentionally cruel. That the popular newspapers refrained from introducing Wallis to the British public was by the King's own wish, but as things turned out it did her untold harm, allowing the development of the scandals about her that were not to die down for many years.

The claim, too, that the newspapers had been independent of pressures was not helped when, in 1937, Julius Salter Elias of the *Daily Herald* received the peerage he had craved. His excitement, according to his biographer, knew no bounds. He happened to be ill in a nursing home at the time, but a visitor, who had been asked to bring him a book on etiquette, found him flushed with pleasure, "his eyes glittering with joy." He could claim that his public services and his charitable bequests were being recognized, but Hugh Cudlipp gave Fleet Street's view when he said bluntly that it was in recognition of Elias' attitude during the abdication crisis: "A grateful Tory Government sent the button maker's son to the House of Lords."

An explanation of why the British press had failed was to be given by the New York *Daily News*. In London, the *Daily Mirror* had complained that opposition to the marriage in the Dominions could be attributed to the mud that had been stirred up by "the newspaper hooligans" of the United States. "Sure it's our fault," the *News* sarcastically admitted. "Must be!" The real culprit, it claimed, was the British press, which had handled the Simpson story "clumsily, mistakenly and cravenly." The trouble with Britain's newspaper publishers, the *News* went on, "is that most of them think of themselves as statesmen first and publishers second—a long way second. They feel that they must mould public opinion through their papers, by telling the public only what the public should hear."

It was a just assessment. Beaverbrook and Dawson both used their newspapers for propagandist purposes. Beaverbrook avowed his anti-government propagandist aims, but Dawson remained unaware of how far the *Times* had become a government organ—departing from the concept of the purpose of the fourth estate, as it had been propounded by the great Scots advocate Thomas Erskine nearly a century and a half before: "Other liberties are held under government, but the liberty of opinion keeps governments in subjection to their duties."

It could at least be said on behalf of the press, though, that when the story broke, it was tackled in the newspapers with energy and a sense of the occasion. The British Broadcasting Corporation could not even make that boast. The *History of the Times* permitted itself a passing sniff: the BBC, it recalled, "throughout published colourless official statements. The ordinary citizen gathered his information from the newspapers."

"THE GOLD BAR OF HEAVEN"

For Baldwin, the outcome of the abdication crisis won a respect and admiration greater than he had ever previously enjoyed. True, he was named by the dissidents as the head conspirator, but the charge won no responsible support. Even Compton Mackenzie, though he felt that the British ruling class had been glad to get rid of Edward because he represented a threat to their complacency— "For years he fired his bullets at the sandbags of bureaucracy, bullet after bullet buried in that dead-weight of administrative inertia until at last, disarmed by love, they found him powerless to fire another shot"—dismissed the conspiracy hypothesis. So did others who might have been tempted by it. In *The Gathering Storm,* so critical in other respects, Churchill repeated and amplified the verdict on Baldwin he had given in the Commons at the time: "Undoubtedly he perceived and expressed the profound will of the nation. His deft and skilful handling of the Abdication issue raised him in a fortnight from the depths to the pinnacle." And Attlee, though later concerned to point out that he had approached Baldwin on the Mrs. Simpson issue rather than vice versa, continued to hold that the country owed Baldwin a debt of gratitude for the way he had dealt with the affair.

At the time, the remarkable success—as it seemed—of Baldwin's handling of the abdication meant that even his "appalling frankness" revelations were for a while forgotten and forgiven. He was able to retire with a peerage after the coronation in May 1937 feeling, as he described it, "tired, happy and at peace. . . . I still have that sense of wonder the Blessed Damosel showed in her face when she leant over the gold bar of heaven." That sense of wonder had worn off, and Baldwin was shrewd enough to remark, "So will mine." It did. After the collapse of the Allied forces in France in 1940, the deficiencies in men and materials uncovered by Hitler's Blitzkrieg were blamed on the Conservative-dominated governments of the 1930s, and the scapegoat was not Chamberlain—whom Churchill magnanimously kept in the Cabinet, and who died a few months later—but his predecessor. Baldwin was actually warned that he had better not come to London, so strong was the hostility to him. "They hate me so," he said, sadly. "They hate me so."

One man certainly hated him so: Beaverbrook. At long last, the opportunity presented itself for revenge. In 1940 Winston Churchill made Beaverbrook his Minister of Aircraft Production, a post in which he had a striking success, providing the fighter aircraft replacements for the Battle of Britain. In 1941 he became Minister of Supply. He knew that among other commodities iron was urgently needed. In September 1941 local authorities were circularized with a request for details of all iron railings and gates in their area so that they could be requisitioned for scrap, unless they were of outstanding historical or artistic merit. Baldwin had some century-old ironwork gates in the grounds of his home; and when he put in a plea for them, the Ministry's architect accepted it, saying, "It would be a tragedy if they were allowed to disappear." But—according to Keith Middlemas and John Barnes, writing in the *Observer* on December 12, 1965—Lord Beaverbrook intervened in person to override the architect's report, and the gates were then "summarily removed by the Ministry of Works, acting as agents for the Ministry of Supply." A.J.P. Taylor suggested in the correspondence that followed that most people at this time were gladly surrendering their gates and railings; Middlemas replied that it was in fact many months before the Worcestershire local authorities were ready to handle the scrap resources disclosed by the investigation. Their collection did not even begin until over a year after receipt of the Ministry's circular.

The front gates of Baldwin's home were exempt from the requisitioning order—the gates having been the gift of his constituents when he retired, an exception made not because of their personal associations, but because drive gates were not as a rule requisitioned. But when this was mentioned in the Commons, a Conservative MP interjected that Baldwin might need them "to protect him from the rage of the people." He lived on in seclusion until 1947. Having once won the admiration and affection of a whole people, he now saw them, in Young's words, "converted to the bitterest hatred . . . there was not much to comfort him in those years."

Even when Baldwin's reputation was at its lowest, however, the assumption remained that over the abdication, at least, he had behaved with matchless probity, tact and skill. When the Duke of

Windsor's autobiography appeared in 1951, with its caustic comments, the impression remained that the Duke had been nursing a grievance, and was now putting the blame on Baldwin that he ought to have laid on his own advisers. Some suspicion remained, though, that there must have been more to the abdication crisis than met the eye; and eventually the charges against Baldwin were spelled out in detail with the serialization of Beaverbrook's abdication commentary in the *Sunday Express* in December 1965. Baldwin, Beaverbrook claimed, had deliberately deceived the House of Commons in his speech on December 10: "If a man wishes to mislead and deceive his hearers, he need not be driven to the telling of a direct and simple lie. He can achieve the same effect by using the suggestion of the false and the suppression of the true. These were the means that Baldwin employed."

Beaverbrook made sixteen specific charges, but few of them could be sustained. It was unfair, for example, to claim that Baldwin deceived the House by failing to mention that Hardinge had consulted him and Dawson about his letter to the King. In doing so, Hardinge was doing no more than his routine duty as the King's private secretary. It was also hard to credit the allegation that soon after George V's death, Baldwin knew that Edward intended to marrry Mrs. Simpson—considering that the Duchess of Windsor by her own account did not herself yet know of that intention. In their *Observer* article countering Beaverbrook's charges, Middlemas and Barnes had little difficulty in disposing of them. Six, they showed, were demonstrably false, and the rest contained misrepresentations. Clearly, when Beaverbrook wrote the memoir he was still smarting from recollection of his humiliating defeat. True, he insisted that his intervention in the crisis was to help the King: "I did not enter the struggle to dislodge the Prime Minister from Downing Street. That would be a welcome by-product of my efforts." But he continued, "My meditation led me to believe that on the political issue the King must prevail, and Baldwin must be destroyed." Would Beaverbrook have known at the time of the crisis whether helping the King or destroying Baldwin was his primary aim? All his career suggests that he would not. He was far too easy a prey to self-deception to be a reliable judge of his motives.

Beaverbrook's account of the abdication, therefore, must remain suspect. But this does not preclude the possibility that his instinct was right about Baldwin, even if his rationalizations were wrong:

right, for example, about the unreliability of the speech to the Commons as a guide to Baldwin's motives. The speech, Beaverbrook claimed, was "no more than a recital of the empty and insincere gestures he had made . . . while professing to serve the King, he had worked to destroy him." And there are indications that Beaverbrook may have been right.

Baldwin implied in the speech that he had been unaware of the vast volume of correspondence from America and the Dominions, "expressing perturbation and uneasiness at what was then appearing in the American press," until he came back from his holiday in mid-October. But this is hardly conceivable. He must have known. It was not as if he had been seriously ill, so that the news had had to be kept from him. The most likely explanation is that he knew, even if he did not fully appreciate the extent to which what was being written in the American press was presenting a danger to the Commonwealth, but that he deliberately decided to wait. Even after he had spent a day at his office at the beginning of October he still waited: when he saw the King in the middle of the month, the subject was not mentioned. Their first confrontation on October 20 could hardly, then, have been—as he claimed—"because it was my duty, as I conceived it, to the country, and my duty to him not only as a counsellor but as a friend." A true counsellor and friend would have spoken to the King months before, or, if unwilling because of embarrassment to speak earlier, would have at least given him more helpful informal advice than Baldwin, by his account, attempted to give when they met. The most likely explanation is that Baldwin was pushed into the first confrontation by his friends' concern, not because of any desire to help the King.

On his dealings with the Dominion premiers, too, as Beaverbrook observed, Baldwin did not tell the whole truth. His questions to them were framed without reference to the King, and apparently in a manner that intimated no great anxiety that the King should stay. But the most damaging of all Beaverbrook's charges was that in his account of the final stages of the crisis, Baldwin deliberately misled the Commons. He made much of the fact that as late as Wednesday December 9, the day before the abdication, he and the Cabinet had sent Edward a message begging him to reconsider his decision—the clear intention being to convince the Commons that the Cabinet had been anxious to the last that the King should stay. But what, then, of Baldwin's admission to Young that Tuesday, December 8, was the only time he was frightened because "I thought he might change his mind"? That Baldwin had been alarmed by this possibility was to be confirmed by a remark he made a few days later to Brownlow. In a letter to the *Evening Standard* during the Baldwin-Beaverbrook controversy in 1965, Brownlow recalled that he had seen the Prime Minister at Chequers and had told him of the advice he had given to Mrs. Simpson to leave both the King and Europe immediately. "If your advice had been accepted," Baldwin replied, "I would have sent you to the Tower of London for the rest of your natural life." Obviously Baldwin was being jocular, but the words, Brownlow thought, were nevertheless revealing: "Such was his loyalty and friendship for the King."

The evidence, then, strongly suggests that Baldwin did not make any positive effort to keep Edward on his throne and that in the final stages of the crisis he was anxious to ease him out as expeditiously as possible. But was this desire to end the crisis the consummation of a plan to get rid of the King that Baldwin had hatched long before? It could have been simply the logical and inevitable outcome of a policy that Baldwin had decided upon earlier as the best, or the safest, in the difficult circumstances in which he found himself, with no preconceived end in mind other than the best interests of the monarchy, of the nation, and of the Conservative Party—bearing in mind that for Baldwin, the best interests of all three were inseparable.

The most satisfactory explanation for Baldwin's actions during the crisis is, in fact, that he determined from the start not to work to any plan, but to allow his political instinct to take charge and to obey its promptings. True, it had let him down over the Hoare-Laval pact, and was to do so again during the crisis, in connection with his "appalling frankness" speech. But it was still his most effective political weapon. Whenever he had planned, consciously, to take a specific course of action it had usually led him into trouble. Over the King's matter, therefore, he let hunch take over. And although it proved a slow and tortuous business, it worked.

Four stages can be traced. In the first, even before Edward came to the throne, Baldwin realized that there were going to be difficulties. In the second—the first few months of the reign—the difficulties accumulated, culminating with the differences of opinion over the King's holiday plans, which compelled Baldwin to realize that a constitutional crisis might be impending. In the third, that autumn, it arose—over Mrs. Simpson. But Baldwin, though he may have been aware that Mrs. Simpson might be an excuse to get rid of the King, did not immediately begin to work to that end. Instead, his dealings with the King were of such a kind that if he decided to renounce Mrs. Simpson, he could have no ground of complaint against his Prime Minister, but if he did not renounce her, he would put himself in an untenable position should a constitutional crisis develop. Only after the "appalling frankness" speech, and the efforts of the popular press to make capital from the King's visit to South Wales, does Baldwin appear to have taken advantage of the mistakes the King made to speed his departure. Even then, he still refrained from taking positive steps of the kind Chamberlain recommended—presumably because Baldwin sensed that if the King realized that he was being eased out, he might accept the conspirators' advice, pretend to renounce Mrs. Simpson, and bend his energies to getting rid of his Prime Minister, in order to regain her, later.

As a result, all the moves that led up to the abdication were made by the King. Baldwin did not need to intervene, because events were moving so inexorably toward it even without his intervention. But equally, he did nothing effective to lead the King away from the destructive course on which he had embarked. As James Agate perceptively noted during the crisis, "Asquith would have 'gentled' the King in his present extremity"—gentling being a technique of breaking in a horse firmly but sympathetically. Baldwin's gentling, at least in the closing stages, was pretence. At some stage—perhaps when the story broke, perhaps even before, when the returns from the Dominions came in—Baldwin surely must have begun to realize that the wheels could not be reversed. They could only be lubricated—as even commentators who disliked Baldwin's politics were later prepared to agree. After the Hollywood-style publicity, Kingsley Martin conceded in the New Statesman, "It was difficult to see how he could remain King with dignity, or work with his ministers." And, whatever Baldwin himself thought, it is extremely unlikely that his Cabinet would have tolerated Edward's continued presence on the throne if, bowing to the decision of the Dominions, he had intimated his readiness to renounce Mrs. Simpson.

Perhaps, though, Baldwin never consciously made up his mind that Edward must go. To the end, he may have convinced himself that he was doing his best to enable Edward to stay. What to Beaverbrook, and later to Edward himself, was to appear a hypocritical pretence of sympathy when it was all over was probably genuine enough. According to Baldwin's account to his son about his parting from the King, Edward told him that although he realized Baldwin and his wife could not approve of what their King was doing, they must remember that he belonged to a different generation. Baldwin, moved, replied that "there are no two people who hope more sincerely that you may find happiness where you believe it is to be found." And the King, also moved, said that Baldwin and his wife seemed the only people to show they cared about his happiness. Even allowing for exaggeration, the story does not ring false.

It is theoretically possible, of course, that Baldwin deliberately deceived his son; but it is highly improbable. And his son was far from being alone in the impression that Baldwin had an avuncular fondness for the King. Two of his closest friends, Lord Davidson and Lord Crathorne (who as Thomas Dugdale was his parliamentary private secretary at the time of the crisis) wrote to the *Times* during the Baldwin-Beaverbrook controversy in 1965 to say, "We who were very close to the discussions in Downing Street during those tragic days know how much the Prime Minister, Mr. Baldwin, suffered at this period." And a few days later Sir Alan Lascelles, who for years had been on Edward's staff as a private secretary, and who was associated with the day-to-day developments of the crisis, asserted in a further letter to the *Times* that "the King had no more loyal and devoted subject than Mr. Baldwin, then or at any other time." And if Baldwin did not feel sympathetic, why should he, on his retirement a few months later, have written to the Duke to say, among other things, "through all that time in the early winter you ran dead straight with me, and you accomplished what you said you would do; you maintained your own dignity throughout; you did nothing to embarrass your successor"? There was no political advantage to be gained, at that time, from flattery.

The most reasonable hypothesis is that Baldwin throughout the crisis, and after it, had a genuine feeling for Edward. When Edward's departure became inevitable, Baldwin did not think of it as victory over an adversary in the contest which circumstances had made inevitable. He regarded Edward more as the owner of a lovable dog might do, if the dog gets too big and too restless for the family's peace of mind.

This interpretation—that Baldwin did not work to a preconceived end, but allowed events to run their course with a shrewd idea of what the end might be—also fits the picture of him presented by those who were to be accused of "conspiring" with him. The Archbishop of Canterbury, in particular, saw him infrequently; and Geoffrey Dawson, though he saw more of him than Lang did, saw much less of him than he wanted to. When they did meet, too, Dawson could sometimes barely disguise his irritation, as the reference to Baldwin's "sealed lips" indicated. The only time that Baldwin really unburdened himself during the crisis, Dawson claimed in his memorandum, was when he was shown the "Britannicus" letter. He then described what had happened at the confrontation with the King, speaking "more fully than he ever did of later events." Dawson, admittedly, had an interest in his memorandum in proving that he had not conspired with Baldwin against the King, but his diary confirms that he was actually a little hurt over Baldwin's failure to confide in him.

Baldwin knew what he was doing. Shortly before the war broke out, Duff Cooper wrote to him for his birthday, making the point that Chamberlain had fallen into an error his predecessor had avoided: "He believes public opinion is what the *Times* tells him it is." Baldwin was shrewd enough to realize that the *Times* was not a mirror of public opinion, but he also knew from the Hoare-Laval episode that Dawson could be a dangerous adversary. He therefore saw just enough of Dawson, and gave him just enough information, to prevent him from being tempted to break out. Beaverbrook's picture of Dawson sitting with the Prime Minister, comforting and encouraging him whenever he lost his nerve, was very far from the reality.

As the King had asked him to do—but not because the King had asked him—Baldwin handled the crisis alone. Few Prime Ministers would have been able to do so, because few would have trusted their own hunch sufficiently. But Baldwin did not even keep all his ministers informed: "You can't tell a thing like that to the whole Cabinet," he complained to Tom Jones. "Out it would come!" He confided what was happening—belatedly—only to his inner Cabinet circle: Chamberlain, MacDonald, Halifax, Simon, and for safety's sake, Runciman. He sometimes confided in Tom Jones, because he liked to have somebody to talk to. But otherwise he unburdened himself only to his immediate staff circle—Horace Wilson, for example, and Dugdale, and to the Davidsons, his closest friends.

THE APPLE CART

Baldwin, then, did not get rid of the King. At most, he simply facilitated the process by which the King made his departure inevitable. The question that remains to be answered is whether the King need have gone—whether, if he had accepted the advice of his friends (or of Baldwin's enemies), he could have outmanœuvred his government and stayed on his throne.

There can now be no doubt that he would have liked to. Of all the accusations levelled at him while he was in exile, the one that appears most to have irritated the Duke was that he had found in Mrs. Simpson an excuse to relinquish a job he did not enjoy. "There has been criticism in some quarters," he told the magazine *Parade* in 1957, "that I did not want to be King, that I put my personal feelings above the throne and above my duty, that I left because of a craving for private happiness. This is a lie. I say it now and for all time: all my life I trained for the job and for twenty-four years as Prince of Wales I served my country and the Commonwealth devotedly. For a year as King I worked as hard and selflessly as I knew how. Of course I wished to be King. More, I wished to *remain* King." Nothing that has emerged before or since casts doubt on that assertion. It is, of course, possible to surmise that there were also unconscious forces at work, but that can be no more than speculation. All the indications are that the story that rapidly gained currency and acceptance—that he had not really wanted to be, or liked being, King —was false.

Connected with this was another criticism that justifiably riled the Duke: that he put his private happiness before his royal duty— his "sacred trust," as Lang called it. "What seems most incredible," the *Times* argued on the morning after his departure, "is that any man who was born and trained to such high responsibilities, who had clearly the capacity to undertake them, and who had in fact begun to exercise them with the complete goodwill of the nation, should sacrifice it all to a personal preference for another way of life." But as Edward was to argue on his own behalf, although he married because he chose the path of love, he abdicated because he chose the path of duty: "I did not value the Crown so lightly that I gave it away hastily. I valued it so deeply that I surrendered it, rather than risk any impairment of its prestige."

His was not one of the spectacular romances of history. James Agate had a point when he remarked after the abdication announcement that the affair should be looked at in terms not of Shakespeare's Antony, but of H.G. Wells' Mr. Polly: "Man comes into life to seek and form sufficient beauty, to win and increase it." History, Agate thought, would record that Edward had found the Kingship—without Wallis—to be of insufficient beauty. As for Wallis, her photographer Cecil Beaton observed at the time, "She loves him, though I feel she is not in love with him." But the course the marriage took was sufficient answer to those who thought that Edward and Wallis were in the grip of a temporary infatuation, and that he should pull himself together and think of his duty. It is possible to argue that Wallis could have made him an admirable consort, had public opinion permitted, but nobody could now seriously suggest that Edward would have been capable of relinquishing her and continuing to reign without her.

Could he have reigned with her? Two possible courses of action had been open to him. One would have been to play it cool, as Duff Cooper and others advised—letting Wallis leave the country, and waiting for the rumours to die down, in the hope of establishing himself so firmly on the throne that she would be able to rejoin him after her divorce was through without the risk of a constitutional crisis. The other was simple defiance: an appeal to the country over the heads of his ministers, with the idea of creating a King's movement—if not a King's party.

In *The Apple Cart*, first produced in 1929, Bernard Shaw had shown how a monarch might react in a constitutional crisis, where he was reluctant to take his ministers' advice. Confronted with their ultimatum, he could threaten to resign, telling them that he proposed to go forward as a commoner for a seat in the House of Commons at the next election. Shaw's *Evening Standard* article during the crisis amounted to a broad hint to the King that he might examine the possibilities of thus appealing from his government to his people. Lewis Broad discussed what might have happened in such circumstances in his book on the abdication, and in a paper to the Shaw Society John Grigg, son of Edward's former friend Edward

Grigg, claimed that the situation which Shaw had put on the stage was not entirely unreal: "It presupposes an improbable set of circumstances but it is one which could, in such circumstances, occur. In fact—and this is perhaps the most fascinating point about *The Apple Cart*—an almost identical situation did occur within ten years of the play's appearance."

Grigg's thesis was that with the help of such allies as Lloyd George and Churchill, Edward could have refused a dukedom in order to be eligible, as Sir Edward Windsor, to enter into public life. Then "as a left-wing politician, with Lloyd George's ideas for home policy and Churchill's for foreign policy, he would have been a well-nigh irresistible force." Whether this would have been a good thing was a matter for speculation—"but I am at a loss to see what Baldwin could have done if King Edward had made *The Apple Cart* his blueprint." This may sound far-fetched, but that Edward's successor was not unmindful of the possible risk is clear from his memorandum on the abdication crisis, quoted by his biographer Sir John Wheeler Bennett. Reith, apparently, had intended to introduce the former King before his farewell broadcast as "Mr. Edward Windsor." That George VI told his advisers, "is quite wrong: he cannot be Mr. E.W. as he was born the son of a duke. . . . If he ever comes back to this country he can stand and be elected to the House of Commons. Would you like that?" If he were a royal duke, however, he would not be eligible—he would not even be allowed (as he would if he were an ordinary duke) to speak or vote in the House of Lords. So a royal duke he became.

The idea of Edward Windsor solemnly contesting a seat in Parliament cannot be taken seriously, but by his own account, the prospect of a King's party did momentarily exercise his mind. On the evidence, however, it never stood a chance—so long as he was determined to marry Mrs. Simpson. Lloyd George and Winston Churchill may in restrospect sound a formidable combination, and at the time, suspect though they both were, the possibility of an alliance between them to fight on the King's behalf caused some alarm. But they could not have formed and led a King's party— Churchill, for one, was too good a House of Commons man to have even contemplated doing so. And if a King's party had emerged, it would have found little backing. By the time the King had placed himself in a situation from which he could extract himself only by defying his ministers, it was much too late. If he had had any idea of defying the government, he would have needed quietly to secure the support of some other potential allies, as well as Lloyd George and Churchill, much sooner, and he would have had to submit to being guided by their advice.

But that would have meant playing it cool, and this, as he made clear in *A King's Story,* he was incapable of doing. He lacked the patience, he lacked the guile. No doubt if he had arranged that Wallis should discreetly withdraw into the background from the moment he made up his mind to marry her—before the press speculation about them began—she could have obtained her divorce in America and then come back and been married to him in secret, thereby enabling him to introduce her to the government and to the people as his lawful wife. It would have been a shock, but he might just have got away with it—in theory. But there is little point in pursuing the speculation except out of curiosity, because there was never the slightest chance that he would be sufficiently far-sighted—or, he might have added, sufficiently hypocritical. He would have thought the project dishonest.

Edward's inability to plan ahead can be traced in part to his personality—he lived for the moment in all he did, with a touching directness and spontaneity—but also, in part, to his popularity as Prince of Wales. He was one of the first people, perhaps the first, to receive internationally the treatment that was to become a commonplace for famous film stars and later for pop singers: uncontrolled adulation, which led his admirers to break through police barriers, to try to touch him (sometimes with a rolled newspaper, he complained, if he was out of hand's reach), and to pillage his clothing of removable objects, handkerchiefs or buttons, as souvenirs.

A shrewd member of the court felt that this was the main cause of his downfall: "The public, all the world over, loved him too well and most unwisely. No man in history has ever been so fulsomely adulated as this modern Stupor Mundi, and the result was his unshakeable conviction that he could get away with murder." This was also the belief of Hannen Swaffer, for over a quarter of a century one of Fleet Street's best-known characters and a spokesman for the uncommitted left wing. He blamed the press for "that tuft-hunting and title-seeking which made us flatter so much and grovel so completely, that Edward VIII, believing it all, lost his head and thought himself greater than the people."

Edward, too, lacked friends of the type that could have steadied him, not so much by their reprimands, or even their advice, but by the continuing stability of their opinions. It was not only the Archbishop who criticized Edward's circle of friends. The day after the abdication the otherwise sympathetic *New Statesman* claimed, "It is an open secret that much of the society which has surrounded King Edward has been irresponsible and politically, as well as morally, undesirable." But this appears to have been the work of rumour, denied knowledge of who Edward's friends actually were. His immediate circle appear to have been quite an agreeable, even a conventional, group, but they lacked weight. The *Times* came close to the mark when it quoted the historian Clarendon, about a popular favourite of three hundred years before: "His single misfortune was (which indeed was productive of many greater) that he never made a noble and a worthy friendship with a man so near his equal, that he would frankly advise him, for his honour and true interest, against the current, or rather the torrent, of his impetuous passions." The trouble with Edward's circle, the *Times* thought, was that it "was too largely composed of men and women, some of them of high birth and all of them remote from 'the people,' who cared far less for his welfare than for their own amusement."

What this amounted to was that Edward, from the government's point of view, was an unsatisfactory monarch, and had Baldwin not been presented with a way of compelling him to abdicate, by rejecting his proposal of a morganatic marriage to Mrs. Simpson, a clash would have come over some other issue. But how far was the common view at Westminster at the time—that Edward did not do his homework satisfactorily, and that he interfered in state business—really justified? Or were such stories spread around, both during his reign and after it, in ministerial self-justification?

On this issue it is still not possible to be dogmatic; the relevant Cabinet papers may in due course give a clearer answer. But Edward himself was to provide clues in his later career in exile, when he sometimes behaved, to put it charitably, with conspicuous lack of tact.

For this he had some excuse. He might reasonably have expected, having left his throne to the accompaniment of what at the time seemed like a handsome testimonial from the Prime Minister, that he would be remembered with sympathy and affection. But rumour had created prejudice, and effective though the abdication speech was at the time, the effect soon wore off. The Archbishop's intervention, too, by helping to create the impression that Edward had been removed by a conspiracy, encouraged the Establishment to react by emphasizing Edward's unsuitability as King. Wilson Harris, editor of the *Spectator*, was among those who were assured that Edward had been drinking heavily—the most common of the smear stories going the rounds. He mentioned this to Baldwin, and Baldwin "quickly and emphatically" disposed of it. But not all who heard the rumour had access to the Prime Minister.

Nor was it only Edward's enemies who turned on him. Sir Philip Gibbs reported a scene in an air force mess on the afternoon of the abdication: on hearing the news, the young pilots denounced the King—" 'He has let us down,' they shouted, 'He has thrown up the sponge.' " It must have been disconcerting, particularly for one so long accustomed to adulation, to hear echoes of such sentiments—particularly during the long weeks he had to wait before rejoining Wallis to get married.

Edward also had some reason to be offended at the way he was treated by his family. He had naturally assumed that as he was to be His Royal Highness the Duke of Windsor, Wallis would become Her Royal Highness. But when the title was given legal form at the time of the coronation, it was expressly stated that he would be entitled to hold the title for himself only: his wife and descendants, if any, would not be eligible. The effect, the Duchess recalled in her memoirs, "was to debar me in defiance of all custom from taking my place alongside my royal husband." Her royal husband was understandably enraged: "Nothing in the aftermath of the Abdication hurt David more than that gratuitous thrust. In his eyes it was an ultimate slur upon his wife, and, therefore, upon himself." It remained a barrier to reconciliation between the Duke and his brother's family until 1965, when Queen Elizabeth and the Duchess were introduced at his hospital bedside.

Edward, too, could not persuade his mother that the course he had taken was the right one. Her attitude was to be set out in a letter written in July 1938, in reply to his request that she should set down her feelings about him:

You will remember how miserable I was when you informed me of your intended marriage and abdication and how I implored you not to do so for our sake and for the sake of the country. You did not seem able to take in any point of view but your own. . . . I do not think you have ever realised the shock which the attitude you took up caused your family and the whole Nation. It seemed inconceivable to those who had made such sacrifices during the war that you, as their king, refused a lesser sacrifice. . . . All my life I have put my country before everything else, and I simply cannot change now.

Edward, then, had cause to feel hard done by. But by some of his actions over the next few years, he was to lend justification to those who continued to view him with suspicion—and also to alienate people who would have been on his side.

There was a revealing glimpse of him in Douglas Reed's *Insanity Fair*, published in 1938—a description of Reed's work as a foreign correspondent, chiefly in Germany during the years immediately after the Nazis came into power. Reed was in Vienna at the time of the abdication. He listened to Edward's farewell speech, and liked it. He had no strong feelings about the monarchy, and he was rather proud of the way that the abdication crisis had been resolved: "England might have lost her grip on foreign affairs, but she could still handle abdications." But though it had been done efficiently, it had not been done very creditably. Why the righteous indignation, the vindictiveness to the departed King? "The contrast between the tone of oleaginous adulation used by the ruling classes in England towards the King as long as he was the plastic instrument of their will, and the venomous dislike of him which they showed when he wished to marry a woman they did not like, was more than I and most of my acquaintances could stomach." And with some of his English friends, Reed composed a valedictory sonnet in the contemporary Poet Laureate-ish idiom, which expressed their feelings:

> The hand that blew the sacred fire has failed,
> Laid down the burden in the hour of need,
> So brave begun but flinching in the deed.
> Nor Mary's power nor Baldwin's word availed,
> To curb the beating heart by love assailed.
> Vainly did Delhi, Canberra, Capetown plead
> The Empire's ruler flouts the Empire's creed
> By princes, prelates, people sore bewailed
> The triple pillars of the Empire shake
> A shock of horror passes o'er the land.
> The greatest throne in all the world forsake

To take a favour from a woman's hand?
The hallowed pleasures of a kingly life
Abandoned for a transatlantic wife.

Reed was prepared to be sympathetic—until he met the Duke
in Vienna, where he was staying until he could rejoin Wallis. The
Duke chose the occasion to complain about newspapers, and a few
months later he complained about them more publicly at a press
lunch in Paris. Reed, irritated, recalled the thousands of journalists
all over the world who had spread the Prince's fame: "I thought of
the perfect tact and sympathy, the complete absence of *Schaden-
freude*, with which hundreds of newspapers big and little all over
Europe had written of his crisis and abdication. I had hardly read
a niggardly or even a seriously critical word. No man ever had such
selfless service from men of all nations completely unknown to
him, who took him completely on trust. Through the press, he had
become more popular throughout the world than any king in history.
And he complained of the press!" Of all the Duke's mistakes, this
sniping at the newspapers was perhaps the most unwise.

But it was not the most serious. The rumour that had lost Edward
most support, particularly on the political left, had been that he and
Wallis were Fascist sympathizers. They knew it was false; and it was
consequently very much in his interest to avoid any action which
would appear to justify it. Yet they chose to have their wedding and
honeymoon at a chateau owned by Charles Bedaux, an industrialist
whose methods and views on employer-labour relations had already
won him notoriety and whose Fascist sympathies were known (at
the end of the war, he took poison to avoid the fate which he
knew would be in store for him as a collaborator).

Later in 1937, Bedaux arranged a trip to Germany for the Duke
and Duchess, ostensibly to study German housing methods. Beaverbrook actually flew to Paris to beg them not to accept, because of
the effect their visit would have on opinion in Britain. The Duke
replied that as he had no official position, he was free to go where
he pleased. The Foreign Office, embarrassed, decided to take no
official cognizance and the British ambassador was diplomatically
absent from Berlin, but the Nazis gleefully exploited the visit.
Bedaux had told the Duke and Duchess they would be meeting industrialists. In fact, they were met by the drunken Robert Ley,
of the German "Strength Through Joy" movement, and by him in-

troduced to Goering, Himmler, Hess and the other Nazi leaders, and eventually to Hitler himself. The Duke and Duchess found the Nazi leaders almost uniformly repulsive, but they could hardly publish their opinion and the visit was taken to be a deliberate calculated snub not only to the British government but also to those who, far more strongly than the government, loathed Nazism and all it stood for.

Bedaux had also arranged for the Duke and Duchess to visit the United States; but early in November the project was formally denounced by the Baltimore Federation of Labor, with the approval of the A.F. of L. President, William Green. The complaint was that Bedaux had been responsible for the introduction of an industrial efficiency system, adopted by a number of firms but loathed by the American unions. Bedaux had also been responsible for the Windsor's tour of Germany, under the auspices of Ley—"the man who ordered and ruthlessly directed the destruction of the German trade unions"; and he was known for his Fascist sympathies. When this attack appeared, the Duke immediately decided to postpone his U.S. tour because of "the grave misconceptions which have arisen."

The *Times* reported his decision and the reasons for it on November 6 without editorial comment; though, as if out of nostalgia for past intimidation in code, one of its editorials that day was given over to a eulogy of Baldwin, who had been presented with a gold casket containing an address of appreciation by the City of London. Later, the President of the A.F. of L. was to insist that his unions' strictures were directed at Bedaux, not at the Windsors, but the damage had been done. Even his staunch ally Josiah Wedgwood felt let down. In his memoirs, he claimed that he was still glad that he had spoken out at Westminster, "if only for the reputation of Parliament." But he had been perturbed by the intimations of Fascism that he received in his fan mail at the time, and "the subsequent career of the Royal Duke in Austria, Germany and France inclines me to think that Baldwin was wise."

The mistaken impression created that the Duke was a potential friend to the Nazis was to have a curious consequence. At the beginning of the war, the Duke returned to Britain, but no posts of a kind that the government considered suitable, and which he considered acceptable, were available there. Eventually he returned to France, as a liaison officer between the British and French armies, and at the time of the fall of France he and the Duchess made their way to Spain. There he was the subject of a comical plot, later to be described by William Shirer in his *Rise and Fall of the Third Reich,* with the Franco government delaying the Duke's departure for Portugal as long as possible in order to give the Germans time to get to work on him, in the hope they could use him at some later stage as a puppet alternative to his brother.

The Duke, as it happened, was in no hurry to leave for Britain. He refused to return until he knew which job he was returning to because he wanted to be sure it was suitable. "I won't have them push me into a bottom drawer," the Duchess recalled him saying. "It must be the two of us together—man and wife with the same position." Eventually the two of them moved on to Portugal but there he stayed, refusing to board the flying boat sent for him. It was characteristic of him, Wallis thought, to hold such a view—it was "one of the reasons why I know that he is a finer person than I can ever hope to be. But his stubbornness worried me." Her instinct was once again sound. His determination to bargain over his return was to have unfortunate repercussions.

Not unnaturally, the Germans assumed that the Duke's reluctance to go back to Britain was attributable to his views about the war, and they contemplated kidnapping him to transfer him to Spain, and give him an excuse for staying. Even when the Duke agreed to become Governor of the Bahamas, the Nazis took the appointment as confirmation they had gauged his attitude correctly. The German minister in Lisbon told his foreign office that the new job was intended to keep the Duke away from England, "since his return would bring with it very strong encouragement to English friends of peace," and he went on to report, "The Duke is convinced that if he had remained on the throne war would have been avoided, and he characterizes himself as a firm supporter of a peaceful arrangement with Germany." Inevitably, the news of German "negotiations" with the Duke in Spain and Portugal filtered back to London, helping to revive old suspicions, and it was not until Shirer's book appeared that the affair was unravelled.

From the reports of the German ministers in the peninsula, which Shirer quoted, it is easy to see how the Duke was misunderstood. He had always been friendly to Germany. He had believed that the war was unnecessary, and until the Blitzkrieg, he appears to have hoped that it might be ended by negotiation (a view shared by Lloyd George, though not by most of the appeasers, who at last realized that business could not be done with Hitler). The Duke may, too, have made remarks about British politicians that would have been perfectly acceptable at a London dinner table, but which in Lisbon were indiscreet. But the reports of what the Duke was believed to have said, and the interpretation put on them by the German ministers were a ludicrous misinterpretation of the Duke's attitude—"complete fabrications and, in part, gross distortions of the truth" was his own comment.

The Duke, though, bore some of the responsibility for having created in the minds of the Nazi leaders the impression that he might allow himself to be used in their peace campaign in the summer of 1940, when they hoped to overthrow Churchill and secure a docile government, of a kind that would support Hitler in his projected campaign against Soviet Russia. The excuse, for example, that the Duke had given for his visit to Germany in 1937—that as he held no official position, he could go where he liked—was only reasonable so long as he did not contemplate holding an official position at some later date. As things turned out, the prejudice aroused against him by the visit, and by his connections with Bedaux, appears to have been partly responsible for making it difficult for him to come back to Britain, as he wished, in 1940. If there had been general sympathy for him, some suitable work would surely have been found for him to do. But he had forfeited sympathy.

The Duke's refusal to return until suitable work had been found worried the Duchess. It was scarcely, she thought, "for us to make an issue of so private a matter when the rest of Britain was fighting for its life." What Churchill, busy directing that fight, thought of the stream of cables from Portugal, ariving at a time when Britain was hourly expecting invasion, is not recorded. Had the Duke come back and offered to work in a voluntary capacity—as a member of the Auxiliary Fire Service, say, in the Blitz—his later career could have taken a very different course. As it was, he was offered the Bahamas post, and when he went there, he drifted out of the mainstream of British life, never to return.

ACKNOWLEDGEMENTS

As my intention has been to re-assess the accepted sources for the period, rather than to present new findings from hitherto untapped sources, an array of footnotes giving references would have seemed a little ponderous. I have, however, ordinarily mentioned sources in the text, not simply to identify them, but also for cautionary purposes. Many of the writers on this subject have had an axe to grind, and in such circumstances evasions and distortions are apt to slip in. It would have been impossible to evaluate every statement, but the qualification "according to so-and-so's account" will, I hope, have enabled the reader to gauge its worth.

Of necessity, mine is an interim assessment. The materials for a definitive study will not be available for many years. Some of the relevant papers are in the royal archives. State papers, too, are withheld under what used to be known as the "Fifty Year Rule," banning inspection for that period. This regulation has recently been modified, but at the time of writing it seems unlikely that all the papers relating to the abdication will be released.

Of the central characters in the story, the Duke and the Duchess have written their various memoirs, and although they have left some problems unresolved, it is unlikely that they will have much more of significance to add. My thanks are due to Mr. G.W.L. Morley, of Allen and Overy, the Duke's legal representatives in London, for reading the typescript and proposing a few amendments, and to Jack LeVien, producer of the film *A King's Story*, who also read the book in type, and who had made some very helpful suggestions in the early stages before I had begun to write it.

The Baldwin papers are not available for inspection, but I have had invaluable help from John Barnes, of the London School of Economics, who is currently engaged with Keith Middlemas on a biography of Baldwin. Mr. Barnes has also been preparing the memoirs of Lord Davidson, Baldwin's closet friend, and his knowledge of the period is alarmingly encyclopaedic. We did not always see eye to eye on the interpretation of the the material, but I found his comments and criticisms extremely helpful.

The limited role of Cosmo Gordon Lang, Archbishop of Canterbury, has been adequately described by his biographer, J.G. Lockhart. I have followed his account of Lang's career in general—and in particular, of Lang's relationship with the royal family and with Baldwin.

The role of the other alleged "conspirator"—the editor of the *Times*—has been described in Sir Evelyn Wrench's biography, which carried extracts from the memorandum compiled by Geoffrey Dawson about the crisis. There were some gaps, however, in Sir Evelyn's account, and I am very grateful to Mrs. Cecilia Dawson, the editor's widow, for allowing me to consult not only the full text of his memorandum, but also his diary and letters and press cuttings of the time. The memorandum in fact adheres closely to his day-by-day diary. His object, clearly, was simply to demonstrate that he had *not* been involved in a conspiracy with the Prime Minister and the Archbishop. Where the diary failed to make this absolutely clear, he was occasionally tempted to insert a word or phrase to point it up. But there can be no doubt, comparing memorandum with thesis, that his only object was to clarify, not to disguise, his role. His correspondence also helps to confirm the overwhelming endorsement of the *Times* position during the crisis.

The death of Lord Beaverbrook meant that access to his collection was temporarily suspended. I knew that he had written, and actually printed, an account of the crisis, but then laid it aside. I therefore asked A.J.P. Taylor, to whom the papers had been entrusted, whether it would be possible for me to examine it. He looked it up, and immediately realized that it was suitable for publication—for which, presumably, Beaverbrook had intended it when he had it printed. A few weeks later it began to appear in serial form in the *Sunday Express*. This was particularly useful to me, as the resulting controversy in the *Times*, the *Observer* and the *Evening Standard* helped to clear up a number of points which had remained obscure.

One man who might have made a significant contribution to the story declined to do so: Ernest Simpson. But it is impossible not to admire the determination with which he resisted what must have been extremely lucrative offers to tell all.

For the rest, I hope that some of those who played a part in the events of the time, and who are still living, will write their memoirs —or leave correspondence and diaries for future biographers. Two biographies which will certainly throw further light on the period are already in preparation: Lord Birkenhead's life of Walter Monckton, and Randolph Churchill's life of his father Winston.

My thanks are due to Data Research, who made a preliminary survey of the available material; to Virginia Makins, for lending me her entertaining collection of off-beat American newspaper cuttings of the period; and to Raye Farr, who went through the first draft producing many ideas for revision and, in some cases, re-casting, helping to get the book into presentable shape; to John Grigg, who read the typescript, and made some valuable suggestions; and to Bernard Levin, who read the proofs and contributed, among his corrections, some caustic comments which I would have liked to incorporate in the text.

I wish also to thank the following, with whom I spoke or corresponded on points treated in the book. Their assistance varied from general reminiscences of the period to the elucidation of individual points which they knew about, or events in which they were concerned. Although I have used such material with caution, mainly to confirm or rebut earlier speculation, the reminiscences of those involved directly or indirectly in the crisis have been most valuable, not least in helping to give a "feel" of the period. My thanks, then, to Sir John Aird, Lady Asquith (formerly Lady Violet Bonham-Carter), Lord Attlee, Lord Avon, Sir Gerald Barry, Alan Beattie, Lord Boothby, Lord Brownlow, Lord Crathorne (formerly Sir Thomas Dugdale), Lord Citrine, Roger Falk, Sir John Foster, Tony Foster, Lord Francis-Williams, T.R. Fyvel, Peter Goldman, John Gross, Lord Hardinge of Penshurst, Professor Richard Hoggart, Sir Alan Lascellus, the late Lord Layton, Sir Compton Mackenzie, David Marquand, Kingsley Martin, Lady Alexandra Metcalfe, Lord Mountbatten of Burma, Malcolm Muggeridge, Oliver Whittey, Professor Desmond Williams and Sir Horace Wilson.

BIBLIOGRAPHY

Aga Khan. *Memoir* (1954)
Agate, James. *Ego 2* (1938)
Airlie, Countess of. *Thatched with Gold* (1962)
Amery, Leo. *My Political Life* (3 vols.) (1953–1955)
Astor, Michael. *Tribal Feeling* (1963)
Attlee, C.R. *As it Happened* (1954)
Avon, Lord. *The Eden Memoirs* (Vol. 1) (1962)

Baldwin, A.W. *My Father* (1955)
Beaton, Cecil. *The Wandering Years* (1961)
Beaverbrook, Lord, *The Abdication of King Edward VIII* (Ed. A.S.P.
    Taylor, 1966)
Betjeman, John. *Collected Poems* (1958)
Birkenhead, Earl of. *Lord Halifax* (1965)
Blythe, Ronald. *The Age of Illusion* (1963)
Boardman, Harry. *The Glory of Parliament* (1960)
Bocca, Geoffrey. *She Might Have Been Queen* (1955)
Bolitho, Hector. *King Edward VIII* (1938)
Bonham Carter, Lady Violet. *Winston Churchill* (1965)
Boothby, Lord. *I Fight to Live* (1947)
———— *My Yesterday, Your Tomorrow* (1962)
Bowle, John. *Viscount Samuel* (1947)
Briggs, Asa. *The Birth of Broadcasting* (1961)
———— *The Abdication: 25 Years After* (1961)
Broad, Lewis. *Sir Anthony Eden* (1955)
———— *Winston Churchill* (1956)
Brockway, Fenner. *Inside the Left* (1942)
Brodey, Iles. *Gone with the Windsors* (1955)
Brown, W.J. *So far . . .* (1943)
Bullock, Alan. *Ernest Bevin* (1960)
Butler, J.R.M. *Lord Lothian* (1960)

"Cato." *Guilty Men* (1940)
Chandos, Lord. *Memoirs* (1962)
Christiansen, Arthur. *Headlines All My Life* (1961)

Bibliography

Churchill, Randolph. *Lord Derby* (1959)
Churchill, Winston. *The Gathering Storm* (1948)
Citrine, Walter. *Men and Work* (1964)
Clynes, J.R. *Memoirs* (1938)
Cockburn, Claud. *In Time of Trouble* (1956)
Cole, G.D.H., and Raymond Postgate. *The Common People* (1946)
Cooke, Colin. *Stafford Cripps.* (1957)
Connell, Brian. *Manifest Destiny* (1953)
Cooper, Lady Diana. *The Light of Common Day* (1959)
Coote, Colin. *A Companion of Honour* (1965)
———— *Editorial* (1965)
Cudlipp, Hugh. *Publish and Be Damned* (1953)
———— *At Your Peril* (1962)

Dalton, Hugh. *The Fateful Years* (1957)
Day Lewis, C. *The Buried Day*
Decade (1931–1941)
Driberg, Tom. *Beaverbrook* (1956)

Edwards, Cecil. *Lord Bruce of Melbourne* (1966)

Feiling, Keith. *Neville Chamberlain* (1946)
Flanner, Janet. *An American in Paris* (1940)
Foot, Michael. *Aneurin Bevan* (1965)
Furness, Thelma, and Gloria Vanderbilt. *Double Exposure* (1959)

Gibbs, Sir Philip. *Ordeal in England* (1937)
Gilbert, M., and R. Gott. *The Appeasers* (1962)
Graves, Robert, and Alan Hodge. *The Long Week-end* (1940)
Grigg, Sir J. *Prejudice and Judgment* (1948)
Guedella, Philip. *Winston Churchill* (1941)
Gunther, John. *Inside Europe* (1936)
Guttsman, W.L. *The British Political Elite* (1960)

Halifax, Lord. *Fulness of Days* (1957)
Hardinge of Penshurst, Lady. *The Path of Kings* (1952)
Harris, Wilson. *Life So Far* (1954)
Herbert, A.P. *Holy Deadlock* (1935)
———— *The Ayes Have It* (1937)
Hesse, Fritz. *Hitler and the English* (1954)
Hoggart, Richard. *The Uses of Literacy* (1957)
Howard, Peter. *Beaverbrook* (1964)
Hyde, H. Montgomery. *Norman Birkett* (1964)

Jackson, R. *The Chief* (1959)
Johnson, Alan Campbell. *Lord Halifax* (1941)
Jones, Sir Roderick. *A Life in Reuters* (1951)
Jones, Tom. *Lloyd George* (1951)
———— *A Diary with Letters* (1954)

Kilmuir, Lord. *Memoirs* (1964)
Kirkpatrick, Ivone. *The Inner Circle* (1959)
Kirkwood, David. *My Life of Revolt* (1935)

Laver, James. *Between the Wars* (1961)
Lee, Jennie. *This Great Journey* (1963)
Leeds, S.B. *Cards the Windsors Held* (1957)
Lehmann, John. *The Whispering Gallery* (1955)
Leighton, Isabel (Ed.). *The Aspirin Age* (1949)
Lockhart, J.G. *Cosmo Gordon Lang* (1949)

McElwee, William. *Britain's Locust Years* (1962)
McGovern, John. *Neither Fear Nor Favour* (1960)
McKenzie, Compton. *The Windsor Tapestry* (1938)
Macleod, Iain. *Neville Chamberlain* (1961)
Maine, Basil. *Edward VIII—Duke of Windsor* (1937)
Martin, Kingsley. *The Magic of Monarchy* (1937)
———— *Harold Laski* (1953)
Minney, R.J. *Viscount Southwood* (1954)
Mitford, Jessica. *Hons and Rebels* (1960)
Morrison, Herbert. *Government and Parliament* (1954)
———— *An Autobiography* (1960)
Mowat, C.L. *Britain Between the Wars* (1951)
Muggeridge, Malcolm. *The Thirties* (1940)

Nicolson, Harold. *King George V* (1952)
Norwich, Viscount. *Old Men Forget* (1953)

Orwell, George. *The Road to Wigan Pier* (1937)
———— *The English Revolution* (1940)
Owen, Frank, and R.J. Thomson. *His Was the Kingdom* (1957)
Owen, Frank. *Tempestuous Journey* (1954)

Petrie, Sir Charles. *Monarchy in the Twentieth Century*
Pope-Hennessy, James. *Queen Mary* (1959)
Postgate, Raymond. *George Lansbury* (1951)
Pritt, D.N. *From Right to Left* (1965)

Bibliography

Raymond, John (Ed.). *The Baldwin Age* (1962)
Reed, Douglas. *Insanity Fair* (1938)
Rees, Goronwy. *A Bundle of Sensations* (1960)
Reith, Lord. *Into the Wind* (1949)
Rose, Sir Francis. *Memoirs* (1961)
Rowse, A.L. *The End of an Epoch* (1947)
———— *All Souls and Appeasement* (1961)

Samuel, Viscount. *Memoirs* (1945)
Sencourt, R. *Reign of Edward VIII* (1962)
Shaw, G.B. *The Apple Cart* (1930)
Shinwell, E. *Conflict Without Malice* (1955)
Shirer, William. *The Rise and Fall of the Third Reich* (1959)
Simon, Lord. *Retrospect* (1952)
Smith, Janet Adam. *John Buchan* (1965)
Somervell, D.C. *The Reign of King George V* (1935)
———— *Stanley Baldwin*
Spender, Stephen. *The Creative Element* (1953)
Strauss, Patricia. *Cripps, Advocate and Rebel* (1945)
Sutherland, Stella. *American Public Opinion and The Windsors* (1938)
Symons, Julian. *The Thirties* (1960)

Taylor, A.J.P. *The Origins of the Second World War* (1961)
———— *English History 1914–45* (1965)
Templewood, Viscount. *Nine Troubled Years* (1954)
Thomas, Hugh (Ed.). *The Establishment* (1959)
Thomas, J.H. *My Story* (1937)
Thompson, Dorothy. *Let the Record Speak* (1939)
The Times, A History of (Vol. IV) (2 vols., 1954)
Toynbee, A.J. *A Study of History* (1934)
Turner, E.S. *The Court of St. James'* (1959)

Vansittart, Peter. *The Mist Procession* (1958)
Von Ribbentrop, Joachim. *Diaries* (1954)

"Watchman." *Right Honourable Gentlemen* (1940)
Waugh, Evelyn. *Vile Bodies* (1930)
Watson, Francis. *Dawson of Penn* (1951)
Wedgwood, C.V. *The Last of the Radicals* (1957)
Wedgwood, Josiah. *Memoirs of a Fighting Life* (1940)
Wells, H.G. *The Shape of Things to Come* (1933)
Wells, W.B. *Why Edward Went* (1938)
Wheeler-Bennett, John. *King George VI* (1958)

White, J.L. *The Abdication of Edward VIII* (1937)
Williams, Francis. *Ernest Bevin* (1952)
———— *A Prime Minister Remembers* (1961)
Wilson, Edwina. *Her Name was Wallis Warfield* (1936)
Windsor, Duchess of. *The Heart Has Its Reasons* (1956)
Windsor, Duke of. *A King's Story* (1951)
———— *The Crown and the People* (1953)
———— *A Family Album* (1960)
Winterton, Lord. *Orders of the Day* (1952)
Wood, Alan. *Beaverbrook* (1955)
Wrench, Sir Evelyn. *Geoffrey Dawson* (1955)

Young, G.M. *Stanley Baldwin* (1952)

INDEX

INDEX

(421)

Index